The World War II Combat Film
Anatomy of a Genre

THE WORLD WAR II COMBAT FILM
Anatomy of a Genre

JEANINE BASINGER

New York   COLUMBIA UNIVERSITY PRESS

All photos courtesy of Museum of Modern Art Film Stills Archive.

Library of Congress Cataloging-in-Publication Data

Basinger, Jeanine.
The World War II combat film.

Filmography; p.
Bibliography: p.
Includes index.
1. World War, 1939–1945—Motion pictures and the
war. 2. Moving pictures—United States—History—20th
century. 3. World War, 1939–1945—Motion pictures and
the war—Film catalogs. I. Title. II. Title: World
War 2 combat film. III. Title: World War Two combat
film.
D743.23.B36   1986   791.43'09'09358   85-22326
ISBN 0-231-05952-3
ISBN 0-231-05953-1 (pbk.)

Columbia University Press
New York   Guildford, Surrey
Copyright © 1986 Columbia University Press
All rights reserved

Printed in the United States of America

For John

Contents

ACKNOWLEDGMENTS

In Fall 1978, I planned a class which was organized to work from film history toward an understanding of how a specific genre functioned. Using the World War II combat film, I set up a great many screenings so that students could see a certain type of film evolve chronologically. I wanted to see if what I thought I had observed about genres would hold up under a test condition.

I gave the class no initial guidance, but let them "define" and "trace" for themselves. During the first two weeks 40 movies were screened, with students recording what they saw on objective sheets in which they filled in information as to Hero, Enemy, Objective, etc. Then we set about analyzing and discussing, and comparing the observations against a second genre, the woman's film, and looking at films from both genres across a time span of 25 years.

The class did their assignments with enthusiasm and intelligence. They made discoveries, argued definitions, followed the evolution of the genre, and made connections with remarkable clarity and insight. Under the direction of three outstanding teaching assistants, Nancy Katz Colman, Alicia Springer, and Richard Teller, this class verified with their hard work something about genre and history that I had been thinking about for many years. To them, and to Wesleyan University, where I have always had wonderful students, I owe a great deal of this book. This was the class that said to me at two in the morning, when we were still talking after an extra screening, and I was tired and thought we should stop, "Well, you just go on home then. We'll carry on without you." And they did. My Senior Seminar repeated and verified the experiment in Spring 1985.

A book like this, for which so many films must be screened, also requires that many people must be thanked. For Pat Moore, formerly at United Artists, all the people at Films, Incorporated, and Leslie Levy at Swank, I express deep thanks. For excellent help with research, I thank Richard Teller, Audrey Kupferberg, and Marsha Maguire, and especially Mary Corliss at MOMA. For colleagues who screened films with me and shared thoughts—especially Richard Slotkin and Joe and Kit Reed—I am grateful. For others, some of whom I do not know personally, but whose work has meant a great deal to me over the years, I am indebted: Bill Paul, John Belton, Robin Wood, Andrew Sarris, Joe McBride, Stanley Cavell, V. F. Perkins, Thomas Schatz, Frank Capra, and many others. In particular, I want to thank all those people in my life who have shared their amazing knowledge of film history with me, and who have kept the cause of film history alive through years when no one cared, and when those of us who screened films—and then screened more films—were considered lunatics and film study was not chic in any area, academic or otherwise.

These intrepid film historians deserve mention: William K. Everson, who shares time and films generously; Leonard and Alice Maltin, who are always ready with answers to research questions; Ray Cabana Jr., a generous spirit who told me about *Crimson Romance*; Bob Smith, a kindred soul who loves *China Doll*; and David Mallery, who is always ready to talk film long distance.

I also want to thank my sisters—Rosemary, who took me to see my first silent film (Rudolph Valentino in *The Eagle*) and made me aware old movies were wonderful; and Pat, who came home from the movies to tell our family the news on December 7, 1941 and who later held my hand during *Cry Havoc*.

People always ask me why I want to study war movies. It's hard for me to answer, other than to say that I was a child during World War II, and I think that means I will always be "lookin' for the old Arizona." Others who were children then will understand that. I felt it was my personal responsibility to be organized for attack, and I worried alone at night in my bed, hideously aware that the rest of the family did not seem alert to the impending arrival of the Japanese and Germans in our back yard. I expected them because I went to the movies every Saturday and Sunday—and God knows, there they were. I can still remember my absolute conviction that I would be forced to leave South Dakota on a submarine and, while submerged in Tokyo Bay, most likely have my appendix taken out by the Pharmacists Mate. (My friend Mary was lucky. Hers was already out.) These powerful and dark films about war stayed with me for years, and by studying them I came to understand that they taught me many, many things about myself and America and people and death. Contrary to what many believe, they very definitely taught me that war is a terrible thing, a lesson I've never forgotten. The best anti-war film has always been the war film.

Thanks to my excellent word processer, Debbie Sierpinski, who worked hard and with remarkable accuracy and good cheer. She was a reliable and supportive help during the summer of 1984. And thanks also to my equally excellent editors, William F. Bernhardt and Leslie Bialler. And finally, thanks to my husband John, to whom this book is dedicated, and to my daughter Savannah, both of whom help me everyday in many ways, and for that I am as lucky as I am grateful.

Jeanine Basinger

The World War II Combat Film
Anatomy of a Genre

"Bang! the fieldpiece,
Twang! the lyre.
Mars by day,
Apollo by night."

Mr. Jingle on War

INTRODUCTION

If you sit down to watch a movie in which Maureen O'Hara plays an ambitious young woman trying to marry her way upward into financial security, would you inevitably label it a woman's picture? Suppose it is set in the desert, and O'Hara wears harem pants. Could it be a woman's picture anyway? What if it is called *Tripoli*, and co-stars John Payne as a United States Marine. Is it a combat movie? But how about if it has Howard DaSilva as a pirate? Maybe it's a swash-buckler. And it's set in 1805, so it must be a costume film . . . or maybe a historical drama.

Tripoli exists, and it does star Payne and O'Hara. Watching it, one can recognize elements from many types of films—musicals, Westerns, service films, traditional war films, and even the woman's film. It's a story about the marines fighting the Barbary pirates. It contains within its running time traditional events that have come to be associated with all the genres named above, and probably more. It's a grab bag of plots, a crazy quilt.

It's also a distinct failure as entertainment, cinema, narrative, and anything else you might care to mention. You can imagine a group of screenwriters sitting around the studio, each with a particular specialty, and going through a "now it's your turn" game and coming up with *Tripoli*. These plots are not fully developed or resolved; they exist as a rogue's gallery. But what is significant about them is that an audience recognizes them as familiar elements from other films. Each is a part of a larger, remembered whole. People know the rest of the story. The pirates are from pirate movies, and the Marines from military films. O'Hara is from a long tradition of desperate dames trying to climb the social ladders of the woman's picture. Audiences associate certain cos-tumes, plot contrivances, characterization, settings, and events with specific kinds of films.

Tripoli presents a lot of these abstracted referential moments. An audience can supply the rest of the details for the pirates, marines, and O'Hara. If you have seen a group of pirate movies, you remember how

A mix of genres: Tripoli

pirates (on film) dress, talk and act. Since film is a powerful visual
medium, crowding out any sense of reality, you accept the images of
a pirate movie as a picture of how pirates were. You remember the
images, and use this acquired knowledge to explain pirate behavior
whenever a "pirate" appears on film. Furthermore, film makers, consciously or unconsciously, begin to use and repeat and refer to this
"knowledge" of the audience's. Even though the story in *Tripoli* is
boring and intellectually sterile, and *Tripoli* is not an important film,
the recognition of it as a collection of things seen and understood from
other places, *is* important.

   Tripoli is not the only film that mixes generic components. *Honky
Tonk*, a 1941 film starring Clark Gable and Lana Turner, is a romantic
woman's picture empire-building historical costume epic star vehicle
frontier comedy rags-to-riches success story Western. It is almost always
classified as a Western, however. It spends more time indoors than out

and is closer to *Gone with the Wind* than *Stagecoach,* but people call it a Western. Why? *Tripoli* and *Honky Tonk* are both mixtures of established genres, but the latter film is readily referred to as *one* genre— the Western—and the other film is not defined as a genre movie at all.

Why should one film be identified as a specific genre and not the other? In this case, one might speculate that Lana Turner and Clark Gable are big stars, and John Payne and Maureen O'Hara are not. Thus, the studio, critics, theater owners, and customers alike did not simply make a designation for this big budget, successful movie—they needed such a designation for convenience's sake. But probably *Honky Tonk* is called a Western because the Western is a very strong genre. If you put Gable in a saloon and on a horse, and Turner in bustles and behind a runaway wagon, people will call it a Western because they recognize such signifiers as the saloon, the horse, the bustles, and the runaway wagon. Despite these things, however, *Honky Tonk* is not really a Western film in the popular sense of that genre's definition. It is a film set in the West, with characteristics of the Western, but it is actually a movie about Clark Gable taking Lana Turner to bed, and about his ruthless climb to riches. It's not hard to imagine M-G-M, the producing studio, saying, well, we have Gable and Turner, a hot combination, so let's put them in a lusty film together. What's a really lusty setting? The West? Good. But let's do it like *San Francisco* crossed with *Gone With The Wind.* We'll keep Gable as Rhett Butler . . . and Turner can be half Scarlett and half Melanie . . . but we'll put in a saloon, some horses, bustles, and a runaway wagon and say it's a Western so it won't look like we're ripping off GWTW [*Gone with the Wind*]."

So *Honky Tonk* is labeled a Western in M-G-M's ad campaigns and reviewers follow suit. "A lively, lusty Western," says *Variety,* and the audience accepts it, at least, as "sort of a Western with Gable and Turner." They do this, even though GWTW, a "Southern" if there ever was one, also had a saloon, horses, bustles, and a runaway wagon. Years pass, and *Honky Tonk* is labeled forever as a Western. Nobody questions the label because everyone, of course, knows what a Western is.

A Western, after all, is a Western. But one does not have to dip too far into that most complicated of genres to know that it can be a musical (*Red Garters*), a film noir (*The Halliday Brand, The Furies, Pursued*), an epic (*Duel in the Sun*), a comedy (*Destry Rides Again*), a historical drama (*They Died with Their Boots On*), a biography (*Buffalo Bill*), a woman's film *(Cimarron)*, and even a combat film *(Ulzana's Raid)*. It can be a family saga *(Broken Lance)* or a social document *(Devil's Doorway)*. Its action can be partially psychological *(Left-Handed Gun)*, and even its famed iconography and traditional shootout can be unexpected, as when Sterling Hayden, playing a Norwegian sailor, harpoons the villain in the streets at the climax of *Terror in a Texas Town*. Futhermore, some Westerns have been remade directly "as is" from other genres (the *film noir House of Strangers* remade as the Western *Broken Lance*, and the gangster film *High Sierra* remade as the Western *Colorado Territory*). More to the point of this book, a desert adventure film with a remote World War I background can also be remade as a Western and later become the prototypical World War II combat film *(Lost Patrol* remade first as *Bad Lands* and then as *Bataan, Manila Calling*, and *Sahara)*.[1]

Most film viewers know that some Westerns *are* combat films, just as they know some combat films are Westerns, and that some gangster films are Westerns and some Westerns are gangster films. Trust the steady filmgoers to know. They can recognize content they've seen before, and so can reviewers, who constantly complain about having "seen this one before." Many films are not genre films at all, of course, and many others are too hybrid a form to be classified as one thing or another.

In film study, most scholars have accepted the labels placed on films by the industry itself. They have assumed the presence of the genre they are discussing. They have also tended to work with a relatively small list of popular titles that are agreed upon by critics, audiences, and the industry as one thing or another generically. They have overlooked films such as *Tripoli*, which mix many genres, or *A Yank in the RAF* which mix only two (romantic musical comedy and combat), and they have not dealt with the difficulty of classifying movies such as *Bombardier*, which contain no combat until the final minutes of the film, but which are definitely about military forces in wartime. They have not catalogued every film they felt fit a genre's assumed definition and thus have not confronted the very tricky nature of genre. Given the problems of historical research in film study, this is not surprising. Time, energy, money, and in some cases thorough knowledge of film history and availability of films and studio documents, have prevented such research. This has led to a sense among some people that generic families are apparent and rather clearly definable. It is assumed every-

one knows the definition of any particular genre. And why not? Genre
is the known definition. But how and when does that definition beome
known? How does a genre grow, evolve, and endure? Why does it stay
alive over different historical periods, and how does it differ from 1945
to 1965, if at all? To my knowledge, no one has ever attempted to define
a genre specifically, based on the actual viewing of the hundreds of
films involved. What would happen if someone did that? What would
be learned?

This book is the result of such questions. It is a book based on the
history of the films themselves. It assumes that by taking an analytical,
thorough approach to one genre, particularly one with a specific beginning point in film history, and by tracing it forward in time, one
might learn something about the larger topic of genre itself.

I am comfortable with the idea that film can claim for itself what
other art forms claim—the right to study the objects themselves for
various kinds of information and meaning, and for the rules and non-
rules that govern the form. This does not mean that I think a book that
is a detailed piece of historical research on a genre is the full picture
on genre. The careful viewing of a great many films for a list of recurring
characteristics with which to prove the observation of—and thus existence of—a genre definition is only one aspect of genre study, a re-
spectable piece of historical scholarship. However, tracing that
definition forward, seeing how it changes and undergoes an evolutionary process over a period of years, should be of interest to anyone
studying genre. Such tracing is hard to do, because the films are difficult
to locate and see, and because it takes years of viewing. It is difficult,
also, because genre is alive. The films don't always behave the way
they are supposed to. They change, shift ideology, vary themselves,
merge with other genres, hide their stories in new clothes, lie dormant,
and then reappear. This book is offered as an example of what can be
learned from an intense observation of a single genre, but it does not
presume to provide the answer to all the questions of genre. Others will
want to add to it, examine the information from other viewpoints—
both internal and external to the film—and test the information against
other genres and specific theories.

There are many approaches to a study of the combat genre:

- Study of the films themselves.
- Study of the system that produced them—in this case the Hollywood

studio system, both as it existed when the genre first emerged and as the system changed. The evolution of the combat genre that grew out of World War II can trace its development from the heyday of the studio system through its collapse, an important factor in the history of all genres.

- Study of the various individuals who contributed to the films through writing, directing, producing, art decoration and costuming, etc., by tracing their individual and collective contributions to these films, as well as other nongenre films, other genre films, including their private experiences of combat and noncombat.
- Study of the development and change in the technology used to produce these films. The World War II combat film's history is influenced by the developments in sound, and the use of color and wide-screen. Its evolution is further influenced by the development of mobile equipment that easily went into the combat zone as well as by the impact of television on combat reporting.
- Study of the audiences who received these films: individual or collective psychology, sociology, anthropology.
- Study of the changing and developing history into which these films are released: social, political, economic.
- Study of other representations of the combat experience during the relevant years, such as comic books, novels, *Life* magazine, biographies, autobiographies, newsreels, letters, radio, television—all forms of both high and low culture.
- Study of parallel generic developments and histories in other fields, such as literature, art, music.
- Study of anything and everything else that is relevant by any and every critical theory of genre and/or cinema.

Because one book cannot do all of the above, this book is based on study of the films themselves. It will present a history of World War II combat films, tracing their origin and evolution and indicating important information about the system that produced them, the individuals that created them, and the technological developments that changed them. For instance, my reading of the various script rewrites on the film *Bataan* (at the Louis B. Mayer Library of the American Film Institute in Los Angeles) was particularly illuminating. So were such items as Dorothy B. Jones' definition of combat films published during the war years and a 1939 issue of *Photoplay* that explained genre to its readers ("you know the film stories you want to see"). Anything directly relating to the films—production, technology, authorship, critical reaction—will be incorporated in the text. Factors lying outside the direct examination of the films and their surrounding circumstances will be referred to where appropriate, but will not be the direct concerns of this book. However, these matters are, obviously, of great importance, and a total understanding of genre must include work on this topic by others whose area of study prepares them to tackle the questions. Since I believe that films can be validly studied from many different viewpoints, I look forward to these other books on the same subject. I am offering this careful research for consideration by those who wish to see genre evolution documented and analyzed. It is solidly based on actual viewings of the films.

Someone once told me that "nothing could be learned from staring at the screen." If that were true, the world would be a simpler place, and we could all stop worrying about MTV.[2] Things *are* learned, and thus we need to figure out not only *what*, but also *how* and *why*. Some of these things we know about, and some of them we don't realize until it's too late, and there we are, married to a girl who looks like Marilyn Monroe but acts like Blanche Yurka.

To some, it may seem a melancholy, even crackpot thing to have screened more than a thousand films over a five-year period in order to see what happens to one presumed genre. However, it fascinated me. I believe scholars who want to understand film have to watch films. Years ago, I also interviewed many of the people who worked on these films. I learned as much as I could about the studio system, the working collaborations involved, the background planning of who made them and why, and how they were received by audiences and why. I read the histories and novels of World War II, and looked through the old *Time* and *Life* magazines, but I concentrated on the films themselves when the time came to do the work. It is the films I love, and the films I want to understand. Once I saw a curator at the British Museum, preparing to piece together what looked to me like shards of a Greek vase, found on a dig he had participated in. Outside his office were hundreds of other vases, already intact and viewable. Yet he was full of enthusiasm—and convinced of the importance of his task. This book is my Greek vase, and if, when it is assembled, we have only another Greek vase—or if we thought all along it *was* a Greek vase anyway— I can still say, but now we have *proof.*

Dudley Andrew has written, "Today. . . everyone is aware. . . genre is not a set of rigid characteristics." He's right; but we have to prove it.

And in proving it, we have to consider why everyone once thought it *was* such a thing. When the theory of human evolution was first being considered, Darwin and Wallace both found insight in an essay of Malthus, which led them to state (independently of one another) the theory of natural selection. Wallace's statement was the inspiration and insight of a moment, while Darwin amassed the evidence it took to convince others. Both made valuable contributions.

The value of historical research is that it destroys certain inaccurate clichés that have been passed around and gives proof to ideas that scholars have known for a long time. Clichés about genre include the idea that they are easily defined and recognized, that they are fixed and never change, that they are based only on recognizable literary devices—such as characters and plots—and that films are either one genre or another. Actually, genres are hard to define, tricky, and contradictory. The cinematic form in which they are contained—the way they are presented through cutting and composition—and the use of color, sound, and wide-screen are as significant as their plots and characters. They are inconstant, moving their stories from place to place, and demonstrating curious affinities for one another. The Western loves the gangster film, and the comedy loves the horror, and the musical loves the combat, but the combat can love the Western, and the musical the horror and the comedy the gangster.

Genres seem to exist for certain purposes, but they linger on long after the purpose is accomplished. World War II on film is still with us, and so is the Western, despite its oft-announced demise. Items that define a genre can remain fixed while their meanings change, or the meanings can remain fixed while the items vary. Oh, perfidy! Genre is that damned elusive pimpernel, always in a new disguise, always slipping away.

Other clichés about film history include ideas such as "the Western disappears during World War II" and "World War II films celebrate the war." To view the films is to refute these ideas, and to suggest that new thinking is needed about Hollywood movies. The history and archeology of American film have been neglected by film scholars, and they must be given their rightful place among other scholarly approaches before it is too late and the films are lost and erroneous ideas become legend. More scholars seem to be attracted to the ideology of genre, or to the why of its appearance, than to its historical development. But as Leo Braudy wrote in *Post Script*, we need to approach genre through both theory and history. His words point up a current lack in serious film study—the frequent absence of a solid grounding in the primary facts of film history, as well as a distressing lack of acquaintance with the films themselves. Surely serious film study is now accepted enough so that we need not fear the dread label "film fan," just because we are engaged in thoroughly exploring all the artifacts of an era.

The purpose of this book, then, is to study a genre through historical research—"historical" in the sense of the history of film on screen, using the World War II combat film to accomplish the following:

1. To establish a definition of the World War II combat genre.

2. To use this definition to trace the evolution of that genre from its pre-World War II influences, past the war, and into its various historical "waves" that reflect its shifting ideologies and usages.

3. To indicate what happens to the basic definition when it is altered by comedy, music, and female variations.

4. To demonstrate how this definition, as it evolves and varies, transforms itself, commingles with other genres, disguises itself as another genre, and allows other genres to enter itself.

I have selected the World War II combat genre because, unlike most other presumed genres, it has a clear and specific marking place for its beginning. Triggered by a catastrophic historical event and the resulting social upheaval, this genre filled the needs of the wartime public for information placed in a narrative, and thus more personal, context. Juxtaposed as it was with actual newsreel and documentary film, as well as with numerous newspaper and magazine photographs of "reality," this genre provided comparison, contrast, and emotional relief. The World War II combat genre existed for the period of the war, but by virtue of its popularity has remained a genre (or accepted story pattern for films) until the present day. Furthermore, once established, the combat film influenced the entire concept of the war film. The pattern of the World War II combat movie is now the most common pattern for all combat movies.

Basic Assumptions

There Is a World War II Combat Genre

A question may arise here—why isn't it just a subgenre of the war film? This, of course, assumes there is a genre called "the war film." Most people, when asked what the war film is, promptly describe the World War II combat genre. Others look vague, and speak of Napoleon, or General Custer. One elderly lady I asked told me solemnly that the best war film she ever saw was Danny Kaye and Dinah Shore in *Up In Arms*. The irony is that she wasn't wrong because of genre, only taste.

"War" is a vague category, and is too broad to contain a basic set of characters and events, the hallmark of genre. Furthermore, the combat genre tends to have its own subcategories, such as military biographies and the commando raid.

There are just too many World War II combat films, and too many of them appeared *after* the war was over, for them not to be recognized as a genre. The war film itself does not exist in a coherent generic form. Different wars inspire different genres. "War" is a setting, and it is also an issue. If you fight it, you have a combat film; if you sit home and worry about it, you have a family or domestic film; if you sit in board rooms and plan it, you have a historical biography or a political film of some sort. It's very hard to be in war and not be in combat (although the effect of the war on civilians has become a familiar genre-type in foreign films, since when civilians sat home they were still in a war zone). "War" can be a metaphor, or it can be a background to other stories. Combat always implies a war of some type or another, but the question of whether or not the combat film is a genre, or a subgenre, is the subject of this book. And to answer the question, one must turn to the films themselves.

It Is a Representative Genre

The second assumption is that even though historical events inspired the beginning of the World War II combat film, it is nevertheless not isolated too much from other genres to be useful for research. The musical, too, had an abrupt beginning (with the advent of sound), and the combat film, as we will see, has a rich prior history on film.

Certain Films Can Be Eliminated

The purpose of such eliminations is not to narrow the number of films down to a manageable quantity (it in fact merely narrowed them only to a nearly unmanageable quantity), but rather to help illustrate the difficulty of genre definition. Right at the beginning of thinking about a body of films that are designated as a genre, a problem of definition, and thus selection, arises. As has been noted, many patterns of tangled story units move from genre to genre, so many films are not easy to label. However, the Catch-22 of defining any genre is, of course, that you must define it before you can define it. A working definition must be generated. I therefore had to establish the parameters of what I thought the genre would or should be in order to find the films to put under the microscope. I had to decide what films that contained World War II combat as only a small part of their storyline would be acceptable and what films would not—and why.

This donkey work, which involved viewing a great many lousy and often irrelevant films is, to my mind, a necessary part of genre study. By its nature, the study of genre requires a solid grounding in film history. One cannot learn about genre by examining ten films set in the West, calling them Westerns, and defining their common elements. And one cannot justify the definition found that way by systematically searching for ten more films that fit this pattern and conveniently discarding the rest. Faulty assumptions are easily made about what genre is, or what genres are, when you have not seen the films or carry in your mind a hazy, incompletely remembered definition of what such films were and thus are. The faulty assumption of genre is in and of itself *a* (if not *the*) definition of genre. However, even that faulty assumption requires definition. The films eliminated are in the categories of (1) Misleading Titles; (2) Newsreels; and (3) Foreign Films.

1. Misleading Titles. I have carefully tracked down and eliminated a great many misleading titles. For that film nut in Peoria who wants to write in that I forgot to include *Aerial Gunner*, I have the definitive answer. *Aerial Gunner* is not a combat movie, nor are *To the Shores of Tripoli*, *Army Surgeon*, *True to the Army*, *Action in Arabia*, *Remember Pearl Harbor*, and a long list of others I have carefully preserved against denunciations. I am well-armed here, and have the combat scars of endless hours of wasted time viewing most of these turkeys to prove it.

2. Newsreels. For the purposes of this book, newsreels have been eliminated, because this is a genre study of fiction films. However, the book will discuss the famous combat *documentaries* in terms of their influence on the fiction films that *are* under consideration.

3. Foreign Films.   Because of the nature of this study, which is about American generic patterns of film—our world, our culture, our artists, our movies—foreign films were eliminated. It was easy enough to wave off the Russian, French, and Chinese movies, but eliminating such successful British movies as *In Which We Serve* and *Above Us the Waves* was difficult. Difficult, but necessary. There is a limit to human endurance, and I screened films, including many foreign titles, almost daily for five years to cover this genre.

> *Military films not involving active combat should not be included.*

The truly difficult areas to decide on involved films which touch on World War II and the military, but which really do not involve active combat. I viewed scores of such films, always asking how they related to the combat genre. These "problem areas" fell into place as I worked. Ultimately, research indicated them to be of most importance in the prior history of the genre (see chapter 3), and of much less importance after the genre was fully defined by the war years. These films fall into groups which may be loosely designated as (1) Wartime Films, (2) Military Background Films, (3) Training Camp Films, and (4) Military Biographies.

1. Wartime Films.   Films about being in a time of war sometimes contain combat sequences, but these are mostly used to demonstrate the pressure of war on the noncombat life. (Example: Douglas Sirk's *A Time To Love and a Time To Die.*) "Wartime" can also mean films with no combat whatsoever, such as *Since You Went Away*, the epic home-front drama of World War II in which the pressure of war (that is to say, the faraway combat) is exerted on typical American family life. "Wartime" can also mean many other wars—from the Ancient world through Napoleon, the Civil War, World War I (see prior history section), and outward into the Star Wars. It can also imply a pacifist film but, although many of the later combat films take up the "war is hell" theme, they provide viewers with ambivalent satisfaction and thus are not truly pacifistic. What all these films of "wartime" do is influence the combat genre in terms of what the characters out on patrol think about regarding home. Later, the combat genre influences *them*. Here is where one sees the problem of definition in full flower. It is possible that such films are actually a subgenre of combat, rather than vice versa. It is the war, after all, that dominates them, and war during World War II means the combat film.

2. Military Background Films. Many musicals, comedies, and adventure films are set against a military background. Any film which presents the military setting without going into actual combat obviously is not a combat film. Yet these films, as we will see, teach us about military life—something you need to know in combat.

3. Training Camp Films. The problems of categorizing films are well-illustrated by trying to separate the film which takes place in a training camp from the military background films defined above. During World War II, many films that must ultimately be designated as belonging to the combat genre *begin* in training camp *(Gung Ho!)* and thus many later films follow that pattern as originally established *(Sands of Iwo Jima)*. Because these films make it clear that the men-in-training are headed for a specific combat situation, and because they do, in fact, present battles, they are combat films. However, if the men never go into combat, but remain in the training camp, the film obviously does not fit. *(Take the High Ground* is an example of such a film.) Yet a serious training camp film is very different from a musical with West Point as a background. (And a serious West Point musical is very different from an Abbott and Costello training camp movie.) But since all these films present or maintain the conventions of combat in a noncombat situation, they are significant. Although they contain no actual combat, they contain fist fights, war games, and conflicts of many other kinds. These conflicts represent the war these military men are being trained to fight. Films such as *Bombardier* and *Marine Raiders*, both made during World War II demonstrate the problem. *Bombardier* is 90 percent a training camp film, but contains an armageddon of actual combat as a finale. *Marine Raiders* starts briefly in actual combat, then sends its troops back for retraining and a long series of noncombat events, before finishing, again briefly, in combat.

4. Military Biographies. Although many true combat films are based on the exploits and experiences of real-life war heroes *(Merrill's Marauders* and *To Hell and Back)*, the biographical war film about events from World War II tends not to be about combat, but about a personal sacrifice, a religious fervor, or a human crisis of some sort, such as a veteran's adjustment to a handicap or to a psychological crisis developed during combat. Combat is thus used as a remembered event (a nightmare) or is presented as the basis of the problem, one section of a larger, noncombat story. (*Battle Hymn, Pride of the Marines, Thirty Seconds Over Tokyo* all fit this.) There are also war stories of noncombatant heroes who are drawn into the conflict (*Story of Dr. Wassell*), sacrifices made in combat by those who sit at home (*The Fighting Sullivans*), and complex character studies of our war generals (*Patton, MacArthur*). The latter, by virtue of being about the men behind the scenes, are not laid entirely in the slogging-through-the-mud settings of the combat film.

Conclusions

In taking the time to screen so very many films, I observed an evolutionary process in which the genre was defined, and then repeated, and then shaded to fit changing times. I am offering the results of this research, which is specifically historical, and which both led to and is based on these conclusions:

That World War II gave birth to the isolation of a story pattern which came to be known and recognized as the combat genre, whether it is ultimately set in World War II, in the Korean War, or in Vietnam, or inside some other genre such as the Western.

That, before World War II, this combat genre did not exist. Certain of its characteristics may have been present in earlier films of various kinds, but although war films did exist, and combat in war on film did exist, the combat film genre did not.

ONE

Definition

The rudimentary (and practical) study of genre begins with the simple observation that a great many films appear to have similar settings, plots, characters, and events. In fact, it is this very awareness that makes genre what it is. This is no secret; it was understood and welcomed by audiences and filmmakers alike. "Are you playing a Western tonight?" we were frequently asked over the telephone at the movie theater I worked in throughout the 1950s.

The industry advertised films as "the greatest musical since *Singin' in the Rain*" or "an epic Western," and articles in film magazines of the 1930s actually defined genre for fans. *Photoplay* ran a monthly column called "Brief Reviews" designed to give readers a quick reference guide to the genre of current films. The September 1939 issue indicates how easily such labels were applied: "social message picture" (*Back Door to Heaven*), "Western" (*Dodge City*), "madcap comedy" (*Bridal Suite*), "gangsters" (*Big Town Czar*), "musical fantasy" (*Wizard of Oz*), "mystery" (*Clouds Over Europe*), "propaganda" (*Confessions of a Nazi Spy*), etc. Films were also identified as being like other films ("kind of a *Mr. Deeds*" or "another *Informer*") and as star vehicles ("Shirley Temple film") or imitative of another star ("miniature Sonja Henie film without Henie"). In 1939, *Photoplay* also wrote an article on genre itself, explaining how studios, who wanted to please audiences, repeated types of films that viewers seemed to like and want repeated.

Almost anyone you ask to define a genre such as the Western will come up with a list—the saloon girl with heart of gold, the school teacher, the good guy in the white hat, the bad guy in the black hat, the Indians who try to buy rifles, the sheepherders who try to fence off the cattlemen's grazing land, and the inevitable final shootout. A simple test for any genre is whether or not you can, in fact, generate such a list. If you can, it's a genre. If you can't, it probably isn't.

The combat film from World War II can indeed generate such a list:

The hero, the group of mixed ethnic types (O'Hara, Goldberg, Ma-towski, etc.) who come from all over the United States (and Brooklyn), the objective they must accomplish, their little mascot, their mail call, their weapons and uniforms.

Therefore, to begin this historical survey, first the combat film defin-iton must be found. When we speak of such a genre definition, we are actually speaking of two kinds—the basic assumed definition, which more or less remains constant, and the evolving definition, which uses the basic one to construct new meanings for the changing times. To understand genre, one can never assume the set of recurring charac-teristics is all one needs. Genre is a kind of Lego set. It is a bunch of pieces that stay the same, but out of them you can build different things. The combat film pieces can be put together as a propaganda machine or as an anti-propaganda machine, as an "America is beauti-ful" or an "America is an imperialist dog" message. "War is necessary" or "war is never necessary." Over a long period of history, these shifting messages indicate what audiences of a particular era learned or wanted from these familiar genres. Deciphering those messages and meanings is a major part of film study today, because this shifting ideology is central to genre's purpose and construction.

Consider some items common in World War II combat films—boots, mail call, stopping to enjoy nature, and adopting a little dog (or cat or child) as a mascot while on patrol. All of these items, taken together, might be seen as the man in combat's attempt to link himself to sanity, to order, and to the remembered life from before he went into combat. They are a collective meaning which says—one must hang on to one's humanity in this situation, if at all possible. As Cornel Wilde warns his troops in *Beach Red*, after punishing them for need-lessly breaking a prisoner's arms, "This isn't the end of everything out here. Some of us are going back home, and we can't leave all that's decent on this battlefield."

Once established as links to order, however, they can also be used as warnings about combat behavior. Leave your boots outside the foxhole at night, and you'll get shot when you stick up your head to reach for them in the morning. Stop to pick some flowers, and the enemy sniper in the long grass will shoot you. In other words, remember home through your mail call if you want to, but never forget your military training. Thus boots become a symbol of military discipline or order, and losing them means losing your life (or your legs). Not having a pair that fit well makes you vulnerable on patrol. Taking them off all the time can be seen as a rejection of the combat situation, and so forth. In later genre stages, your own comrades can shoot your little mascot as a hideous joke. All this shows how basics are established and used, and how meanings shift and change and reverse themselves, but how, in the long run, they shift against something, change from something, and reverse the thing they have been established as. As audience familiarity increases, the basic definition grows increasingly referential and abstracted, because people KNOW it and can fill in the blanks.

Therefore we begin to trace the genre by establishing the basic definition. There are two aspects to the basic definition—what it is, and what people think it is. These two are not incompatible, but the difference between them is the area of flexibility the genre must maintain if it is to endure, and the cultural phenomenon that genre represents. The moviegoing public is sure that they know what any genre is and that all the films within it are the same. Scholars know this is not really true, but is true enough in people's minds. Because a genre story is a kind of shell to be filled, many subtle variations of plot are presented from film to film without damaging the basic units of its presentation. Although everyone thinks of all the films of a given genre as "the same thing," they are in fact, ingeniously altered to both reaffirm the genre and keep it fresh. A shootout in a Western can involve two men, three men, a man and two women, or two full gangs. It can be stark (man to man in the street) or complicated (two men sneaking around a complex geographical space, upstairs and down, inside and out). One participant can have a gun, and one can be unarmed. Instead of a fight with weapons, it can be a fistfight. Participants can go on foot or ride at one another on horses or in wagons.

Thus, in accumulating the description of what becomes the World War II combat film, one attempts to create a story that contains *all* the remembered elements from *all* the remembered films. This isn't possible. What *is* possible is to create a story that contains the basic repeated elements, and these in turn become what is used when later filmmakers want to make a film about combat. The sense of repeated elements solidifies, and filmgoers then imagine that a single film had contained them all. The later films refer to these elements as if they were all present, and as if all prior films contained all these elements. This is not true, except that, since our collective filmgoing consciousness agrees that it is true, it therefore is true. This agreement on the part of audiences and filmmakers about their accumulated and amalgamated *story* from a group of films might be called the Kilroy Test for Genre.

The Kilroy Test is what its name implies. A signature appears which everyone recognizes and accepts. In accepting it, we give credence to its having been written, and since it says "Kilroy was here," there must be a Kilroy. Later, we write "Kilroy was here" ourselves on the wall, and not only does that mean we believe in Kilroy, but that we have accepted his reality to the extent of being willing to take up his burdens and write his name on the one wall he seemed unable to find. Genre is like this. No one film ever appears that is quintessentially *the* genre. A group of films with very similar characteristics emerge, blend, and become one film in memory. When later, filmmakers create films of the same type (because they were popular and made money and can still speak to an audience about issues they want to hear) they make the memory of the accumulated film. They take up Kilroy's burden, and if challenged about the characteristics tell you in effect that there is, too, a Kilroy; they saw him. At least they saw his name on the wall. We live in times when names appear on walls, all put there by believers in a phantom Kilroy.

Land, Sea, or Air: They Journey On

The combat film naturally breaks into three areas from which to fight the war: on the ground, on the sea, and in the air. Each has its own particular spaces, costumes, weapons, real battles and heroes to emulate, as well as its own unit of generic action. Obviously, a sea combat presents a ship or submarine, with sailors dressed in naval uniforms, using depth charges and torpedoes, while an air battle in-volves bombers, fighter planes with pilots in airman's dress dropping bombs or spewing bullets out of tail guns and belly guns. The ground forces have several sets of possibilities: foot soldiers with rifles and bayonets, or tanks with guns, or cannon fire from a distance. Also, there are possible mixes of sea-air (aircraft carriers), air-ground (bombers helping foot soldiers), sea-ground (submarines taking combat patrols into battle).

Each area of combat has its own particular generic unit, or event, that marks its narrative. For instance, the sub must dive and leave someone up top. The combat patrol must leave behind a wounded comrade, with no chance of survival, in the jungle or the desert or the frozen north or wherever, with only a few salt tablets, his rifle, and a little water to hold him until discovered by the enemy or destroyed by thirst and starvation. The pilots must fly home, leaving behind their shot-down or paratrooper comrades. This is all the same event—leaving a fellow combatant to his fate because the pressure of war dictates the survival of the fittest, or the need to press on no matter what, even to the sacrifice of members of the group. In the same way, the captain who remains behind on his sinking ship, or remains until all crew members are safely off, is the equivalent of the pilot who remains at the controls of a burning plane until all crew members have jumped to safety, or a combat patrol leader who waits to go last after his men "run zig zag" to safety across a minefield, or an open field watched by the enemy.

When you watch *Sahara*, for instance, you see a tank progressing across the dry wastes of the desert. When you watch *Destination Tokyo*, you see a submarine progressing through the watery depths of the ocean. When you watch *Air Force*, you see an airplane flying onward through the unmarked skies. What's the difference? You're not being told any narrative verbally, but visually, you are. "They journey on," you record in your mind, consciously or unconsciously. The tank across the sand is the sub through the water is the plane through the sky. The machinery of war, carrying its cargo of men, moves forward toward and away from danger/combat.

These units are the equivalent of the patrol walking forward through whatever terrain they walk through—desert, jungle, snow, etc. The men on foot in *Sahara*, walking the desert wastes, hot and dry, are like those of *Objective Burma*, hacking through the steamy jungle, hot and wet, and also like the skiing commandos of *Heroes of Telemark*, sliding over snow and ice. "They journey on." The difference is that the men in tanks, subs, and planes fight the mechanized war, and the man on foot fights the old war. All are attacked not only by the enemy, but also by nature—sandstorms or heat or rain or fog or snow. They suffer the specific dangers of their separate geographic environments—thirst, suffocation, gravity, or disease (desert/underwater/skies/jungles), but their basic problem is the same—threat of death from various sources. The combat film is about death and destruction, and how we have to fight to avoid it.

This "they journey on" property is partially attributable to a unique

Destination Tokyo

property of film—editing. The ability to remind a viewer constantly of the circumstances of war, nature, and containment—the conditions under which the characters of the film move forward—is one of the tools of cinema. Genre study should not ignore such properties and their contained and implied meanings. One of the primary character- istics of the World War II combat genre is the use of cutting to remind viewers of the overall situation of the war. By cutting from a personal view of characters involved in a dialogue and action as individual human beings to a more distanced and impersonal view, the film shows us the larger situation its characters are in. You see an image which reads as "these are human beings like me contained inside that sub- marine which is itself contained under a large body of water and which is trapped in the big picture of World War II"; but in spite of this, "they journey on." These images of the machines in a particular terrain also link a viewer's experiences to other visual material, such as the newsreels at the local movie or the photos from the war in newspapers and magazines. "They journey on" by its implication of perseverance under difficult situations implies the possibility of victory, or at least endurance. "They journey on" tends to be the variation of the combat genre in which we win, instead of the trapped, last stand variation, in which the journey ends in stasis, and ultimately death. Thus, editing and its sense of progress or change becomes an important aspect of genre definition, to be used one way in films of movement and another in films of entrapment. The long takes in which men sit trapped in a submarine on the bottom of the ocean stretch out the length of the moments for viewers, as do similar instances of men sitting tensely in foxholes at night, straining to see the enemy approach in the dark. The long take provides no release, a sense of endless time, and an additional realism to the event. A similar property of genre involves narrative variations which are cosmetic: dress, weapons, settings, locations, actions which are on the surface different but represent the same information transmitted to the audience.

Subtle Variations

Where the ground/sea/air formats differ is in the subtle variations they transmit via coding of spaces contained within image. For instance, the truest and purest combat format is the infantry film, followed by the submarine film, with surface navy and air force films vying for third place. Obviously, the infantry out on patrol are in the midst of the war, and the submarine, although a self-contained home-like unit, is also in the midst of danger from both nature and the enemy. The surface ship, with its big kitchen, dormitory style living, and abundance of air to breathe, is less frightening for viewers than the underwater boat. The air force, with its ability to fly in and out of combat, sets up a pattern of safety and danger, attack and fly away, yet its vulnerability to crash means danger, too.

It is interesting to consider the various spaces assigned by reality to the three basic formats of combat: air, sea, and land. Those who fly can return to safe havens and the occasional foray into nightclubs or private homes in England or China. The spaces they occupy tend to be *professional*: offices, barracks, briefing rooms. On the ocean when not in combat, men occupy *domestic* spaces: their bunks, bedrooms, kitchens, galleys, as well as bridges which are porchlike in their capacity to provide seating arrangements and places for conversation. There is a doctor on board, and his office is a place to discuss domestic problems and feelings. On land, men occupy foxholes or tents, which are purely *combat* spaces. Consequently, the air force film is often about *professionalism*, the pressure of duty, the responsibilities of leadership. The navy film is about *domestic* strife, not only the kind that grows up among the men on board (as in family life), but also the kind they left behind with women who resent their long months at sea. The land/ infantry film is about *combat*.

Thus, the infantry film almost always becomes the pure combat movie, whereas the navy film tells the story of the domestic lives of military men and the air force film that of the problems men have in the chain of command.

Previous Classifications

The simple classification of films by military force was one of the first ways anyone ever tried to organize the combat genre. In 1945, Dorothy B. Jones, head of the Film Analysis and Reviewing Section of the Hollywood office of the Office of War Information, was asked to compile and classify all the war-related films made during the combat, according to a series of categories first defined by President Roosevelt in his annual address to Congress on the State of the Union in January 1942.[1] These classifications were The Issues, The Enemy, The United Nations, The Production Front, The Home Front, and The Fighting Forces.

The films classified under The Fighting Forces contain those films made during the war years which involve combat. Jones subdivided them into Armed Forces groupings, with the Marine Corps, the Medical Corps, and the Women's Corps as subcategories of all three. She further separated them according to whether they were training films or actual combat films. As stated earlier, this was easier said than done in some cases, such as *Bombardier* and *Marine Raiders*. Her list is also not free of omissions and errors, as she includes *two* noncombat comedies, *Abroad with Two Yanks* and *Two Yanks in Trinidad*.

Dorothy Jones' list is not just an example of how to define and catalogue groups of films by a set of assumed characteristics. It brings legitimacy to the existence of the combat genre, and also indicates that genre was a language understood by an entire nation in the 1940s. In order to make her list, she had to consider all the films made that touched on the presence of war, and the war permeates the films made in Hollywood during the years of actual combat. Even films which seemingly have nothing to do with war, the so-called escapist films, frequently are touched, however lightly, by its presence. Musicals are about soliders and sailors on leave, or about women waiting for their men to come home. Swashbucklers have villains with Nazi-like characteristics, and even cartoon characters confront the enemy, as when Bugs Bunny "Nips the Nips."

The problem of listing all the films which are combat films appears to be somewhat easier than the task Jones undertook. Combat is only one type of film, and she was listing six types. Moreover, her categories are broadly generalized, whereas the combat film is specific, and thus restrictive. However, classifying it is actually *more* difficult, and much harder to do, than one might think. Someone told me, "All that anyone need look for is the presence of combat in a World War II context." This illustrates the easy assumption that any genre is what it is— that it never grows or changes or appears as part of any other genre or incorporates another genre into itself or, in fact, that it comes from anywhere other than history. There will never be any problem in identifying it—no questions about including comedy versions or films that have only one short battle and no other combat scenes.

However, to deal with a mass of material, one must begin somewhere, so to begin the historical analysis of the combat genre, I began by screening the films of World War II itself. Obviously, I had a prior conception of what the genre would be. The peculiar nature of genre study, in which one seemingly knows the definition one is looking for, allowed for my making comparisons from an informed point of view. What I knew in advance was what presumably every member of our culture would know about World War II combat films—that they contained a hero, a group of mixed types, and a military objective of some sort. They take place in the actual battle zones of World War II, against the established enemies, on the ground, the sea, or in the air. They contain many repeated events, such as mail call, all presented visually with the appropriate uniforms, equipment, and iconography of battle. They employ the full usage of the tools of cinema (lighting, camera movement, composition, and cutting). In them, people die. This knowledge, which is essentially correct, was enough to guide me through the films without limiting new discoveries.

Obviously, these films did not appear without borrowing some characteristics from earlier films, and this tendency will be described in chapter 2. Influences on these films would naturally come from many other sources, too: real events; newspapers, newsreel, and magazine images of real events; earlier real events of other wars; novels, stories, and comic books; plays and paintings. Out of many sources, groups of filmmakers (writers, directors, producers, art directors, et al.) began to make films which told stories about the war our nation was fighting as the war unfolded and as we fought it.

Emergence of the Genre

In screening the films released between December 7, 1941, and August 8, 1945, I saw the combat genre emerge. The definition appeared out of the fog of war, as it were. From the development I observed in these films I discerned three divisions:

- *Introductory Stage*: December 7, 1941–December 31, 1942.
- *Emergence of the Basic Definition*: 1943.
- *Repeat of the Definition*: January 1, 1944–December 31, 1945.

It is striking how few actual combat films were released during this time period. From December 7, 1941 to January 1, 1944, the primary list of pure combat films, by which is meant films that take place *totally* in combat, contains only five films, and none of these five appears before 1943. Even allowing for films which contain combat only as part of a larger, somewhat unrelated story, there are only approximately twenty A-budget features (see Filmography). Many films, of course, are difficult to classify, because they contain only small bits of combat. But the hard-core movies which are either pure combat or mostly combat are remarkably few. Considering the number of films released in those days (as many as 400 to 500 titles per year), this is a small group of movies. Since these films are the basis for a genre that is still alive today, their power and importance is obvious.

In thinking of these films, it is important to remember that the filmmaking process, even in the swift days of the well-equipped studio system, takes time. To conceive, budget, write, shoot, edit, process, and release a film of the nature of the combat film (which involves special effects, and special costumes and equipment) took enough time so that the first A-film of the genre (*Wake Island*) did not reach audiences until September 1942. The first year's releases were inevitably small, and perhaps a little cautious. After all, the news in the early days of the war was not good. We were losing. Studio heads and personnel also worried about whether or not Americans really wanted to see combat films. With sons and brothers and husbands fighting and being killed, would people want to pay money to see it happening? The answer, as we shall see in chapter 3, turned out to be yes.

Of course, all Americans who went to the movies were seeing the weekly newsreels that covered the combat in the field. This was not the instant, "as it happened" daily television news coverage of the Vietnam War, but it was current visual coverage of events. In addition, various documentary films were being released to viewers: *We Are the Marines* (December 14, 1942), a full-length, "fact film" from the "March of Time," and John Ford's shot-on-the-spot *Battle of Midway*, a color film made during the actual chaos of combat during the attack (see chapter 3).

British combat films were also appearing in New York during this time span. Such titles as *Suicide Squadron, One of Our Aircraft Is Missing,* and *In Which We Serve* were being seen. Russian combat films, too, appeared.[2]

Introductory Stage:
From December 7, 1941–December 31, 1942.

A review of all the films released from Pearl Harbor to the end of 1942 turns up a strange list of movies difficult to categorize. Here in the beginning stages of the war, in which the industry had to turn around and begin production on a new basis, there are many films which could involve endless discussions about definition. A large number of films were released which carried titles implying topicality but examining them proves they were not really combat films at all. *Remember Pearl Harbor, Parachute Nurse, To the Shores of Tripoli, Wings for the Eagle, Call Out the Marines,*[3] *Atlantic Convoy, Two Yanks in*

Trinidad, and *Thunder Birds,* for example, are not combat films. Inevitably, the films of this period are transitional, and the facts indicate that, while war was on everyone's mind and references to it were contained in many films of many different types, those which involved the presentation of combat or involved combat as a story premise were sparse during this time period. The films released before the end of 1942 which contain actual combat or which concern some form of military action and thus introduce the genre are: A *Yank on the Burma Road, Submarine Raider, Eagle Squadron, Wake Island, Desperate Journey, Manila Calling, Flying Tigers,* and *The Navy Comes Through.* Out of these eight films, not one is yet pure combat.

Looking at each of these films, one can see how the pattern of hero, group, objective, etc. slowly develops and solidifies. One can also see the transitions which link the old and the new. In retrospect, 1942 is clearly a transitional year. Of the eight films of combat from 1942, A *Yank on the Burma Road, Submarine Raider,* and *The Navy Comes Through* are low-budget films, designed to exploit current headlines. *Manila Calling* is interesting only because it appears to be a variation of John Ford's 1934 film, *The Lost Patrol,* written by Dudley Nichols. This was not the first time *Lost Patrol* was used as the format for a film, nor would it be the last. Remade in 1939 as a western entitled *Bad Lands, The Lost Patrol* would be resurrected yet again as the model for the seminal film of the formation of the genre, *Bataan,* which would be released in 1943. The *New York Times* review of *Manila Calling* clearly indicated its predecessor: "Sol Wurtzel, the film's producer," the reviewer noted "has seized upon the idea of using the Japanese invasion of the Philippines as the background for a story similar to that of *Lost Patrol.*" Reviewers of the 1930s and 1940s easily identified generic sources and conventions. People in those days went to the movies steadily, and they remembered what they had seen. Although scholars today assume the public wanted familiar stories told and retold, reviewers constantly complained about it at the time.

Desperate Journey is an unusual case. Released near the end of 1942 (reviewed September 26),[4] it is an energetic film that illustrates clearly the differences between early examples of the war film as opposed to what would emerge later. It is a Rover Boys-Go-to-Germany adventure/ comedy in which the Germans are dolts, and in which the heroes face serious danger as if it were a lark. World War II is like a panty raid on a dormitory by a particularly enterprising group of fraternity boys.

Desperate Journey has lasting fame as the film in which the three survivors steal a German plane and fly happily home toward England, with Errol Flynn cheerfully saying, "Now for Australia. . . and a crack at those Japs!" Well-directed and paced, *Desperate Journey* is a transitional film because of its treatment of the war as a madcap adventure. It also presents both "good" Germans (those who help our flyers) and "bad" Germans (the Nazis) in a highly oversimplified way. In a sense, *Desperate Journey* is to war films what *To Be or Not To Be* (directed by Ernst Lubitsch, written by Edwin Justus Mayer, 1942) is to comedy— all wrong for the times and for what was coming, an alleged insult to a serious issue. Seen today, *Desperate Journey* is quite a bit of fun, and its breathtaking pace is delightful. (And *To Be or Not To Be* is a masterpiece.)[5]

It is *tone* which marks *Desperate Journey* as separate from the genre about to develop. First of all, the men are not really involved in combat; they are involved in adventure. They are behind the lines in Germany by accident, as their plane has crashed on a bombing mission. They do have an objective—which is to get home—but on the way, they find other fun-type objectives such as blowing up a chemical plant. They are captured and escape. They connect with the underground. They go here, and they go there. What larks! Despite some heavy propagandizing about what swine the Nazis are (and what idiots), the film is more a comedy than anything else. It is in the tradition of the Errol Flynn movie—lighthearted adventure with a graceful hero who never loses his sense of humor despite the seriousness and immediacy of the danger. *Desperate Journey* is partly related to films which will come later, such as *Dirty Dozen* and *Kelly's Heroes*, which make fun out of the adventure of war, and superimpose that sense over real death and destruction.

Where *Desperate Journey* fits the new emerging genre is in the idea of a group working together toward a military goal. The implication is that members of this group, no matter what their varying skills and experiences, are equal heroes in the action. Errol Flynn is the star of the film, but his companion, played by Ronald Reagan, is his equal in heroism, if not in billing. Importantly, it is a group of five representative types: an American (Reagan), a young and inexperienced Englishman (Ronald Sinclair), a World War I veteran from Scotland (Alan Hale), a Canadian (Arthur Kennedy), who provides plot conflict, and the central hero, an Australian (Errol Flynn).

Desperate Journey also illustrates the difference between our cultural viewings of Germany and Japan during the war years. In film terms, the Japanese are linked to the sea, the Germans somewhat more to the land. The Japanese war, if not on the sea, is on an enclosed and isolated island, whereas the German war is on open farmland, in forests, and villages. The majority of the very early films concern themselves with the Japanese war. The dramatic shock of Pearl Harbor, and the sense of outrage Americans felt, made that story the more important one. Besides, we had already fought the Germans in World War I, and films such as *All Quiet on the Western Front* had humanized them for us. "Our" group might have a German in its midst, but, during the war itself, never a Japanese. When we met the enemy, it was somewhat plausible to assume Germans could speak English, or that we could speak German. It was less plausible to make such an assumption about Japanese. This created the fabulous "I was educated in your country" explanation from the Japanese leader who takes an American prisoner, which again implies a kind of treachery—using our educational system for nefarious purposes. (Some of Japan's best naval officers *were* educated at Annapolis.) The plain fact of all this is that we viewed the war with the Japanese as a race war, and the war with the Germans as an ideological war. When we disliked Germans, it was the Nazis we meant. When we disliked the Japanese, it was all of them.

Wake Island and *Flying Tigers* are the two most important films of the transitional year, 1942. With the key film *Wake Island*, what is going to happen begins to happen: It is the first film based on an actual World War II battle, and the first to reach the public as an A-production from a major studio. *Wake Island*, nominated for best picture of the year by the Motion Picture Academy, was enormously successful. It was favorably reviewed by major critics. You can trace in it clearly the transition from the older military films of the 1930s toward the new tradition of the World War II film. The characteristics that define it are a mingling of "old" and "new"—with "new" being old plot devices updated by linking them *specifically* to Wake and the war.

Wake Island thus is not total combat. Its opening scenes appear to be a typical 1930s military film, in which the traditional problems of the service comedy are in full swing. But this familiar plot is exploded by the attack of the Japanese, and the film blows itself up. When the men fight back—and fight they do—the kernel of the combat films which would appear in 1943 can be seen. In fact, *Wake Island* is perhaps the one film in which we can still see it happen. Here's the old—out with the old! Blow it up! Fragments fall down. We gather them like old planks of wood (rivalries, a little mascot dog, mail call) and use them in building the new. Old planks beside new planks—the new structure. And not just the new structure—also the new emotion, the new propaganda.

These "old" traits, seen in earlier films and used by *Wake Island*, will continue in the genre films to follow:

- An adversary relationship between two characters (played by William Bendix and Robert Preston). This competitive friendship between two men in military service may be called the "Quirt/Flagg" relationship, as it grows out of *What Price Glory?* (see chapter 2).
- An internal conflict on our side—between military men on the island and a group of nonmilitary construction workers
- The plan of a character (William Bendix) not to re-enlist when his time is up (later familiar to fans of John Ford's westerns, in which Victor McLaglen faced similar decisions).
- The arrival of a tough new C.O. who forces the military personnel to undergo a difficult inspection
- An illegal fistfight between a military man and someone he should not be hitting (in this case, a civilian), followed by a scene in which the two enemies join together to hide their fisticuffs from authorities
- One character's being deeply attached to a little dog, who has become a mascot. (This one has puppies!)
- The fabulous Armageddon of conflict which ends the film, and in which all the characters the audience has come to know are killed, in accurate representation of our first losing battles of the war.
- An opening frame in which a printed set of words speak to the audience of historical events and to the authenticity of the film. "From the records of the United States Marine Corps . . . in this picture the action at Wake Island has been depicted as accurately and factually as possible . . . America and Americans have long been used to victory, but the great names of her military history . . . Valley Forge . . . Custer's Last Stand . . . The Lost Battalion . . . represent the dark hours. There, small groups of men fought savagely to the death because in dying they gave eternal life to the ideas for which they died." These bold and dramatic opening words are further bolstered by a documentary-like narration, which refers to the marines building a military base on Wake Island. Printed dedications, references to past historical events, official advisors or references to military files, and voiceover narration all become conventions of the combat films which follow.

- The "last stand" format, familiar from such Westerns as *They Died With Their Boots On* and other Custer stories as well as films about the Alamo. (*Lost Patrol* is also a "last stand" movie.)
- The military unit of enlisted men and officers—separated by rank, education, background, and lifestyles
- A poetic burial at night
- The sacrificial pilot, this one willing to die because of the death of his wife at Pearl Harbor. He takes his plane up to bomb the Japanese warship successfully.

As stated earlier, *Wake Island* begins to relate the meaning of these "old" devices directly to World War II. Thus, they are reborn as "new" to World War II. For instance, the characters played by Brian Donlevy and Albert Dekker represent conflict between the military (Donlevy) and civilian life (Dekker). Whereas in a pre-war movie this might stand for duty vs. irresponsibility, or the group vs. the individual, here it demonstrates the need for each side to understand the other, to respect each other's various skills (both of which will be needed in wartime), and to work together. The wartime metaphor is obvious. In the end, these two men are together in a foxhole sharing memories of playing football ("Notre Dame '28" and "V.M.I. '28") "To '28" is their final toast, with the last bottle of beer on the island. Once separated by occupation and university, they are united in the war effort.

Another example of "old reborn new" is the reenlistment conflict of William Bendix, a familiar ploy skillfully updated by the dramatic use of SUNDAY, DECEMBER 7TH, 1941. If there is one thing anyone familiar with films set in those days knows: December 7th. Over the years, filmmakers have shown it on calendars, on desk pads, in invitations, and on bulletin boards. It has been announced over the radio, over loudspeakers, and on intercoms. We all know what it means— The Day of Infamy, Pearl Harbor. "Where were you when you heard about Pearl Harbor?" people used to ask, and everyone, everywhere knew. Pearl Harbor Day stands as our most commonly remembered and shared date. As the film runs, the audience knows it is moving inexorably toward that date. All meaning is linked to it. As *Wake Island* provides transition from the old to the new, the date stands as the changeover point—for the narrative, for the viewers, for history. When Bendix circles it on his calendar near the opening of the movie, he does more than turn a calendar page. He flips *Wake Island* over from the 1930s to the 1940s.

Wake is also "new" because it identifies an enemy, presenting Japan in clearly propagandistic terms, as a strong and powerful force. Furthermore, the Japanese are seen in closeups as real flesh and blood people, not some distant inhuman thing. The film obviously seeks to stir up the viewer's hatred for this enemy, by presenting him as a frightening figure who would shoot a radioman in the back, and who would gun down a brave pilot who had to parachute out of a burning plane. (The latter image recurs in *Air Force*.) The sense of the enemy as a sneak is enforced by a sequence in which the Japanese envoy and his entourage arrive by plane, en route to Washington for a Peace Conference. In stopping over at Wake, they are seen at the evening's celebratory banquet, candlelight playing menacingly on their faces, while the envoy offers a toast to Roosevelt. Later, the radio is heard, and a newscaster, says, "On this peaceful Sunday A.M., December 7, 1941, the Japanese are in Washington with a message of peace."

The propaganda goes beyond the presentation of a menacing enemy, however. It includes a patriotic reference to our historical battles, not just in the opening dedication, but also in the final battle itself. "Don't fire till you see the whites of their eyes," Donlevy tells his men, pointing out that he is quoting Colonel Prescott from the Battle of Bunker Hill. Donlevy's character also points out the reason we must fight: "We've got to fight to destroy corruption," he says, in some vague reference. (This man is quite a philosopher. He tells the young pilot whose wife has been killed in the raid on Pearl that, "A man's main memories are given him by a woman—his mother, his sisters, his wife—even the women you want to forget. You're like me, now. A man with a memory." Some comfort!)

The two best scenes for emotional power, other than those of combat, concern death. More than anything else, this separates *Wake* from the earlier films of 1942. There is no glamor and glory, just *death*. The two scenes concern a young couple, newlyweds, both of whom are killed. Since the wife is a character we never really know, her offstage death is less poignant than it might have been. For that matter, the young husband (Macdonald Carey) is also a character we hardly know, so we have nothing invested in a love for him. Yet his death is dramatic. Because his wife's death has left him nothing, he decides to avenge her by flying out alone to bomb the off-shore ship that is shelling them. Here we see two motifs of World War II combined—it will be a war on women and children as well as on soldiers, and it will require the

The burial at night: Wake Island.

sacrifice of certain individuals. Over and over again, a woman or child will be killed, while the men who are out in the war, expecting to die, will survive and suffer the irony that someone they loved has been killed behind the lines. Over and over again, a brave pilot will fly out alone to bomb the enemy, conscious he will never return. In *Wake Island*, the pilot manages to both bomb the ship and bring his plane triumphantly home. But when his comrades run to greet him, he is dead in the cockpit. His burial at night is a visually beautiful scene, scored by the haunting playing of taps. The lighting is soft, its darkness a comfort from the harsh explosions and hard sun of daylit Wake. Yet its comfort is cut by the beam of a flashlight, which Brian Donlevy must hold to read from the Bible. There is the urgency of war about the service, the sense of men trying to do the expected thing in a situation that soon won't have any time for convention.

Despite the effectiveness of this scene, and despite the real excitement of the combat, *Wake Island*, from today's perspective, is flawed by a lack of character development. There are too many people, and we never really get to know any one of them as a human being. However, this movie helps contemporary audiences to understand those of 1942; the critical reception then indicated no such flaw. At the time, audiences knew the situation and its deaths first-hand. They probably fleshed out the characters themselves with people they knew and loved. They brought characterization into the theater with them. They came to learn about the new war, with its enemy and its death—basically to see what it looked like and to hear told the story of World War II.

Still, despite its changing "old" to "new" before our eyes, *Wake Island* is not really the typical combat film of World War II. In it, we observe the process of change, not the new product. The language of the combat genre is not yet spoken here, although its words are known. The film is a dramatic reenactment of a historical event, done documentary style in terms of its final combat, with narrative only as filler and touchstone (not to mention enticement) for the audience.

Today the iconography looks wrong to the viewer familiar with the equipment of World War II. It may indeed have been accurate that those who fought at Wake Island were wearing World War I style helmets and using out-of-date weapons, but the war films to come, which would live in the minds of viewers, would look different. The geography of Wake Island, both real and filmed, does not relate to the later films audiences would remember. It is neither that of the European patrol, passing hedgerows and villages and farms, nor that of the Pacific jungles or the barren desert wastes of the African campaigns.

Wake Island has the look of World War I at its finale, with Donlevy and Dekker out in a foxhole with a barren stretch of beach in front of them, dotted only with brush that looks almost like barbed wire. The command post is a lookalike for the old trench world of World War I. World War I had a designated space on which to fight the infantry war—"no man's land," between the opposing sides' trenches. That barren space, fortified with barbed wire, is the visual place of World War I. One can leave the war and go back behind the lines to a French inn and find love, romance, food and wine; but the no man's land is the World War I infantry combat space.

World War II's visual presentation is constituted quite differently. As was true in real life, its space of war is anywhere and everywhere.

Although there are places where combat is not happening at that moment, such as a village or farmhouse, it can intrude very suddenly. To get out of it, one has to leave the whole theater of war—return to America, fly back to a safe base, or die.

Wake Island, like the war films which follow it, concerns itself not only with history and battle, but also with the underlying issue of what it means to be an American: Here is a nation that seeks to whip its populace into patriotic fervor by showing them films based on *defeat*, not victory. As the introductory words of *Wake Island* indicated, both Valley Forge and Custer's Last Stand, not to mention the Alamo, represent great moments in American bravery or folly (or both), depending on your point of view. It is significant that Americans seek to glorify these last stands, or failures, in many ways and in many formats, not just the combat film, but also in Westerns and in gangster films.[6] Donlevy's final message sent out from Wake is "The enemy has landed. Issue still in doubt." The issue in doubt can only be World War II, not the battle of Wake Island. When *Wake Island* ends, the message is clear: "This is not the end. There are other marines. Other leathernecks." And there will be other World War II combat films, that's for sure. The clouds of smoke that blur the final images of the deaths of the last men alive on Wake Island are cut by hundreds of marching marines emerging out of the fog. We may be losers, but we never give up—and losers who never give up will finally win.

In 1942, air warfare was still relatively new, having begun in World War I, celebrated by such famous films as *Wings, Hell's Angels, Lilac Time*, and both versions of *Dawn Patrol*. Its premise is the glory of it all, and the ability of the air combatants to return to a safe base inevitably requires a story with a strong subplot which can be enacted back at the base. (A notable exception to this is *Air Force*, in which the plane enters a state of total combat.)

More than *Eagle Squadron, Flying Tigers* is really the first of the actual World War II air combat films. Combat takes up more than half its running time. It carries a dedication that is a quote from Chiang Kai-shek: "They have become the symbol of the invincible spirit." The combat is intense, and the film builds to DECEMBER 7, when those volunteers for freedom, the Flying Tigers (others might call them Nosy Parkers), find the justification for their early involvement. Nevertheless, the film contains familiar plots from the 1930s. In addition to the romantic triangle (the responsible man, the trusted nurse, and the dashing devil-may-care flyboy), there is also the sense of acceptance of duty, and a subplot right out of *Only Angels Have Wings*, one of the most successful airplane movies of the late thirties. This story, a direct steal, involves an old man who wants to keep flying but who can't see well enough anymore. At a crucial moment, he goes up anyway and loses his life (as does the Thomas Mitchell character from *Only Angels*).

Through its two heroes, *Flying Tigers* demonstrates the conflict of individualism that will be resolved within the new definition of the combat film. The two men are played by John Carroll and John Wayne. Carroll, a poor man's Clark Gable, is carrying on the Gable persona in his role. (Gable was such a strong star that he established not only a persona for himself but also, by extension, one for his lookalike, Carroll). Carroll's character is jaunty, irresponsible, a wolf with women, and a daredevil. Wayne is sober and responsible, a good and true leader of men. The film implies that the skills of both are needed to win the war by establishing that, to accomplish the final mission, both men must be in the plane which sets out on a suicidal objective. America, a maverick country that was started, settled, and built by a rebellious group of religious dissidents (and also by a ragtail group of misfits and outlaws), always contains the elements of rebellion and outlawry in the national persona. This is perhaps why we always favor the underdog, and why so many of our favorite stories have losers who turn out to be winners. (It's also the source of some of our national guilt and ambivalence. We deserted our families and countries to come over here.)

In the finale of the film, Carroll, knowing he is mortally wounded, lures John Wayne into bailing out of the plane. Then, he skillfully steers it downward, bombing the supply train below. (A similar event will take place in *Bataan* and other, later films.) According to some historical sources, Americans were not initially informed about the Japanese kamikaze pilots. This news was considered too horrible, too demoralizing for the people at home. Yet our filmed stories of the war from the beginning used the concept, but always with our side in control of it. As if to demonstate that we, too, could sacrifice ourselves in war, films presented the noble sacrifice as a choice good men could make for their country. However, no American pilot ever chooses this road unless he is already mortally wounded or seriously flawed (too cowardly, too old, too cheeky, too just plain bad). He uses his last effort for the collective good. In *Flying Tigers*, it is the irresponsible side of the dual heroes who goes down. We must use this irresponsibility, says the film, because we need that kind of courage, skill, luck, and daring to win this war; but we must put it under the control and direction of the sober leader, who will survive. *Flying Tigers* is about our country's having to grow up: "A whole lot of us don't grow up," Carroll tells Wayne. "We stay kids." But, he adds, change the streets that are being bombed into the streets of his home town, ("Call it Texas"), and that changes everything.

In retrospect, then, in 1941 and 1942, only *Eagle Squadron, Wake Island* and *Flying Tigers* qualify as true military force combat films significant to the development of the genre. *Yank on the Burma Road* and *Manila Calling* involve guerrillas and civilians, although *Manila Calling* is interesting because of its *Lost Patrol* format. *Submarine Raider* and *The Navy Comes Through* existed to expolit, not to define or inspire. Who remembers them? They are part of that large bunch of low-budget films that Hollywood always turned out to make a buck, as opposed to the big-budget films they made carefully and thoughtfully to make big bucks. *Desperate Journey* is not the story of an actual military operation. It is an action adventure story *set* in enemy territory. Later, after the genre is clearly defined, this format will return to importance, but at this point in history, it does not help shape the genre. This leaves *Eagle Squadron, Wake Island,* and *Flying Tigers* as the films which mark the beginnings, and in them we see the transitional period. The old and the new intermingle in various ways. In ranking their importance, *Wake Island* is clearly the most significant, followed by *Flying Tigers* and then *Eagle Squadron.*

Because *Eagle Squadron* takes place in Europe and celebrates the glamor of the air service, and because it tends to be molded in the World War I tradition, it is less significant than the other two films despite its hero, group, and objective configuration, and despite some authentic battle footage producer Walter Wanger secured from the British government. *Wake Island* and *Flying Tigers* both contain news of December 7, and a true combat engagement between military men and the Japanese. They have heroes, groups, and objectives, as well as other traditional events of the genre. However, they cling to the past with their heroes in pairs having a personal competition, instead of a military or political conflict that is personalized through their characters.

In these early stages of 1942, what we learn is how very important the concept of the unified group is to the World War II combat film. It is that unique group of mixed individuals, so carefully organized to represent typical Americans, that we find missing in these films. It is this shifting from a single individual, or a pair of competitive individuals, over to a unified group as a hero (although not without its leading man, the hero of the heroes) that marks the war years and the new genre. The obvious interpretation is that the war brings a need for us to work together as a group, to set aside individual needs, and to bring our melting pot tradition together to function as a true democracy since, after all, that is what we are fighting for: the Democratic way of life.

Emergence of the Basic Definition: The Calendar Year, 1943

The films which initially define the combat genre appear in 1943. During that period, the narrative films which opened in New York City were *Air Force* and *Immortal Sergeant* (February 4), *Stand by for Action* (March 12), *Crash Dive* (April 30), *Action in the North Atlantic* (May 22), *Bataan* (June 4), *Destroyer* (September 2), *So Proudly We Hail* (September 10), *Corvette K-225* (October 21), *Sahara* (November 12), *Guadalcanal Diary* (November 18), *Cry Havoc* (November 24).[7]

Of these, *Bataan* is clearly the seminal film. It marks the point at which a film appears that contains the primary characteristics of the genre—a film totally set in the combat situation, with no escapes or releases of any sort. The year 1943 may be divided into Before *Bataan* and After *Bataan* to illustrate how the genre emerges and how the presentation of combat finally takes complete charge of the military picture. Of the five films released before *Bataan*, four clearly contain a visual denial of the war. These four are *Immortal Sergeant, Stand by for Action, Crash Dive,* and *Action in the North Atlantic.* All four movies contain the traditional characteristics that will come to be associated with the genre, and that were observed emerging in 1942. However, they each find ways to remove their heroes from combat, to take them away from the military situation into civilian life. This visual denial of combat does not happen in *Bataan* at all, and to a certain degree does not happen in *Air Force.* However, of all the films released from December 7, 1941 to June 4, 1942, only *Bataan* contains no release from the combat situation whatsoever.

Immortal Sergeant, Stand by for Action, Crash Dive, and *Action in the North Atlantic* reflect the idea that audiences may be unwilling to submit themselves to movies that give no relief from the war. Film-makers must have thought it necessary—as it may well have been—to provide outlets for viewers of combat movies. They may also have felt that such outlets helped to build connections and links between life on the home front and life in the combat world, important links in the emotional lives of American civilians who needed to feel connected to their friends and relatives who were fighting in combat.

The ways these four films deny combat are both visual and narrative. They find plot structures which provide excuses for the heroes to return home from combat, as in *Action in the North Atlantic,* when the heroes have their merchant marine ship torpedoed out from under them, or in *Crash Dive,* when the heroes return home after a successful mission. These two films tell their different stories—one of defeat and one of victory—but in both cases, the combat event provides an excuse with which to return the heroes to shore, and thus to romance, excite-ment, typical American home life, or a noncombat experience.

Stand by for Action also finds a plot that allows for the intrusion of the noncombat experience, but its variation is slightly more imaginative than the predictable return to shore. The story of a destroyer on active combat patrol, *Stand by for Action* tells how the crew of the destroyer picks up a lifeboat loaded with babies and two pregnant women, both of whom proceed to give birth. The sailors have to feed babies, rig cribs for them to sleep in, diaper them, and of course deliver the two new recruits. It would be one thing for "signs and meaning in the cinema" if they picked up two philosophers—or a plumber and a mechanic—but they picked up women and babies, a clear statement about removing the men of the destroyer from their traditional military concerns and restoring them to the concerns of the American home front. *Stand by for Action* also demonstrates how some of the earlier films unified the old and the new, in that it begins with the statement "The Day of Infamy" and a replay of December 7, followed by a montage of Amer-icans beginning to arm to retaliate. Then it drops a military stance entirely, and opens up on a tennis court, with the handsome hero (Robert Taylor), splendid in his whites, meeting two adoring girls and making a date with one for a cocktail party. He is assigned to a destroyer that saw service in World War I and that has been lovingly cared for by a civilian watchman who once served on her crew in active combat

(Walter Brennan). The story of how both Brennan and the old ship are refurbished to fight and win anew makes an obvious metaphor about America's preparation to fight the Germans a second time in a great World War.

The most interesting denial of the total combat situation is visual. The combat film has its own light and dark, its own explosive images, its own weaponry and uniforms and spaces inside foxholes, tanks, subs, and planes. Whenever such iconography is removed from the screen to be replaced by tennis whites and cocktail parties, or small town city streets, or train rides to Washington, D.C. and lovely New England girls schools—all of which appear in these four films—then the audience is not only released from the combat experience, but it is also involved in a new set of signifiers and meanings. Combat disappears, and by disappearing ceases to be. A different genre takes its place. This is particularly true in the early stages of the genre's development, in which it is obvious that the removal of combat is specifically done for audience release and relief. After the war, the continuation of the genre usually finds such scenes much more directly connected to the combat story. For instance, the home front story may then establish the theme of the character's cowardice, which will be used in the combat section of the movie.

The unique devices of the film medium are put to use in this visual denial through the filmic device of the flashback. In the most common form of the flashback, a specific character "remembers" or "flashes back" to past events in his life. These events then appear on the screen, removing or replacing the "present" in the character's life. This device is put to full use in *Immortal Sergeant*. This movie, which stars Henry Fonda, purports to be a film of total combat. It begins in a combat situation in North Africa, and ends with a brief return to England in which Fonda is reunited with his girl, Maureen O'Hara. Otherwise, it is set totally in the North African desert campaign, a story of how timid young Fonda must face death and the pressures of leadership after he is unexpectedly left in command when his tough old sergeant dies. In his mind, his lack of courage in wooing the girl he loved back in England is linked to his fear that he cannot lead his troops safely through the desert. As he fights the war, he remembers his courtship of her, and these courtship scenes appear on screen as flashbacks.

Set on patrol in the African desert in the midst of total combat, *Immortal Sergeant* thus may be the only combat film with a Cuban musical number! What a great device to give the audience a war movie and not give them a war movie! The use of the flashback would become increasingly important in the combat film in the postwar years, as it offers a way to present the traditonal genre but not leave audiences completely stranded in a conflict that has been resolved.

Narrative stucture also indicates the commitment of film to the emerging genre. *Crash Dive* begins with a victorious return of the hero (Tyrone Power) from a sucessful PT boat mission. The film then follows his onshore life, romantic involvement, transfer to another service, conflict with a fellow officer, etc., until it returns to total combat in the form of a dangerous submarine mission. By beginning with a statement of combat, and setting up a story that must head directly back to combat, *Crash Dive* marks itself as a combat film with shoreline interludes.

Action in the North Atlantic opens with a ghastly combat sequence in which the ship carrying the heroes is torpedoed and destroyed by German subs. This necessitates a return to shore, and a waiting period while the representative group of men live their lives until a new ship is prepared and they return to combat. They are in the Merchant Marine, so their job is not to partrol the ocean, but to cross it carrying supplies. This allowed for shore stories to be easily incorporated in the plot, but the film returns the men to shore through the device of defeat and necessity.

If *Immortal Sergeant, Stand by for Action, Crash Dive,* and *Action in the North Atlantic* all find a way out of combat for viewers, why are they combat films? Is "combat film" nothing more than an arbitrary designation? Once defined, its characteristics are so specific that it is anything but arbitrary. Even in these early stages it isn't really arbitrary either. It's something that kind of sticks its head out slowly, waiting to see if it gets applause or raspberries. First it appears a little bit, then a lot more, and then finally, it becomes the total running time of a film. This means the movies that contain combat initially are not all combat movies, unless one wishes to say that any movie that contains combat is a combat movie. This, of course, makes *For Me and My Gal* with Judy Garland and Gene Kelly a World War I combat movie, which it isn't. So finally, one has to decide how much combat needs to be present to constitute a combat film. Initially, this can be decided by a simple running-time estimate. This is not a mindless factual formula— sixty minutes of combat means a combat film, five minutes does not—

even though one can almost use such a formula as a guideline. It has to do with purpose, representational meanings, and attitudes. A combat film that won't tell the audience the full story seeks to deny what it is. It may not be able to, but, on the other hand, it may. One can only view the film, analyze, and decide. One is watching something grow, and what is the moment when the berry is ripe? Later, after the definition has formed, it is much easier to designate a film as combat or not combat, because it defines itself for a viewer through its presentation of what the viewer understands *is* the combat film. This is a primary problem of genre study. It involves not only understanding a list of characteristics of a certain kind of film, but also realizing what these characteristics stand for and how they are being used and received by viewers. It is part of what we are seeking to learn about genre. In 1943, we are in the primitive stage of discussion.

Perhaps a comparison of two films will help. Based on my viewings of *Crash Dive* and *A Yank in the RAF* (1941), I would say *Crash Dive* is a combat film with lots of noncombat action, and that *A Yank in the RAF* is a noncombat film with lots of combat. (I never promised you a rose garden.)

Why do I see these films this way?

Betty Grable, the female star of *A Yank in the RAF*, was the top female box office draw in the history of film. She ranked in the top ten for a full decade from 1942 on. A Betty Grable film was a Betty Grable film, and that meant a musical. Although she only does two low-budget numbers, her story is as important as the story of Tyrone Power, the hero, and his combat raid on Europe. In fact, his raid is what makes him worthy of her, and it might be said that raids on Europe were what it would take to win her. The film is as much about Betty Grable as about anything else. Where *Immortal Sergeant* was set in a state of total combat but returned to the romantic story via flashback, *A Yank in the RAF*, a similar story about the man's need to become worthy of the girl, makes the girl's portion of the film active through present tense. Grable is simply more important on screen than O'Hara. She must be more than a memory.

In addition, the film does not begin in combat. It moves toward it for a fitting climax. Furthermore, audience expectation is always involved in genre. Audiences going out to see a film with Betty Grable expected music, romance, glamor, comedy—and would accept some combat, especially if Tyrone Power were her costar.

In *Crash Dive*, there is an entirely different situation. First of all, the film begins in combat, with a victorious return of a PT Boat. The female star, Anne Baxter, was not a top box office draw. She was not even a star, but only beginning her career. This automatically made her less important, and the story connected to her less important. She is a device, not an entity. The two men in conflict are both stars (Dana Andrews and Tyrone Power), which was not the case in *A Yank in the RAF* in which John Sutton, the other man, was a minor figure and never reached stardom. Furthermore, he was British, and if there is one thing we know from movies, when a Britisher and a Yank vie for a girl, the Yank will win. (Thus it is we keep fighting the Revolutionary War. Oddly enough, this appears to be the only way we do fight the Revolutionary War in genre.[8]) In *Crash Dive*, two Americans fight for the girl. This makes it a male story, and relates it more closely to the combat genre. *Crash Dive* also contains a great deal of combat, with a tense commando raid and real climactic fighting.

Bataan and *Air Force* both accept the war. They embrace it. There are no flashbacks, no safe returns home, no ways out but to fight. As a pop song of the time put it, "No love, no nothin'." They contain the new genre. In fact, they *are* the new genre. They are the two most important films of the emergence of the definition, because they are the first that are totally in and about World War II combat.

What do *Air Force* and *Bataan* have in common? Although one is about the air force and one about an eclectic mix of military forces, they share the Pacific war, a mixed group of types, a person in their midst who is not enthusiastic about the combat, a leader who dies, a hero out of necessity, death of valued members, and much more. *Air Force*, however, is about a group on the move, and *Bataan* is about a group trapped. If you consider that the air group is *enclosed* within their plane, however, you have almost a parallel situation. The *Bataan* group will make a last-stand effort on the plot of ground they occupy. All will die. The *Air Force* group will make a last stand from within their bomber, successfully piloting it on and on until they reach safety, bomb the enemy, and endure.

Air Force is perhaps the purest combat film ever made about the air service. Its journey, from San Francisco to Pearl Harbor to Wake and Manila, is a miniature replay of the first months of the war. It is like some hideous wagon train west, with problems of supplies and hostile forces constantly attacking the wagonload of heroes. It fits perfectly

The crew of the Mary Ann *in* Air Force.

with the tradition of American films, and yet it is a unique and original film, not quite like any other.

It is curious how these films of 1942 and 1943 work. *Wake Island* and *Flying Tigers* both begin before Pearl Harbor. The news of December 7 hits the characters more than halfway into the running time. This is not true for *Air Force* and *Bataan*. *Air Force* begins on December 6,

1941, with a group of men saying goodbye to friends and families as they prepare to fly to Hawaii, and thus straight into combat. *Bataan* begins not only after December 7, but after the fall of Manila. As an audience, we have been escorted forward, taught, and initiated. Like soldiers who have undergone training, we are ready to fight. We are *prepared* for combat. (The preparation process included not only the films of 1942, but also the films discussed in the next chapter. It also included more than just films, obviously.)

The *Air Force* group has only one star name, John Garfield, and his part is downplayed to make him really one of the group. In fact, his sucessful initiation into the group, his acceptance of the need for combat and for turning away from cynicism, is the key plot ingredient. In *Air Force* we see a hero, a group, and an objective. We see all the battles of the early days of the war. We see the ignominy and shame of our defeat at Pearl Harbor, and the civilians who died there are mourned. We see a smart and dangerous enemy, and we learn the rules of combat. We experience death and sacrifice, but we fight on to ultimate victory in which our bomber, the intrepid Mary Ann that represents America, bombs the heck out of the entire Japanese fleet.

Air Force does not shirk its task of telling an audience about the war, nor does it fail in its other job—to entertain us. It is a great film, still powerful today. In it, one sees the visual strength a genre must have to endure. The powerful sense of a journey is physically demonstrated, and the coherence of the group takes place in the enclosed space before our eyes. Once separate in the frame, man by man, they become a working force linked visually by composition or united by cutting where once they were isolated.

Personal involvement is inspired through functional use of the camera, keeping a viewer at an eye-level, participatory relationship to the events on the screen. Like the men in the story, we are put through incredible tension as we believe the Mary Ann cannot get back in the air after being damaged. In a race against time, we move to the edge of our seats as the crew fights to avenge her and get her airborne as the Japanese advance through the jungle. When finally she soars, in the nick of time, we celebrate and feel victorious. Later, we feel release and relax with the men. This organization of plot and narrative, matched with a visual equivalent through the tools of cinema, lifts the genre into a coherent experience with a dramatic effect on a viewer. *Air Force* takes off—in every sense of the expression. This use of film technique to present generic conventions visually will be fully developed in the next stage, January 1944 through December 1945.

Reviews of *Bataan* began to appear in early summer of 1943, a little more than a year after the peninsula fell, just as our nation plunged into the depth of the war. Its reviews were uniformly excellent, and its box office was good. There is no doubt but that it was modeled after John Ford's 1934 film, *The Lost Patrol*, written by Dudley Nichols. Originally, it was even to be called *Bataan Patrol*, and the similarities between the two films are striking.

Four versions of the *Bataan* script are held in the Script Collection of the Louis B. Mayer Library at the American Film Institute in Los Angeles, so that one can note the subtle changes that take place as a script is rewritten. One of the most significant is the elimination of a Native American character named Private Edward Evening Star, whose dialogue makes explicit the "last stand" implications of the story:

> EVENING STAR: Didn't you ever read about the Indians?
> SERGEANT: Yeah. What's your tribe?
> EVENING STAR: Sioux. I was brought up on the reservation at Fort Belknap, Montana. (Chuckles) My grand-dad always claimed he was with *Sitting Bull* at *Custer's Land Stand*. I always doubted it. But he talked a swell Wild West.
> (The underlining is in pencil on the script.)

The inclusion of a Sioux in the original script links *Bataan* firmly to the tradition of the Western film, where frequently an Indian scout is a part of the Cavalry team, and where, at the very least, Indians play an important role. Historically, the fall of Bataan is linked to such American defeats as Custer's Last Stand and the Alamo, events which have been filmed often, usually as Westerns. Since Bataan itself was a "last stand," and since the filmed version of *Bataan* ends with the annihilation of the heroes in a determined, but doomed "last stand," it is no surprise that the original script contained an Indian.

This character was eliminated in the final script, apparently because the link to the Western seemed *too* obvious, the characterization was weak, and there were already thirteen men to characterize and kill off. The other major script revision involved the film's ending.

The second to last version of the script does not have the hero, Sergeant Dane (Robert Taylor), standing in his grave at film's end. Instead, he seems to see the men of his patrol standing at attention, each man beside the cross that marks his grave. This negates the total "last stand" effect the actual movie has, since the Sergeant has survived. As he marches out a voice over ("the voice might be General Douglas MacArthur's own voice," says the script) pays tribute to the fighting men of America. As the Sergeant and the men who rescued him march, filling the screen, they are joined by close-packed ranks of American fighting men who come on and on, seeming to march straight out at the audience, superimposed with graves and crosses. The flag comes up big as the voice says, "That their flag and ours will rise again— where they made their last stand." Changing the script to show no rescue—just total death—not only influenced the genre but made the film much more powerful.

Since the most common form of the combat genre is that of the ground forces, usually the infantry out on patrol, *Bataan*, which typifies such films, emerges as the single most important film for the development of the genre in the first year and a half of the war. This is true not only because of its box office success, its place in moviegoers' memories, its relationship to one of the most important battles (and grimmest defeats) of the early years of the war, but also because of its presentation of a situation that is *totally* in combat, and because of its clear and precise presentation of the genre's characteristics.

The story of *Bataan* contains all the various characters, situations, iconography, and formal presentation of the traditional World War II combat film. The story of the real battle of Bataan is a story of loss and defeat, as is the story of *Bataan*, the movie. Although it is obvious that the battle itself inspired the movie, it is important to realize that the story the film tells is one audiences had seen before in *Lost Patrol*.[9]

It requires no special insight to make this connection, because over and over again, reviewers of the day commented, "Just like *Lost Patrol*"; "we've seen this before, only it was *Lost Patrol*," etc. *Lost Patrol* was supposed to be a film about desert warfare in Mesopotamia during World War I. However, it is not cheating to say that the war really is so distanced, so abstracted, as almost not to exist. First of all, the heroes are fighting Arabs, and therefore seem not to be connected to World War I at all. Furthermore, they are dressed in the manner we associate with foreign legion movies, and the desert sands take us so far away from what we think of as World War I that nine out of ten people will

Lost Patrol

tell you *The Lost Patrol* is a Foreign Legion movie. In fact, having seen it numerous times and despite an opening title which locates a viewer in time and place, I am still shocked when World War I suddenly flies in out of nowhere in the shape of a fancy airplane. (This element is quickly dispatched. The pilot is shot as he jumps down with a tally-ho air. He is shot, and that's that. So much for the reality of War. It's as if someone from *Dawn Patrol* flew in, and the cast and crew said, "Hey, get out of here. That's not the movie we're making.")

This patrol really *is* lost—lost from history and reality—and that's probably what makes the story so useful for later films. In fact, just how this patrol got lost in the first place is rather unclear in the narrative. When we meet them, they are already wandering, which gives the film an eerie, horror-movie-like effect. It even stars Boris Karloff in a key

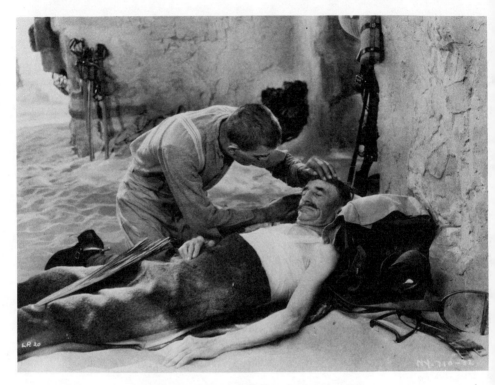

Lost Patrol. *Boris Karloff tends the wounded.*

role! The lead, Victor McLaglen, is "the sergeant," apparently a man with no name, and the enemy have an invincible, unreal quality. *The Lost Patrol* is the *Moby Dick* of combat films—they're out there on the desert seas, all right, and they're after something; but what it represents goes beyond the issues of World War I and patriotism.

The enemy is the "unseen Arab enemy that always struck in the dark—like a relentless ghost." No doubt this sense of a racially different enemy that sneaks up on you in endless droves helped filmmakers in the forties to link films such as *Bataan* to *Lost Patrol*. The format of *Lost Patrol* is strikingly similar to *Bataan* in numerous ways. The men end up on an oasis where they make a last stand, slowly being picked off one by one. They talk about what they are doing and why, and whether or not they understand it. They share memories, and fears, and conflicts break out among them. There is comedy relief. Equipment fails them, this time a horse that collapses and has to be shot.

There are thirteen men in this group, also, and they die in a ritualistic, specific order.

First of all, the young leader is suddenly shot, the initial dramatic event at the film's opening, leaving them leaderless, so that the tough old Sergeant, a rigid disciplinarian, must take over. Next, an inexperienced young man who loves Kipling is murdered during the night. A second man is wounded at the same time, and he dies from these wounds later. Then, a man climbs a tree to see what is happening and is shot in the head. The men tease him that he is looking for "Molly's red hat on the dock"—his version of a device that will appear as "lookin' for the old Arizona" in John Ford's later World War II film, *They Were Expendable*. Two men push off to bring help, and their dead bodies are later returned. One goes crazy from the heat and wanders towards the Arabs, hatless, and is shot. Later, another will also go crazy and, thinking he is Christ, wander out to the Arabs, carrying a cross. He, too, is shot. (This character is played by Boris Karloff.) Everyone else, dies one by one, until the hero, Victor McLaglen is left alone. "Come on, you swine!" he cries. In the morning, he is seen burying the last of his men. Each man's sword marks his grave. McLaglen carefully dons his uniform jacket and takes his sword as the Arabs come over the sand dune. He shoots at them, laughing and talking to his dead companions. "We got 'em!", but he's shot and falls. He gets up again, however, and walks toward the edge of the oasis. At this point over the hill come the British. He is a survivor! When asked, "Where are your men?" he points to the swords. "Auld Lang Syne" is heard on the sound track.

There are many parallels with *Bataan*. Some basic rules of the combat film emerge: don't climb a tree; don't try to go alone for help; keep your wits or you'll go crazy; don't go out to bring in a dead body (a lesson from *All Quiet on the Western Front*, too); be a professional and accept the situation; there is no room for religious epiphany here because the enemy has another God, and so forth.

However, the war of *The Lost Patrol* is a vague desert war, and these troops are British. There is also a strong religious undercurrent (Karloff calls the oasis "the garden of Eden") and the traditional World War I sense of glory is the underlying issue. The young innocent who loves Kipling says about his fellow soldiers, "They're so modest. They don't see the glory in it, do they?" "No." is the firm, meaningful reply of old soldier McLaglen.

The important point is that Holloywood was, contrary to popular opinion, a frugal place. Plots and characters and events were saved like old pieces of string, and taken out of the drawer and re-used. Audiences presumably were glad enough to see old friends back on the screen doing the old familiar things. That, after all, is a very good explanation of stardom and star persona. Useful things were—tough sergeants, raw recruits, old veterans, diary-keeping writers, colorful immigrant types; mail calls, Christmas celebrations, barroom brawls; dead men crying out to be brought in, and, when rescued, dying anyway; brave men going up in planes to sacrifice themselves. The list is long, but the important thing is the context in which the conventions are used. From the most successful films, producers, writers, directors, et al. took the most memorable parts and brought them forward for the new war. Into them they added something fresh that they took from everywhere— novels, newsreels, poems, comic books, radio shows, other kinds of movies, the works—and created a new type of film that became a genre: the World War II combat movie that would then recur and recur and recur.

Critics of the day, who almost unanimously gave *Bataan* favorable reviews, referred to the film's "gritty realism." It is interesting to see a film like this, filmed entirely inside a studio on sets, referred to as "realistic." The production work is superb in the Metro-Goldwyn-Mayer tradition, yet the use of matte shots and rear projection was obvious even in 1943. Above all, the artificial, expressionistic use of swirling fogs and mists coupled with the almost magical onslaught of the Japanese crawling on their bellies toward their own proscribed enemy gives the film its eerie power. In its own way, *Bataan* is realistic. Its anger, determination, and passion for the fight are very real. It's as if that passion were sealed in the film cans, and to open them is to feel some of what Americans felt at the humiliating defeat of Bataan. This is to suggest not that we feel good about the propaganda *Bataan* contains, or that we believe that propaganda now, or subscribe to it in any way—but only that we can clearly see and feel what it was at the time. *Bataan* is sure of its task as a film. Everything that the cinema has to offer—lighting, cutting, composition—is placed in service of the main message of propaganda. *Bataan* does not seek to make subtle meaning out of the tools of cinema. It puts them at the service of its message and story. Thus, *Bataan* is indeed an effective work of propaganda, of storytelling, and, as history has proved, of genre. It told a story we would want to hear again and again. It influenced and affected the way the story of World War II combat would be told in the future. *Bataan* has *commitment*. It *is* the definition, clarified, focused, and presented with passion.

Bataan is the story of a group of hastily assembled volunteers who, through their bravery and tenacity, hold off an overwhemingly large group of the enemy long enough to buy important time for the American forces. The raw emotional power of the combat, along with the intense presentation of sacrifice, makes the film a disturbing one. Its format is the hold-the-fort variation of the basic story pattern as opposed to the take-the-objective roving format of such films as *Objective Burma*.

Thirteen men are trapped in a situation. They come from different parts of the United States, and from different branches of the service. They are different in age, background, experience, attitude, and willingness to fight. "They're a mixed group," says the Captain. "They've never served together before." In establishing such a collection of misfits (who will be assembled into a coherent fighting group), the film confirms and makes specific the foundation of the combat patrols to follow. These men obviously represent the American melting pot, but the representation is not a simple-minded one. Our strength is our weakness and vice versa. We are a mongrel nation—ragtail, unprepared, disorganized, quarrelsome among ourselves, and with separate special interests, raised, as we are, to believe in the individual, not the group. At the same time, we bring different skills and abilities together for the common good, and from these separate needs and backgrounds we bring a feisty determination. No one leads us who is not strong, and our individualism is not set aside for any small cause. Once it is set aside, however, our group power is extreme.

The group consists of:

1. Sergeant Bill Dane (Robert Taylor). An Infantry career man, who has been in the Philippines two years.
2. Captain Lassiter (Lee Bowman). A West Point Cavalry man, who has been in the Philippines four months.
3. Leonard Purckett (Robert Walker). A Navy band musician who used to be an usher in a movie house.
4. Ramirez (Desi Arnaz). A Private from the 192d Tank Corps. A Californian. Was part of National Guard.

The seminal combat group: Bataan

5. Jake Feingold (Thomas Mitchell). A Corporal from the 4th Chemical Corps.
6. "Barney Todd" (which turns out to be a pseudonym). (Lloyd Nolan). From the Provisional Signal Battalion. Enlisted February 5, 1941 and volunteered for the Philippines on November 11, 1941. Corporal. (His real name is Dan Burns.)
7. Yankee Salazar (J. Alex Havier). A Philippine scout. Former boxing champion.
8. Steve Bentley (George Murphy). An Air Force Lieutenant.
9. F. X. Matowski (Barry Nelson). Engineer. From Pittsburgh.
10. Sam Malloy (Tom Dugan). Motor Transport Service. Acts as group's cook. Private.
11. Gilbert Hardy (Phillip Terry). 4th Medical Battalion Private. A Conscientious Objector who enlisted as a medical aide. Carries no arms.

12. Corporal Katigbak (Roque Espiritu). A Philippine Air Force Man. Mechanic.
13. Wesley Eeps (Kenneth Spencer) Was studying to be a minister before the war broke out. 3d Engineer. A demolition expert.

They are, respectively, WASP, WASP, WASP, Mexican, Jew, WASP, Philippine, WASP, Pole, Irish, WASP, Philippine, Black. The two Philippines are sub-divided into Philippine primitive (Salazar, the scout, a former champion boxer, who plays the role an Indian would play as scout for a cavalry group) and Philippine nonprimitive (an Air Force mechanic). The WASPS are subdivided into an elite West Point man (Lassiter), an innocent farm boy (Purckett), an unidentified "gangster" (Todd), a natural, graceful leader of democratic tendencies (Bentley) and a noncombatant (Hardy). They are from everywhere: West Point, Middle West, California, New York, Pittsburgh, the South, and nowhere. They are geographically mixed, as they are racially and intellectually. For purposes of narrative development, each of these men plays a traditional role that defines the internal structure of the combat story.

The Dead Father Figure (Lassiter/Bowman). The officer who originally rounds up the group of volunteers for an important mission is the official ranking officer, and thus the leader or father figure of the group even if, as in this case, he is a young man. As the film opens, he has just secretly wed a young nurse from Kansas, and he is seen saying goodbye to her in a restrained manner. Lassiter represents a kind of American nobility, having gone to West Point (class of 1940). In his brief scenes in the film, he has a generous bearing, intelligence, and grace. His correct sense of things is demonstrated when he tells Robert Taylor, the true and natural leader and the man with the most experience in the group, to "just tell me when I make an error." He also tells Taylor to give orders direct if needed, and not to waste time getting his permission.

The first thing that happens to the group is that this man, their leader and "father" figure, the best educated among them, is suddenly, unexpectedly, and, without much being made of it, killed. " We'll stay as long as we can stand up," says Lassiter, just before he dies. His words are the meaning of the film, but he dies saying them. This becomes a basic unit of the combat genre. The metaphoric meaning is obvious. In war, one will lose security, home, and comfort. A sacrifice will be made, and this initial loss in the story line depicts this for the viewing audience in narrative terms.

The Hero (Robert Taylor). Taylor plays the role of the natural leader, the professional soldier who has already seen two wars. He is a slightly tarnished version of the classic romantic hero, a man of experience and intuition. He is so capable that he "would have been an officer" except that he "trusted a man" who went AWOL from him during his time as a military policeman. As a result of this betrayal, he lost his chance for a commission. However, because of his having been tested and found wanting, this character has learned that the world is not an easy place. He has proved his ability to withstand the hardships that lie ahead, because he has withstood those from his past. Not only is he personally ready for trouble, but he can guide others through difficulties. This man will be the last to die. In fact, the audience does not see him die. Instead, we see the film end in a blur, with Taylor bravely, defiantly continuing to machine gun the oncoming hordes of the enemy in an image reminiscent of gangster films.

The Hero's Adversary (Lloyd Nolan). This man is the group cynic, an important stand-in for audience doubts, and for its unwillingness to face the hardships the war will bring. Such a character becomes an appropriate initiation figure into the change-of-attitude that will be required for the task at hand. He can voice dismay, disapproval, disgust—anything negative—and siphon off audience ill will. He can *be* unpatriotic. He becomes the foil against which the issues of the film are played. In the plot line of *Bataan*, this character is operating under a false name. He is, in fact, the man Taylor, the hero, once trusted. Thus, they appear in the film operating under a plot conflict from their pasts. It is significant how genre, from the beginning, indicates other films, other stories. Their story might easily be a military service film from the 1930s. The structural device of having a hero and an adversary carrying forward a conflict acts on audience awareness as a sort of updating of the old familiar service film/training film/plots. All that's over now. We must win the war. In this way, one old genre (or formula) is used to help the audience locate itself in the new. There is also the hint that Nolan is that American tradition, the outlaw hero, as he is almost a gangster type.

The Noble Sacrifice (George Murphy). Murphy's character is a brave and good man, who is the most likable and understanding of all the men. He is an officer in the Air Force who, when the official group leader dies, does not take over command but defers instead to Taylor's natural leadership. This man, mortally wounded, elects to die for the group by flying his plane out and crashing it into the bridge between them and the Japanese, to destroy it and buy time. (Note similarity to ending of *Flying Tigers*.) Murphy is a WASP type, and thus represents the price white middle class America will pay in the war.

The Old Man/The Youth. The war film inevitably portrayed an older man in the midst of combat, usually one who fought in World War I (the sobriety of such a thought made its own point) and whose feet hurt (as this one's do). The old man character of this group, played by Thomas Mitchell, is Jewish, and a chemical engineer. He is also a kind of comedy relief, and a semiparental figure to balance the one lost by the death of the original leader. The young man, Robert Walker, represents initiation into battle and the question of bravery/cowardice, as in the novel *Red Badge of Courage*. Walker's young man is innocent, dreamy, a former movie usher who entered the Navy as a musician. When his ship was shot out from under him, he swam ashore, and joined up with this motley group. Walker's character is naive, but not unwilling or incapable. He talks of his former life ("reminds me of when I was a cowpoke!" or "did I tell you about when I was a cab driver?"), but it is clear it is a life that not only never existed, but under the circumstances, never will. It is the remembered life of the movie usher, a series of filmed touchstones from a Walter Mitty-like youth. Walker plays this character brilliantly, and the poignancy is all the more painful for its comedy. The youth character represents the best of the group, which is to be totally wasted and which, if it would only be allowed to grow and develop, would make us a better nation. The old man, on the other hand, is what we are. We've been through this, and our feet hurt. The contrast of youth and age is both shattering and uplifting for the audience. It shatters us to lose the youth, but on the other hand, maybe we'll live through it, like the old man. (In *Bataan*, of course, everybody dies.)

The Immigrant Representative. Barry Nelson plays the man with the unpronounceable name, F. X. Matowski. Such a character (and such characters are almost always Polish) overtly remind everyone of the melting pot tradition. This man, who is from Pittsburgh (the steel mills?), dreams of his mom's lima bean soup, "made with vinegar." (This is a candidate for one of filmdom's worst recipes.)

The Comedy Relief. Both the old man and the young man character provide comedy relief. A film of such grim nature requires more than one porter knocking at its door! In this film, the official comedy relief is the cook, played by Tom Dugan, and frequently thereafter, the comedy relief *is* the cook.[10] The man in war who is there to do unwarlike (and thus unmanly) things is a suitable subject for comedy.

The Peace Lover (Phillip Terry). In this film, the man who speaks of peace is an actual noncombatant, a figure seldom seen in the early World War II combat films, for obvious reasons.

The Minority Representatives. A Mexican from California (Desi Arnaz), a jitterbug who loves jive music; two Filipinos who are not American citizens; and a black man who sings, prays, and delivers himself of such folksy insights as, "You can promise your mind, but you gotta deliver something to your stomach."

Bataan opens with credits which appear against a map of the Philippine Islands. BATAAN! screams the title, jumping out of the frame and coming at the viewer in all its implied horror, defeat, and sacrifice. For the audiences of the day, the word practically dripped American blood and shame. Its impact was directly emotional, linked as it was to a current event that no one in the audience could be unaware of. Seen today, the impact is visual, and it becomes emotional by extension.

The objective of the above mentioned volunteers will be to demolish a bridge and prevent a Japanese breakthrough at all costs. In so doing, they will buy time for MacArthur so the war in the Philippines won't be "over too soon." The film's printed dedication said it all:

"When Japan struck our desperate need was time—time to marshal new armies. Ninety-six priceless days were bought for us—with their lives—by the defenders of Bataan, the Philippine Army which formed the bulk of MacArthur's infantry fighting shoulder to shoulder with the Americans. To those immortal dead, who heroically stayed the wave of barbaric conquest, this picture is reverently dedicated."

The Japanese flag being raised is the opening image, and then we are plunged into Manila. In the chaos of war, women and children and soldiers are mixed in a mass of evacuees. This first sequence speaks to us of the horror of World War II—it will be a war waged as much on women and children as on soldiers.

As the band of volunteers is assembled, they are told to join the 26th Cavalry for their special detail. The cavalry, a film metaphor of heroism and dashing bravery, is a familiar military group for viewers. They fought the barbaric Indians, as this group will fight the barbaric Japa-

nese. ("Those no tail baboons," says Taylor, "they're no. 1 skillful. They can live and fight for a month on what wouldn't last you guys two days.") In fighting the "no tail baboons" (also referred to as "yellow skinned, slanty-eyed devils"), the thirteen men will lose their lives. The order in which they die, as well as the methods by which they die, are significant to later narrative structures. After the loss of the leader, the minorities die first, and then the weak and the mentally sensitive. Later genre stages will create new meanings by varying this structure.
The order of death is as follows:

1. The father figure, the captain, as discussed earlier. He is shot in the head as he walks away after giving his volunteers their orders. It is sudden, swift. (The first death must always be a significant one.)
2. The Pole from Pittsburgh. Immediately after the nostalgic conversation about his mother's soup, he climbs a tall tree and is shot by snipers. This is one of the film's most memorable moments, and it is practically axiomatic from then on that he-who-climbs-tree-in-war-film dies. (A further implication is included in the juxtaposition of the climb and the home-front conversation. Sink into the past, the film seems to say, and lose your life. No time for warmth and nostalgia here. Keep your mind on war.)
3. The Philippine Air Force man. A mechanic, he is last seen walking back to their camp to get the carburetor repaired. He dies off-screen. He is found in a swirling, deadly mist, a samurai sword sticking out of his dead body, its ornate top visible in the fog. (This is a horror film image, and a horrible death becomes traditional for minority figures who act as fodder for the film's narrative.)
4. When Japanese planes fly over and bomb their camp, the cook, in a fit of personal rage, picks up a machine gun and brings down one of the planes. Immediately after his joyous triumph, he himself is mowed down. (You can't feel pride and joy in the work of killing. When you take a moment to act as a selfish and prideful individual, they'll get you.)
5. The other Filipino, the former boxer and present scout, strips down to native wear and sets out through the jungle. His body is later seen hanging across the ravine, stripped and barbarically killed. (This man's obvious stripping down to his primitive self invited such a death, and linked the viewing audience to the film tradition of cowboys and Indians.)
6. The Mexican jazz lover, Desi Arnaz, dies of malaria. "He's jitter

buggin' himself to death" observes the black man, as Arnaz shakes and sweats.

7. George Murphy, dying of wounds, crashes his plane into the bridge, making a noble sacrifice.

8. The noncombatant from the medical corps goes mad and runs toward the Japanese, throwing grenades. (His ultimate acceptance of the need for combat is an obvious lesson, with its underlying implication that he was a noncombatant because he just couldn't take it, as his madness overwhelms him).

9.-13. The final section of the film is reserved for a powerful presentation of the ultimate total combat these remaining five men are subjected to. The black man dies first, then the Jewish old man, then the youth, then the hero's adversary, and finally, of course, the hero.

In this thunderous finale of combat, all five men demonstrate incredible bravery, skill, and heroism. They fight fiercely, running up out of their foxholes and charging the enemy in hand-to-hand combat that includes any method of dirty fighting they can manage—throwing dirt in Japanese faces, tripping them, cheating, and both garroting the enemy and beating their dead bodies with rifles after the garroting. They shoot already fallen bodies to be safe, and ruthlessly use a corpse as a decoy. It is not a prettied up barroom brawl, and the enemy does not lie down and die easily.

In a horrible clash of cultures, the black man runs forward from frame right toward a Japanese soldier, who runs with equal speed toward him, on a diagonal from the left. The black man strikes this oncoming soldier with his rifle, and bayonets him after he falls. As he accomplishes this, a second Japanese soldier runs in full speed from frame right, the upper right hand corner, and swings a sword (and/or bayonet—repeated viewings still cannot separate the distinction in the blur), hitting the black man solidly in the back of the neck. The victim's face is seen to respond, contracted in horror, with a scream frozen on his mouth. The blade enters halfway through his neck. Although we do not actually see the head fall, or blood spurt out, this is one of the most graphic and violent killings of the pre-sixties period of film history. Involving us as it does in the swift action, the effect, even today, is breathtaking. This death finishes out the bad news for the minority figures in the film—for them are reserved the most brutish deaths.

A brief respite occurs. The surviving men, Thomas Mitchell, Lloyd

"This is our last round of ammunition...but those Japs will know they've been in a fight before they get us!"

Bataan, *with Lloyd Nolan, Robert Taylor*

Nolan, Robert Taylor, and Robert Walker gather together. Mitchell walks into their area of shelter, enters his foxhole, sits down, and dies. In this aftermath of battle, the final conversations about why we are fighting occur. The peace and sustaining nature of this interlude is destroyed when they hear on their radio the words, "America! You are beaten." "You stink!" cries out Walker, standing up and demonstrating the famous edict, never stand up in a foxhole. He is shot and dies.

This leaves only the hero and his adversary, Taylor and Nolan. "It's you and me now, Sarge," says Nolan, and "We've been headin' for that for a long time," he replies. Nolan is stabbed in the back by a supposedly dead Japanese body, leaving Taylor alone, standing in the grave he has knowingly dug for himself. "Come on, you suckers. Come and get me." He dies alone, firing his weapon and laughing. "Didn't think we were still here? We'll always be here."

The film's propaganda values are prominently displayed. Not only are the Japanese referred to with insulting epithets, but screen time is devoted to discussions about why we are fighting. When, just before the film's ending, Walker asks Taylor, "Can I write a letter?" the ensuing oral dictation of what he wants to say, put in the form of a letter to his mother ("Dear mum," he begins), is the vocalizing of the youth's fears. "There were thirteen of us, and now they're only three. Maybe there won't be any of us ever to get out of here alive. . . ." When he breaks and cries, Taylor takes over, finishing the thought by adding purpose to it: "Maybe it don't seem to do a lot of good, for men to get killed in some place you never heard of, but we figure . . . the men who died here may have done more than we'll ever know . . . to save the world ["He died a long way from home," said the black man in an earlier scene, as he prayed over a grave] . . . . it don't matter where a man dies as long as he dies for freedom." A voiceover speaks: "So fought the heroes of Bataan. Their sacrifice made possible our own victories in the Coral and Bismarck Seas, Midway, New Guinea and Guadalcanal. Their spirit will lead us back to Bataan!" (A film called *Back to Bataan* was in the works, albeit made by another studio.)

The Japanese of *Bataan* are an almost invincible force. Not only are there seemingly zillions of them (they keep coming and coming in endless waves of undervalued humanity), but they also have planes, tanks, trucks, ammunition aplenty, searchlights, and everything it takes to make modern war. They are both totally sophisticated with their mechanical skill and up-to-date equipment, and totally primitive, with their barbaric methods of killing. It is significant that when the Filipino scout sets out to go through their territory, he strips down to native dress, a symbolic acceptance of the attitudes he must have to deal with them in what has become their territory. "Get civilized again," Taylor orders the scout, but he slips away into the ravine before this can happen. Taylor constantly warns his men about the strength and cunning of the enemy. He must not be underestimated. At the same time, he speaks of the Japanese in the most brutally racist terms.

The Japanese are seen as an impersonal, faceless enemy. They are a mindless group, as opposed to our collection of strongly delineated individuals. Walker, the beardless youth, wants to prove his worth by killing one of the enemy. "If I could only get ONE Jap for myself," he says over and over. His Jap, the one he bayonets, is the one exception to the facelessness of the players who represent the Japanese army in the film. When Walker hesitates before bayoneting a man on the ground, he is himself tricked, tripped, and thrown. Walker, with skill and cunning, recovers himself and *does* kill this teacherous enemy. It is not only *his* Jap, the one he longed for during the film, but it is also *ours*. His is the only one we see in the film with a real face.

After the volunteers establish their camp on a high shelf of rock, from which they will make their last stand, they undergo periods of night and day, rest and work, combat and noncombat. From time to time, there is mist around them, presumably rising from the heat and humidity of the jungle and the river across which their objective, the bridge, stretches. This eerie white mist provides a sense of danger, coming as it does from images in horror films. It also provides a sense of the mist of myth and of history. The dead die and fall into the mist, tumbling away into legend. It surrounds their graves. Their situation is one of a symbolic act—a few men sacrificing their lives for the many. The misty look does much to enhance their historic importance.

The realities of war were seen and absorbed by viewers: the iconography of the military—guns, helmets, uniforms, quinine tablets, K rations, planes, radios, etc. The practicality that is required is spelled out. You don't play taps when a buddy dies, because it alerts the Japanese as to how many of you are dying. And you don't leave his helmet to mark his grave if someone needs to wear it to keep his own head from being blown off. All the action helps both to entertain and to educate the audience.

In summary and in retrospect, it may be said that with the release of *Bataan*, the foundation of the World War II combat film is in place. Using *Bataan* for guidance, these are its generic requirements:

- The group as a democratic ethnic mix, in this case a motley group of volunteers from several service branches who really have no other choice (the basic immigrant identification).
- A hero who is part of the group, but is forced to separate himself from it because of the demands of leadership.
- The objective (hold the bridge, delay the Japanese).
- The internal group conflicts (Nolan vs. Taylor, and the need for the men to accept Taylor's hard-nosed ways in combat).
- The faceless enemy (with the one exception).

- The absence of women (after opening scenes).
- The need to remember and discuss home, and the dangers involved in doing so.
- The typical war iconography and narrative patterns of conflicting and opposite natures.
- The journeying or staying nature or the genre: in a last stand, they win or lose; in a journey, they also win or lose.
- Propaganda, the discussion of why we fight and how justified it is.
- The events combatants can enact in their restricted state: writing and receiving letters, cooking and eating meals, exploring territory, talking and listening, hearing and discussing news, questioning values, fighting and resting, sleeping, joking.
- The attitudes that an audience should take to the war are taught through events, conversations, and actions.
- The tools of the cinema are employed to manipulate viewers into various emotional, cultural, and intellectual attitudes, and to help achieve all the other goals.
- Information the audience already has in terms of prior films, stories, newsreels, magazines, comic books, experience, etc. is put to use, as when images associated with horror films surround the death of Espiritu and engulf the five final survivors.
- A location in time, place, and military service is established, aided by maps, military advisors, and official dedications.
- Death.

All these items are clearly repeated in the films which followed rapidly after *Bataan*.

In film history, *Bataan* is rather like *Citizen Kane*. It wasn't that audiences had not seen *Kane's* devices before: Deep focus photography, out-of-sequence narrative, low ceilings had appeared in Hollywood cinema before. But *Kane* fused them together in one film, and told a powerful story by using all of them to one purpose. *Bataan* is not the work of art that *Citizen Kane* is, but what *Kane* did for form and narrative, *Bataan* does for the history of the combat genre. It does not *invent* the genre. It puts the plot devices together, weds them to a real historical event, and makes an audience deal with them as a unified story presentation—deal with them, *and* remember them.

1943 After Bataan

After *Bataan*, the other 1943 combat films that were released are *Destroyer* (September 2), *So Proudly We Hail* (September 10), *Corvette K-225* (October 21), and three dramatic November releases, *Sahara*

(November 12), *Guadalcanal Diary* (November 18), and *Cry Havoc* (November 24). The year ended with the release of *Destination Tokyo*, reviewed in the *Times* on New Year's Day of 1944. With these titles, the genre of World War II combat was firmly established and repeated, solidifying the characteristics and attitudes that constitute its core.[11]

Tables 1 and 2 are comparison charts which contrast *Bataan*, *Sahara*, *Guadalcanal Diary*, *Destination Tokyo* and *Air Force* in terms of recurring characteristics. The similarities are striking despite the obvious differences of setting, military force, and enemies faced. The chart could easily have included *Destroyer* and *Corvette K-225*, two minor films which also fit the definition. *So Proudly We Hail* and *Cry Havoc* also follow the *Bataan* format, but they concern themselves with women in war, and thus will be discussed in chapter 4.

In closely observing *Sahara* (desert tank warfare against the Germans and Italians), *Guadalcanal Diary* (jungle war against the Japanese), and *Destination Tokyo* (undersea war against the Japanese) one can see how the basic definition has no difficulty remaining constant whether on land or sea, in dry or wet climate, based on a real event or an imaginary one, against Germany or Japan.

The flexibility of genre, which is seldom discussed, is well demonstrated by these films. As the charts indicate, all four films are the same, yet different enough to please filmgoers. If these films were *exactly* the same, no doubt movie goers would have turned away. They are instead enough the same to serve emotional needs, match audience expectations, relate to common perceptions about war (and war movies), and yet provide enough variation and singularity to attract new audiences.

Each film maintains an area of uniqueness. *Destination Tokyo* was the first big-budget submarine movie of World War II combat, and it became a famous and fondly remembered film. It lives in people's memories partly because it clearly establishes the dramatic world of the combat submarine. It shows people how men lived in subs and made war. It shows how a submarine works, how it dives, how its machinery functions, and how it defends itself from attack from above as well as from the inevitable crushing danger of the ocean. It presents in detail the harrowing life aboard a tiny sub under combat conditions. The challenge of limited space to be explored by the camera, coupled with the various possibilities for dramatic action—both above and below the sea—make it a natural for the film medium.

In addition to the explicit presentation of the unique submarine world, *Destination Tokyo* dramatizes and emphasizes a special element

Table 1. Comparison of Five Films

Element	Sahara	Guadalcanal Diary	Air Force	Destination Tokyo	Bataan
DEDICATION	Acknowledgment: IV Armored Corps of the Army Ground Forces	"Appreciation is gratefully acknowledged to the Marines. . . . Army, Navy." "A new chapter in the history of America: by the correspondent who landed on Guadalcanal with the first detachment of U.S. Marines"	"It is for us the living to be dedicated. . . to the great task remaining before us." —A. Lincoln Gettysburg Address	"To the Silent Service"	"To those immortal dead. . . . the defenders of Bataan"
TIME	June 1942	July 26-Dec. 10, 1942	Dec. 6, 1941 onward through Pearl and beyond	Christmas Eve 1941 through Doolittle Raid, April 18, 1942	Just after the evacuation of Manila, which Japan entered on Dec. 31, 1941. Americans and Filipinos then prepared for a last stand in weeks to come
PLACE	North Africa	Guadalcanal, Pacific	San Francisco to Pearl, Wake, Midway, etc.	San Francisco to Aleutians, Pacific Ocean on to Tokyo	Manila
MILITARY FORCE	IV Armored Corps Also: British, French Sudanese	Marines	Air Force. B-17s	Submarine Service	Mix of services

PRIMARY OBJECTIVE	Survival in retreat	Capture Guadalcanal	To fly to Hickam Field, Hawaii	Put men ashore in Tokyo Bay	"Buy Time"
SECONDARY OBJECTIVE	"Buy Time"	Hold Guadalcanal	To survive	Survive combat entanglements	Survival in retreat
HERO	Career military man. Sergeant	The group as a unit	The group as a unit	Not a career man. Captain	Career military man. Sergeant
STAR	Humphrey Bogart: "A loner from nowhere"	—	—	Cary Grant: An Oklahoman—social, but lonely in leadership	Robert Taylor: "A loner from nowhere"
GROUP	Inexperienced youth High-ranking man who'll die Comedy relief Cynic Medical men — Quirt/Flagg — — Mix of international forces	Inexperienced youth High-ranking leader who dies Comedy relief Cynics Medical men Chaplain who prays Quirt/Flagg 2 older men War correspondent — 	Inexperienced youth High-ranking leader who dies Comedy relief Cynic — — Quirt/Flagg Old man Correspondent (log keeper) — 	Inexperienced youth Father figure who dies Comedy relief Cynic Pharmacist's Mate Man who prays Quirt/Flagg Old man Correspondent (log keeper) — 	Inexperienced youth High-ranking leader who dies Comedy relief Cynic — Man who prays Quirt/Flagg Old man — Mix of military forces
ENEMY	Germany/Italy Personal	Japan Impersonal	Japan Impersonal	Japan Impersonal	Japan Impersonal
WOMEN	None	None	None in central combat story	None in central combat story	None in central combat story

Table 2. Comparison of the Narrative Elements of Five Films

	Sahara	Guadalcanal Diary	Air Force	Destination Tokyo	Bataan
Burial or Funeral	Y	Y	Y	Y	Y
Death	Y	Y	Y	Y	Y
Combat	Y	Y	Y	Y	Y
Enemy Deception	Y	Y	Y	Y	Y
Outnumbered Heroes	Y	Y	Y	Y	Y
Nature as Enemy	Y	Y	Y	Y	Y
Humor Among Heroes	Y	Y	Y	Y	Y
Roll call of Living or Dead at End	Y	Y	Y	Y	N
Need To Maintain Equipment	Y	Y	Y	Y	Y
Talk of Wives and Home	Y	Y	Y	Y	Y
Minority Sacrifice	Y	N	N	N	Y
Discussion of Why We Fight	Y	Y	Y	Y	Y
Journey/Last Stand	Y	Y	Y	Y	Y
Music other than Score	Y[a]	Y[b]	Y[c]	Y[c]	Y[c]
Mail	Y	Y	Y	Y	Y
Big Combat Finale	Y	Y	Y	Y	Y

a. Harmonica
b. Harmonica and Song
c. Radio

of its own—that of the concept of family. The crew is the traditional representative group of mixed types, but it is also presented as a family. As the sub sets out on its secret voyage, the men sing Christmas carols and exchange gifts and greetings (while Alan Hale, playing the comic cook, dresses up like Santa Claus) and their enclosed world, separate from the one they left behind, is clearly established. These men have a kitchen, bedrooms, places to relax and talk. They have a cook who acts as a mother to them, and they have each other. Theirs is the world of combat, but it's a family world. When appendicitis strikes a crew-member and there is no doctor on board, the family gathers around. Using American ingenuity, they make the necessary instruments: the cook's knives are ground into scalpels; a tea strainer is used to administer an anaesthetic; the cook tells the sick man that, when he comes out of it, he can have anything he wants to eat. "Start cooking a pumpkin pie" is the response. As the operation takes place, one man reads aloud the instructions from the Anatomy book and the Doctor's Manual, to help guide the Pharmacist's Mate who performs the surgery. The victim (how else can we view him?) recites the 23d Psalm as he goes under, and it apparently helps. He survives. Supported by friends and his surrogate family, he *can* survive, a wartime lesson for viewers.

As the sub moves toward Japan, the movie virtually turns into submerged soap opera. The men chat, eat, have coffee together at the kitchen table, listen to the radio, exchange philosophies. Alan Hale gets a haircut. They discuss life after death, and religion. "Pills," their Pharmacist's Mate, believes in only what he can see, he says. (He'll have plenty of time to find God in his foxhole later, when he has to take out the appendix.) Dane Clark tells an anecdote about a girl he tried to pick up and Cary Grant thinks of his son's first haircut. These last two episodes are seen in flashback. The difference between these flashbacks and those in *Immortal Sergeant* is the difference in the acceptance of the war. In *Immortal Sergeant*, the flashbacks are themselves a miniature movie, a unified collection of scenes which, if removed from the film and spliced together, would make a traditional romantic comedy. They exist separate and whole, and tell a story the audience waits to have finished. They recur more frequently as the film moves forward. They actually explain the combat portion of the film to us, in that we know the hero must learn to have enough courage to court the girl or he will lose her to the smooth other man. Will he find his courage, asks the film? Combat capability is linked to home,

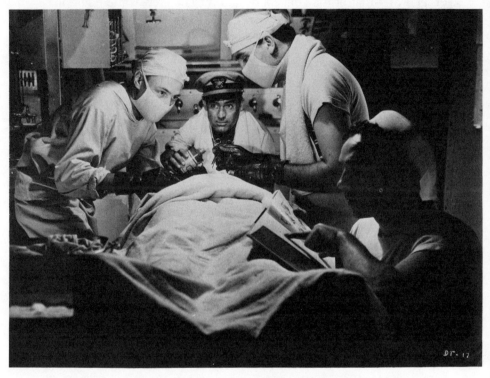

The appendicitis operation: Destination Tokyo

to sex, and to romance. In *Destination Tokyo*, the tiny, fragmented flashbacks are brief, and disappear as the film progresses. They tell us a little bit about the men. That's all. They do not form a complete story on their own.

After leaving the Aleutians, the sub enters maximum danger and the combat begins. The basic units of the submarine film are established: planes attack them up top; an unexploded bomb drops and becomes wedged on the aft deck, followed by a slow and intense sequence of defusing the bomb to save the sub; a burial at sea takes place; they go through nets into the Japanese harbor and sit on the bottom of sea; they hear Tokyo Rose on the radio; a group must go ashore on a mission; the appendicitis attacks; they attack ships with torpedoes; they undergo a destroyer attack with depth charges; they have to sit on the bottom again for a long period of time. These units of story appear over and over again in later submarine films. They represent the need to work against time (defusing the bomb, or emergency diving when someone is still up top); the constant threat of death; the need for patience during long periods of intense helplessness; and the primary importance of working well together.

Although they are indigenous to the submarine film, and dependent on the submarine setting, they are not really different from the basic units of *Bataan*. For instance, in *Bataan* a burial takes place in the ground, instead of at sea. There is malaria instead of appendicitis. The men in *Bataan* have to sit and wait for the Japanese to attack, knowing they will come, as the men in the sub await the depth charges. Both listen to Japanese propaganda on the radio; both work against time; both must repair equipment to survive; both must cook and eat; both must be patient and learn to work well together. The group going ashore on a mission is like the scout who goes out for help in *Bataan*. Precious group members die, and there is the constant threat of death. Combat is different if you are inside a submarine, and so are uniforms, battle conditions, and physical settings. However, key elements are the same. The group, with its leader, must work together, setting aside differences to withstand danger, The men share fear, but exhibit grace under pressure. The ideas of why we are fighting the war are discussed, and heavy propaganda is established as to the cruelty and treachery of the enemy, as well as to its intelligence and its worthiness as an adversary.

At the beginning of *Destination Tokyo*, Cary Grant speaks to his men as the sub leaves home. The audience sees all the men, meeting them fully for the first time. As the film ends, we see the sub sail back in under the Golden Gate, and each man says what he most wants: "Cold cider back on the farm," "Dinah Shore records," "Green vegetables," "Girls," "Someone else to cook." Order is restored. Watching this triumphant return, with the group intact despite its tragic loss of "Pop," its official father figure who has died in combat, one may feel that *Destination Tokyo* is the family that succeeds because its crew knows how to cohere into a group, how to become a family, whereas *Bataan*'s did not have enough time together to do more than try. Both films say we must fight unto death, and by never giving up we will win. Both tell us that some have to die to win this war. The audience has learned about death and sacrifice, but also about the possibilty of endurance and victory.

Sahara and *Guadalcanal Diary* also demonstrate both the maintenance of the basic definition and subtle variations that mark its flexibility. The most interesting comparison between *Bataan* and *Sahara* is in their two groups of 13 men from representative backgrounds, in *Sahara*'s case a miniature U.N., instead of the more common mix of Americans:

1. The tank man hero, Humphrey Bogart, American, former Cavalry man, a pro.
2. The American radio man from the tank, Dan Duryea.
3. The tank's American machine gunner from Waco, Texas, Bruce Bennett.
4. A British medic.
5. A Frenchman.
6. A cynical Britisher who has corns and aching feet.
7. Lloyd Bridges, young and naïve, who carries a photo of his girl and shows it to everyone. (With British troops, his accent is Australian.)
8. A black man, a British Sudanese, from the 4th Sudanese Battalion, who knows the territory—the location of wells and depth of the sand (the Indian scout character).
9. An Italian, whom the Sudanese has taken prisoner and who speaks English—his wife has cousins in America.
10. An Australian.
11. A captured German pilot.
12. A South African originally from Dublin.
13. A Britisher from Sussex.

Where *Sahara* differs from *Bataan* is that it presents a "last stand" that ends sucessfully. The international group—that is, the two left alive—effect a surrender from hundreds of German troops. (This is a variation of the real-life story of World War I hero, Sergeant York.)

The credits of *Sahara* indicate that it is based on a Soviet novel, *The Thirteen*. Like *Bataan*, however, its plot is very similar to *The Lost Patrol*. The desert setting is the same, and the slow elimination of the group by the enemy fits well with the John Ford film. It is a somewhat more optimistic presentation in that, although only two survive, they have captured what appears to be the entire Germany Army. Neither *Bataan* nor *Sahara* officially credit the original author of *Lost Patrol*. Neither is officially classified as a remake. Yet the similarities are striking. The *New York Times* review said *Sahara* was "in a class with that memorable picture which it plainly resembles, *The Lost Patrol*."

In terms of location of combat and general setting, *Guadalcanal*

Diary is the most like *Bataan* of these late-1943 films. It is based on the bestselling book of the same name by Richard Tregaskis. Its credits acknowledge its "grateful" appreciation to the military forces that helped make the film. Its title is seen as the cover of the book, and after the cover is lifted, the credits appear as pages in that book. We read about "a new chapter in the history of America by the correspondent who landed on Guadalcanal with the first detachment of U.S. Marines." Then we see drawings of the stars of the film, with their characters' names and ranks underneath their images. After the rest of the credits, the film opens on a troop transport ship in the South Pacific, headed for combat. "Today, Sunday, July 26, 1942," says a narrator, and we are plunged into a filmed re-creation of Tregaskis' diarylike book, a motif which will recur all through the film.

Guadalcanal *Diary*, like the book, captures a sense of the democratic amalgamation of people going off to fight. It is perhaps the first really conscious mythologizing of the fighting men, characters who are brave, jaunty, funny, and who sing. Oh, boy do they sing! "Rock of Ages," "Genevieve, Sweet Genevieve" "Bless 'Em All" and many more. It's the combat film Hit Parade.

The opening sequence on board the troop ship introduces the film's group, and acquaints viewers with who and what they are through their conversation. As the action of the film unfolds, it is carefully linked to the reality of the actual event through the device of announcing the dates: "Friday, August 7, 1942." The film seems to work from the assumption that the audience would already know the basic story, from newsreels and newspaper accounts.

A mythology of the men who fight the war for America is beginning to take hold. Here are events we already recognize: mail call, conversations about future plans, talk of women back home, burials, and prayers. Here are the kinds of characters we appreciate as "typically" American: William Bendix from Brooklyn (Bendix qualifies as an icon of the World War II movie, combat or otherwise) and the brave minority figure, Anthony Quinn, as a Mexican. Here is the attitude of humor and resignation, the acceptance of the burden the enemy has laid on us. This represents, says the myth, the American pioneer spirit, the ability to go to a strange land and take hold of it. We show our American character through griping and complaining, but also through singing and praying. We talk bad, but we're really swell!

One sees this mythologizing in the usage of film references. A man wets the end of his rifle with his thumb, as audiences had seen Gary Cooper do in *Sergeant York*. "Tex, this ain't no turkey shoot," says tough old sarge. "Make em all count." Later Tex is asked, "Who do you think you are? Sergeant York or Gary Cooper?"

"They were good, too," he replies, and then gobbles like a turkey, which was a diversionary trick of Cooper/York. When a Japanese hears and raises his head, he is shot.

We see the tools of war, and how they are used: guns, machinery, uniforms, and the jaunty jokes our soldiers make, such as the road sign that says, "3380½ miles to Tokyo." We are linked back to the home front in the same ways that "our boys" are linked, through popular culture, baseball games that come in on shortwave radios, and pin-up pictures of Betty Grable. (Bendix shaves before a cover of *Modern Screen* magazine on which her face appears. Grable was the pin-up queen of World War II, and references to her abound throughout the evolution of the genre. Whenever she appears, in name or image, she *represents*—sex, glamor, love, affection, beauty, both attainable and unattainable. Her persona was that of the blonde who was nice enough to meet the folks and sexy enough to inspire dreams. Bendix's act of shaving is practically an obeisance to Grable.)

The combat of *Guadalcanal Diary* is memorable for its amount and its passionate intensity. It is brutal on both sides, culminating in the hideous battle which finally secures the island. A miniature last-stand unit is contained within the action, in which the only survivor, Anthony Quinn, gets away by swimming underwater. There's a bit of a Tarzan feel to this, and the implication that, for once, the minority can endure. The relationship between Indian Scout, black man, Indian, and Mexican is a sort of Gunga Din relationship. The white troops have their assistants from the lands they exploit: the fey, imaginative, and in-tune-with-nature creatures that guide them through the jungles and hostile terrains they have set out to exploit in true white-man tradition. On board the troop ship, when the men want ships identified, they summon a black man. Like an Indian scout on a high bluff, he identifies the stuff on the horizon for them.

At the finale, the new troops coming in pass by the old, a ritual that will become a familiar sight in films to come. Unlike *Bataan*, this group survives, although not without losses, of course.

Summary: Elements of the Genre

From these films of 1943 comes a list of elements to be found which repeat and recur in the combat genre. We know *Guadalcanal Diary* to be an on-the-spot-correspondent's account of an actual battle. And yet the story might as well have been thought up in Hollywood by someone who had never been there. Setting aside differences in military uniform and weapons, and thus the attendant differences in mission and type of combat, *Destination Tokyo, Bataan, Air Force, Sahara* and *Guadalcanal Diary* are the same movie. This "list" can be put into two forms:

A. As a "story" of a film—the "story" which becomes what everyone imagines the combat genre to be, but which, in fact, does not exist in a pure form in any single film. It is this "story" that the satirists use in TV skits, but it is also the thing that filmmakers would later use to create new genre films.
B. As an outline of elements and characteristics, to be used in analyzing films of the genre.

A. The "Story"

Here is the "story" of the universal World War II combat film, with its primary units in bold face and indications of how they can be varied without violating the basic definition in brackets.

The credits of the film unfold against a military reference. [A map, a flag, an insignia, a photo or painting of battle, a military song, for example.] **The credits include the name of a military advisor.**

Closely connected to the presentation of the credits is a statement that may be called the film's dedication. [It may be printed or narrated. It may be a reference to a military battle of the past or present. It may contain thanks to a military service which cooperated in the making of the film, or an emotional tribute to a gallant fighting force, our allies, or a quote from a famous World War II figure, with Churchill and Roosevelt being particular favorites.]

A group of men, led by a hero, undertake a mission which will

accomplish an important military objective. [The group of men is a mixture of unrelated types, with varying ethnic and socioeconomic backgrounds. They may be men from different military forces, and/or different countries. They are of different ages. Some have never fought in combat before, and others are experienced. Some are intellectual and well-educated, others are not. They are both married and single, shy and bold, urban and rural, comic and tragic. They come from all areas of the United States geographically, especially the Middle West (stability), the South (naïveté but good shooting ability), New England (education), and New York City (sophistication). Favorite states are Iowa, the Dakotas, and Kansas for the Middle West; California and Texas for recognition; and Brooklyn. (In the war film, Brooklyn is a state unto itself, and is almost always present one way or another.) Their occupations vary: farmer, cab driver, teacher. Minority figures are always represented: black, Hispanic, Indian, and even Orientals.]

This group contains an observer or commentator. [A newspaperman, a man keeping a diary, or a man who thinks in his head or talks out loud.]

The hero has had leadership forced upon him in dire circumstances. [The highest ranking officer may have been killed, placing him in command. He may have been forced into his role simply by having been drafted or having felt he had to volunteer for the role. He may have been a career military man who received an odious assignment. The assumption of enforced responsibility, however willingly or unwillingly accepted, is present.]

They undertake a military objective. [They may have to hold a fort and make a last stand. They may have to rove forward through jungle, desert, forest, the ocean, both on top and underwater, or in the air. But whether holding the fort or journeying to destroy the enemy's fort—or waiting for returning comrades or going out to rejoin comrades—the objective is present. The objective may have been a secret, or it may have been planned in advance, or it may have grown out of necessity.]

As they go forward, the action unfolds. A series of episodes occur which alternate in uneven patterns the contrasting forces of night and day, action and repose, safety and danger, combat and noncombat, comedy and tragedy, dialogue and action. [The variations are endless, as inventive as the writers can make them.]

The enemy's presence is indicated. [He may appear face-to-face, fly over in airplanes and bomb, sail by in other ships and shoot, crawl forward in endless numbers, assault from trees, broadcast on the radio, whatever. He is sometimes seen in closeup, and is sometimes faceless.]

Military inconography is seen, and its usage is demonstrated for and taught to civilians. [Uniforms, weapons, equipment, insignia, maps, salt tablets, K-rations, walkie-talkies, etc.]

Conflict breaks out within the group itself. It is resolved through the external conflict brought down upon them.

Rituals are enacted from the past. [If a holiday comes, such as Christmas, it is celebrated. If a death occurs, a burial takes place.]

Rituals are enacted from the present. [Mail is read, and weapons are cleaned. Philosophies of life and postwar plans are discussed.]

Members of the group die. [This has many variations, including the death of the entire group. The minorities almost always die, and die most horribly.]

A climactic battle takes place, and a learning or growth process occurs.

The tools of cinema are employed for tension *(cutting)*, release *(camera movement)*, intimacy and alienation *(composition)*, and the look of combat *(lighting)* and authenticity *(documentary footage)*.

The situation is resolved. [It will be so only after sacrifice and loss, hardship and discouragement, and it can be resolved either through victory or defeat, death or survival.]

THE END appears on the screen. [A "rollcall" of the combatants appears, either as cast names or pictures of the actors with their cast names or as a scene in which they march by or fly by or pass by us in some way, living and/or dead.]

The audience is ennobled for having shared their combat experience, as they are ennobled for having undergone it. We are all comrades in arms.

Anyone wishing to write a combat film can follow this story and make an appropriate script. Just to show how it can work, here is the first one-third of an imaginary combat film, entitled *War Cry!*

The insignia of the Marine Corps is seen, and "From the halls of Montezuma" is being sung by a male chorus. *War Cry!* jumps out from the screen. The credits appear, including the name of Col. Marcus B. Everson, Technical Advisor. As the credits finish, a map of the Solomon Islands is seen, and these words are on the screen:

"This film is dedicated to the ferocious fighting men of the American Marine Corps. From the halls of Montezuma to the shores of Tripoli

. . . and now to the heat and humidity and horror of the Pacific . . . these men, ordinary people with extraordinary ability to fight. . . guard our American way of life. We owe them our deepest gratitude and greatest respect, because, no matter what, they always do the job with the rallying cry, "Marines Let's Go!!"

Semper Fidelis. . .

On a troop ship heading into battle on the Pacific is a combat platoon consisting of Feinstein, O'Hara, Thomas Jefferson Brown, Kowalski, Rinaldi, Andy Hawkins, Bruce Martinson, Pop Jorgenson. They are under the command of Captain Charles P. Jenkins, and their tough professional soldier top sergeant is Kip McCormick. With them is war correspondent David C. Davis.

On board ship as they await battle, they talk of their lives and homes. Pop's feet hurt. He tells about the night before his first battle in World War I. Martinson, a Harvard graduate who had planned to go to medical school, is reading A Farewell to Arms. Feinstein talks about wishing he was back home going to Ebbetts Field to see the Dodgers, driving there in his cab. Hawkins, a young and unsophisticated boy, has never been away from home before, his home being his father's farm in the mountains of Tennessee. Kowalski and O'Hara hate one another, and are arguing about how to make a good stew. Kowalski says no potatoes, use cabbage. O'Hara says no cabbage, use potatoes. Thomas Jefferson Brown sings "Swing Low, Sweet Chariot," and Jenkins tells him how they always sang "Rock of Ages" at their little church in New England, but he guesses it's all just the same song. Jenkins notices the little dog Hawkins has hidden beside him, but decides to ignore it. Jenkins talks about his wife, a Sunday school teacher, and his two kids. Davis is keeping a diary. His voiceover talks about his fears of combat, and about how brave the other men seem. McCormick says nothing. He keeps his own counsel. Rinaldi is sleeping.

Going ashore, Jenkins is killed, and after their small band is isolated from the main group, McCormick assumes command. To survive, they must rejoin their main forces while avoiding the Japanese patrols. They have only enough salt tablets for half the group. Their maps were lost in the landing. Feinstein has been wounded and cannot walk. Kowalski and O'Hara prepare to carry him. Davis's voice is heard saying, "If we ever get out of this alive."

Here you have the first one third of a perfect combat movie, based on what you already know.

B. *The Outline*

Because so many variations of the basic definition can be created, and because of the process of evolution the genre will undergo, the story may be transferred into an outline form with which to compare films easily. Since characteristics can be the same, only different (group of mixed military forces, group of ethnic mixes, group of mixed international forces), and since what they represent will shift in the evolutionary process (how tragic to lose the good father leader, how good to get rid of the evil father who forced us to fight), we need an objective format with which to identify the basic definition:

The Outline
A. CHARACTERS
    1. The Hero
    2. The Group
    3. The Enemy
    4. The Women (if any)
B. SETTING
    1. The Theater of War (Date and Place)
    2. The Military Force Involved (Air, Sea, Ground)
    3. Relationship to History (true event or not)
    4. The Objective
C. NARRATIVE STRUCTURE
    1. Episodes
        a. Credits, Dedication, and Opening Sequence.
        b. Combat/Non-combat (Action and Repose)
        c. Familiar Events (This refers to events, such as mail call or Christmas celebration that occur from film to film.)
        d. Night/Day
        e. Comedy/Tragedy
    2. Organization of story pattern
        a. Time sequence (present, past, use of flashback, etc.)
        b. Place sequence (Change of geographical location, etc.)
        c. Plot Sequence (Order of events)
        d. Narrative viewpoint (Objective/Subjective)
D. CULTURAL ATTITUDES
    1. Death/Sacrifice/Loss
    2. Propaganda
    3. Humor
    4. Home/Family/Country

      5. The Situation At Hand
   E. LANGUAGE
      1. Film and visual language
         a. Technique (cutting, camera movement, etc.)
         b. Image (Includes what is seen as event, gesture, action)
         c. Iconography (Includes all possible coded information)
      2. Dialogue

By using this outline and applying it to a particular film, the relationship of that film to the rest of the genre (its inconsistency or matching qualities) can be determined. Also, its position in the evolutionary process is established, as well as its overall relationship to history and reality. It demonstrates how a primary set of concepts solidifies into a story—and how they can be interpreted for a changing ideology. From the films came the list. From the list comes the story. Out of the story you can make a screenplay. Out of the total accumulated screenplays (films) can be made an outline. Out of the outline one can study the films to see where they differ and vary the basic pattern of the genre.

To simplify and condense, *Bataan* has been used here as the sample film from which to generate the list. In actual research, all the combat films screened were used for the basic definition. The important aspect of these characteristics is obviously not just the list itself. For a genre to live, it must in some way tell a story the audience needs to hear told after the war is over. This means its characteristics must contain meanings that an audience needs further information or involvement with in the postwar era.

Can the characteristics be made to represent the concerns of another era? We can see from the basic definition that the concepts may be varied, but that their function remains the same. Can they be varied and also have their functions inverted or adjusted ideologically, and still remain the genre? We know that genres have eras of particular popularity, and that some seem to disappear. Currently, we talk of the disappearance of the Western, and the suggestion is raised that, since the geographical frontier is no longer an important concept for filmgoers, we see no more Westerns but instead turn our attention to the science fiction movie and the new frontier of space. Of course we quickly see that the science fiction movie tends to give us the Western format in space clothes, but a discussion of that will come later.

Now we are concerned with basic definition. If the primary characteristics can be used to answer questions that are concerned only with
the war, presumably the genre will have no use, no appeal, for viewers
when the issue of the war is settled by its successful completion. When
we look at the list of questions the war combat genre generates, it is
obvious that some of them are settled once war is over, but that
most of them are basic to our understanding of ourselves and our history.
They are eternal questions, and this makes the genre one that can (and,
in fact, will) live on.

The primary questions which inspired the basic characteristics of the
combat genre—the storytelling process of hero, group, objective—
were straightforward concerns of a nation at war. Could we win it?
What would we have to do to win? What was each individual's responsibility in the fight? We all would have to do our part—whether in
combat or on the home front—but how? What things would we have
to know in order not to become separated eternally from one another
if some went to fight and others stayed behind? Who were these strange
enemies, and what attitudes should we take toward them now? Since
America was a nation of people from many countries, what would we
do when some of us were suddenly designated as enemies? We had to
be taught what to think, and what aspects of the enemy we should fear.
In order to do this, we had to reconsider the concept of Americanism.
What did it mean to be American? What was America's history, and
who were her heroes? We had to think about what nice guys we were,
and about how we always played fair and about how much we liked
our moms and apple pie. If we were reluctant to fight, we had to be
taught why we must. We were preserving our democratic system and
our cultural attitudes. We were defending a precious and unique heritage. To do this, we were going to have to work together as a real group
of equals, or we weren't going to make it. Oh, we needed the individual's
bravery and guts, but only if it could be sacrificed to the good of the
group. And if our families were separated and torn apart by war, this
group could become our substitute family—a kind of big, national
family of other Americans. More than anything else, we needed that
group.

All these questions and lessons were basic to the war combat genre
of World War II. When the war was over, however, these issues were
resolved, and we had no further need for the information. If these had
been the only questions ever asked by the World War II film, perhaps

it would have died. But there were other issues involved in these stories, issues that made them of continued importance, because they were issues we would always need to think about. World War II films were all about living and dying. What makes a good life and what makes a good person? What should we be willing to die for—and how do you die right. If you had to die young, what would make you a noble sacrifice and what would make it all a waste? What about killing? If you had to do it, did that make you a killer? What about when the war was over, and you returned home, having killed? Would it change you forever? It was one thing to agree cheerfully to work in a group, and to accept the group over the individual for the war effort, but how did you do this? How did you resolve group conflicts and differences of opinion, background, and attitude? Could you really make family relationships and thus preserve a form of civilization in the midst of combat? How could you be a good American, and furthermore, was that really a good thing to be? Could you suffer loss and defeat and still survive? Could defeat really be victory in disguise? Was it wrong to be selfish, and not want to make sacrifices, or was it exhibiting sanity to reject wartime attitudes?

There are doubtless more questions, enough to fill a volume themselves. But in these one can see why the genre survived and was repeated. Long after the primary issues were resolved (we did win the war; we did learn to play our roles well; we taught the enemy they were wrong about it, etc.), the other issues have remained. The evolutionary process the genre has undergone happened because some of these issues are still relevant. We continue to need to learn what it means to be Americans, and if that is a good or bad thing. We continue to need to learn about living and dying, and about loss and defeat, and about what our way of life really means. Furthermore, these issues are flexible, and can be used to demonstrate differing ideology and political attitudes in the years to come. It can be bad or good to be American, right or wrong to kill. All this allows for the evolutionary process. And all this is typical of all genres, not just the combat film. It can be observed operating in the gangster films and Westerns over the years as they reflect a celebration of American violence or shame about it, as they repress women or liberate them, and as new wars come along to be understood and evaluated.

Since World War II is one of the biggest events of American history, it is natural that films about it would continue to be of interest. However, the same might be said about the Civil War, World War I, and even the Spanish American War.

Consider the films about other great wars of American history. We have almost no films about the Spanish American War although sometimes in Westerns or musicals the hero has to leave town to go fight it for a time, as in *Pursued* or *Stars and Stripes Forever.* The Civil War, too, has fewer actual combat films than one might suppose. It was *very* popular in silent films, but the two World Wars tend to crowd it off the screen. Although many Civil War films are set in the South, these are films about a way of life, and about issues such as slavery and sex more than they are about combat. The combat of the Civil War is actually seldom depicted on the sound screen. Perhaps the greatness of *The Birth of a Nation* took care of the presentation once and for all. *Gone with the Wind* has no actual combat, just its aftermath and the effect of renegade soldiers in the lives of women. *Horse Soldiers* (1959) is one of the few combat films of the Civil War, and the combat occupies perhaps half of its running time. It has a Westernized format, and is directed by a man closely associated with World War II films and Westerns, John Ford. *The Red Badge of Courage* (1951), that notorious flop, is a miniature patrol film, and its influence, both as a novel and as a film, might be felt, but the film was not released until *after* World War II. John Huston, its director, had already made documentary combat films, as he participated in the battle of San Pietro and went forward, camera in hand, to record the events. Here is a case of reality and fiction blurring indeed. Perhaps we do not care to see our Civil War depicted in any way but as what it is: a quarrel in the family over material matters. *Tap Roots* (1948) effectively carries this idea out by telling the true story of a Mississippi county that seceded from the secession. Thus, the combat is seen more as them-against-them than as us-against-us—a larger type of family quarrel. The World War I film, discussed in the next chapter, also seems relatively limited in appeal.

World War II seems to be the combat that speaks to the American soul. Perhaps it is our total victory, or the sense of our righteousness, or the conviction that it wasn't our fault, or the influence of technology on art—in which the ability to take cameras into the field created images of power that would and could not be forgotten—or the simple thing that a great many cracking good stories came out of WWII, or that the studio system was alive and well and could turn out many films. There are many possibilities and no doubt they all apply.

But all or nothing at all, as the World War II-era song says. Whatever the reason, the combat film was born in World War II, and it grew, lived, and evolved during the conflict.

TWO

Prior History

The great advantage of using the World War II combat film for a study on the evolution and definition of genre, is that it has an obvious beginning place. No World War II combat film could be made until there was a World War II.

To locate the first Western, or the first woman's film is a more difficult task. (*The Great Train Robbery*, a piece of what would become the Western, may or may not be "first.") The problems of film preservation, in which nearly 50 percent of all the films made in America before 1950 have disappeared, make studying films from the silent period particularly difficult. Starting a study after December 7, 1941, simplifies the task, since more films exist, more films are accessible, and more reviews and written records have been kept.

It makes it simpler, but it doesn't make it easy.

We may easily say "once the war begins, the genre begins." This is history. But just as the War came from somewhere, so did the films. The Evolution can be traced clearly once the war began, but where did the genre come from in *film* history?

It would be ridiculous to suggest that combat films of WWII sprang out of the early months of 1942, and the dark days of 1943, without any reference to what had come before. There is a prior history of war, of war films, and war combat films, to be considered first.

The World War II combat genre underwent a process in which it was born from or out of something. And presumably this is true for all genres. Perhaps it is an event, or a technological breakthrough (as when the coming of sound brought the movie musical) and/or other types of films. The World War II combat film was born out of an event, influenced by technological developments, but created in story form not only from history, but also from parts of earlier movies.

For instance, in *Hell Below* (1933) combat is part of a total story that includes elements of family conflict (between father and daughter), a raucous service comedy (in which Jimmy Durante boxes a kangaroo, if that's raucous enough for you), a teacup romance (Robert Montgomery and Madge Evans), and a typical service drama about a code of honor (should the sub have dived down and left poor Robert Young up there alone?). A decade later, *Destination Tokyo* was released. In a sense, it is the actual submarine warfare section of *Hell Below* dilated to become the entire movie. The dangerous underwater events, which were only a part of the plot of *Hell Below*, are the entire story of *Destination Tokyo*. Yet the characters of the later film seem to come from the sorts of stories *Hell Below* presented in full detail.

Some of these characters' stories are briefly presented in *Destination Tokyo*'s flashbacks, in particular the romance of Cary Grant and his wife and the service comedy story of Dane Clark. Other stories are merely implied. The flashbacks of *Destination Tokyo* indicate a prior life for the characters, just as they also indicate a prior film. The statement made by the use of these flashbacks is that the prior life, the prior film, and the prior audience life, must all be jettisoned for the war effort. Narrative richness, à la *Hell Below*, must be ditched so we can buckle down to winning the war. We must all make a sacrifice, and for the viewer that means taking Cary Grant out of his tuxedo and subjecting him (and us) to the full combat experience.

After the war, when the genre was established, submarine films would reappear, and this time redevelop a shoreline story. However, both audiences and filmmakers now clearly considered such a film a submarine combat movie. The shoreline events are a buildup for the combat sequences, and what happens on shore is going to be related to what will happen in combat. If other parts of the film include a teacup drama or a family conflict, these events are now closely tied to the combat experience that is the heart of the film.

An example of this is *The Deep Six* of 1958. The hero (Alan Ladd) is a Quaker. In the early part of the film, he is an advertising man. When war comes, he joins, but everyone, including him, wonders if his religion will be a problem in combat. Can he kill or not? Ladd serves on a destroyer, and two crisis situations demonstrate the conflict between combat and his Quaker sensibility: when he hesitates to fire on what appears to be an attacking plane, and when he goes ashore on a patrol and is reluctantly forced to fight.

Throughout the movie, both before war and after war, whether in the advertising world, in romance, or on the destroyer, the problem of his religion ties the different sequences together. The audience knows the issue will be resolved where it belongs—in active combat—because whatever else this film is about, and wherever else it may be set, it is a movie about a man fighting World War II to resolve his problem. *The Deep Six* demonstrates how, once the war is won, the genre can be used to tell a story about an individual with a personal problem.

To summarize: first there is a film with a group of related or unrelated story patterns. A time of need or stress causes one of these story patterns to break off and dilate into an entire film. This portion grows and strengthens (or dies, as the case may be). After the time of stress passes, the portion grows a new, broader story around itself. It does not recede back into the same sort of unrelated series of stories that it emerged from. The new stories around it *are* related, however loosely.

This does not mean that combat as a story pattern cannot reappear in a formulaic[1] film, or that battle scenes do not appear in films besides those set in World War II. This characteristic is true for genres other than the combat film, too. The studios had continuity in terms of working personnel and studio policy. They reused costumes, furniture, whole sets, and certainly entire plots. They also knew how to update the images of favorite stars, providing new roles in new genres that still maintained the basic persona the audience had come to know and love. For instance, Humphrey Bogart, associated with gangster roles at the end of the thirties, was placed in a movie in which gangsters fought Nazi fifth columnists in New York City. The film, *All Through The Night*, handily united Bogart's gangster years with the war years, showing how skills with violence and weaponry could easily move into a new genre. The new Bogart was the old Bogart. The Bogart of World War II combat films was the gangster Bogart, using his old skills for war instead of crime. Alan Ladd made a similar film, *Lucky Jordan*, and so did Cary Grant (*Mr. Lucky*).

Obviously, films depicting internally declared or recognized *war*, specifically combat on the ground, at sea, and in the air, existed before Pearl Harbor. War has been depicted in all its variety. Films have presented wars among cave tribes and in the times of ancient Greece and Rome. Audiences have been treated to spectacles of medieval crusades, the Napoleonic Wars, and the Boer War. The U.S. Revolutionary War, Civil War, and Spanish-American War have been re-created, as have such conflicts as the Indian wars and the Mexican wars, and so, of course, has World War I. And then we have seen on the screen imaginary wars between mythical Kingdoms and in outer space. In these films, war might be said to be *war*, an officially declared act. Such forms of "war" as union strikes, the Hatfields and the McCoys, and all types of undeclared conflicts are obviously not included, since we are moving toward the definition of the combat portion of an internationally declared and recognized *war*. (Any conflict, of course, is "war," and that includes love!)

Each of these types of war films has its own conventions, and might be properly catalogued in another genre. The Napoleonic Wars have been presented on film as historical dramas (*Desiree*), costume films, epics, and literary adaptations (*Becky Sharp*). Ancient wars and major European wars are usually epic films and/or costume pictures. Indian wars are usually Westerns. In some cases war may appear in a film not properly a genre film at all. It is important to remember that not all films are genre films.

Eliminating generalized war films does not, however, say that none of these films influenced the combat genre. Some of them can be discussed as important indirect influences. Such films include the Western about General Custer's last stand, *They Died with Their Boots On* (1941); the British Empire film, *The Charge of the Light Brigade* (1936) about the ill-fated "last stand" at Balaclava during the Crimean War, and *The Real Glory* (1939), about Moro native uprisings in the Philippines. And, of course, *Lost Patrol*, which has already been discussed. These are only four examples, but it simply isn't possible to discuss every related film. Discussing any film with a group, a hero, an objective, and even a last stand would take research farther and farther away from the combat genre. There is no doubt that the same story can be told against a changing background. Stories about groups of men who undertake difficult objectives, led by a hero, existed before World War II. It is possible to say that the Western Cavalry troops became the World War II fighting unit, and then returned to their Western format after the war. Or that stories about gangsters, pirates, and revolutionaries underwent the same redressing. Again, however, speculations return one to a basic examination of film history. One has to look at the films themselves to trace these transformations. The results might be analyzed culturally or psychologically, but, as stated earlier, this book is about the combat film and its historical development. A phenomenon of genre is that what describes one can fit into another if you change the clothes and the setting. This is one of the things research on combat reveals. This phenomenon—*cross-genre influence or transformation*—will be analyzed later in the book.

This chapter will concern itself with direct influences, or the obvious prior history of the genre, which lies in films about World War I and about life in military service. Even with this restriction, selecting these films and cataloguing them was difficult. The truth is that where a genre comes from is difficult to pin down, given the thousands of films made in America during the golden days of the studio system. This is one of the reasons I have chosen to trace a genre that has a clear beginning place.

The main influences most directly involved in the prior history of the combat genre can be divided into World War I films; the Noncombat Military Service Films of the 1930s; and the Films of 1940-1941, made after war was declared in Europe but before the United States entered.[2]

World War I Films

The American filmed versions of World War I are very important, because the inevitable questions arise—Why wasn't the World War I combat film the generic prototype? What was its influence on the World War II combat film? The stories of World War I definitely contain characteristics that reappear in World War II combat films. In them, one finds Quirt and Flagg, as well as beardless youths, old professionals, and noble leaders. One sees the men receive their mail, fight their wars, and argue among themselves. They, too, wear uniforms and carry weapons, and above all, they, too, die. At bottom, both WWI and WWII films are about death.

However, the two wars do not evolve historically into a single unified genre. There are a great many reasons why this should be true—different enemies, different political issues. There is also the evolution of film itself—the addition of sound and the advancement of film grammar. It is entirely possible that the core explanation of genre development is linked to these technological and artistic developments. The coming of sound certainly inspired genres such as musicals, gangster films, and teacup dramas. The ability to add song and music, the rat-a-tat of machine guns, and lah-di-da salon discussions to film brought on films which took advantage of those opportunities. Color changed the look of violence in combat films and westerns, and the entire advancing of the history of film shows the development of meanings through cutting, camera movement, narrative ellipsis, and the expressive uses of devices such as the zoom lens and the widening aspect ratio.

The depiction of World War I on film was obviously interrupted by World War II, with its new needs and concerns, and new attitudes. This makes it difficult to assess whether or not the World War I film is usually an antiwar film (except for its brief rehabilitation as a recruiting poster in 1938-1941) because its basic definition was less flexible than that of World War II, or whether the advent of the new war simply froze it in its pacifist stage. Observe, by way of contrast, that when the Korean conflict broke out, its films were constituted in the basic format of the World War II genre, with minor variations. The Korean film and the World War II film were closely related, but the World War I film grew increasingly separate from both, and became associated almost exclusively with an antiwar statement. It is possible that the World War I film has undergone its own evolutionary cycle.[3]

An overview indicates that the world wars both taught audiences about combat—about training men to fight, and about what happens to them when they do. To portray this, they use similar characteristics, but the films of the two wars are not the same in their basic attitude toward the war or in their look. An average filmgoer can quickly identify the two wars from a single frame, not only by uniforms and weapons, but also by the landscape of war. The reason the two types of narrative film don't look the same is because documentaries, newsreels, and photographs showed audiences and filmmakers what each war really *did* look like, and the two wars *were* different. Filmmakers had to match their stories of war to the real images of war that audiences were seeing.

World War I was the first war to be recorded by the moving camera. However, bulky equipment and the shortage of telephoto lenses (which allowed the photographer a safe distance) prevented easy in-the-field coverage. There was also censorship in effect regarding the photographing and showing of bodies, and the majority of the photographing of the war had to be done by the Signal Corps. As a result, the American public was not in the same position as in World War II, when the sight and sound of documentary combat footage, as well as news photographs of battles, was a common, everyday experience.[3]

It is notable, however, that World War I was the first war that could be watched on film by those who were not taking part in it, even though such viewing was not the shared mass experience it would become in World War II. Photographs were more readily available, and these images were seen.

Film, of course, was still in a relatively early stage of development during the first World War.[4] Such famous epics as *Civilization* (1916) and *Intolerance* (1916) were great antiwar epics, while *Battle Cry for Peace* (1915) demonstrated what would happen if the United States were invaded. The majority of war-related films during the actual period of the war were propaganda films such as *The Kaiser: The Beast of Berlin* (1918), *My Four Years in Germany* (1918), and *Heart of Humanity* (1918), with Erich von Stroheim as a bestial Hun who throws a baby out a window. For his great World War I film *Hearts of The World* (1918), D. W. Griffith used a few scenes he actually shot in the battlefields of France, but he returned to Hollywood for the major reenactment. "Sometimes one does not know whether what he is seeing is a real war or screen make believe," observed the *Times* review, sounding a prophetic note. 1918 was the key year for films during the war itself (as 1943 was for World War II), with many films and newsreels appearing in major cities.

After the Armistice, war films temporarily disappeared from the screen, presumably because people were sick of the subject. Advertisements for movies even carried the promise: THIS IS NOT A WAR FILM. (It is interesting to note that a similar disappearance occurs after World War II, for logical reasons.)

If there were no other way to learn anything about World Wars I and II other than from Hollywood movies, what would we know? First of all, World War I was a flop. World War II was a hit. World War I was supposed to make the world safe for democracy, and it didn't. World War II was supposed to rid the world of Nazis, and it did. World War I was all about glory and the waste of youth and the need for pacifism. World War II was all about bravery, the dedication of youth to democracy, and the need to get together and fight. Frequently, the World War I film, American made, is about Germans or Frenchmen or the British. The World War II film is about Americans, except maybe in the later, more decadent states of its development. World War I is about Europe, and World War II is about America. World War I talks about the troubles of officers, and World War II talks about the troubles of the common fighting man. World War II teaches us how to make order out of chaos, and World War I says leaders go crazy because you *can't* make order out of chaos. The hero of World War II *probably* won't die, but members of his group will. The hero of World War I may have to sacrifice himself and die by his own choice.

Examining the use of World War I as a genre setting for films, one can see that, no matter how gloriously entertaining or exciting the combat is (particularly in the air films), the genre is developed as a pacifist message throughout the twenties and thirties until just before World War II. Despite this unifying pacifism, the films of the silent era, the transition-to-sound era, and the 1930s have subtle differences linked to the presentation of the combat force involved. If the film is an airplane movie, it is inevitably more exciting and glorious than if it is an infantry movie. Furthermore, the air movies celebrate the individual, and concern themselves with the burdens of elite leadership. The infantry films are more involved with death, futility, and the waste of youth in war.

Each of the three WWI-film historical periods—the silent era, the transition-to-sound, and the 1930s—contributes something to the later World War II film, despite the fundamental differences between the two genres. For instance, three famous and successful silent World War I films are *The Big Parade* (November 20, 1925), an epic story, involving romance and comedy, which takes a wealthy young man away from his home town to combat overseas and then returns him home, crippled; *Tell It to the Marines* (December 24, 1926), a classic training camp-into-combat film, which teaches an audience what a professional marine is, how he is trained, how he fights, and how he finds romance and comedy along the way; and *What Price Glory?* (November 24, 1926), a story of the professional soldiers who fight World War I as yet another war in their lives, and who experience comedy and romance while in war and whose experiences are contrasted to those of young men who are not professional soldiers. The three films are actually three different prototypes of war stories, each one of which makes its own contributions to the later, more streamlined World War II genre.

Collectively, these films teach an audience what war is for—how you train for it, how you fight it, and how you live through it. In each one of these films, the heroes not only fight a difficult war, but they also find women to love and much to laugh about. The World War II combat film in its pure form usually has no women, or presents them as "memories" in a flashback form. Its comedy grows out of the men's ability to joke in the face of death, and is part of their cynical, mocking attitudes toward their situation. In later World War II films, comedy (and romance) will appear, but in the pure form combat film, comedy is an attitude taken toward an unfunny situation and romance is a memory or a wish.

The Big Parade is a powerful antiwar statement. Its combat is intense, but it also tells a fully developed noncombat story, which is traditional of the great World War I films. It begins in America, and returns to America, showing a total picture of war's effect on the life of one young man. Thus, it is not just a story of combat, but a story of history, a demonstration through one example of how American youth were changed by a war that billed itself as a war to end all wars, but failed. This young man's life is ruined emotionally and physically by the experience of war. Like many other heroes of World War I films, he will be crippled. (Most World War I heroes go blind. This one's leg is amputated.) The model for the World War I epic story of wasted youth is set by *The Big Parade*. Its contribution to the later genre is that of the death of youth, and the memory of home.

Tell It to the Marines (1926), filmed with the cooperation of the United States Marine Corps, is the key film that sets up the story pattern in which rookies spend a long time getting trained and then go off to combat. (*Sands of Iwo Jima* is a World War II example.) It is set initially in a training camp, in which young recruits come into boot camp, run up against a tough top sergeant (Lon Chaney as Sergeant O'Hara), and have to learn to pull their own weight. It teaches an audience what the Marines are—a tough group who stand for no nonsense, no breaking of the rules. Strict discipline is a must, the audience learns. The audience watches the young hero (William Haines) become a Marine, but still he falls in love and marries. The old dog, Lon Chaney, remains alone. This sense of the true military man as a man without home or family endures in later films.

Tell It to the Marines contains a marine top sergeant who is ruthless with his men, a detailed presentation of Marine Corps life, and all kinds of fighting. In training films, a barroom brawl traditionally takes place. Such brawls, which also occur in Westerns, are linked to military movies of all types. When a man is trained to fight, he fights.

What Price Glory? (1926) is one of the most successful films of World War I, and a popular film on any terms. There may be another film as influential in determining the basic definition of the hardcore professional enlisted man, but it's hard to imagine just what it would be.

Based on a successful stage play written by Laurence Stallings (who helped create the screenplay and who also wrote *The Big Parade*), *What Price Glory?* sets the pace for the sense of the swaggering, rough, tough macho men who fight the American wars, wherever they may be. Directed with pace and flair by Raoul Walsh, it was a huge success and a much remembered and beloved movie.

What Price Glory? (which was remade by John Ford in 1952, during the Korean War) tells the story of Quirt (Edmund Lowe), the hardboiled professional soldier, and Flagg (Victor McLaglen), who was "soldiering for wages, and who loves life and fun." These two marines are seen throughout the film's action in a series of conflicts. Theirs is a male friendship that is fundamentally a competition, an adversary relationship. Such a relationship is perhaps the single most important contribution of the World War I film to the World War II film.

Quirt and Flagg may be represented as the two main characters in one of the later World War II combat films, or they may be minor characters or even comedy relief. They may be seen to be like Robert Taylor and Lloyd Nolan, in primary conflict in *Bataan*, or as a basically loving but competitive friendship, as that between Robert Preston and William Bendix in *Wake Island*. But whether they are lower class, or educated, main characters or supporting actors, they are involved in a fight or argument with one another that provides a running commentary or leitmotif to the film. Perhaps they best represent the last of the individualistic tendencies that the World War II film seeks to convert into a group consciousness.

In *What Price Glory?* the Quirt/Flagg fight is over women, but in the later films the conflict becomes representative of a differing attitude toward combat, toward politics, toward life—whatever. It becomes a familar relationship on which new issues can be superimposed. This illustrates a quality of genre—the recognizable device, the Quirt/Flagg relationship in this case, will later be presented for the audience as a marking point, a familar place with which to enter a film or connect to it. The Quirt/Flagg device is used to present a different issue, but an issue related to the overall meaning the genre presents. In even later genre stages, it sometimes appears for no real reason. It serves no purpose, has no ideological use. It's there because it's always been there. It becomes vestigial.

In *What Price Glory?* other basic events of wartime combat are defined. There is a mail call. There is the iconography of war: uniforms,

What Price Glory?—*Victor McLaglen, Dolores del Rio, Edmund Lowe*

guns, etc. There is the terrible weather one must slog forward through: "Rain—Muck," and the usual boy who plays a harmonica. There is a mix of people who come up to fight the war (a farmer, an artist, a comedy figure, and a man who has an awful mother-in-law and was glad to get away). There is a soldier who keeps a diary, and his writing appears as titles with appropriate dates: "August 14, 1918, will this bath of blood cleanse the world?" All of these elements will reappear in World War II films. However, *What Price Glory?* doesn't really present a viewer with a sense of a democratic group, a microcosm of American types. In general, World War I films usually have characters that seem to be wealthy, more aristocratic, and thus English, than those of World War II. Quirt and Flagg are exceptions to this, and this may be another reason why they have remained with us in American war films. They were a breath of fresh air among all the Arrow Collar ads.

The similarities in content, character, plot and event between films from the two wars can be catalogued, even though their attitudes toward the group and the individual or toward death and victory, toward the very fighting of the war itself (should we be there or not?), is markedly different. However, it is in the *image* itself that one finds the basic difference. These two wars don't *look* alike.

In a typical World War I battle scene, hundreds of men are seen in long shot, running, charging, and dying, giving the subliminal impression that all the young men in the world are being killed. The long shot adds to this sense of number and impersonal death. The waste of youth theme is strongly played.

The World War I film also depicts gas war. The men of *What Price Glory?* have mice with them in the trenches, so that when gas comes near them, and the mice die, they know they are under a gas attack. Gas and mice, however, did not become a genre convention, even in the World War I films that come later. Some things just don't get popular with audiences no matter what, and gas and mice may fall into that category!

One of the key differences between the look of the World War I and II films is the clear demarcation between a battlefield and a behind-the-lines world. In *What Price Glory?* we see defined the real look of the "no man's land" image of World War I—a bare landscape, dissected with barbed wire, burned out trees, and, frequently, dead and abandoned bodies. Coming across it are small figures, the soldiers who fight the war, heading back to their trenches, semi-secure behind barbed wire and inside the earth. Inside the trenches is the home space of the war, and back behind the lines is the safe space outside the war, this time a bar called Cognac Pete's. The field of war is this naked, barren and sparse landscape. War is still a soldier's game. He leaves the women and kids and goes up to the front, and thus there is a "landscape of war." World War II is a total war against everyone, women and children, too.

Perhaps the main narrative difference between the silent World War I films and the World War II film is summed up by the word *glory*. "What price glory now?" asks the leader at the end of the big battle, nearly mad from the strain of leadership and the death of so many young men under his command. Whether decrying it as an empty thing, as in *The Big Parade*, or indirectly selling it, *glory* is an issue of the first war; it is *not* an issue in the next one. Survival will be the issue, not glory. The romance of battle, the code of bravery, is part of what they were all fighting for in World War I. "This war and glory racket is kind of like a religion" says Flagg. *What Price Glory?* and *The Road to Glory* are the names of World War I films. In World War II, in later stages, we get a film called *The Glory Brigade*, but the use of the word is ironic.

The tradition of silent combat films is carried forward into the transition-to-sound, but with a split personality. Perhaps inspired by the new possibilities of sound and perhaps by the need to depict the war as our heroic effort to "make the world safe for democracy" and thus to justify the sacrifices we made for it, the transition era of the early thirties produced a spate of World War I films: some that presented the glory of World War I in memory and retrospect, and some that were powerfully antiwar. How to categorize such movies? The "glory of war" films are remarkably few, and tinged with ambivalences. The messages I see and hear may not be the ones you do—even if you were meant to. For instance, a film which says "war is hell," but makes it thrilling to watch, denies its own message. A film that says war is fun, but shows too much violence and death, may not deliver what it intends either. In film study, too often this problem is overlooked. It makes the medium extremely difficult to categorize generically.

At any rate, there was a brief period of popularity for such ambivalent films during the transition-to-sound. All of them carry on the basic attitude of the World War I movie—war is hell and it kills our youth— but they seem to pay only lip service to that theme. They actually gloriously celebrate male bravery and heroism, and visually present exciting scenes of combat. It is significant that the majority of "glory" films are about what was then called the Air Service. Without those silvery mechanical birds so perfectly beautiful on film, the "glory" films might not exist at all. It may be that the Air Service kept these films alive, and that World War I was just a background excuse to put planes in the air. The "glory" films include *Today We Live* and *The Dawn Patrol*, both of which are related to the silent film of the same period, *Wings*.

The Dawn Patrol is one of the most famous movies ever made about airmen, the first version of which was released in 1930, directed by Howard Hawks, with the original story written by John Monk Saunders. Today, this film has been retitled, *The Flight Commander*, for television release, so as not to confuse it with the 1938 remake, starring Errol Flynn and David Niven and directed by Edmund Goulding.[5]

Dawn Patrol is a movie that is generic in every sense of the word. Television skits imitate it. Comics imitate it. Movies with satiric comedy use it, such as Danny Kaye's stiff-upper-lip version in *The Secret Life of Walter Mitty*. *Dawn Patrol* tells us that we should never send men out there like that, in those awful flimsy crates, and it also says gamely, "Hurrah for the next man to die!" It's an adventure story about men and their comradeship, their grace under pressure, their nobility to their enemies, and their efforts to serve their countries in difficult situations. It is a film that boys like and men remember fondly. (It has no important female character.) It sets a standard for the kind of story it tells, and it lays ground rules about how men behave in air combat. Actually, these ground rules were probably established with silent films like *Wings* and *Lilac Time*, but *Dawn Patrol* dropped out the key women characters who appear in those films, and focussed an audience on air combat.

In a sense, it is probably *Dawn Patrol* that the World War II film is working against when it appears. The inherent sense of the elite that is related to men who go up into the air, that place where men are not supposed to go, is deeply engrained in the air combat films of World War I. World War II helps to wipe that out by democratizing what is now the Air Corps with its group of mixed ethnic and social types. This is pointed up by the practical individual vs. group nature of the air craft being flown in the two wars. A World War I ace is usually alone, his scarf flying behind him, and he salutes his enemy, another elite, individual ace. A World War II flyer is usually part of a large crew, a group who work together and who can't even see the enemy's face. (Fighter pilots are the exception.) The earlier airmen were noble, brave, elite, and usually British. These are men in a desperate war, and yet they are boys—boyish in looks and behavior, with a schoolroom naughtiness and dash. This idea is even spoken for reinforcement, when a young flyer, going out to fly against veterans, is told: "If you should lose, be a good loser, just as you would in school." This spirit is juxtaposed with tragic events, for poignancy and a basic antiwar attitude, but its appeal, combined with the gladiatorial nature of the air combat scenes, makes such activities glamorous and masculine. This is the spirit one sees later in *Desperate Journey*, which is why that later film is all wrong in tone for the new war of 1942. Films like *Dawn Patrol* explain why the World War I film could *not* be the format for the World War II film.[6]

Today We Live (April 15, 1933) illustrates the thematic concerns that become linked to the World War I combat film: gallantry, glory, waste, and romance, both the romance of adventure and the romance of love. *Today We Live* is a World War I combat film about the first PT boats and the Air Service, a hardcore nucleus of a male adventure film, surrounded by an outer layer that can only be defined by calling it a Joan Crawford movie. One could spend a lifetime sorting this out, and making stacks in which one scene is labeled 'woman's film' and one scene labeled 'combat film.' In the end, what you would know was: here's a hardcore combat film surrounded by a Crawford movie. The sorting wouldn't be worth the effort. Crawford wears great clothes, and she plays a rich aristocrat, British type. She goes up front to drive an ambulance and to be near the three men she is involved with: her brother (Franchot Tone), her childhood sweetheart (Robert Young), and the American she has fallen in love with (Gary Cooper). Young and Tone are in the torpedo boats, and Cooper is the flyer. People go blind and sacrifice themselves, and what we get out of that is that World War I is a waste and a losing game. These same people, however, go to sea in battle and up in the air in battle, and that's the "today we live." We don't just survive. We also enjoy. The combat sequences are excellent, so despite its attempt at a pacifist message, *Today We Live* can be seen as a "glory" film out of the transition period.

Whether their focus is "glory" or antiwar, all these films are about the waste of youth, the burdens of leadership, the inability to win in a wartime situation, the need to give up a light-hearted attitude and understand the horrors of war and yet be jaunty and pretend death is a bad joke, but you'll laugh anyway. They are about love and romance and sex and, except for *Dawn Patrol*, women. The primary importance of women in these films is another main difference between them and the pure World War II version.

The best known film of the transition-to-sound period is an antiwar film, *All Quiet on the Western Front* (April 30, 1930). In the long run, the chief use of World War I became to serve the pacifist tradition in such films as *Paths of Glory* (1957), *The Blue Max* (1966), and the musical film *Darling Lili* (1970).

The most respected of all World War I films, *All Quiet on the Western Front* solidified this tendency. Unlike *Bataan*, which achieved the nonpacifist tradition for the World War II genre, *All Quiet on the Western Front* is based on a literary success, the 1929 novel of the same name by Erich Maria Remarque. It is one of many plays and novels about the horror of WWI that appeared in the late twenties. It presents the war from our enemy's point of view, a phenomenon that inevitably marks it as an "after the fact" film. Nevertheless, it is an important film for reflecting what makes the World War I combat film, and how it differs from that of World War II.

The film illustrates the horror of war, not only in its death and destruction, but also in its wasting of a nation's youth, both physically and mentally. It traces an idealistic young boy from the schoolroom, where he's inspired to patriotic frenzy by his professor, outward into his recruitment, experience of combat, and ultimate death. It stresses the futility of war and the psychological pressures on the men who fought in it.

All Quiet on the Western Front is a war film, *and* a combat film, because it moves directly into a fierce presentation of total warfare: hand-to-hand fighting, bayoneting, and a running attack which shows that, when the horror of combat sweeps over you, all you can do is fight like an animal for survival. Such scenes suggest that war is hell and we shouldn't be doing it, as opposed to World War II's war is hell but we have to do it and win. The end of *All Quiet* presents the familiar "Parade of the Dead" in which the characters of the film all pass in review before the audience. In World War II upbeat films, this will be amended into the Parade of the Survivors, and turned into a strength, or an optimistic characteristic.

All Quiet teaches an audience what it needs to know about what happens when young men go to war. They must be trained, after which if they are lucky, they will meet an old soldier with the experience to guide them during combat. And they have hard lessons to learn. When someone risks his life to go out to no man's land and bring in a dead comrade, the old soldier is stern: "Why did you do that?"

All Quiet on the Western Front

"Why, he's Dave. He's Dave."

"It's just a corpse. Whoever it is, don't any of you do that again."

The pacifist tradition of these films was violated in the late 1930s and early 1940s. As war clouds gathered over Europe, Hollywood produced a group of films set in World War I which were obviously to "get us in the mood" for war in Europe again: *The Fighting 69th, Sergeant York,* and *Submarine Patrol* are examples. These films served a very important function for viewers. They refought the earlier war on a new, more optimistic basis, to detach it from its former downbeat tradition. They reversed its original purpose. To do this, the World War I story was united to biography *(Sgt. York, Fighting 69th)* and to upbeat service comedy/dramas. Here is seen the tricky nature of genre. Having spent more than a decade teaching audiences that World War I killed our youth, the genre moves away from itself toward other genres to change audiences' ideas about war. By uniting with service comedies, the genre automatically becomes more positive, more upbeat, more action oriented. By uniting with biography, it makes itself more true than the earlier, downbeat films, and it seems to say that if the men of these biographies survived war, then it will be okay for your young sons. Furthermore, it implies, "Unlike the earlier films, I am truth."

Sergeant York (July 3, 1941), one of these biographical films, is set in the Tennessee mountains of York's youth. It is only partially a combat story of World War I. Its power lies in its ability to persuade viewers that it is the story of a nonprofessional soldier who is drawn into the fight out of necessity and appropriateness. It is a very important film of this transition period, because it teaches us we must fight. We don't want to, but we have to, just like York. We watch his struggle to overcome his religious beliefs, and his ultimate understanding that war is necessary and it will take his skill to win it.

Thus we see how movies have to reorganize. If we spend ten or fifteen years teaching people through films that war is bad and it kills our youth, then we must have an important film that resolves the problem. *Sergeant York* cleverly gives us a pacifist—persumably someone who has learned the lesson—and shows him slowly realizing that is not the appropriate attitude to have. We can sit in the theater and see him go fight a better World War I for us. When York fights and wins, we see him receiving the ultimate reward from his country—all the ultimate rewards: fame, medals, success, money, the girl, and his own home, right where he wanted it, just as he dreamed of it. If we fight, the film teaches, we will win and get our girl and get our own home. It's not so bad, after all. This youth wasn't wasted. Thus, films wipe out earlier images and replace them with new ones, appropriate to the times. New lessons are learned as World War I is fought with a much better plot, and a much happier ending. And this time it's *true*. We were just kidding before, folks!

The film shows that the real Sergeant Alvin C. York was taught he must fight by a company major, who explains that violence is sometimes necessary to preserve our free way of life. To prove this, he gives York a book on American history. In 1941, Hollywood gave people a movie instead of the book, and that movie was *Sergeant York*. Not only did Gary Cooper, playing York, receive the Oscar as best actor, he also won the New York film critics award. *Sergeant York* was given another Oscar for best editing, and nominated for nine others: best picture, best supporting actor (Walter Brennan), best supporting actress (Margaret Wycherly), best director (Howard Hawks), best score, best sound, best cinematography, best art and set decoration, and best screenplay. It was the top grossing film of 1941, and Gary Cooper was the top money-making star. "I wish to emphasize that this is in no sense a war picture," said Jesse Lasky, the film's producer. Then he added, "It is a story Americans had to be told today."[7]

Those who want to label films should take a good look at *The Fighting 69th* (January 27, 1940), a preparation-for-war film. It is so much like a World War II movie that in some sense it might have been one, yet in other ways it is so much unlike a World War II movie that it really can't be.

Like *Sergeant York*, *The Fighting 69th* uses World War I differently. Instead of being a loser's war, with the hero going blind and all the youth being wasted, it becomes a war in which a misfit can redeem himself. He may die in doing that, but better death than blindness. Instead of living a cripple, he dies a hero. And the true hero of the film is the historical regiment itself, not a man, and if a man, then it is the Chaplain—pure proof that God is on our side. It changes the melancholy, downbeat sense of a war that kills youth and blinds brave men and that no one can win into yet another opportunity for Americans to prove their fighting ability. World War I ceases to be the old war we used to know, and becomes something else. We're not sure what, and neither is it, because the thing it will become isn't happening yet. So it is preparing us for what is to come. Whatever it is, it can't be World War I, because the old form tells us the wrong story. It says, don't fight. And we must fight.

The opening to *The Fighting 69th* is exactly like what will be seen in World War II combat films. A photographic insert of each actor, with his character's name underneath and the appropriate military insignia above, is shown. "To all the men of the last war . . . to the Rainbow Division, which represented all our states and territories. . . the 69th New York. . . 1165th Reg. AEP. . . Warner Brothers respectfully dedicates this picture," says the dedication. In other words, to a representative group of people and types from all our nation, that group of ethnic mixes that will form the fundamental group of the World War II film.

It's tempting to call *The Fighting 69th* the first American combat film of World War II, except that it's set in World War I and was released in 1940, before the United States entered the war. Also, it doesn't have much combat! But it contains so much that will become part of the genre that it cannot be overlooked. Here we see a World War I that *looks* like the one we saw before, but it's *purpose* is different. Gone is the misery and waste, and a new, resolute attitude and optimism takes its place. It tells us some of the story units we are going to carry forward, and it tells us how we will be using old ones in new ways. It's almost as if *The Fighting 69th* knew about World War II in advance, and with Jack Warner in charge of production, who is to say?

New York's famous Irish regiment, known as "the fighting 69th" and also as "the fighting Irish," fought together in the Civil War, and were incorporated into the Rainbow division in 1917. This film celebrates the famous regiment by placing in it a young man (James Cagney) who does not at first appreciate its great traditions. His initiation into its world constitutes a similar lesson for an audience that would all too soon have to face the problem in real life.

Since this is an Irish regiment, the group "mix" would presumably all be Irish, but much is made of a character named Moskowitz who pretends to be "Murphy" in order to join up with the group he admires. The mix comes from other directions: old and young, tough and gentle, experienced and inexperienced, religious and nonreligious. Key characters who represent types that become standards of the genre are:

- The tough drill sergeant (Alan Hale).
- The equally tough major (George Brent) who is a real life hero, Wild Bill Donovan.
- The understanding chaplain (Pat O'Brien), also based on a real person.[8]
- The cynic who must be taught by danger to understand the nobility of the cause and of the group (James Cagney).
- The war correspondent figure, or man who keeps a diary, in this case the real poet, Joyce Kilmer. (The use of Kilmer here foreshadows that of people like Ernie Pyle in the World War II film. It is significant that this character in the World War I film is a poet, while in the World War II film, he is a newspaperman.)

The Fighting 69th tells us a lot of information in narrative terms. "No man has ever let the regiment down." "Get him or he'll get you." "An Irishman never needs a prayer in a fight." It also teaches what happens when men go to war and why and how they have to be trained first. They have to have medical checks, read eye charts, get shots, be issued uniforms. They have to march and drill, and they have to have bayonet training. They go on night maneuvers (which we don't see, but do hear about), and they have to learn to obey and get along with one another. In 1862, the 4th Alabama "shot the pants off" the 69th's New York Irishers at the Battle of Fredericksburg. When these groups are meshed in the Rainbow Unit, a fight breaks out between the two former Civil War enemies. The stern major lectures them: "We're all one nation now, a team, The Rainbow Division." We hear that they "rose above their hatreds to be one country again . . . all come here as Americans."

The wonderful thing about Warner Brothers is the economical use always made of old plots. Someone once said that Warners remade the same movies so many times that the writing department was known as the Echo Chamber. In some ways, Warners invented genre. In *The Fighting 69th*, a transition film in a brink-of-war time slot, Warners not only makes a get-em-ready-for war film, but, just to hedge its bets, throws in familiar devices from other popular movies they had made from the 1930s. For instance, when a German bombing run causes some of the group to be buried alive under tons of rubble, O'Brien insists on going down through a tunnel to give them last rites. This is like a coal-mining movie. When Cagney gets into trouble and is about to be transferred out, O'Brien takes the responsibility for him, as he would if he were the warden in a Prison Movie and Cagney were a troublesome inmate. (Later, Cagney is court-martialed and sentenced to be executed!) There's funny business with a donkey who won't budge, like the good old service comedies, and the trusty device of a fist fight between Cagney and his sergeant, Alan Hale, as in *What Price Glory?* (As is traditional, when caught, both men will deny the fight to save one another. This recurs often, as in *Sands of Iwo Jima*.) It can be counted as a biography because of Donovan, Kilmer, and Duffy. There is the bravery crisis, in which a man who turned yellow in combat later has to prove himself (a plot of the service musical, *Shipmates Forever*). Ultimately, however, *The Fighting 69th* is an Irish movie, or maybe a Catholic movie. There is a great deal of praying and discussing God, and the film ends with a monument—a statue of Father Duffy (Pat O'Brien), and the list of wars he fought in (Spanish-American, Mexican borderwars, World War I).

Whenever I see *The Fighting 69th*, I have a strong sense of "The Genres Go to War." Just as Lucky Strike Green went to war. Just as women went to

Fighting 69th, *with Pat O'Brien, James Cagney*

war, marching in front of us in fashionable clothes which remarkably disappear, to be replaced with work fatigues and military uniforms. Here I see prison movies, gangster movies, Irish Catholic movies—the whole works from Warner Brothers—marching before me, with their appropriate costumes disappearing into World War I uniforms that are really World War II uniforms. The Genres Go to War.

In a sense, all this plot hodgepodge proves there can actually be no World War II movie until World War II despite the many similarities. Here we have the mixed group fighting the war and saying the things they ought to say, even doing some things they ought to do. They celebrate Christmas, and, at the end, pass by us again in a "rollcall" of men who fought and either lived or died. But there's the old trench warfare, the no man's land look. And, instead of knowing how to get the men out on patrol and keep them there, the film suddenly falls back on other genres, other plots. Instead of making a World War II movie (and how could they have?), Warner Brothers just mixed together some old standards. The combat is there—explosions, the eerie light of bombings, the danger and the death—but, again, the language of the World War II genre is not yet spoken. To authenticate the new genre, reality must play a role, adding in true stories and real battles.

The Fighting 69th ends with a supposedly pacifist message—a prayer for "the lost generation" who gave their lives "that an ideal might live— don't let it be forgotten, America—be a citadel of peace, peace forever more, this I beg of you" says the Pat O'Brien character. However the film glorifies bravery and glamorizes combat by making it exciting and fun to watch, despite the deaths which take place.

In discussing *The Fighting 69th*, one sees the difficulty of simplifying genre. One might make a list of characteristics that will appear later, create a sort of grid, apply it to the film, and claim it as typical of the combat films to come. On the other hand, one might make a list of characteristics that are *wrong*, and do the same thing. What *The Fighting 69th* represents is something that will be discussed at the end of Chapter 3—that familiar story patterns can appear in more than one type of genre, and that genre is a living beast that grows and shifts and changes. It is not a fossil, a dead and fixed thing.

Another pre-war movie that is of interest is John Ford's *Submarine Patrol* (November 19, 1938), written by Brian James, Darrell Ware, and Jack Yellen, and based on a novel *The Splinter Fleet*. It is a kind of service comedy, but it has an integrity about military combat and a respectful attitude toward the enemy (in this case, the Germans) that will reappear in Ford's later film *They Were Expendable*.

Submarines had always been popular with filmmakers. As early as November 15, 1915, A *Submarine Pirate*, starring Syd Chaplin, was released in New York. According to press releases, it showed the sub "above water, submerging, and firing a torpedo . . . and the use of the periscope is also illustrated." Even soap operas could be set in a submarine, as in *The Devil and The Deep* (1932), in which Tallullah Bankhead's husband, played by Charles Laughton, goes loony because she's really in love with Gary Cooper. (Not only that, Cary Grant was lurking around the periscope in a small part, too. This woman had choices!) *Hell Below* had a dramatic submarine portion, and "inventor movies" such as *Submarine D-1* (1937) also demonstrated the dangers and inevitable appeal for audiences of the stories set under water. It took World War II to make the submarine into a real genre setting for viewers, yet it is remarkable to see how many elements of later stories appear in *Submarine Patrol*. (Here, of course, the enemy are in the subs, and the heroes are on top of the water in a subchaser). For instance, in addition to the comedy attitude taken by the crewman (and the film really *is* a comedy to a large degree), one may see these typical characters, relationships, and events:

- The rich young man from an elite family who has to learn to be one of the common men, and thus one of the group, after his enlistment (Richard Greene plays this part, which might be called the Tyrone Power role).
- The mixed group who form the crew of the sub chaser, the "Cook" who owns a restaurant in town, the "Professor" who is studying for a master's degree while at sea, the former taxi driver, etc.
- A conflict between the civilian life, represented by the sea captain father of the girl, and the military life, represented by the subchaser's new skipper, Preston Foster.
- The cowardice theme, which in this case involves Foster, who lost his former command because of "cowardice."

Submarine Patrol has the visual beauty associated with Ford's work. When the subchaser pulls out of New York harbor to go into combat patrol, the sight of the men's faces as they take a last look at the Statue of Liberty and the New York skyline speaks eloquently of the uncertainty that lies ahead. This departure, with the faces of the men against the sky, may have influenced the departure and return of the U.S.S. *Copperfin* in the later film *Destination Tokyo*.

When films like this began to appear, they revised the issues of World War I for the mass viewing audience. They began to reteach characterization, ritual event, ordinary plot event, and setting, with a new attitude which was preparatory in nature. What *Submarine Patrol* tells an audience is the key to later combat films: when there is military work to be done, one must set aside an idle life and civilian concerns and learn to sacrifice, to work with a group for the good of all. This is represented not only by the rich young man's need to prove himself worthy of the common good, but also by Preston Foster's need to redeem himself from the taint of cowardice, by the crew's need to forget their shoreline occupations, and by the girl's father having to accept his military son-in-law and having to himself rescue the ship when the subchaser is hit by the enemy. The girl, of course, does her part by loving the rich young hero. Sometimes being a girl was the easy part.

There are, however, no patriotic issues in *Submarine Patrol*. The story might have been told without the war, as indeed it was in many service comedies or adventure films of the day. Perhaps the most significant aspect of *Submarine Patrol*, as a transition-to-war film, is that it is putting World War I back into the stories it was removed from for most of the 1930s. Without the war, it would have been a service comedy.

Noncombat Military Service Films of the 1930s

There is more to the prior history of the combat film than films about World War I. There are also a confusing array of noncombat films that concern military life. In an era that does not call forth the need for combat movies, do films nevertheless keep the relevant issues of military service, competition, male camaraderie, patriotic responsibility, duty, war preparedness, combat capability and procedure, and inventiveness[9] before the public? Yes. This illustrates a phenomenon of generic development: that genre recedes and emerges as needed or desired, and that it also lies dormant in other forms (musicals, comedies, adventures) until needed. This is seen in examining the noncombat military films of the 1930s.

The Thirties Tradition contains several types of military service films: *Comedies, Musicals, Adventure Films*, and *Military Preparedness Films*. These films illustrate how many variations can appear in something that is called a "genre." Suppose you decide that there is a genre called the "military service film." The differences between one that is a musical comedy and one that is a dramatic adventure film are enormous in terms of viewer response. Yet they have striking similarities in their attitudes toward discipline, sacrifice, and romance. Again, as with

Fighting 69th, one might make a grid of similarities and claim them as alike, or a grid of dissimilarities and claim them as separate.

What they illustrate is a commonness of purpose. They contain the issues that any association with the military must have: bravery, conformity, discipline. They show the events such a life brings to an individual: death, sacrifice, danger. They are stories about men. Sometimes these men fight over women, and sometimes they don't even meet women in the plot; but whatever they do, they keep certain issues alive for viewers.

These films show how the combat genre behaves in an era in which there is no war. As the thirties progressed, fewer and fewer World War I films were made, until they were reborn as "transition-to-war" films at the end of the decade. These service films stand in for combat. As the presentation of war becomes unnecessary, the genre strengthens itself by forming a relationship with another type of film. Thus we do see military service musicals, military service comedies, and military service adventure films.

Comedy

Here Comes the Navy (July 21, 1934) is in every way a typical noncombat military comedy of the time. It stars James Cagney and Pat O'Brien, two men associated with one another in gangster films, and with *The Fighting 69th.* It also takes place on the battleship *Arizona.* Many scenes were actually filmed aboard her. The *Arizona,* of course, was destroyed on the Day of Infamy and lies at the bottom of Pearl Harbor today—a monument to what happened there. Her name is frequently mentioned in films as a marking place and as a symbol of what was lost that day, and what we were fighting for afterward. This is most beautifully evoked in John Ford's *They Were Expendable,* in which men stare out to sea, just "lookin' for the old Arizona."

The story is typical: Chesty O'Connor (Cagney) is a civilian riveter who enlists in the Navy to get even with his enemy, Biff Martin (O'Brien), who is chief petty officer on the *Arizona.* Cagney falls in love with O'Brien's sister, and ends up marrying her. The Navy and the stories of the sea always present these familial entanglements. Sometimes it is a sister and brother; sometimes a father and daughter. There are many who feel these stories are about male love, and thus the

"Lookin' for the old Arizona": They Were Expendable

substitution of a sister for one man solves the problem by heterosexualizing it. At any rate, the adversary male relationship is solved through the love of a woman which unites the two enemies. *Here Comes the Navy* is true to that tradition, as well as to the tradition in which a maverick without respect for the service (Cagney) must learn discipline. As the review in the *New York Times* noted, "This story has a familiar ring."

There was no war in 1934. However, there are "battle maneuvers." Use of a war game to stand in for war will recur later in the evolutionary process, and is a standard device of war combat comedies. It's called how to have war without having a war. The Navy Department cooperated with Warner Brothers in this production, and scenes were filmed with the Pacific Fleet on battle maneuvers, as well as on the *Arizona*, at the dirigible field at Sunnyvale, California, at the Naval Training Station in San Diego, and at the Navy Yard at Bremerton, Washington.

Musicals

Shipmates Forever (October 17, 1935) illustrates the musical variation. It was filmed at Annapolis, and the Navy Department once again
cooperated with Warner Brothers, assigning an officer and two mid-
shipmen to advise filmmakers on naval regulations and naval life.
Although this film has Dick Powell singing and Ruby Keeler dancing
up a storm, it once again puts forward what one might now recognize
as the standard issues. Powell's father is an admiral but Powell wants to
be a crooner. Forced into the Academy, he does well, but thinks it's all
meaningless. He has to be shaped up, taught respect for the military,
ritual, and discipline.

This film is different from a service comedy like *Here Comes the
Navy*, because it involves musical numbers. Yet it's not merely a "puttin'
on a show" vehicle with the academy as a background; and it's not
entirely a lighthearted romp. It's sad and touching, and the theme of
sacrifice is very strong, especially in a subplot about a young seaman
who flunks out. He proves his mettle in a crisis during battle maneuvers,
and he loses his life in doing so. Again, the issues of death and discipline
are kept alive in the military setting, despite the musical format. Conventional wisdom has it that musicals have fluffy plots, and nothing
serious ever happens in them. Yet dozens of them could be listed that
have death, suicide, despair, and, yes, combat. The George Raft–
Carole Lombard film, *Bolero*, has more combat than *Thirty Seconds
Over Tokyo*, yet the average person would quickly put the latter picture
in the combat category and never list the former at all. This is not to
say that *Bolero* is a combat film. It is not. But it contains a rather
lengthy sequence in which George Raft goes into combat during World
War I and is severely wounded. (See *Thirty Seconds Over Tokyo* in
Filmography.)

Service Adventure

Typical examples of the 1930s service adventure film are *Sea Devils*
(March 16, 1937), with Ida Lupino, Victor McLaglen, Preston Foster;
and *Hell Divers* (December 23, 1931), with Clark Gable and Wallace
Beery. One of the authors of *Sea Devils* was Spig Wead, an ex-navy
man who wrote many such films and whose own biography was made

into *Wings of Eagles*, directed by John Ford. *Sea Devils* is about a Quirt/Flagg relationship involving Victor McLaglen (as Medals Malone) and his opposite and equal, Preston Foster, as Mike O'Shay. These men are in the Coast Guard, and a thank you and dedication to this service appears printed at the opening of the film. The movie is a kind of adventure-comedy-romance. The adventure is the part involving the dangers of military service, including a dramatic rescue of people on a burning ship (the fine opening sequence), and a long sequence with a ship on "ice patrol," which goes out to dynamite icebergs. On that patrol, the true conflict between the two men breaks out, resulting in Foster's court-martial. When McLaglen admits he is the culprit, he is demoted to chief petty officer and applies for retirement. The whole thing culminates in an exciting and well-done sequence in a hurricane.

Comedy is interlaced throughout, involving all three major characters. McLaglen hates Foster because he's "just like me" and considers him an unsuitable son-in-law. The romance is the love story in which Lupino chooses to marry Foster despite her father's wishes. Foster and Lupino "meet cute" when he opens a door as she walks toward it, and she gets a bloody nose. (In Hollywood, a rule of thumb was that if the hero beat up the girl, she was his forever.) Lupino and Foster trade snappy dialogue throughout the film.

Foster (About Shakespeare): "He's a great writer, that guy. Wonder why he doesn't write a movie?"

Lupino: "Oh, he has."

The issues are those of duty and responsibility, loyalty to the service, family relationships, and the acceptance of maturity. Guys like Preston Foster have to settle down and marry girls like Lupino. Guys like McLaglen, essentially a loner even though he has his daughter and a girlfriend, pay for their aloneness through sacrifice, most frequently involving death. A subtext to all these films is—if you disobey the rules of your service, you will be demoted or drummed out, and you regain status by saving innocent people through your own death.

Hell Divers is about a Quirt/Flagg relationship personified by Wallace Beery (named Windy, possibly the most appropriate character name he ever had) and Clark Gable (Steve). They are Navy aviators, and besides brawling and arguing and wrecking saloons in fistfights, they also go on top of the water, above the water, and under the water in all forms of naval craft. There is no war, so maneuvers once again stand in for combat. The *Film Daily* stated it clearly: "There is no story. What composition is present has a *What Price Glory?* basis from which springs the formula that has governed such pictures as *Cockeyed World, Flight,* etc." It is interesting to note that the transition-to-sound period inspired both films set in World War I and films like this, which were not set in any war, but which did much to keep the military issues alive until they could be incorporated into the newer World War II genre films.

Military Preparedness

The military preparedness films, although similar to the service comedies, musicals, and adventure films, are marked by a stronger sense of war. They appear at the end of the decade and into the early 1940s, and are parallel to those in which World War I was used for the same purpose.

Wings of the Navy, released in New York City on February 4, 1939, is one of the most typical of these films. It, too, contains no combat. The United States is not at war. However, it is practically a textbook on the machinery that can be used for war, and on what military aviation is like at the time. There is no question but that it is helping to educate Americans about war, war equipment and the need for more of the latter in case there's more of the former. One can note how the Hollywood studios, Warner Brothers in particular, had the help of the armed forces in photographing and making so very many films set against the background of the armed services during the late 1930s. Obviously, Hollywood was doing its part to get America prepared.

Wings of the Navy was filmed at military air fields at Pensacola, Florida and San Diego, California. The full cooperation of the Navy department is acknowledged. The story is by now too dull to repeat—two brothers who are from a Navy family in a rivalry for the same girl—all three with their chins lifted to the sky, while the stirring title song roars on the soundtrack. But the rest of the film is modern for the time, showing in detail the training of a young man in the latest naval air equipment, including his postgraduate training in a huge PBY-2 sea-going bomber. He learns all kinds of tactics, including flying blind, defensive maneuvers, and tricky formation bombing.

Films like *Wings of the Navy* glamorize and sell the service. They also teach Americans directly about new equipment and methods.

Although they don't talk too much about war, it is an ever present threat, and by war is meant a *new* war. These films break with the old service comedy/adventure/romance films by using the service as a setting to prepare us for something unspoken that is clearly coming. Another striking example is *I Wanted Wings* (1941), which begins with a mock bombing attack on Los Angeles—it's a film made and released before Pearl Harbor!

The Early Forties Films

There is one final category of films pertinent to the prior history of the combat film—that of specific usage of established genres by linking them, familiar as they are to viewers, to the new war. The support for the new combat film is built by these films. Audiences are brought along and taught, made comfortable by seeing the new combat linked to what they already know about and are familiar with. They are lured into theaters this way, too. Such films cannot be discounted in generic development. They are an important part of the continuing storytelling relationship with the audience. They build and connect, and, above all, they prepare. This usage comes in two types: the *hybrid film* and the conscious *updating* of an old military form with new war equipment.

Hybrids

Research and extensive viewing uncovered a curious type of early forties transition film which is schizoid in nature. This "hybrid" was the romantic comedy/combat film, in which a traditional love story was exploded or destroyed by a combat film. Structurally these films are a metaphor for the situation of the shattering of the peace, or status quo, since they act out a narrative in which one traditional generic form is replaced by another. The plot line is that a young couple has their time together destroyed by war. Through this device, the romance audiences are taught that they, too, must give up romance for sterner stuff. (They refused, and the fluff flowed on, of course.)

Such films include *Somewhere I'll Find You* (1942), in which Clark Gable and Lana Turner are two cheeky reporters who embark on a rocky love affair but who end up on Bataan, *They Met In Bombay* (1941), in which Clark Gable and Rosalind Russell are two selfish jewel thieves who end up with the Victoria Cross, and the aforementioned *A Yank in the R.A.F.* (1941).

A Yank has a curious parallel in the Warner Brothers film, *International Squadron*, which was released a short two months after the Grable/Power film in 1941. *International Squadron* is a low-budget variation of the same plot, this time starring Ronald Reagan, who plays a stunt pilot—American, of course—who accepts a job ferrying a bomber over to England for the RAF. He then decides to join up himself when he sees a small child killed in an air raid. He's still irresponsible, however, and his girl-chasing prevents him from going on a patrol. The man who takes his place is killed, and Reagan atones for this by going on a dangerous bombing mission in which he himself dies a dramatic death.

International Squadron is safely forgotten, and plays no key role in genre development. It was a minor B film of the time. Yet it illustrates the reality of the filmmaking business in Hollywood, an important thing to remember when analyzing trends from a distant viewpoint. The film handily uses old plots from World War I air hero movies (the death and sacrifice of the hero), and from the studio's own successful civilian air-hero movies of the 1930s (such as Cagney's *Ceiling Zero*). It links them to what it knows is going on in the news, that is to say, Americans and men from other nations going to England to join the Royal Air Force. It, by its nature as a quick, cheap, ripoff movie, illustrates how genres originally are formed and made.

Updating Old Genres

The other type of early forties transition film involves putting an old genre into play, and rehabilitating it with new military equipment. These films retrain viewers. They send us to camp and teach us the visual basics we will need to watch the new movies. They do more than hint at needing to know about war. Their whole plots are given over to a story that says—Americans, get ready to change. Inside the military or out, you've got to learn new ways. *The Bugle Sounds* (April 3, 1942) updates the old service comedy/adventure film, and *Captains of the*

Clouds (February 13, 1942) does the same for the "working men" movies Warners made in the 1930s.

It is one thing to single out such films as *Captains of the Clouds* from others as hybrids, since it is about civilian pilots who enter the service after war breaks out. It is, however, drawing a fine line to separate *The Bugle Sounds* this way, since it is totally about military service. Where does it differ from *Wings of the Navy*? *Wings* also prepares viewers to use new equipment, to be proud of their country, and to see the military life as glamorous and romantic. *The Bugle Sounds*, released a little over two years later, overtly prepares them for war. The film was made after Pearl Harbor, and shows it. It is a far more deliberate preparation for a war that is now real.

The credits of *The Bugle Sounds* carry a reverential announcement that it was made "with the gratefully acknowledged cooperation of the U.S. Army." After the credits, against an image of military vehicles converging and moving rapidly down a road, these words are heard on the sound track:

> This picture is dedicated in gratitude and proud affection to the officers and men of the United States Army, who, from the brass-works at Bunker Hill to the thunders of the Meuse/Argonne have never yet flinched or failed or slept in their ancient holy watch along the ramparts of American freedom. Now our war planes launch flight after flight into skies darkened. . . .
>
> Upon the ground below men wearing the uniform we honor turn with the old fidelity and the familiar courage to hard new tasks. Infantry, artillery, engineers, signal and quartermaster. Not the least, is the Cavalry, performing still its immemorial dashing function. . . .
>
> Is there any here who will not say God bless and keep them?

The film which follows represents clearly the war preparatory theme of these transitional years. It shows us the new icons, the new uniforms, and helps us understand the old stories are the wrong ones for the new wars. We've got to rewrite them a bit. It is a story of the old Cavalry (the 19th Cavalry, in this case) being mechanized, In order to activate a new armored force unit, the 198th Armored Regiment Light is to be turned into a tank division. "Presto," says a character, "and we're steel Cavalry." In this sense, it is also a reoutfitting of an audience to accept stories on film about machinery, not horses, and brave men who fight inside tanks instead of from the backs of horses. At the beginning of

the film, these old soldiers ("I was aimin' to die in the Army," says the
hero, played by that old crock, Wallace Beery) talk about the old days,
about "the ones who started with him at the Border . . . the Meuse/
Argonne," a noble and brave group. Now they must reorganize themselves into a new force, with colors that include yellow for cavalry, blue
for infantry, and red for fire power. The film follows the traditional
form of male rivalry over a woman (Marjorie Main!) in the Quirt/Flagg
tradition and presents the typical bunch of green recruits who arrive in
camp and are told by the tough old Beery—"And for your information,
you're lookin' at a soldier." The crisis of the story occurs when Beery's
beloved horse is injured in a barn fire (caused by sabotage), and Beery
wishes to shoot the steed himself, after marking his head with chalk in
the old manner. It is now against regulations, as injured horses are
injected with fatal drugs. Beery is given permission to kill the animal
the old way, and the symbolism is obvious.

The Bugle Sounds is not a combat film. It is a transitional presentation
of how an old soldier, with 9 wounds from service, with a DSC, a
Purple Heart, Croix de Guerre, his medals from "The Border, the
Meuse, etc." becomes modernized for a new kind of warfare.

Captains of the Clouds is also a film of this type. It, too, carries a
dedication: "This picture is respectfully dedicated to the Royal Canadian Air Force . . . with sincere appreciation of their cooperation and
admiration for their abilities and courage. . . . To those student pilots
in this picture who are now in actual combat overseas, and most
particularly it is dedicated to those many in the Service who have trailed
the shadows of their wings over the vastness of Canada from the 49th
Parallel to the Arctic Circle. . . . The Bush Pilots." Its first half is a
familiar Warner Brothers adventure film, the story of three bush pilots
(played by Dennis Morgan, Alan Hale, and George Tobias) who find
their business being threatened by James Cagney, a newcomer to their
area. Joining with another pilot, improbably played by the debonair
drawing room comedian Reginald Gardiner, they track him down. The
film establishes Canadian men of strength and courage, the kind that
will be needed to win the war. It demonstrates that the skills they need
to live and work and fly the wilderness are those they'll already have
honed for war.

There is the usual romantic rivalry over a girl (Brenda Marshall),
but she turns out to be bad, selfish, and money-hungry, hot for the fast
lane. She must be gotten out of the plot, dropped, a wartime sacrifice,

and this actually happens approximately half way into the film, when the scene is moved from the rural wilderness to the city (Ottawa).

Marshall more or less disappears, left behind somewhere in the night clubs and hotels of the city while the story becomes a military training film. Dunkirk appears in the news headlines, and Churchill is heard on the radio. ("We shall not flag or fail . . . we shall defend our island . . . we shall fight in the hills . . . we shall never surrender.") "Now there's a man who knows how to word an invitation," one character says, and all join up. Our heroes are retrained, taught to fly a different kind of plane in a different style. As the recruits are interviewed at the RCAF Service Flying Training school, it almost becomes a documentary. Bush pilots become teachers, and are seen flying in formation. This image, contrasted with the earlier flights we have seen of their rolls and dives, free and easy, over the Canadian wilderness, explains more about World War II movies than anything else in the film. From freedom to conformity. From the individual to the group.

The Canadian military tradition is paraded. Troops, bagpipes, war memorials, recruiting posters—all tell of The Black Watch, the Princess Pats, the Winnipeg Rifles, the RCHA Artillery, the Tank Corps, and finally, "the fighting Canadian tradition exemplified by the RCAF." Ultimately, the great Canadian World War I flying ace, Billy Bishop, (playing himself), is introduced as the man who shot 72 planes down and "flew by the seat of his pants." He is now an Air Marshal present to pin white wings on pilots in a big outdoor ceremony. He reviews the troops, and gives a speech referring to the American men who have come to Canada to join up (the film is set before Pearl Harbor). Ironically, it is over this speech and presentation that Cagney and Hale, half drunk, choose to demonstrate their marvelous flying ability, representing individualism. Bishop himself was the iconoclastic ace of the first war—the maverick flyer like those now presented as needing to change their ways for the new, more disciplined war. Showing Bishop endorsing the change was a powerful thing at the time.

Ultimately, Cagney is washed out for nonconformity, but through a plot device he is allowed to reenlist under an assumed name and join a group ferrying bombers over to England on an emergency basis. (Here is the Lloyd Nolan character from *Bataan*, who also reenlisted under an assumed name.) Dennis Morgan and the old group, minus the dead Alan Hale whose identity Cagney has assumed, are flying the planes. Morgan and Cagney are reconciled, a theme of war, and Cagney is welcomed back into the fold, a reformed and chastened man, a major convention of the combat film. As they fly toward England, Reginald Gardiner, Cagney's co-pilot, talks of his native land (and the explanation of his casting in the film becomes clear). "Funny, I had a hunch I was never going to see it again," he says one and a half hours away from England. (Words like these are the kiss of death in a war film.) Out of the clouds come German war planes, and since they are in unarmed planes, Cagney flies straight at the Germans, sacrificing himself to save the bombers. (Gardiner has already been shot.)

This sacrifice of the flawed group member becomes a convention of the combat film, particularly the air variation. As the planes fly on, Dennis Morgan says over the radio, "The land fall straight ahead of you, gentlemen, is England" and Churchill's voice is heard saying, "We shall never surrender." A final thank you to the military services involved appears at the end, with a note that such people as Billy Bishop, V.C. "are portrayed in the actual performance of their duties."

Summary

In summary, the World War I films—both at the time and after the time—and the service comedies, adventure stories, and musicals—all add up to one thing. There was no World War II combat film before there was World War II combat. There were issues, events, and relationships that would prove useful when updated: the Quirt/Flagg friendship, the tough old sergeant, the mail call, the young recruits who come up looking green and unprepared, the war materiel, the sense that one must leave a frivolous life and learn discipline, and that men from all walks of life from all backgrounds could and would do this. All this existed—but the World War II combat format did not.

What can be observed happening is logical, even predictable. When war exists, we make films about it. When it goes away, we make films about military battle maneuvers, or films about how awful the war was (awful, even if glamorous). We also make other genre films that serve similar purposes, of course. As war nears, we change our minds, and get involved in the new mechanized war and a new understanding of it. To do all this, we tell stories in the old way, updating them with new equipment and new ideology, slowly moving toward a period of time when the new war breaks out and the issues it will provide can be amalgamated into the story. After World War II, we know we need the group—the definition emerges, and never goes away. Once defined, the genre is strong, and although it undergoes an evolution it never disappears. Onward to that evolution. . . .

THREE

Evolution

By speaking of "evolution" of a genre I do not imply a sense of progression, a development toward a higher order. I mean only to suggest a state of change. Since I first began my research for this book, the word "transformation" has become prevalent in genre study. As used, it refers to ways in which genres have "transformed" themselves over time in response to various cultural and social pressures. My sense of evolution is similar, but since I am observing and tracing a historical phenomenon, rather than placing emphasis on the cultural and social forces themselves, I have decided to retain my original word, "evolution." Throughout this book I am, in fact, observing various kinds of transformations of genres—ideological changes; transfers of a story pattern from one genre to another; cross-pollination of genres with each other; and various hybrid and hidden forms.

Genres have to change to remain popular. At the same time they have to stay the same to be genres. How can this work? In order for it to be considered a genre, a story with a list of familiar characteristics is repeated often enough for an audience to recognize it, expect it, want it, and fill in all the missing details. If a particular narrative formula such as the World War II combat film is to become a true genre, it must, of course, remain popular past the event that inspired it.

It is possible to think of story patterns that emerged briefly and then disappeared, popular for a short time, but locked into one time period. These "hula hoop" films might be called stillborn genres. This phenomenon does not apply to such things as screwball comedies, which are associated mostly with the Depression, because crazy comedies about eccentric people existed before and after the 1930s. It might be possible to trace the "crazy people" comedy for its own pattern of evolution, in which the screwball comedy is only one variation. A stillborn genre would be a group of related films which appear, are imitated by a sudden crop of others, and then disappear. Examples would be the initial O.S.S. films of the postwar period and the student revolutionary movies of the mid-to-late sixties, even though it might be claimed that these story patterns reappear later in, respectively, the popular spy movies of the sixties and the investigative reporting movies of the late seventies and early eighties. However, such faddish movie types do not endure because they have no long range flexibility. They are the result of moviemakers imitating one another to make a buck, to cash in on headlines. These are not to be confused with genres.

To be a true genre that lives and is repeated, a story must be able to represent new issues without losing the basic pattern that inspired its popularity in the first place. After it undergoes the process of presumed accumulative meaning (The Kilroy Test), it must *evolve*.

The combat genre definitely undergoes such an evolution. From its first appearance in World War II to its present appearance as such television movies as *Dirty Dozen: The Next Mission* (1985) and as the Vietnam variation, *Uncommon Valor* (1984) it has proved a favorite story for filmmakers. It maintains the basic definition which emerged during the war, although the attitude taken toward it, or the purpose for which it is presented, varies as the years go by. By looking at the films based on the typical World War II combat movie over the decades from the forties to the eighties, one can see and trace a true genre evolution. This evolution can be seen as various "waves," to use an appropriate combat terminology:

> *First Wave*. From the beginning of the war until the end of 1943, the basic definition of the World War II combat film is formed.
>
> *Second Wave*. From 1944 to just past the end of the war, it can be seen that audiences and filmmakers have accepted the basic definition. Filmmakers use visual shorthand to refer to the concepts, and they translate them into totally effective cinematic terms.
>
> [A period of respite occurs from just past the end of the war until the end of the 1940s, during which combat films more or less disappear.]
>
> *Third Wave*. A new decade of combat films happen from the end of the '40s to the end of the 1950s—a complicated decade which puts reality into the genre in significant ways, in order to unify an audience that is made up of people who know war only through films and people who experienced it directly. The Korean interruption occurs, bringing the Korean variation and a renewed interest in the World War II films.
>
> *Fourth Wave*. The early 1960s bring epic re-creations, officially replacing "reality" with "filmed reality."

Fifth Wave. A period of inversion occurs, partly inspired by the Vietnam war which, unlike Korea, does not create a large group of Vietnam combat films.

These "waves" cannot be carved in stone. The inversion process that emerged in the 1960s can be observed in a few movies in the mid- to late 1950s, and the epic wave continued onward even though the inversion started in the 1960s. However, this evolution is a clear and observable historical process. Obviously, the ideology represented in the basic definition shifts accordingly.

First Wave. December 7, 1941 – December 31, 1943
Creation of Current Historical Events in Narrative Terms

The emergence of the basic definition is really the "first wave" of its generic evolution. In it, films which depict the first disastrous losing battles of America's entry into the war were released. These films were an attempt to create stories about the real event, incorporating a narrative line and a set of characters, thus making the events alive and personal for the moviegoer. Viewers participated vicariously in war, and, by extension, were educated to the new combat process. Presumably, this process also created patriotic pride and fervor, a desire to win the war. This "wave" has already been described in chapter 1.

Second Wave. January 1, 1944 – January 31, 1946
Creation of Current Historical Events in
Established Genre Terms

It might be said there is just one big first wave of war movies—those made during the war itself. Yet actually watching the movies one by one indicates that by the end of 1943 the basic definition was in place, and that the 1944 and 1945 movies are subtly different. That difference is accounted for by the awareness within the films themselves that they are all one type. This is significant enough to genre that it seems important to separate the two sections of the war years. Although the second wave overlaps with the first, it is dependent on the establishment of the first to exist. It begins as *part* of the first, but separates from it and continues past it. This observable—but subtle—difference is demonstrated largely through the formal means of film itself. A film such as *Objective Burma* contains lengthy sequences which have almost no dialogue, and which tell the combat story visually. This is done not only as if the people making the film knew how to use the medium for specific meanings, but also as if they knew the audience already knew and understood such concepts as the group of mixed ethnic types. *They Were Expendable* tells its story as if it were not about the war, but about the aftermath of war, in which we would look back and understand that people did what they did out of a sense of duty, and that they paid for that obligation through suffering and death.

These second wave films have an *awareness*—whether of the earlier "first wave" films, of newsreels and documentaries, or of a long-range historical view—although *reality* is still the key factor. This self-consciousness on the part of the filmmakers will later be developed more fully in the third wave. The filmmakers begin to use the conventions as if they believe them to be recognizable to audiences. They begin to use an image—presumably familiar from first wave combat films—as a kind of visual shorthand for viewers. The power of the purely visual is that it demonstrates the belief that an audience can look at a group, a hero, or an objective and supply dialogue and meaning it *knows* from prior films. As E. L. Doctorow says, "When you use a genre, you are playing against the music already in the recorder's head."[1]

Thus, we begin to see that when a genre convention is established in the minds of viewers, it becomes possible for filmmakers to find a visual or formal equivalent for it. The crudest films can know the familiar concepts, or language, of any genre, and use it—even use it well. Some films, however, translate it into filmic terms, thus making generic language fully cinematic. It is progression which moves the verbal/visual toward the visual/verbal. It cannot happen without the establishment of the genre definition, the recognition of that definition by the audience, and the usage of it by people who understand both film *and* genre fully.

Two influences on this self-conscious second wave in terms of visual development were *documentary films* and the *contributions of individual producers, writers, directors, and stars*, whose work carried its own baggage into the process. Documentaries taught viewers what real combat looked like, while filmmakers created a formal, visual shorthand for narrative concepts the audience had learned.

Documentaries

Thanks to the extensive, rapidly processed newsreel, World War II really was the first war that could be seen on film soon after it happened by the public at large. These weekly newsreels, which were very brief, also covered sports events, fashions, celebrity life, and human interest features. Scenes of combat were tempered by these safety valves. Although newsreels helped teach audiences what combat really looked like, it was the documentaries of World War II that linked such footage to a sense of great drama. These films were frequently feature-length, allowing for an involved viewer participation, and although they *were* documentaries, they contained their own kind of passionate storytelling. The United States spent more than $50 million annually for making documentary movies during the war. Combat photographers, a noble group of unsung heroes, filmed every major military campaign.[2] The National Archives today estimate the *uncut* combat film of World War II alone at over 13.5 million feet!

Some of the footage was used in the making of documentaries by a talented team of Hollywood directors who enlisted in the armed services and were assigned to film units—Frank Capra, John Huston, John Ford, George Stevens, and William Wyler among them. Today, the National Archives distributes a film rental booklet that carries these words: "It has been said that war is the stuff of which great films are made, and World War II proved to be no exception. Although Government motion pictures were made under the exigencies of wartime morale and education, it was the unifying vision of their Hollywood directors that elevated them above the level of mere historical records. At their best, they are highly personal statements on the realities of war—remarkable for their power, intelligence, and democratic approach."[3]

To consider these documentaries is important, because they influence the look of the combat film in three ways: home audiences, having seen them, now had an idea of the physical look of combat and thus would expect films about combat to look that way; filmmakers, having the same experience as these viewers, would react similarly and could and would perhaps use some of that same footage in combat films; and those filmmakers who made the documentaries in the field would return to Hollywood to make combat films when the war was over.

The key documentary films which influenced the look of combat-on-film are: *The Battle of Midway* (1942), *The Fighting Lady* (1942), *Memphis Belle* (1944), *Thunderbolt* (1945), *Report from the Aleutians* (1943), *The Battle of San Pietro* (1945), and perhaps most interesting of all in terms of genre development, *December 7th* (1943). Although they were made from 1942 to 1945, and some were released in major cities during the "first wave," the majority of the audiences would have seen them during 1944 and 1945. Thus, they fall into "second wave" influence.

The first documentary that found wide release and popular response was *The Battle of Midway* in 1942. It was an accident of fate. John Ford, a commander in the Navy, was on Midway when the Japanese attacked. He ran out, placed three 16mm cameras in the sands, and shot as much film as he could. Two of the cameras were destroyed, some of the remaining film was unusable, and Ford himself was wounded in the experience. However, the resulting film, *Battle of Midway*, showed Americans clearly what it looked like to be in the midst of the chaos of combat. There is no doubt that American audiences saw it, because 500 copies were made at government expense and shipped all over the United States, free of charge to theater owners.

The Memphis Belle (1944) is a cinematic record of the final mission into combat of a Flying Fortress named "the Memphis Belle." Directed by William Wyler (who in 1946 would make a celebrated film about the return to civilian life of the kind of men who flew such missions, *The Best Years of Our Lives*), *Memphis Belle* makes the experience of being inside a bomber during combat vivid and real. It influenced the look of air films which followed, because the point of view of the combat experience is from inside the plane.

This is an important consideration because it changes the role of the viewer from observer to participant. Previously, the viewer typically experienced air combat by looking at a mockup of the actor sitting inside a plane, or at an exterior of an airplane seen from the air or the ground. In 1945, another Wyler air combat film, *Thunderbolt* (made with John Sturges), was released to theaters. It showed the 57th Fighter Group during "Operation Stranger," which destroyed supply routes deep inside German lines. These sequences, which place a viewer inside a P-47 Fighter-Bomber as it swoops and dives, are some of the most exciting and spectacular views of war ever filmed from the air. They, too, teach a viewer what it looks like to be in the air during real combat.

Report from the Aleutians (1943) and *The Battle of San Pietro* (1945) were both made by John Huston. (A third documentary Huston made, *Let There Be Light*, is about battle shock, not combat, and its resulting mental condition among soldiers. It was considered taboo for civilians, and has only recently been declassified and made available for general viewing.) *Report from the Aleutians* shows real soldiers involved in activities that audiences could recognize from war films: mail call, a funeral and burial, joking camaraderie, and a shared singalong. By seeing that real soldiers at the front actually did the things their fictional counterparts did in war films, audiences had their movie-story experiences verified. They saw active combat in *Report from the Aleutians*— a tense bombing raid from which not everyone came back—and they saw how the men acted while waiting to go into combat again. *The Battle of San Pietro* shows the hard fighting that took place in Italy. It's a remarkable film. The horror of war is real—dead bodies, devastated towns, shocked civilians and war-weary soldiers. In watching it, viewers could see that war was not a glorious thing, and they could also form an accurate sense of what it looked like. Narrative movies were put to the test by the reality of *Battle of San Pietro*.

The Fighting Lady (1945) was also photographed during major battle campaigns. Louis de Rochemont, the film's producer, put it together from 60,000 feet of 16mm film taken over a 14-month period during 1943 and 1944, when the filmmakers were aboard the 3000-man ship, *Fighting Lady*, a 27,000-ton Essex-class aircraft carrier. An outstanding group of cinematographers, headed by no less than Edward Steichen, took spectacular footage of aerial combat, and did solid work on the everyday life of a ship's combat crew. Viewers learned about the men who fought the war—their fears, their ways of living and eating, the things they had to do to protect themselves, not only against a fierce enemy, but also against injuries, infections, and debilitating tensions. The famous Battle of the Philippine Sea (June 1944) was recorded on film in detail. Sitting in one's safe theater seat, one could watch torpedoes, rockets, dive bombers, dogfights in the air, bombings—all real.

Perhaps the most interesting of all the war documentaries is the 1943 *December 7th*, made by John Ford for the Navy, which well illustrates the blurring of reality with filmed versions of reality. On the day itself, few cameras were ready for what was, after all, the surprise attack of the century. When John Ford and his director of photography, Gregg Toland, set out to make a "documentary" on the subject, they had to recreate most of the action in the studio. The scenes which many now believe to be photographs of sailors and soldiers running through the chaos of combat, firing their weapons desperately at the enemy, are, in fact, scenes with actors playing those roles. In addition there is process photography, the use of miniatures, and rear-screen projection. In short, *December 7th* is hardly a documentary at all. It is a more of a short narrative film, anything but a dispassionate presentation of facts. It is highly emotional, and its purpose is to incite and enflame. "Always will our nation remember the character of the onslaught against us," FDR had said, and he is quoted here. "A date that will live in infamy . . . horror and disgust. . . . amazement and sorrow. . . ."

The National Audio Visual Center's booklet on the films it offers for distribution says, "Thus, the film represents one of the rare instances where moments of illusion have become, for most of us, the documentary reality. However, because the fact and fiction of *December 7th* are blended together so skillfully, its impact is not seriously diminished. On the contrary, the film stands as an almost textbook example of the use of a succession of edited images to involve and overwhelm an audience."[5] Over the years, television news shows and other filmmakers, both narrative and documentary, have borrowed footage from Ford's film as if it were pictures of the real morning of the attack on Pearl Harbor. When *Tora! Tora! Tora!* (1970) and TV's *The Winds of War* (1983) set out to show what it was like at Pearl Harbor that Sunday morning, they re-created images from *December 7th*. This may not be the actual beginning of the modern age in which image supplants reality, but it certainly marks a place where it can authentically be pointed to and defined. The version of *December 7th* that was released to theaters in 1943 won the Academy Award for best documentary. It was a 20-minute version, but the original full 85 minutes is held by the National Archives, who sell a 34 minute version in both 16mm and on videocassete, so that all future generations may see what Pearl Harbor "really looked like."

In addition to the re-creation of events that Sunday morning, *December 7th* reinforces the emerging language of the genre: It presents a representative mixed group of young men. "Who were these young Americans?" the narrator asks, as viewers see a row of graves and are told 2343 American serviceman were killed that day. "Speak, some of

December 7th

you." A list of names is carefully recited, with photographs of the dead, and posed images of each man's parents and family. The list will match those democratic groups of the World War II combat film:

- Robert R. Kelly, Army, Findlay, Ohio
- Alfred Aaron Rosenthal, Navy, Brooklyn, New York
- Theodore Stephen Zabel, Marines, Castelia, Iowa
- Moses Anderson Allan, Navy, from a farm near Cove, North Carolina
- James Webster Lake, Navy, Huntington Park, California
- Antonio S. Batoya, Army, Albuquerque, New Mexico
- William R. Schick, Medical Corps, Chicago, Illinois

Schick's young wife is seen holding his baby, born three months after Pearl Harbor on what would have been his own birthday. The narrator asks the voice that spoke for these dead men: "How come you all sound alike?" "Because we *are* all alike," it replies. "We are all Americans."

December 7th also teaches viewers how the former island paradise becomes fortified for combat. Windows are taped, houses camouflaged. Barbed wire is strung on the beach; shelters are built; blackouts scheduled, air raid systems established; and school children are taught to use the gas masks and evacuate their schools into slit trenches. War has come. Even civilians must learn to cope. As a final hideous symbol, inadvertently funny, a man changes the sign outside his restaurant: *The Banzai Cafe* is now the *"Keep 'em Flying!"*

At the end, the narrator tells viewers that "this is a war of survival, a people's war, even a little people's war." There are no credits, just a simple statement: "Photographed by U.S. Navy photographers." We are all Americans. *December 7th* reminded viewers of that, and taught them how to prepare for war.

Individual Contribution

In analyzing Hollywood films, one must remember the studio system that produced them. What one is dealing with is an ever-changing system of personnel and business pressures. These are in turn set within an ever-changing society. What evolves is a portrait of America, her changing culture and ideology, but it is evolving within the evolution of a minisystem (Hollywood studios) that is changing its own structure and reflecting those changes (all of them) in a narrative system.[6]

This book does not seek to resolve the great "who did what?" question. It is an important question, but without picking apart specific contributions, it is necessary to base the development of this second wave on the idea that individuals could contribute. More importantly, it is necessary to say that Hollywood filmmakers, all of them, could and did do their jobs well. That means that after a basic genre was established, some of them got together and made films that transformed concepts that were spoken aloud into concepts that were presented purely visually. The literary became the visual. Content became form.

The reason this is important is simple enough. It allowed for the full participation of the viewer, and was, in fact, dependent on his cooperation in the understanding of the process. As genre evolves, it grows more referential, less detailed, This can happen because viewers already know its conventions. It is facilitated by skilled filmmakers who find the visual equivalents for the concepts, and who present them so viewers can "read" them for themselves.

Let us accept that men and women who are creative, whatever their jobs on the film, can make a contribution to generic development. Let us admit that anyone who comes to make a film uses all the sources available, whatever they may be—literary and nonliterary, filmic and nonfilmic, real and unreal. Let us acknowledge that all contributors and all sources are multi-influenced, intricately cross-pollinated. Then let us survey all the people, all the sources, including perhaps the government, lurking behind it all in some mysterious and threatening way. Finally, then, let us ruefully admit that sorting it all out after the fact is not only difficult, but nearly impossible—at best, speculative. Then, let's speculate a bit.

For instance, a historian might say that the plot device of having a submarine dive before a crew member can get inside was influenced and created by a real event of history. On February 7, 1943, Commander Howard W. Gilmore ordered his executive officer on the submarine *Growler* to "Take her down!" The order was loud and clear, and while the men at the sub aperture waited and precious seconds ticked by, the Commander himself did not appear. He was badly wounded and clinging to the bridge frame, having waited to give the order while four other men got safely below.

The Naval Institute Press' official book, *United States Submarine Operations in World War II*, says: "Gilmore and Growler. In the memory of the U.S. Submarine Force the names are welded, inseparable. Mention either, and submariners think of gunfire and chaos in a roaring sea—a submarine's life threatened—and a voice speaking out of the night. 'TAKE HER DOWN!'" This dramatic story, illustrated with a beautiful full-color drawing, was written up in *Life* magazine.

The movies copied this story. Right? Yet *Hell Below* (1933) has a story in which a submarine must dive and leave a comrade up top. How can one sort these things out? Do we credit history, *Hell Below*'s screenwriter, or the director's Aunt Mabel who told him the idea the night before?[7]

Although the role of the individual in the development of genre is controversial, it has to be acceptable to say that there *can* be individual input. This might come from anyone from the group who collaborated on the film. Deciphering such input is a valid part of genre study, because it is inevitable that the men and women who made these films not only used established conventions, but added to them, varied them, reshaped them, out of personal vision and experience as well as business concerns. Who did what, and where these visions came from is, needless to say, very difficult to establish.

For this reason, many people speak only of the director as the creator of any given film, since the director was presumably most responsible for what ultimately appeared on the screen. The relationship of any individual—director or otherwise—to the development of genre cannot just be ignored because it is a difficult area to analyze. In discussing the relationship of genre study and the role of the film artist, Thomas Schatz writes, "These two critical methods do complement and counterbalance one another in that genre criticism treats established cinematic forms, whereas auteur criticism celebrates certain filmmakers who worked effectively within those forms . . . Analyzing a genre director's work, which has grown along with a genre, represents . . . the complexity involved in criticizing Hollywood genre films."[8]

Presumably an auteur is an auteur if he is a film director who shapes scripts or ideas into a personal film in a pattern that emerges over a period of time. Therefore an auteur would be a director who may or may not make genre films but if he does, he makes them his way. "His way" would mean that he would use the many talents and ideas of the script writers, cinematographers, actors, designers and producers working with him on the project. I do not mean to suggest, here or ever, that I do not recognize the many contributions of collaborators to those men designated "auteurs," nor do I mean to suggest that I think only a director can be (or has been) an auteur. Actors are auteurs, and producers are auteurs. Studios are auteurs, and art directors are auteurs. Certainly writers are auteurs. In fact, individual input into the generic format includes the works of the writers (of primary importance to genre), the art directors (who contribute iconography), stars (who create meaning through persona and who have persona created for them from generic tradition), as well as master directors who, if they are effective, tend to create their own genres: "The Hitchcock thriller, the Capra comedy." For any member of the filmmaking team who is an artist, genre is never formula.

Many people were influential in making war movies. The list is endless, and includes producers such as Walter Wanger,[9] writers such as Spig Wead, Laurence Stallings, and John Monk Saunders, studio heads such as Jack Warner, cinematographers like James Wong Howe . . . on and on. Three directors who made effective war films were John Ford, Howard Hawks, and Raoul Walsh. Each made a key World War II film: Walsh, *Objective Burma*; Hawks, *Air Force*; Ford, *They Were Expendable*. Each had made a prior film that was important in the shaping of the genre: Walsh, the silent *What Price Glory?*; Hawks, *Dawn Patrol* (as well as *Today We Live*, *The Road to Glory*, and *Sergeant York*); Ford, *Lost Patrol*. John Ford later remade Walsh's *What Price Glory?* and he was also responsible for the key documentaries, *The Battle of Midway* and *December 7th*.

Of the three, only Ford participated in actual combat. However, they overlap in their usages of stars, writers, studios, and cinematographers, so presumably they shared influences and collaborators to a large degree. Each director worked in many genres, some of which cross-pollinate with the combat genre. Each of these men eventually developed a set of recurring thematic and stylistic characteristics that mark his work, and if these coincided with the needs of the genre film being made, they used them appropriately. For instance, Hawks liked films about a professional group of men. Thus, *Air Force* was perfect material for him. Walsh made films about men who moved fast across country, as in *Objective Burma*, and Ford liked movies about the nobility of defeat. Their skill in telling such stories helped, no doubt, to strengthen these attitudes in genre. Certainly their skill as directors of films which made the most use of visual and formal possibilities contributed to this wave of genre. It is possible that unless it has contributions from auteurs—whatever the production job—no genre can really become a genre. The relationship of auteurism and genre is a subject for a full-length book itself.

Four Key Films of 1944–1946

The films of 1943 which defined the genre were films that used colossal defeats for patriotic inspiration. The films of 1944 tend to repeat this pattern, or to inspire by a sense of we ain't licked yet. As American forces began winning the war, our films grew even darker. Even when we survive and take our objectives, the overall sense is one of death and sacrifice. Four films, made near the end of the war, by people who believed in what they were doing, are noteworthy. They have a tension that the times themselves had. There's excitement and danger, tinged with sadness and pain, that later movies do not and cannot have.

The four films are *Objective Burma*, *They Were Expendable*, *The Story of G.I. Joe*, and *A Walk in the Sun*. Taken together, they are a kind of last hurrah for the combat films of the era. Each was well-appreciated by critics and audiences at the time; each has a solid grounding in reality. Two (*They Were Expendable* and *The Story of G.I. Joe*) are based on writings by or about men who were in the wars described. The other two are based on actual combat, with *Objective Burma* being a story similar to that of Merrill's experiences in Burma, and *A Walk in the Sun* a story of the landing in Italy by American forces. They share a dark force, a grim sense of war as a no-win situation, in which we will hang on and endure, but not without suffering.

All have a touch of the poetic—*Objective Burma*, the poetry of movement and courage in difficult times; *The Story of G.I. Joe*, the poetry of men trying to hang on to human meaning in an inhuman war; *They Were Expendable*, the poetry of loss and defeat; and *A Walk in the Sun*, the poetry of poetry. All indicate the knowledge that viewers knew the "real look" of war from newsreels and documentaries. All reinforce the basic generic definition but add in visual development: the kind of cinematic shorthand which also provides an attitude of distance toward the basic definition.

Both *Objective Burma* and *They Were Expendable* illustrate a situation in which a unit of fighting men must divide themselves in order to go on. In both films, one half dies. We do not see the death of those left behind in *They Were Expendable*, but we know it is coming—either death or imprisonment or both. In both films, the men are cut off from the equipment that links them to their duties. The men of *Objective Burma* cannot signal their airplane after their radio is gone, and the planes cannot spot them on the ground. The men of *They Were Expendable* lose their boats. In *The Story of G.I. Joe*, the man who leads them is dead at the end, his body flung over a mule, and in *A Walk in The Sun*, the leader goes mad and must be left behind. The man who takes over finds no glory in it, and he must press on to the next objective until, one feels, he himself will go mad and the next man will step into his place.

In a basic way, all four of these films are about defeat and failure. Despite the success of the initial mission in *Objective Burma*, the men are left stranded, unable to reach their rendezvous point before the Japanese catch up with them. Although the film ends on a seemingly optimistic note, the war still has to be won. Furthermore, the hero displays a ring of dogtags collected from those who have died on the mission. "Here's what it cost," he says. (This grim note will be repeated in later films, such as *Men in War*.)

In *Objective Burma* (January 7, 1945) we perceive that the filmmakers believe our role in the war is justified. This is reflected in the script, which contains blatant propaganda that portrays the enemy as truly barbaric. Seen today, these embarrassing pronouncements flaw an otherwise superbly crafted and exciting movie. There is a coherent reality to this film's war. It may destroy men's lives and men's minds but it exists to be won, and for good reason. This attitude is reflected in the character of the hero (Errol Flynn) and in the presentation of a true objective, clearly defined and mapped. The leaders carry these maps, and they are able to pinpoint and locate rendezvous points as directed from a plane overhead. Although the patrols become cut off from supplies and rescue, they do not become *lost* in the sense of being unable to read their maps or in the larger sense of "why are we doing this?" They question, but they understand there is a higher order of understanding to the war and that their job is to slog onward, carrying out orders and having faith in their ultimate rescue. They experience fear, and even madness, death, and defeat; but they press onward, following their maps and keeping the faith that they will be rescued. Inevitably, their faith is rewarded, and the film's finale is a sky aburst with airplanes dropping supplies and paratroopers and, presumably, flying straight onward to total victory.

The geographical coherence and reality presented in *Objective Burma* partially reflects the concerns of the director, Raoul Walsh, whose work is generally marked by temporal and spatial continuity. It also reflects the coherence of the true event on which it is based, in which a group destroyed their primary objective but were forced to walk out through the jungle because they were cut off from any rescue by air. [10]

The hero is well played by Errol Flynn, whose star persona is asso-

ciated with the noble romantic hero of such films as *The Adventures
of Robin Hood, The Sea Hawk, Captain Blood,* and, significantly,
General Custer in *They Died with Their Boots On* and the hero who
dies at the end of *Charge of the Light Brigade.* Flynn did not fight in
World War II because of health problems, and thus was available to
play the hero in war films. Yet this is his only combat film of World
War II, unless one counts the Rover Boys adventure story, *Desperate
Journey.* (*Dive Bomber* is not a combat film.) He did, however, portray
war heroes of another type in *Edge of Darkness* and *Uncertain Glory.*
In the former film he was a Norwegian guerrilla and in the latter he
was a criminal who sacrifices himself to save a group of hostages. Both
of these films are set in European villages, and thus afford Flynn the
opportunity for daring and adventure, but, more importantly, for a
concept closely associated with his own screen persona, love and romance. Films like *Objective Burma,* in which not a single woman appears, cut him off from a part of his audience. Although the men of
Objective Burma constantly talk about women, none appear.

Flynn's character in *Objective Burma* is both a father figure to the
men and a hero in the romantic tradition. He is noble, brave, optimistic. He behaves with grace and dignity under pressure. He doesn't
like the war, but he's equal to its tasks. He never fails his men, and he
has an almost godlike sense of direction and purpose. He cries for them,
knows them as individuals, and keeps his sense of humor all through
the disasters.

In *Objective Burma,* Flynn, the noble leader, does not die, as in
Bataan and earlier films. However, a subtle variation of this concept
occurs when the beleaguered patrol splits into two groups, to increase
their chances of survival and to attempt two different routes to the next
rendezvous. We follow Flynn's group, most of whose members survive;
but we learn of the death and mutilation of the other group. The dead
and tortured half of the patrol may be seen to represent the "other
selves" of the group we follow. In that sense, the noble leader *does* die,
as Flynn's counterpart, his loyal and devoted friend who has shared
battle after battle with him, dies horribly.

The objective of the film's title may be seen as twofold: the primary,
assumed objective, which is to blow up a radar and communications
station in the Burmese jungle, an objective which is effectively and
efficiently accomplished; and the enforced objective, which is to reach
a rendezvous point deep in the jungle, in the opposite direction of

Errol Flynn in Objective Burma

safety, where they may be picked up by their rescue planes. Whereas the first objective requires skill, training, and courage, the second objective requires those virtues plus endurance and faith. Many war combat films use the device of the double objective, both assumed and enforced; it is an appropriate structure for films which are in effect saying that war is unpredictable: It can be planned only so far, and after that one must improvise. Destroying an objective is one thing. Getting home safely is another. (Surviving the killing you did and what it has made out of you is something else, too.) This use of the dual objective illustrates the point that soldiers must take responsibility for their own safety and sanity, just as the viewing audience must assume the burden of understanding the sacrifices to be made. Obviously, the dual objective adds dramatic tension, and by affording an audience a grand and glorious victory (in which the patrol blows up the radar station with terrific panache), undercut by a difficult slog through the jungle, it provides dramatic contrast. The traditional foulup of a well-planned mission suggests that war is not simple and cannot be easily planned for and controlled. To fight a war is to unleash a powerful primitive force that may instead control you.

Here the combat genre is not unlike the horror film. It has its Dr. Frankenstein motif. The thing you created can end up destroying you. The affinity of certain genres for one another is frequently cited in terms of the Western and the gangster film, or the Western and the combat film. The combat film also has a curious affinity for the horror movie. As was observed in *Bataan*, the mists of war are visually like the mists of the moors or of London nights when the Ripper is afoot. The enemy attacks at night, and men go mad from the strains of coping—two things which also occur in horror films. People try to explain an insane situation with words in both films, and to hang on to God and reason to see them through what is happening. Above all, each contains a world gone mad with violence, with the unpredictability governing and dominating the best laid plans of attack.

The enemy of *Objective Burma* is presented in a most prejudicial manner. Their faces in close-up are used to frighten a viewer with the sense of alien, unsmiling beings. The narrative suggests a group of truly barbaric men who torture and mutilate. They are called hideous names in a casual manner—"monkeys" and "slanty-eyed devils"—and they are described as "swarming like locusts." However, they are also presented as *smart*, and as very, very dangerous. They are almost an omniscient enemy. They have radar, maps, knowledge of the jungle, and seemingly unlimited forces. Like the enemy seen at the end of *Bataan*, they advance in endless hordes against the band of survivors.

In *Objective Burma*, the enemy is the Japanese army. The jungle is a problem that complicates their escape from that true enemy. In later films, such as *Too Late the Hero*, *Battle Cry*, and *The Naked and the*

Dead, the enemy is the jungle and the the inner psychology of the men. The Japanese become the complication. This may be illustrated by the appearance of that jungle-film staple, the snake. As a child, when I was at a movie set in a jungle, I always waited anxiously for the snake. "Have we had the snake yet?" I used to ask, as I returned to my seat from the candy counter, hoping against hope that we had, so I could relax. The number of times I went to the candy counter was directly related to the time of the snake's appearance. I went as often as I could, hoping to avoid it, but once it had appeared, I settled in and stayed put. (This may be the beginning of my genre study!) But note that the snake does *not* appear in *Objective Burma,* because real war has no time for snakes. It does, however, appear in the postwar *Naked and the Dead,* and it promptly kills one of our group. After his funeral, a comrade ironically intones his epitaph: "Killed in action. By a snake."

The association of jungle and snake is immediately dealt with in Sylvester Stallone's *Rambo* (1985). Shortly after he is dropped into a deep Vietnam jungle, Stallone (as the title character) encounters a huge snake dangling from a tree. With a neat twist of his wrist, he calmly strangles it and pushes on. A lot of things might be said about Sylvester Stallone, but that he doesn't understand the audience's genre expectations isn't one of them. Nobody has time to go to the candy counter.

This all illustrates a point of genre development—the expansion of the basic conventions and plot developments, once the war was won and issues resolved, to include something the audience associates with the setting, and not inappropriate to the story, as a variation to fill in the gaps. The snake does not appear in combat films set in Europe. However, French girls do.

In *Objective Burma,* the presentation of the ethnic group is done with a minimum of referential dialogue that helps an audience recognize types, identify them, and fill in characterization based on already established conventions. The most striking presentation of the group is stylistic. It's done through composition, unifying camera work, and cutting, as well as the use of action, small bits of visual business, and significant gestures—the visual shorthand that is the mark of the second wave.

For instance, as the men wait to jump into the jungle from an airplane, each man is established as an individual. We *see* they are different. The camera moves down the plane, showing each man's private relationship with the impending danger. One reads a Bible.

One fidgets nervously. As the camera roves the tight space, up and down, back and forth, the individuals are united by the camera movement into a group. A group of individuals, but a group. As they stand to jump, this unification of the group is beautifully repeated through camera movement. We learn their ethnic type by closeups of their different faces. We see their attitudes toward combat, their relationships to one another. The camera's final move draws them into a single character, ready to jump as one.

The tension after the paratroopers land in a hostile jungle is so palpable that it still seems to us, after more than forty years, as if the enemy is everywhere watching. The men jump into the dark, hostile jungle below, and the film story picks them up there, the shock of the jump and the fear of the jungle on their faces. Silently they signal one another and begin their walk. The sounds of the alien jungle surround them, as they sneak silently along in the darkness. We must strain our eyes to see in that darkness, just like the men themselves. We must keep alert, listening to the strange sounds, anticipating danger. At any moment, the enemy may descend. Given what we know about films, they probably will come right now. Now! But they don't come. When will they come? What will happen? The men sneak onward, increasingly tense. We watch, increasingly tense. Nobody says a word.

From then on, *Objective Burma* continues to present its men-on-patrol, closely followed by the Japanese, in visual terms. As Flynn and his men wade upstream through a hot and dangerous jungle, one snaps a small branch by accident, and we follow the beginning of its drift downstream. A cut shifts the point-of-view, so that it is as if we turn our heads to watch the backs of Flynn's departing men. As they disappear, the image returns with an almost imperceptible dissolve to the branch, seemingly right where we left it, still moving forward with fluid speed. As it moves it brushes against the legs of a Japanese scout, also forging his way upstream, followed by a horde of soldiers. The film provides tension in this manner by using space to indicate time, and time to indicate space. The sense of the Japanese hot on the trail is enhanced by this skillful manipulation of cinema—estabish forward motion, cut to changed viewpoint, dissolve into continued forward motion which gives a sense of a fluid single-take or the absence of cutting—the visual linking of the pursued with the pursuers in a tight time frame.

Thus *Objective Burma* makes a viewer participate in the combat

Burgess Meredith as Ernie Pyle in The Story of G.I. Joe

experience at a tense emotional level. Although it will have its own share of propaganda conversation, it contains scenes like these in which all understanding grows out of viewing experience. It places the burden of meaning on us. But we can shoulder it easily with the aid of two things: the filmmaking process itself, with its specific meanings of cutting, composition, etc., and with the prior knowledge of other such films. These guides let us create our own narrative and dialogue, but, most importantly, they let us create it by experiencing it more as participants than viewers. Such films contribute to the life of genre through this powerful visual presentation.

The Story of G.I. Joe (October 6, 1945) is about Ernie Pyle, the famous and beloved newspaper correspondent of World War II, who lost his life in Pacific combat. His sentimental, but effective, reporting about the American fighting man was widely read and quoted during the war. These columns form the basis of this film, a definite step in the conscious mythologizing of the war. Made toward the end of the war and released after V.J. Day, the film begins to take a distanced attitude.

Ernie Pyle, played by Burgess Meredith, talks to the audience on the soundtrack, as he is seen typing, writing his column, and learning about the war and the men who fight it. "Only battle experience can produce a combat soldier," he tells us. "Men live rough and talk rough in war." Besides these aural wisdoms, there is an almost reverential visual presentation of what were once simple plot devices. These familiar touchstones of genre are now presented as visual shorthand, little references for us to recognize and understand without full script development. There's a mascot, a dog called A-rab, and there is "Dixie" played on a harmonica. There's a mail call ("Ooooh! I'm a father!") in which a man gets a record of his child's voice, but has no phonograph to play it on. For that soldier, the film and thus the war, becomes a quest for a phonograph, a kind of windmill-tilting journey to link himself back to home. Inevitably, he dies just when the record can finally be played.

"The G.I.," says Pyle's voice. "He lives so miserable and he dies so miserable." This is fully illustrated when the body of their Captain, who has been well played by a young Robert Mitchum, is brought down, slung unceremoniously over a donkey. He's dead and gone. No one knows how it happened. It just happened, and "that's war," as Pyle says. That's war.

The Story of G.I. Joe has the power to take one completely out of the excitement of war, and down into the muck and mud and the human misery. In doing so, it creates a kind of myth and mystery about the experience. This comes out of Pyle's sense of the ordinary fighting man and his courage, his attempt to make life coherent in the midst of chaos. Thus, this film emphasizes human events—a soldier stopping to kiss an Italian girl, a wedding ceremony with the bride in dungarees, and the sad act of the Captain's having to write home to the families of the dead men. When the Americans have secured a village, the people come out to feed them and thank them. (Later, in Samuel Fuller's recreation of the war he actually fought in, *The Big Red One*, a similar scene takes place.) This realism creates a kind of combat poem, and the poetry helps to make the myth.

A major combat sequence of *The Story of G.I. Joe* which is presented in purely visual terms involves the soldiers recapturing a church inside a village. The Germans have holed up inside it, with one acting as sniper from the belfry. This sequence is choreographed, directed, and played out as many such instances had been and would continue to be in Western films. Here is part of the understanding of genre. The war is over now. It is October 1945. Maybe we should begin to think of how action and bravery will appear in films now that we have won the war. Maybe we'll return to the Western format. The way we will do this is through the medium itself—photographing, cutting, and structuring a sequence from one familiar genre, recostumed for another—that is, through visual presentation. If an audience can be taught what real war looks like from documentation, it can also be taught it can look like a Western movie. They already know what Westerns look like. The visual connection can be made.

Some scholars have made the point that the war combat film replaced the Western during the war years. This is convenient, and it sounds good. However, it is a point that does not take actual film history into consideration. Not only were many serials and B-Westerns made, but mainstream release also brought the public such titles as *The Desperadoes, Frontier Badmen, Buffalo Bill* and *Tall in the Saddle*. In fact, more Westerns than combat films were available to the average viewer during World War II. But even if there had been *no* Westerns, history still presents us with the problem that both genres continued to flourish in the postwar period, so that they cannot really be seen as replacements for one another in the long run. In the era of Vietnam the Western *did* take over, but not so much as a replacement for the combat film (which continues), but as a displacement location for a story about Vietnam. Instead of our fighting the Vietnam war as a combat film, we fight it as a western, and also as a homefront problem film.

The two genres are compatible, however, as *The Story of G.I. Joe* shows us in the church sequence—a subliminal indication that if the combat genre will not survive, its stories and actions can be retold for us in the Western format.

A comparison of the titles of war films reveals intention. *Objective Burma* is purposeful, and directional. *Air Force* is proudly professional. *A Walk in the Sun* is poetic and deliberately mythic. *The Story of G.I. Joe* announces itself as celebratory of the American common man, a democratic look at the forces who fought for democracy. On that basis, *They Were Expendable* (December 21, 1945) is probably the gloomiest title of any war film in the history of the type, revealing, as it does, defeat and loss, and an implied attitude toward the men who fight that the necessity of war requires that our government take.

They Were Expendable was released after the war, and perhaps it was only then that viewers could have endured its gloomy message. Yet its sense of defeat is elevated by a triumph of the human spirit, and by its beautiful visual presentation. Directed by John Ford, photographed by Joseph August, and written by Spig Wead, it is based on a book by William L. White about a real officer, Lieutenant John Bulkeley, a close friend of the director's.

They Were Expendable is one of the great films of World War II. It consciously breaks down and reconsiders what has gone before, something that can be done effectively only if audiences and filmmakers know what is being broken down. For example, in *Bataan* and other World War II films, one observes how a motley group of men from different walks of life, and different services, have to band together to participate effectively in the war. Thus, even though the film might end with the destruction of all parties, the sense is one of order grown out of chaos. The lesson is taught that, even if this group seems to lose, they have won by proving their ability to unify, by "buying the time for MacArthur" that was their original purpose, and by demonstrating what a fierce fighting force they have been. They personify and uphold the sense of what it means to be an American and what America is.

They Were Expendable, on the other hand, begins with a strong sense of military order, and slowly descends into chaos. Its opening scenes of the PT boats on display, cutting through the water at high speed with a style and grace that is breathtaking, suggests the coherent system of the Navy and the power that coherence provides in terms of military strength. These beautiful boats go unused in combat for the majority of the film, and ultimately they are broken and destroyed, their crews left on foot, dead, or separated by duty.

The group is not treated as a set of American stereotypes. Although the men are mixed in age and background, they are depicted as individuals, not as concepts. At first one might say this is because the film is based on a book that was a true-life historical account of the war, but the same is true for *Guadalcanal Diary* and *The Story of G.I. Joe,* in which the characters do seem representational.

The leaders of *They Were Expendable* are not able to become members of the group in the same way that Robert Taylor can in *Bataan*. Although we have seen that Cary Grant is the Captain of the submarine, and thus separate, in *Destination Tokyo*, and that Errol Flynn is clearly in command and bears the responsibility for choices in *Objective Burma*, here we have much more rigid concentric circles of distanced leaders. Robert Montgomery as the counterpart of Lieutenant Bulkeley (renamed Brickley) bears the loneliness that leadership brings, and is seen distanced from his men, with the exception of his second-in-command, played by John Wayne. Montgomery's own superior is distanced from him, and the ultimate distancing is that of General MacArthur, seen only in long shot as he is taken away from the Philippines on the first leg of a journey to Australia. Who can fail to be moved by the scene in which Ford, presenting MacArthur as a mythical figure, skillfully weaves photographs from *Life* magazine and sights of him from the newsreels of the day, walking alone, ahead of his men but behind his family, with the stirring music on the sound track? Ford has proved in *December 7th* his ability to replace reality with image, or perhaps to create reality through image, and this film is no exception. This visual power of *They Were Expendable* extends the genre, and proves it through its eloquent comment on established patterns. With its sense of dignity and truth and its rejection of false battle heroics, *They Were Expendable* is almost an anti-genre film—something it couldn't be if the genre were not already fixed.

The release of *A Walk in the Sun* (January 12, 1946) marks the beginning of a legendary attitude toward World War II. As *Bataan* may be seen as the first fully realized pure combat "genre" film for World War II, *A Walk in the Sun* may be seen as the first *overtly* referential film. It is the marker for things to come, but because of the war's end and people's desire to turn away from war and combat, it marks an end rather than a beginning. Although *A Walk in the Sun* is the story of 53 men who start out on a long walk in the Italian sun, it is a key film in the proof of genre. It is self-consciously referential both to the films of the type that came before it, to the reality of the events themselves, and to the audience's knowledge of both.

A *Walk in the Sun* does not seek to destroy the viewer's faith in the nobility of our fighting and winning World War II. Although it has its foot soldiers griping and asking questions as they slog forward on their seemingly undirected and leaderless quest, these complaints form a kind of true American mythologizing. As their ordinariness is presented in event and dialogue, the poetic approach of the film celebrates the common foot soldier, who *would* become the real American hero of World War II. From its opening, A *Walk in the Sun* takes a consciously legendary approach. "This was a story that happened long ago, way back in 1943, the story of the Texas Division that hit the beach at Salerno in sunny Italy . . . it tells of Sergeant Tyne from Providence, Rhode Island, which may not be much as cities go, but was all he wanted."

This voiceover narration speaks directly to the audience in a poetic cadence, with a rhythm that matches the music. This is later matched by the actors, who will speak most of their dialogue as if it were blank verse. The film next shows an image of hands picking up a book. The pages of the book turn into photographs of the characters of the film, as each is introduced, Sergeant Tyne, the hero, is Dana Andrews, followed by the usual representative types:

- Rivera—Italian-American. "Likes opera and would like a wife and kids, plenty of kids" (Richard Conte). "Everything in the army is simple," says Conte. "You live or you die."
- Friedman—a lathe operator, amateur boxing champion, New York City (George Tyne).
- Windy—a minister's son, Canton, Ohio (John Ireland). "Likes long walks alone." He's gotta think, so he writes letters in his head, letters to his sister that comment on the events and the reality of the war.
- Sgt. Ward—a farmer who knows his soil, a good farmer (Lloyd Bridges).
- McWilliams—first-aid man. Slow, Southern, dependable (Sterling Holloway).
- Archaimbault—platoon scout and prophet. "Talks a lot, but all right" (Norman Lloyd).
- Sgt. Porter—he's "locked in his mind." (Herbert Rudley).
- Panella—speaks two languages, "Italian and Brooklyn" (Richard Benedict).

And, as the narrator (Burgess Meredith), adds: "A lot of other men . . . here's a song about 'em . . . listen." On the soundtrack an unmistakably black voice begins to sing:

> It was just a little walk in the warm Italian sun,
> but it was not an easy thing, and poets are writing the tale of
> that fight and songs for children to sing.
> Let them sing of the men of that fighting platoon
> Let them sing of the job that they done
> They went across the sea, to sunny Italy,
> and took a little walk in the sun.
> They took a little walk in the sun.

The treatment of the invasion of Italy as a "little walk in the sun" is both poetic and dramatic, illustrating as it does the American tendency to the "aw, shucks, it was nothing" attitude. This is demythologizing, but of the sort that creates a new myth.

The film is presented via the combination of the song and mythic narration, which make a clear statement that this is a poetic evocation of a genre piece, even though it is presented with images of realism that refer directly to prior films. Notably, the film does not open with an official printed introduction, thanking a military force, quoting a military or national figure, and/or referring to a real battle of military unit. Instead it begins with a series of intense close-ups of the character's faces in the deep dark before their dawn landing. As they wait in the LST, the men talk to one another in a tough and humorous vein, but the words they use have an unreal quality. After a soldier is hit by a bomb, his face blown off because he was standing and looking out, the men make calm, almost deadpan observations:

> "I told him," says one.
> "They'll ship him home," says the cynic, "and we'll be fighting the battle of Tibet. They'll ship him home, give him a medal. . . . in 1956, he'll be a businessman again. . . . we'll be fighting the battle of Tibet. I've got the facts down cold."
> "Maybe he'll die," observes another.
> "Nobody dies," says Conte.
> "Nobody dies," repeats Ireland, and the song breaks out again, referring to all the places the men are from: "Texas, Jersey, Dakota, Minnesota, Maine. But they're all in the Texas Infantry."

At the same time, despite its poetry, the film keeps generic conventions intact. It is present in such characterizations as that of the two Italians, Panella and Rivera, who form a Quirt/Flagg argumentative relationship as the story unfolds. These two men keep up a running conversation about America and things American, a kind of time capsule dialogue where ordinary men are talking about the things that ordinary men would talk about as they hiked along. *Saturday Evening Post* covers, Norman Rockwell, record collections of Bing Crosby, Russ Columbo, the Andrews Sisters, and old movies ("What comes after Tibet?" says one. "Ask Victor McLaglen.") Their arguments form a commentary on events, and so does the comment of the cynic: "We're gonna be fighting the battle of Tibet in 1958. I got the facts."

Other events of *A Walk in the Sun* are also traditional, but with slightly new slants taken. After their landing comes the traditional loss of their leader. However, the "new-leader" that emerges, the next in command, is the character of Porter, the weak, indecisive man who is "locked in his mind."

In the center of the film is a recognizable combat action event, the knocking out of a German tank that approaches them. This attack on the tank, a brief event, is their first offensive of the film. It and the final assault on and capture of a farmhouse, their original assigned objective, are the only real action of the film. Porter, who lives in his head, cries as they plan. Previously he has cracked, falling to the ground and declaring he cannot go on. The film presents this event as if it is not an unfamiliar or uncommon one to the men involved in the story. "You're crying because you're wounded," says Ireland, "You don't have to be bleeding to be wounded. Go ahead and cry. We understand."

The platoon is pictured as surrounded totally by war, but having no clear understanding of its significance "The whole trouble with war is that you can't see nothing, gotta guess what's going on." But when Sterling Holloway climbs up over the ridge to "see war" and watch it through his binoculars, he is killed. He *sees* war, and thus he becomes its victim. Viewers can *see* war and learn through sharing his death.

As the film unfolds, it mixes a recurring series of images, sounds, and observations:

- Realistic battle scenes in the traditional use of bombs, guns, explosions, uniforms, tactics, maps, etc.
- The use of the song on the soundtrack to reinterpret the material and raise it to mythical status.
- The strange, dreamlike observations that characters make as they move along, contributing to the sense of war as a surreal event, catching men in an experience that, unlinked to any former occurrence in their lives and detached from any normal human endeavor, will remain forever

in their memories as an experience of light and shadow; danger and safety; warmth and cold; friendship and enemies, reinforced by the postwar reminder: "Nobody dies." It tells the audience we must not ever let them die in memory.

Although A *Walk in the Sun* presents a myth about the psychology of war more than about its action, the action, when it comes, is dynamic, reminiscent of director Lewis Milestone's earlier film, *All Quiet on the Western Front*, with its camera moving rapidly on horizontal tracks. The climax is a final assault on the farmhouse, which they win in an effective mix of poetry and action. ("How long would it take to crawl around the world?") The men continue their terse humor "Who's that coming up there" asks one, and "Maybe it's Marlene Dietrich" is the reply. They contemplate the soil "no good. . . old and tired" and nature "Just look at this leaf. . . the complications" and the war "there's a lot of good men going down in this war . . . why don't the Germans let us alone?"

In a technical tour de force, the "inside" of Andrews' mind is represented subjectively on screen in three ways: (1) as he waits to enter the combat, he looks up into the sky, and we see the hot sun as he sees it, blinding, overwhelming. (2) as he crawls forward across the field toward the farmhouse, under fire, an intense close-up of his strained face is superimposed over a zoom shot of the farmhouse. A rapid zoom in and zoom out toward the farmhouse is seen at the same time as his blinking and bewildered face responds to what he is obviously seeing. We see what he sees and what he feels simultaneously. (3) as he continues to crawl, his voice on the track is heard saying, "my head's spinning. . . . everything's spinning," and a series of cuts to the world around him spinning rapidly occurs. The fields, the sky, the terrain, all spin, stopped by the blowing up of the nearby bridge. Here viewers were given a visual demonstration of something they had heard about and learned about in earlier genre films: how a man feels in combat. The intense subjectivity of this sequence not only involves an audience directly in the emotion of combat, but also illustrates that characteristic peculiar to the second wave: the translation of what would have been a dialogue sequence into purely visual or cinematic terms.

A continous and dynamic sequence of combat unleashes the final assault, and takes the men to high noon of their day. As they lie about in the aftermath of intense combat, Ireland begins another letter to his

A Walk in the Sun, *with Dana Andrews*

sister: "Dear Frances. We just blew a bridge and took a farmhouse. It was easy. Terribly easy." As the Marine Hymn is heard and the song starts up on the soundtrack, the men walk out of the farmhouse in a typical review of the cast, and Andrews, in Western style, marks a notch on his gun. As we watch them, "nobody dies" is bound to echo in the audience's mind. If it does, the film has successfully completed its task.

> A walk that leads through a Philippine town
> and a highway north of Rome
> it's the same road they had
> coming out of Stalingrad
> it's that old Lincoln Highway back home
>   It's wherever men fight to be free . . .

In its presentation of a long walk, from dawn until noon, made by the men in a single platoon, the film fixes the genre firmly and forever.

It translates the entire experience of World War II into one representative group, one walk, one big battle with a skirmish on the way. It makes all our war combat films into one movie for us to remember more easily. It is a truly allegorical film, consciously mythologizing the war and laying the groundwork for what will come. But in so doing, it proves the importance of the genre in American storytelling and indicates that the World War II battle combat film, especially in its infantry form, will be with us for a long time to come. "Nobody dies."

The four films discussed above demonstrate the second wave. Influenced by documentaries, by talented individual filmmakers, and by the first powerful films of the genre from 1943, these films reflect a realism that is still based on the war itself, but that has taken on an increasingly distanced presentation. Watching these films, one can see the story of World War II turning into legend and myth. Self-consciousness is now present, but *without* violating the realistic nature of the medium and of the historical truth of the material. This is achieved through the skillful manipulation of the medium itself.

What these four films do is "take an attitude." It is a subtle attitude, and should not be confused with the overt propagandizing that is still present in *Objective Burma* (but that has more or less disappeared in the other three films). It is the subtlety of cinema itself, in which technique makes comment. As *Bataan* placed the tools of cinema at the service of its message and story, these films use those same tools to enhance those things and to translate them into visual terms. Things that were previously spelled out now appear on the screen in ways that allow us to "write" them in our own heads. Recognizing them and "reading" them both proves the genre and reinforces it. The genre ceases to be just plot and characters, and takes on the visual power to *represent* for viewers in a wider range of meaning. Without such a wave, it is possible the films of 1942 and 1943 would not have endured to become a genre. All four films employ cutting, composition, camera movement, lighting and cinematic narrative structure to achieve this, but each demonstrates its own particular way of achieving the second wave attitude:

1. TECHNIQUE: *Objective Burma.* The important generic concept of a mixed group of types is presented less through dialogue and narrative event and more through the use of cinematic technique. It is camera movement, composition, cutting, and lighting that not only show the

group's differences in age and type, but also unify the group for the viewer. Whereas before we *listened* to the expression of the group as a democratic force, we now *see* it as a concept. Since we have now learned the generic convention of the group, we can supply dialogue, narrative meaning, and definition for ourselves as we watch the camera present the differing people and weave them into a group. Similarly, A *Walk in the Sun* will show the feelings a man about to go into combat has instead of having him speak of them.

2. NARRATION: *The Story of G.I. Joe.* The narration or voiceover commentary of the legendary war correspondent, Ernie Pyle, himself a World War II casualty, reinforces the treatment of the American common fighting man as a legendary figure. The voice, which calmly and in a low key manner talks of the matter-of-fact bravery of the infantry men, is a distancing device that makes us consider the historical worth of the men at the same time as we are watching their deeds.

There is a distinct difference between this voiceover and *Guadalcanal Diary*, which is also a narration by a war correspondent/observer. The narrator of *Guadalcanal Diary* is a rather nameless creature, presumably the author of the original book, Richard Tregaskis, or the character of the "war correspondent" in the film itself. The voiceover appears and disappears in no logical pattern, and the character himself follows suit. Ernie Pyle, however, is always present in *The Story of G.I. Joe.* He is centrally involved in events. The voiceover is consistent and constant. It offers commentary, but most importantly, it offers the commentary of a distanced attitude. Its view is "the view of history." Tregaskis celebrates event. Pyle celebrates attitude.

3. ABSTRACTION: *They Were Expendable.* The war of this film is deeply felt, and yet it is hardly there physically. It is an abstracted war. Although the men of *They Were Expendable* are in the presence of a combat situation for most of the film's running time, they fight only three brief battles. The treatment of World War II as a situation in which no real victory is possible—defeat and death are its rewards—marks the film as anticipatory of the long-range view of the war. The reduction of the actual amount of physical combat and its replacement by deeper concerns also indicates a postwar sensibility.

4. STYLIZATION: A *Walk in the Sun* seeks to create the new myth of the war by demythologizing its activities. Instead of seeing the events as glamorous, we will learn about the "real" war, one of waiting and no real information for the fighting man. It was just a little "walk in the sun"—taken by ordinary guys for a country made up of other ordinary guys. This movie anticipates the return of *truth* in the sense that it was not brave or glorious—it was just a little walk in the sun.

If all the combat films, first and second waves together, had been about generals and victories, we might have seen the last of them after 1946. But they were about ordinary men and defeat, things that would still be with us when the war was over. Emphasizing despair and death, madness and loss, and with a sense that half of ourselves will die no matter what we do, these four films mark the high point and the end point of the combat films released during the days of World War II itself. It is a striking thing. If our films had been happy, or optimistic, or proud, perhaps the genre could not have lived. It may be here that we find the reasons we wanted more of it, as we moved into an America of Korea, assassination, and Vietnam.

Period of Respite. February 1, 1946– November 1, 1949.

During these years, not a single major film that might be defined as the World War II combat genre opened in New York City, with the exception of *Fighter Squadron* on November 20, 1948. It was an air corps film, directed by that old warhorse of the action/adventure film, Raoul Walsh. With a glamorous name, it featured dramatic actual combat footage, which was presumably its *raison d'être*. That footage is exciting, and it does a great deal to make an otherwise rather tiresome film watchable today. It also represents the first rudimentary coopting of reality into the service of keeping the genre alive. It is a harbinger.

Fighter Squadron[11] illustrates what could happen in filmmaking in the old days. Get a topical subject of interest, a capable experienced director, some first-rate documentary footage, and paste together a story of sorts to carry it along. The script is so referential to such combat films as *Dawn Patrol*, *Eagle Squadron*, and *Flying Tigers* that it's virtually nonexistent. Its own unique contribution is a subplot involving an enterprising sergeant who makes his way around England as a lover, posing as "Sergeant Kinsey" and using a cat to get off the base and into town. (This cat updates the old mascot motif of the war years.)

Fighter Squadron is based in genre. It contains the hero, the representative group, the dedication to duty, the pressures of command, and the conflict between individual initiative and following orders, that were established earlier. Its hero, in a return of the rule-breaking glamor boy heroes of the 1930s, is a former Flying Tiger, played by Edmund O'Brien.[12] He has left the Orient and the maverick Tigers to fly fighter planes over Germany and Europe, but he wears his famous Flying Tiger jacket and still follows the pattern of individual glory that Tigers allowed. He is the jaunty air man who has the guts to "go up in a crate like that." After crashing his plane and walking away from it, he stylishly calls out, "Notify the taxpayers to get me another." The *Dawn Patrol* conflict is established when this flamboyant loner is promoted to a command position and has to face the implications of sending men into danger and death. His life then becomes concerned with the *tactics* of war—should pilots be allowed to dump their extra fuel tanks for explosive purposes, or to go in low to bomb specific targets, or to have the freedom to attempt ground rescues of each other if shot down.

Fighter Squadron is a weak film, except for its magnificent usage of actual combat footage. It might have been better as documentary. (In fact, it *was* better as a documentary, Wyler's celebrated *Memphis Belle*, even though *Memphis Belle* was about bombers and *Fighter Squadron* is about fighter escort planes and political struggle behind the scenes.) The makers of *Fighter Squadron* obviously counted on its dramatic combat footage to carry the film. What is significant is that the story they hung that footage on was set up in the traditional "brave men of the skies" format. Its main point, that of the need for fearless, daring men to break rules, is not fully developed. One could continue to bend *Fighter Squadron* to claim for it certain meaningful generic tendencies but, in fact, it is a minor film, choppily written, but well paced by the skill of Raoul Walsh. It does not do much except test the waters for the next wave of combat films. Perhaps that's why it stands alone in the Period of Respite, waiting for the infantry films to inspire the new wave of combat films.

Third Wave. November 1, 1949–December 31, 1959
(Creation of Filmed Reality Based on Earlier Films and History, with Conscious Use of Genre)

After almost three full years of avoiding the subject of World War II combat, American films began to reexplore the subject. We had won the war. Now we could be proud of it. The reexploration process would help us understand what happened, to whom it happened, and how it happened, and it would also help us understand how it changed and affected us, and to justify what we did during those years. The subject could now be presented for earned national pride, understanding, and justification—not just propaganda. We could *resolve* the war, finish it off once and for all. This was the initial task of the wave, which is interrupted and influenced by the Korean War.

The visual power and beauty of the second wave, manifested in a skilled manipulation of cinematic form, is sometimes present and sometimes not present in the third wave. It appears as if the function of the second wave was indeed to translate the genre into visual shorthand, and ensure that audiences could "read" it without explanation. Once this was accomplished, films could continue that representative method of cinematic presentation or return to the old, more specifically spelled out method, or combine the two.

In this decade, it became clear that the genre was here to stay. Many films were made, and they all conformed to the basic definition that was generated during the war years themselves. Even when the Korean conflict broke out, interrupting the flow, World War II genre films continued to be made, and the films about the new Korean situation followed the same basic generic format despite some appropriate adjustments and the hint of discontent at having to fight another war so soon. The important thing about the third wave is that all its films mix genre and reality.

In screening the films of this decade, the following observations can be made:

- The basic definition remains intact.
- The meanings of the basic definition are adjusted to incorporate the current concerns of the times, such as racial tension, or the threat of Communism. (This is proof of genre: the primary characteristics can be used for new meaning.)
- In many cases, the narrative is expanded to add onto the combat story various subplots which are not necessarily combat stories.

This is what genre is, and how it functions. After it is defined, its characteristics can remain the same and take on new meanings. If the narrative is expanded, the film either keeps the noncombat portion of the story directly related to the combat portion, or it becomes a unit of unrelated episodes in which a miniature combat film is one of the episodes. This is rather like a return to the prior history format, except that, once the combat genre is established, it is too powerful a unit to go unrecognized. As the evolutionary process takes place, this will be explained further. There are additional variations and problems to be discussed also, but for now one wave at a time.

The most important aspect of these films, especially those in the first half of the decade, is that they seem to provide a ritual in which the American audience can watch the war together, celebrate its satisfactory completion, reenact its combat, and come together in their understanding of it. To do this, the films re-create earlier films more than reality, even though they provide real historical reference points.

How does this work?

The public who stayed at home saw the war through film. Those who fought saw it live. After the war, the films that presented the war faced an audience of those who saw reality as well as those who saw war films and accepted them as reality. (This is not to deny that soldiers overseas also saw war films.) This decade of film had to unite the two halves of the audience. Those who fought overseas had to re-fight it through war films in order to share the experience of the home front. These films united the experience of war for those who fought it and those who did not. From this point onward, both groups would share the same combat experience—that of the World War II combat film.

To gain recognition and acceptance, these films relied on earlier films to reach the public. The war was now war movies. The films became a faithful re-creation of a creation. This displacement of fact of history with legend is well known to historians in all fields. In film, we can *see* it happen.

I am not at all suggesting here that men who actually fought World War II denied their memories and readily replaced them with pictures of John Wayne gallantly jumping from an LST yelling "Lock and load!" I am suggesting that some people had only the images of John Wayne and whatever films or pictures they saw. Their images of the war were just that—images of the war. The part of the audience that was in actual combat had true memories of how the war looked. They added to these the images that the other half of the audience had been given, by seeing old films (the same ones seen originally by the home front, now replayed on television), or by seeing the new movies released about the experience. The plain truth is that mental images are memories. As the years go by, if they fade, they are gone. If they become altered by dimming years, they will remain altered. The film images, however, always remain exactly as they were. They remain with us and can be reseen. It becomes possible for the film images to replace the real images even for those who were in combat.

Certainly for the audience that never saw reality, the filmed images have to function as such. The films must tell the new mixed audience the old familiar stories, but not without referring to the reality that those who were in the war can recognize. It is remarkable to see how these films do this. On the one hand, they present the hero, group, and objective configurations of the basic definition, replete with all the familiar plot devices. On the other, they are firmly linked to some part of the real war that would be known to the general audience. For instance, *Fighter Squadron* used documentary footage from a factually accurate situation that already had been documented on films and shown to American audiences in William Wyler's *Memphis Belle*. *Battleground* is about the "Battered Bastards of Bastogne," and *Sands of Iwo Jima* tells the story of the Marine battles of the Pacific, not just Iwo Jima, but also Tarawa. *Operation Pacific* re-creates the Howard Gilmore incident.

This link to true events is not the only factor which separates these films totally from the second wave. They also bring the war down-to-earth, removing the "why we fight" propaganda of the war years and treating those who fought it like fallible human beings who are rising to the occasion out of the instincts of survival.

Fiction met fact, and unification was complete, on film and in the audience. Taking some of these films as examples, one by one, illustrates how this third wave works. What happens to the genre during this decade can be detailed without going into endless repetition about plot and character and how elements are repeated. Once the basic definition is in place, it appears and reappears, and this can be assumed in discussion.

The first true critical and commercial successes that brought the war back, up close, in depth, and down to basic generic references, are inevitably in the patrol format: *Battleground* and *Sands of Iwo Jima*. These are followed by many other films, examples of which will be described in detail: the submarine movie (*Operation Pacific*), Korean movies (*Steel Helmet, Fixed Bayonets*), strange mixes of film and truth such as war hero Audie Murphy's story (*To Hell and Back*), starring none other than Audie Murphy, and examples of World War II combat during Korea (*Frogmen*). This complex third wave made up a decade of great popularity for combat films.

Battleground

Battleground (November 12, 1949) is perhaps the *Bataan* of this wave. It is the key film not only because of its pure combat presentation, but also by virtue of being both a huge critical and commercial success. *Battleground* begins and ends in combat, and is a true celebration of the ordinary infantry man who walks through the snow and mud of war on his own feet. *Sands of Iwo Jima* (December 31,1949) celebrates the marines in a similar manner.

Battleground's cast list includes, in addition to its impressive list of star names, "the original 'Screaming Eagles' of the 101st Airborne Division, who play themselves." As the credits unfold, each actor's character name is given: "Van Johnson as Holley, Ricardo Montalban as Roderiguez, George Murphy as 'Pop' Stazak." These character names prove genre is back—not only back, but also fixed. The announcement of the group proves it. However, as the credits tell us, these characters are now side-by-side with the real Screaming Eagles. Their unit is very specifically located in actual combat forces: I Company, 3d Platoon, 2d Squad. Against the stark images of combat in a cold winter war, a quotation from a German general, Henrich von Luttwitz, of the 47th Panzer Corps is printed: "Bastogne must be taken. Otherwise it will remain an abscess on our lines of communication. We must clean out Bastogne, and then march on." After this opening title, an audience can read "This story is about, and dedicated to, those Americans who met General Henrich von Luttwitz and his 47 Panzer Corps and earned for themselves the honored and immortal name—

Battered Bastards of Bastogne."
The film opens "at a US Army Camp somewhere in France, December, 1944." In other words, on a dark place, in a dark time, before an even darker day of battle. Four or five years had passed since the end of the war. The makers of *Battleground*, realizing that the audience now contained veterans, gave it a kind of tough honesty and grittiness not seen before, even in "realistic" films. Throughout the film there is

an awareness of the actual conditions of combat life, and a masked reference to some of the language used in battle: "Leave your cots and grab your socks," an inspired paraphrase, is bawled out early on by a tough sergeant. When propanganda leaflets are dropped by the Germans (a variation of the Tokyo Rose radio message), I can well remember how the veterans in the audience in my small home-town theater laughed and laughed when "Pop" slowly and carefully gathered up the leaflets and disappeared into the woods, while the civilian audience tried to puzzle it out. "Toilet paper!" one cried out, and the mystery was solved. With the sound of a cadence rhyme and the sight of marching men, a viewer first meets the characters of the film, as the camera moves into camp. There's a true exhilaration in seeing them march and sing out their chant: "Jody's got something you ain't got, it's been so long I nearly forgot . . . Sound off . . . one, two, three, four, one, two . . three, four!" (A chant that became a hit song!)

The men of *Battleground* are all heroes, not only in history but also in the plot. The hero of heroes is Van Johnson, who plays a soldier who has been wounded before the film begins, and has returned to rejoin his platoon. His character is that of the scrounger, a character who will become increasingly important in the genre as it evolves.

This hero is a likeable guy, well-played by Johnson, one of the most popular actors of the 1940s (and, ironically, a young man who came to stardom because he was 4-F during the war). However, it is very clear that this man is not a "noble hero." A realist, he grabs what he can for himself out of the situation whenever possible, whether it's a willing French girl (Denise Darcel) or a half dozen eggs (from an unwilling chicken). "Oh, no!" is his battle cry, the cry of the common man in response to specific orders and to the general situation. Yet he goes forward, endures, and survives. At one point, he demonstrates cowardice and tries to run away, in a parallel to events from *Red Badge of Courage*. His flight is, as was true in the Stephen Crane novel, mistaken as a brave attack and he ends up looking heroic. As a result of this act of cowardice, his platoon wins the skirmish. Later, the greenhorn who yelled, "I'm with you, Holley," to Johnson, and turned him around, admits he thought Holley was running away and was going to join him. A misunderstanding by both brought about an act of true courage. This results in the film's explanation of heroism. "Things just happen. Afterwards you try to figure it out."

The Johnson character is not a total break with the heroes of previous war films, either World War II or World War I, but he is an altered variation. The elements that are stressed are his cynicism, his ordinariness, his tough humor, and resilience. Finally, his bravery emerges, but not in a glorious, romantic vein. Instead, it is demonstrated that ordinary American men like Johnson have what it takes to fight and win a war because of those very qualities—humor, resilience, and practicality.

The group that surrounds Johnson in his platoon are the usual generic collection: Walloway, the football player; the "big brain intellectual" who runs a newspaper back home; "Pop" the arthritic older man whose wife is too sick to take care of the kids, and who awaits, without luck, his dependency discharge; "Lil Abner," the mountainman who has no galoshes of his own because his feet are too big ("That's for sure," he keeps intoning, "That's for dang sure"); Kip, a man with false teeth who is looking for a way to get out of combat and whose cynicism is pessimistic and destructive, the opposite of the hero's ("They don't care," he says. "Nobody cares"); the inevitable minority figure who must die, a Mexican, played by Ricardo Montalban; the typical tough sergeant, James Whitmore; and the young greenhorn, Marshall Thompson, whose initiation into the group and into combat leads an audience through the film. The people in this group are from Illinois, Kansas, California, Maryland, and Ohio, but, to prove its realistic nature, no Brooklyn!

The usual relationships emerge—a father–son friendship between "Pop" and the Mexican, a hero–sidekick friendship between Holley and the young recruit, and a hostile one between the intellectual and the hillbilly. The objective of this group is simply survival. Their film follows the "last stand" format of patrol films, in which they are surrounded and must hold on.

The look of *Battleground* is real. Even the weather seems authentic. At first they are encased in fog, and then the snow, beautiful to see, softly falling, and wet, settles over them, entrapping them. Montalban, the Mexican, has never seen snow, and is delighted, playing, sliding, whooping. Later, he is wounded, and his comrades hide him under a disabled jeep, covering his hiding place with snow so the Germans will not find him. When they are finally able to return for him, he lies frozen in his playground. (Do not play with battle terrain, or assume

Van Johnson and Ricardo Montalban in Battleground

it is as it would be in peacetime, is the axiom, demonstrated once again. The price of enjoyment of nature is death.) It is still a part of generic convention that one cannot relax in combat. Moments of repose are not moments of complete relaxation. A state of total combat exists, and to assume the world one is in is the world of nature is an error that will destroy. One is in the world of combat, a man-made thing, or more specifically, in the world of the combat film where rules of death operate confidently and surely.

Safety lies in being a typical American, with a typical American's knowledge of popular culture. When Germans disguise themselves as Americans and patrol the area, Americans can identify one another as real only through questions about baseball, movies, and comics. "What's a Texas Leaguer? . . . Who's Betty Grable going out with? . . .

Who's the Dragon Lady?" These are the secrets of safety. If you don't know your popular culture, you are not a true American. *Red Dawn* (1984) plays off this by having the high school challenger—"what's the capital of Texas?"—not know the answer herself. "You've seen too many movies," says another character, evaluating her method.

One difference between this film and those which came earlier can be seen reflected in the attitude toward the young. In *Battleground*, beside a Christmas tree bearing the words MERRY CHRISTMAS, 1944, two young recruits stand and talk. They are a tougher, sassier, smarter kind of beardless youth than those of World War I. Those earlier films use the characters to illustrate the tragic sacrifice of a generation of youth as represented by that war. This film is on the side of survival, since it is aimed at an audience of survivers. No beardless youth dies here. On the contrary, Marshall Thompson, who represents the type, learns to survive by studying the ultimate in survivors, the character played by Van Johnson.

A propaganda message is contained in *Battleground*, but it is a message to apply to the late 1940s. It is a message about Russia, for the new cold war. The Chaplain says, "As the years go by, a lot of people are going to forget, but you won't. Don't let anybody tell you you were a sucker to fight in a war against *Facism*. Let us each pray in his own way to our own God." When the fog finally lifts, and the beleaguered men see their own shadows and know they can be rescued by an air drop of supplies and ammunition, a montage of what might be called *war* follows—real newsreel footage of combat. It's like an instant visual replay of everything we all—veterans and nonveterans together—saw from 1942 through 1945. "They shall mount up with wings of eagles. They shall run and not be weary," recites Marshall Thompson, and they move forward into their own war, and are seen killing, running and winning, their personal images superimposed over a general image of total war. This is like instant replay, and it shows how a film like *Battleground* fulfills the reconciliation that is the mark of the Third Wave by bringing together the viewing audience who saw the first combat movies on the home front, and those veterans who may or may not have seen the genre, but certainly saw the real events.

At the end of *Battleground*, their platoon, snatching a weary rest by the road side, is told once again to fall in. ("Oh, no!") They automatically face toward battle, but are told, "About face" and are headed home. As they move out, aching and weary, a new bunch, green and eager, march toward them, moving up to the front. "Do you want these new guys to think you're a bunch of WACS?" bawls their old sergeant, and slowly they pull themselves together. One throws down his cigarette. One transfers his rifle to the proper shoulder, even though its badly wounded. The old sergeant starts moving on the stumps of his frostbitten feet, and even Kip puts in his teeth. They shape up and pull together, beginning their Jody chant:

"You won't get home till the end of the war,
In nineteen hundred and seventy-four."

It's a great moment; and in the tradition of the combat film, a review of all the faces of the group, with the name of the actor and his character name underneath, appears after THE END shows up on the screen. *Battleground* was a pure combat movie that celebrated, finally with the full audience, the fact that we won the war and could dare to be proud of it. It healed, united, and entertained.

Sands of Iwo Jima

This film also makes full use of the audience's knowledge of the events of World War II, as well as of the films about World War II. It also uses real veterans in the cast. "And with the three living survivors of the historic flag raising at Mount Suribachi," say the cast credits— a list which includes the tragic Pfc. Ira Hayes, whose life would later be made into a less glorious story, *The Outsider* (1961). The film opens with the traditional dedication, "To the United States Marine Corps, whose exploits and valor have left a lasting impression on the world and in the hearts of their countrymen. Appreciation is gratefully acknowledged for their assistance and participation which made this picture possible." With the Marine Hymn sung over the credits, and the "Semper Fidelis" insignia behind the dedication, the film announces itself as a tribute to the Marine Corps. As if this were not enough, it opens with a spoken narration: "This is the story of a squad of Marines—a rifle squad . . . We were at Guadalcanal. When that island was declared secure, we were pulled out for . . . retraining . . . in New Zealand." Song, insignia, printed dedication, and narrated reference—an overkill introduction that simultaneously combines the variation of insignia, image reference to reality, and narrated created event. Reference to reality and to movie reality, in fact, is carried further when a character remarks "If he comes out of the war alive," referring to a brave soldier, "I'm going to make him a movie star." This is a reference to Audie Murphy, who had by this time "come out of the war" as its most decorated hero and who was now indeed becoming a big-time movie star.

John Wayne plays Sergeant Stryker, a man "who's got the regulations tatooed on his back." He is the traditional tough-guy top sergeant seen from the earlier films. Other familiar references include:

- Two young brothers who fight with one another constantly, like Quirt and Flagg.
- The typical iconography of the Marine Corps and of battle.
- The training camp-into-combat plot structure.
- The sense that the men will be treated harshly and pushed beyond their capacities in training, but that it will be for their own ultimate good, to prepare them for the rigors of combat.
- Fist fight between an officer and one of his men, later denied by both (Wayne and Forrest Tucker).
- Recognizable events, such as mail call.
- Recognizable characters, such as an ex-fighter, a Smithville, Tennessee mountain type, a young Jewish boy who speaks a Yiddish prayer before dying.
- Re-creation of actual historical combat (Tarawa and Iwo Jima), with some newsreel footage used.
- Reference to the enemy in scurrilous terms ("lemon-colored characters").

Sands of Iwo Jima is firmly based on the first-wave combat films. It mixes elements from *Bataan, Wake Island, Guadalcanal Diary*, and others. However, the story is expanded to include issues that are relevant to the audiences of 1949. Since the war has been resolved, the storyline is expanded to contain a love story and wedding (this adds appeal to those in the audience who might not have wanted to see a John Wayne combat picture); a father–son conflict, represented by Wayne and John Agar, whose father was Wayne's former C.O.; and a long sequence involving the men and their liberty in town. All these stories, however, are directly linked to a resolution in combat, during which the men will understand Wayne's behavior on liberty; Wayne and Agar will be

reconciled; Agar will finally come to understand his father; and the
men will know their loving families are worth fighting for.

Here a film sets out to present a *total* World War II for a set of
characters, the traditional combat group. Like *A Walk in the Sun*, it is
as if all those characters from all those films were put together for the
audience, and their experience of training and moving into combat
through a particularly tough series of real combats (Tarawa and Iwo
Jima) are made whole and coherent for the viewer.

In combat, the unit both makes a last stand and becomes an advancing patrol, so we get both types of combat experience. On Tarawa,
they are told to dig in and hold their position no matter what. As they
sit trapped in their foxholes during the long nights (on the fourth day,
Tarawa is declared secure), they hear a desperate voice calling Stryker's
name. Stryker refuses to go out, or to allow any man to go out, as he
knows to reveal their position or the size of their force is to lose the
battle. An intense close up of Wayne's sweating, weeping face shows
only the audience the price he pays for this dedication to duty. On Iwo
Jima, they advance and attack, delivering a realistic set of purely American speeches about their situation, the litany of the common man:

"Just like Brooklyn!"

"This is the worst soil I ever saw. What do we want with it? Gettin'
shot for this!"

"That's war, boy, tradin' real estate for men."

John Wayne represents officially the "forever and ever" concept of
the tough sergeant, the loner who puts duty before personal life and
who is misunderstood and ostracized by his men. He is hard on them
because he alone knows what lies ahead for them. "Saddle up, saddle
up" he bellows at them, neatly connecting the combat genre to his
more familiar guise of Western hero, and a montage swiftly passes by
the viewer, held together with Wayne's bellowing face superimposed
over specific training events. Wayne has a conflict with Agar, because
Agar had the father Wayne dreamed of having, but Agar embarrassed
his father, because he had "no guts. . . . I'm a civilian, not a Marine."
Ironically, Wayne then becomes the father that Agar needs to become
a man. This does not constitute displacement of the real father, since
Wayne himself was created by that same father in military terms, if not
biological ones. Agar, it is indicated, will go on to become "corps
father" to the younger men he will lead. Thus the "family" of the
Corps is propagated.

Before they go to Iwo Jima, Agar tells Wayne that his newborn son will not be raised to be tough. "Instead I'll try to make him intelligent. Instead of a Marine Corps emblem, I'll give him a set of Shakespeare." On Iwo Jima, however, he comes to understand why men like his father and Wayne are needed, and why making him tough was necessary, at least for war, if not for peace. This leads an audience to understand the postwar message: to avoid this kind of macho mindlessness, they must change the world and prevent war. Like *Battleground*, it contains the new realism, the old conventions, *and* a postwar message—this one about the importance of family life. Wayne himself has a son from whom he is estranged, having divorced the mother under unpleasant circumstances. His letter to his son, read by the men after his death, reveals his own uncertainty and sense of failure.

"Dear Son,

I guess none of my letters have reached you, but I thought I'd better try again because I have the feeling that this may be the last time I can write you. For a long time, I've wanted to tell you many things. Now that you're a big boy, I will. If we could have been together even for a little while, I could have explained many things much better than writing. You've got to take care of your mother and love her and make her happy. Never hurt her or anyone as I did. Always do what your heart tells you is right. Maybe someone will write you someday and tell you about me. I want you to be like me in some things, but not like me in others because when you grow older and get to know more about me, you'll see that I've been a failure in many ways. This isn't what I wanted. Things just turned out that way. If there was only more time, I'd . . . "

"Guess he never finished it," observes one of the men, but it is for the audience to finish it.

It is no doubt intended as a peacetime message, all about responsibility for the future. The sober faces of the patrol, seen in close-up, dirt-streaked and grimy, pained by death, speak of the misery of war. Yet, within seconds, the American flag goes up on Iwo in triumph. The men see it and are stirred. The Marine Hymn breaks out on the soundtrack . . . and "saddle up . . . saddle up . . . let's get back in the war" is heard on the track. Within no time, America had done just that, in Korea.

The combat sequences from *Sands of Iwo Jima* are superbly done, full of tension, explosion, and screamed Marine jargon: "Lock and load!" "Hit the beach!" "Saddle up!" As the men crawl desperately up the volcanic beach, and across Iwo Jima under heavy fire, the presentation of combat is intercut with characterization. A young boy from Cedar Rapids, Iowa, dies with a copy of *Our Hearts Were Young and Gay* in his pocket. One of the two brothers who have fought and scrapped and argued through the entire film runs back to save the other one, who has been wounded. And then they continue arguing. Another soldier, tired and weary, says philosopically, "I'll get a good night's sleep tonight" and then dies. The narration indicates that three days and three nights pass and "we'd barely reached the foot of Suribachi, which is where we were the first night."

Approximately twenty minutes of intense combat are presented, involving hand-to-hand fighting, grenades, shelling, tanks, flamethrowers, the works! Finally, the island is taken. The men are ordered to set up the flag, and a flag is given to Stryker. They sit down to rest and talk among themselves, the men reconciled and united with Stryker; like him, they now understand the need for the cruel training he put them through. They are a group: men in combat. Agar apologizes to Wayne, and Wayne tells the younger man not to listen to the little voice inside that says he may die. Wayne says he himself never hears that voice.

"I never felt so good in my life," says Wayne. "How about a cigarette?" Relaxed and smiling, he reaches for a cigarette and is shot. The suddenness, the unexpectedness of his death, reminiscent of the peaceful moment in which the boy reaches for the butterfly in *All Quiet on the Western Front*, is one of the most shocking and heartbreaking moments in all the combat films. His death is sudden, unexpected, and thus tragic. He is gone! Just when the battle is won! And he's *John Wayne!*

The death of John Wayne helps to mark the film's departure from the earlier wave of combat films. Obviously, Robert Taylor (and everyone else) died at the end of *Bataan*, as did Robert Mitchum at the end of *Story of G.I. Joe*. The death and sacrifice of the leader is integral to the genre, but the death of John Wayne at the moment of climactic victory is quite a different matter and quite a different statement. Robert Taylor is not John Wayne. Even Robert Mitchum is not John Wayne, although he would come close later in his career. When *Story of G.I. Joe* was released, however, he was a little-known beginner, without the persona he later accumulated. John Wayne's persona was already established by the time of *Sands of Iwo Jima*, and it very clearly was a persona

Sands of Iwo Jima, *with John Wayne alive and victorious*

that did not get shot at the moment of triumph. In fact, John Wayne's persona is clearly that of "John Wayne never dies." Wayne, of course, *did* get killed in films: in addition to Sands of Iwo Jima, he died violently in *Reap the Wild Wind, Wake of the Red Witch, The Cowboys, The Shootist,* and *The Alamo.* But nowhere did he die more unexpectedly and inexplicably than in *Sands of Iwo Jima.*

John Wayne is more closely associated with the World War II combat film than possibly any other actor, and it is probably in *Sands of Iwo Jima* (for which he was nominated as Best Actor by the Motion Picture Academy) that this association really solidifies. Clearly, the film revolves around him. Whether bawling out orders or teaching an inept recruit how to handle a bayonet by dancing with him, Wayne is at the center of all action *and* all meaning. A consideration of the character played by Wayne reveals the way in which *Sands of Iwo Jima* reflects its

Sands of Iwo Jima, *with John Wayne, moments later*

evolutionary wave. Despite uninformed attitudes about Wayne's typical
characterizations, he actually plays a three-dimensional character, not
only here but in many of his films. His character in *Sands* parallels the
film's new attitude toward the war. Like the war, Wayne is a necessary
evil. Once again we hear repeated the "we didn't start it, but we have
to fight it" rationale. Wayne is tough, uncompromising, but also hon-
orable and worthy of respect. Ultimately, he is tragic. His personal life
is lonely, disoriented, and his drunken reeling through the streets on
liberty in town is observed with disgust by his men. His personal
problems are as much a part of the film as the combat sequences, and
the suggestion is being made that men like Wayne's Sergeant Stryker
are needed when they are needed, but that they are not needed for
peacetime, and peacetime is now. Furthermore, what we want to strive
for is continual peace, which means a rejection of the Sergeant Strykers
of the world. Ironically, Stryker's letter to his son indicates he would

agree with that view. Compared with many war heroes of these earlier films, this is a sad and pathetic character.

The ultimate demonstration of this is in the random death Stryker suffers. It is an accidental death, not one which is heroic and wins battles. The battle is, in fact, over, and such a death seems initially more tragic than the meaningful sacrifice of combat death. Yet his death unifies his group into an even better family, with a new "father figure," the more tender and sympathetic John Agar. The implication is that Agar is the father we will need for the postwar age, one who could give his sons Shakespeare instead of the Marine manual.

In this sense, we must have a film in which we kill John Wayne, and *Sands of Iwo Jima* is that film. By killing him, we rid ourselves of the war and of wartime attitudes, even though we will still need our stories about it and must respect those who died for us in battle. Now Stryker's dead and it's over—we can go on, more mature and ready for peacetime. This undercurrent of the entire film is duly reflected in the important presence in it of women and of subplots involving women and family structures. Those who think of John Wayne and of all war films as a one-sided affair should see the dark and tragic *Sands of Iwo Jima*, a war film with a subtext which speaks against war and against Sgt. Stryker—speaks eloquently, and with compassion.

Battleground and *Sands of Iwo Jima* are films that are proud of their men and the situation. They tell their stories as if it were still 1943, except for the new attitudes of realism. This realism is not political, and it does not seek to be the realism of the horror of war, its death and destruction. It is the realism of newsreel footage and actual veterans in the cast. It is the realism of the small thing that makes the veteran recognize and remember his situation. No hot food. Constant moving about, just after you dug your foxhole. Sitting in rain and snow. Griping among yourselves. Having to go on, no matter what. And underneath it all, the "nobody dies" from *A Walk in the Sun* has been changed to "nobody cares," the common man's sense of his role in the war. Yet the films are celebratory. We won. We survived.

Thus it can be seen how these new films have it both ways for the audience. They keep the traditional generic combat film configurations in all aspects, but they build in little events and truths from the daily experience of war, and they ground the two things in real battles. Genre will be stronger than truth. It will use truth, take it in, incorporate it. This is how a genre stays alive.

Operation Pacific

Technically, the first Navy film of the Third Wave was *Task Force* (October 1, 1949). Like *Fighter Squadron*,[13] it incorporated real battle footage of World War II into its story, but it really was more of an epic history of the United States Navy from 1921 onward than it was World War II combat film. Gary Cooper plays Jonathan L. Scott, who, on the eve of his retirement, thinks back over his years in service. This includes his attempt to prove the importance of carrier-launched aircraft, his marriage to the widow of a flying friend, his service in Panama, his duty on the U.S.S. *Saratoga*, which he guided back to America after its near-destruction at the battle of Okinawa, and his experience on the *Yorktown* at the Battle of Midway. Although it contains combat, it is a story that covers many years both before and after the war.

More than *Task Force*, *Operation Pacific* (February 3, 1951) is an early example of the third wave film of true navy combat. Although it, too, spends time on shore with a romantic entanglement involving a divorced couple (John Wayne and Patricia Neal), it is primarily a story of submarine warfare in World War II.

Operation Pacific begins with a dedication "to the silent service." It establishes itself as a combat film by beginning in war (the time is early 1942) with John Wayne rescuing a group of nuns and children (including a newborn baby) from an island shortly after the attack on Pearl Harbor. (Nuns and children! Shades of *Stand by for Action!*) On shore, Wayne must act as a father figure to his crew, who are constantly fighting and getting into trouble. Since the film has opened with an image of him running to safety carring a baby in his arms, this film illustrates the family or domestic context built into the Navy branch of the World War II combat film. His submarine is his home, and his crew are his family. This leaves no room in his life for a home on shore, or a shoreline family. This has led to his divorce. The plot presents a typical postwar Navy narrative structure: one half devoted to a marital crisis, and one half devoted to true combat.

There is plenty of combat. Wayne's submarine, commanded by Ward Bond, has nothing but trouble. *Operation Pacific*, like other third wave films, finds its own particular way to incorporate reality into its presentation. First of all, it contains a plot device which is a reference to the true historical fact of submarines having trouble with dud torpedoes during the early years of the war. Secondly, it refers in dialogue to a great deal of Naval history—past heroes like Admiral Dewey, ships like the *Merrimac*, sub disasters like the men trapped under water in the *Squalus*, and to the Naval Academy, its dances and football games. Thirdly, it dramatically reenacts the Howard Gilmore incident in detail. In this film, a decoy Japanese freighter lures the sub up top, and machine guns the commander, Ward Bond, in the Gilmore surrogate role. "Take her down! Take her down!" cries Bond, followed by an effective presentation of the scrambling men and their desperate effort to close the hatches during the dive.

Operation Pacific has another little "real" reference, a kind of Holly-wood in-joke that has to be seen as postwar expansion. When their sub comes alongside another in mid-ocean, the two surface to exchange movies. Wayne's sub has only "a thing called *George Washington Slept Here*" which they are willing to exchange "along with six points." The other sub has "a submarine movie—it's really exciting." The title is never referred to aloud, but later we see the crew of the submarine clearly watching a 16mm print of Cary Grant in *Destination Tokyo*. As they watch, one man falls asleep and one walks out. When asked how he liked the picture, he replies, "Oh, all right, I guess. The things those Hollywood guys can do with a submarine!" To see *Destination Tokyo* and remember its depth charge attacks, its torpedoes, and its crises among the crew, being shown within *Operation Pacific*, with its depth charge attacks and its dud torpedoes, is to see genre being assembled right before your eyes. *Operation Pacific* seems to say it is real, unlike *Destination Tokyo*, and it uses the earlier film to make a conscious point. Yet *Operation Pacific* not only refers to that same Cary Grant film, but it also seems to refer to other combat movies, particularly *They Were Expendable*, when John Wayne once again delivers a hum-ble spoken eulogy for a dead comrade. Where the first one was "home is the sailor, home from the sea" this one is the last part of the Burial at Sea ritual, "and the sea shall give up her dead." They blend together for a viewer, who understands one from out of the other.

The Curious Case of Audie Murphy

In 1955 the merging of historical reality and filmed presentation of historical reality was solidified by the curious case of Audie Murphy. Murphy was officially listed as the most decorated soldier of World War

Audie Murphy in To Hell and Back

II. An authentic and celebrated war hero, he was credited with killing or capturing 240 German soldiers. He was awarded the Congressional Medal of Honor, along with 27 other medals, among them three Silver Stars, the Distinguished Service Cross, the Legion of Merit, A Bronze Star, three Purple Hearts, the Victory Medal, the European Theater Medal, the American Theater Medal, the French Legion of Honor, the Croix de Guerre, and, of course, the Good Conduct Medal. After the war, he became a movie actor, and until his death in 1971, he was a minor star of war movies and Westerns. *To Hell and Back* (September 23, 1955) was a reenactment (fictionalized) of his own World War II combat experience. The film is a curious mixture of what is presumably Murphy's recollection and actual experience, reenacted, and an amalgam of what a typical filmgoing audience would accept as "true" combat experience via generic story telling. For instance, the men surrounding Murphy on the troop ship as they head toward the African campaign are a typical representative group: a Native American, an immigrant with an accent, a wolfish lover who tells the other men many stories regarding "dames" (a direct cross reference to, among others, Dane Clark in *Destination Tokyo*), and a guy from Brooklyn whose mother was born in Italy.

The film's running time includes both events which are recognizable from the first and second waves and events which are recognizable as typically third wave, which adds stories with a wider appeal. For instance, in North Africa, the men visit a night club in which a beautiful girl sings, dances, and flirts with the men. This type of thing was generally omitted during earlier stages. (Maybe it was too threatening for the home girls during the war itself.) A strong sense that there is no uncertainty in the characters about the war prevails. The walk through Italy and the combat they experience is directly linked to the visual presentation of *A Walk in the Sun*, including a "voice of history" narration which intones: "War . . . to the foot soldier. . . . Why? He often doesn't know." When the men talk before battle, however, their concerns appear to be postwar concerns. In fact, the word "postwar" itself is used, an uncommon occurrence in the war years. "What are your postwar plans?" the men ask each other, seemingly confident that there will be such a thing.

To Hell and Back is an excellent example of the third wave's mixture of reality and filmed reality. As its plot unfolds, presumably telling us the story of real-life Hero Murphy's World War II combat experience (and undeniably doing so), the film passes through other films:

1. First, although Murphy gets sick and doesn't fight, the troops arrive in Casablanca to fight (*Sahara*).
2. Second, they arrive in Italy, and begin an advance, with an accompanying narration (*A Walk in the Sun*).

3. Next, they go to Monte Cassino in heavy rain (*The Story of G.I. Joe*).
4. Then, they make an attack on a farmhouse (back to A *Walk in the Sun*).

The incorporation of events from such films does not invalidate the film's accuracy in and of itself. The original films definitely were created out of real events. But bringing a true-life hero back from the war, making a movie actor out of him, and casting him as himself in his own story is a significant meshing for "those who fought" and "those who watched the fight on film as a narrative event." Murphy, it appears, is stepping into his own role to ennoble the stories we have seen by his very real and honest presence.[14] The stories will be retold, amalgamated, unified, and made true by his participation.

Hanging over *To Hell and Back*, based on Murphy's autobiography, is the spectre of *Sergeant York*, both film and real man. One cannot help but wonder if the specter of the man didn't hang over Murphy himself, who probably saw the film at an impressionable age. Just as *Sergeant York* presented the story of York's life in the mountains as a sharpshooting hellraiser who found religion, *To Hell and Back* presents the sober little story of Murphy's early life in Texas. He, too, is presented as a crack shot, but also as a hardworking boy who took over support of his mother and brothers and sisters out of necessity. After his mother's death, his younger siblings are sent to homes while he joins the marines. Pearl Harbor has taken place, so his country needs him, and, as a helpful neighbor says, it could become a lifetime career for him. (The real Audie Murphy found himself another career, of course.)

Watching *To Hell and Back*, one sees a sequence in which his patrol fords a river, and the action is set up very much like that of a Western film, a kind of reference to Murphy's movie career. Not only was he the star of John Huston's adaptation of Stephen Crane's archetypal Civil War battle story, *Red Badge of Courage* (1951), he had also made successful low-budget westerns such as *Kansas Raiders* (1951), *The Kid From Texas* (1950), *Sierra* (1950), and *Duel at Silver Creek* (1952). Murphy provides us with yet another link between the combat film and the Western, one that can be deeply felt when his patrol fords a river to prepare for combat. As in *The Story of G.I. Joe* and the church sequence, the visual link between the Western and the combat film is literally seen on screen. Murphy, the war hero who is also now a Western hero, constitutes as much proof of this affinity the two genres have as anything else. The most interesting connections are all visual ones, when an audience knows it has *seen* the action in another context. Characters ford rivers, and they take churches. If they are wearing cowboy hats, it's a Western, but if they wear helmets, it's a combat film.

The Korean Interruption

The Third Wave is complex because its decade of films is marked by the interruption of the Korean War, which obviously contributed to the popularity of and need for combat films. This brought to American movie screens the Korean combat film, a fact which occurs during the early years of the third wave (1950–1953). Third wave movies are then set both in World War II (*Halls of Montezuma, The Frogmen*) and in the Korean Conflict (*Retreat, Hell!, Bridges at Toko Ri*). Presumably the Korean War renewed interest in the pure combat film, as opposed to films in which combat is there only as a part of a larger story.

An important thing to remember about the Korean War is that it was not a war covered directly by television as it happened. TV cameras were still too bulky to allow for easy while-it-is-happening battlefield reporting, as in the Vietnam War. Thus, major television networks, just taking hold across the United States as Korea unfolded, did not seek to replace the official war coverage provided by the government. Newsreels, of course, did cover the war, reaching the theaters after a necessary time span for processing and releasing. Vietnam thus proved to be the first time instant TV coverage of a war was brought directly to American homes on a day-by-day schedule.

The format of the Korean War film is definitely a replay of the World War II combat film. This is true enough so that the Korean war combat film is swept along in the third wave as a part of it, not separate from it. The political issues have been adjusted, of course, to incorporate a new enemy, Communism, and certain significant variations.

Where are the World War II films and the Korean films the same and where do they differ? The Korean combat film uses these traditional devices from the WWII films:

• The group as a concept, reflecting America's immigrant heritage, and also reflecting the Korean conflict as a United Nations police action
• The hero as the tough, experienced sergeant, usually one who had also

fought in World War II. (Before, it was World War I. How quickly we update our wars!)
- The frequent death of a leader and the resulting need to replace him.
- The traditional iconography of combat, here adjusted to incorporate new weapons such as jet planes.
- The plot which is either a last stand or a patrol on the move.
- A powerful enemy.
- Combat geography and weather, reflecting more of a winter terrain as was true for the Korean war.
- Familiar sequences, such as mail call and Christmas celebrations.
- An opening dedication ("This story is dedicated to the United States Infantry").
- The ending sequence in which the group who have experienced the film are passed in parade for us in some way, frequently as soldiers returning home who pass by the new recruits coming up.

In many ways, the Korean combat film is the World War II combat film set in Korea. These two wars are compatible, unlike World War I and World War II, and they have a mutual effect on one another. However, there are differences, mostly attributable to the new times, the new setting, the new historical facts, the new enemy. There is new technology and there are new weapons of war. All these things influence the Korean variation.

First of all, the group unit now contains new minorities—frequently Japanese, the former enemy, who are now brought back into the fold. The new enemy are clearly delineated as Communists, and the indication is that the enemy is Russia, not China, although we are fighting Communist Chinese. References to Russian rifles, Russian planes, and Russian ideology are frequent. This new enemy is treated with more respect than the enemy of World War II, even though he, too, is treated with blatant propaganda. However, he is seen as an enemy who has an ideology that is threatening because it *is* a political theory that must be discussed and rejected. By considering its ideas as possible, the films give it credibility. This is the opposite of the World War II films, in which the enemy was presented as having an ideology that wasn't worthy of consideration at any level.

In the Korean War, retreat is used as a basic story presentation, similar to, but slightly different from the old "last stand" variation of the World War II film. Retreat was a fact of Korean history, so this is logical. In the same vein, the films present the new jet airplanes, the use of the helicopter, brainwashing, and the Mobile Army Surgical Hospitals (MASH units) as part of the storyline. The latter means that there are more Korean films about doctors and nurses than there are World War II films of that type.

With the Korean War, we begin to see an increased cynicism about fighting wars, a questioning of whether or not we should let ourselves be talked into it. This is demonstrated most dramatically by stories which frequently question military leadership and which often present weak, frightened, or unreliable people in command of troops. This idea begins in Korea, and runs as a dark undercurrent through both the third and fourth waves. It finds its most overt expression in the fifth wave, during the days of Vietnam. However, it is present in some of the Korean War films, and is demonstrated by patrols that are lost, or that simply wander, or go in circles. This loss of direction is a physical equivalent for its obvious narrative meaning. There is a growing sense of futility.

During World War II, the primary issue of the films was always the war itself. Would we win it? Could we win it? Why did we have to fight it, when, after all, it wasn't our fault? The Korean War films are much more eclectic. Technically, it wasn't a "war" at all, merely a "police action," and we were over there with our friends of the United Nations to stop the spread of Communism. As genre evolves, it always uses the same conventions for shifting ideology, but the Korean conflict films present a grab bag of current ideological and social problems that might be on the minds of people in the 1950s audience: Communism, race relations, the morality of killing, juvenile delinquency, divorce, and family conflict.

The development of the themes of family conflict and/or responsibility is particularly strong. When Americans set out to fight in Korea, it would be the second war in less than five years for some of them. They didn't all want to go, and their families certainly were not happy to see them go. There was disapproval in a way that was not the case in World War II when families, however worried and however reluctant, saw it as a duty (at least in films). Many Korean War films begin with a family realizing its father, or son, must return to combat, and the resulting resentment presents an attitude that is entirely different from World War II. Some films, such as I Want You, are totally about this conflict and its resolution. Since films must reach their audience by bringing them stories about what they can relate to, this issue is present in film after film. The Korean combat movies are about American families back home, American families waiting in Japan, and about love and romance in both places. Unlike their original World War II counterparts, they bring these stories directly onto the screen.

An interesting variation of this family responsibility motif is that of placing into the combat storyline a new generic convention—an Oriental child who attaches himself to the hero. The use of caring for a small child to represent an adult's acceptance of responsibility appears in many kinds of films, everything from *The Champ* and *The Kid* to *Shane* and *Meet Me at the Fair*. But the use of civilians, particularly children, appears so often and so clearly as a part of the Korean combat film that it must be identified as a convention of the generic subdivision of Korean combat. Entire films, such as *Battle Hymn*, are about the care of war orphans in the midst of the Korean confict. *One Minute to Zero* concerns itself with the enemy's use of Korean refugees, particularly women and children, to camouflage its agents. The use of women and children in this way proves to us, presumably, that the evil commies have infiltrated their lives and brainwashed them, and this helps to justify our fighting a war in their country. We must take care of them and teach them differently. This responsibility for civilians and thus, by extension, family, implies the inevitable question—why must we fight again, why the same men, why so soon, and why over there where we don't belong in the first place? The Korean combat film is a forerunner to the home front's attitude toward the Vietnam War.

A question inevitably arises—without Korea, would the combat genre prototypically created by World War II have continued in its popularity? Possibly not. The significant thing is that, when the Korean conflict broke out, and the need for combat stories rose, the model of the World War II film was readily available for usage, and was presumably what people understood and expected from the situation. With a minimum of tempering and tampering, the Korean combat film— about an entirely different kind of war—became only a variation of the World War II combat film. This solidified the genre, and makes examining specific Korean films worthwhile.

Samuel Fuller's Korean Films

Two low-budget films directed and written by Samuel Fuller illustrate the Korean variation of the World War II combat genre. *Steel Helmet* (January 25, 1951) and *Fixed Bayonets* (November 21, 1951) show how the Korean genre continues the old and incorporates the new list of ingredients indigenous to the Korean film. Fuller's work is interesting

Gene Evans and William Chun in The Steel Helmet

because he wrote as well as directed his own films, and because he made both Korean combat films and World War II combat films (*Merrill's Marauders, The Big Red One*, both to be discussed later). He also fought in World War II as an infantryman in the First Infantry Division, "The Big Red One." He saw combat in North Africa, Sicily, Anzio, and Czechoslovakia, and landed at Omaha Beach on D-Day. World

War II was a central formative experience of his life, and all his films—whatever their subject—tend to be about war.

The opening sequence of *Steel Helmet* shows a viewer an intense close-up of a helmet with a bullet hole in it, right where the brain would be. But the helmet lifts up, and a pair of shrewd eyes slowly surveys the situation. Inside that helmet, hands tied and lying amongst dead bodies, is the old pro Sergeant who is an obvious survivor of a situation that seems to indicate the shooting of prisoners taken. What a way to demonstrate that this old soldier can survive anything! No matter what, the old soldier survives to war again, and this man represents that tradition, that is to say, the legend of it, not the reality of it. In fact, this film ends, not with the traditional words THE END on the screen, but with a curt note to the viewers: "There is no end to this story." That this is so is capably demonstrated by the opening sequence, which might be the rebirth of a soldier who had died at the end of another film. In a hideous way, it's like seeing war come again. We thought it was over, but like him it gets up and keeps on coming.

The tone of *Steel Helmet* is cynical and tough, but its essence is a kind of disconnected, almost magical presentation of war as an archetypal story. The patrol is lost in the fog, looking for a river, with the loss of direction and a sense of being cut off from any meaningful reality that is basic to the Korean film. "I've got a hunch we're going in circles," "We're lost," and "That's how it is all the time. No one knows where we are but the enemy," say the men on patrol in *Steel Helmet*. In addition, *Steel Helmet* depicts the Korean genre concept of the hero taking charge of the fate of a small Korean child, named "Short Round"—a name that would recur in *Indiana Jones and the Temple of Doom* for a similar canny and tough little kid.

The group is a set of unique characters, unpredictable in genre terms. One is a bald young radio operator, and another carries a portable organ. They are not the traditional characters on patrol, yet their humor, resilience, and very oddness still mark them as a recognizable American group of mixed types and attitudes and backgrounds. They may not be the Irishman/Brooklynite/scholar we know from the past, but they are an American collection of tough misfits. There is a conscientious objector who ends up having to fight, but instead of going mad as in *Bataan* he turns out to be a capable combat comrade. There is the usual downbeat reference to attempting to mark who the dead are as they fall. ("Get his tags," is repeated endlessly.)

The enemy of *Steel Helmet* is a human being, educated, and with a clear political ideology. When the representative enemy character is captured, he appears more like the suave Nazi of World War II films than the leering and grinning Oriental we have come to expect. Yet he is not an upper class figure like that Nazi of old, but a common man, to represent the Communist ideology, and he speaks pure propaganda. However, this one represents a million others. "There's a million Reds out there," and indeed there are.

In *Fixed Bayonets*, a platoon of 48 men—48 of the toughest, most experienced combat soldiers—are left behind to conduct a rear guard action that may save "1500 lives." This situation ("Nothing dirtier than a rear guard action") illustrates the classic pattern of "last stand" American heroism. The 48 men know they are left, probably to die, in order to buy enough time for a larger victory. As their comrades depart, the men are shown in intense closeups, watching friends go, as "On the Banks of the Wabash, Far Away" is heard on the sound track, slow, ethereal, ghostly. The abandoned platoon *knows*. They are human sacrifices to a larger plan of battle. One of the group left behind is Rock, an old soldier who has been there "from Tunisia to Czechoslovakia." Here the experienced combat "old man" is updated from the World War I veteran who appeared in World War II films to a World War II veteran who appears in a Korean film. The rest of the group include an Irish man, a "Bolcheck," a know-it-all who spouts facts constantly, a coward, a full-blooded Cherokee from Oklahoma, a man who fears responsibility—the usual mix of American types with the usual mix of American attitudes and problems. These men talk tough and argue among themselves in an honest and believable way. Conflicts within the group emerge in the traditional manner, and through it all Rock provides what his name suggests, not only finding a cave to shelter them in cold, but also providing a listening post for those who need it, and plenty of practical combat advice. ("Your rifle and your two feet—the only three things you've got to worry about in the Infantry".) Yet he is not omniscient. "I wish I knew the answer" he says when asked why he stayed in the army.

Fixed Bayonets takes place on a winter landscape, amidst snow, ice, and cold. Its hero, group, and "last stand" objective, are tempered by the Korean setting into subtle variations that are unique and most likely come from Fuller's own memories of combat experience and combat comrades. The usual events do occur, such as one man (Michael

The Korean combat group: The Steel Helmet

O'Shea) having to search for a missing comrade. On the way back, O'Shea is hit and must crawl on his belly through a minefield, so someone must now go out for him. When the medic tries, he is blown up, causing O'Shea to yell, "Don't nobody come out to get me—that's an order." But, as is the way of the combat film, the cowardly corporal goes. In an intense sequence that perhaps illustrates why the combat film can last to entertain viewers over the years, the coward picks his way, makes it to O'Shea, and carries him slowly and safely back in. But O'Shea is dead. Didn't we know it? Such a scene illustrates the futility of war at the same time as it pays tribute to the courage and nobility of the fighting man. Fuller's variation seems to indicate a further dimension—O'Shea would have died anyway, but by going for him, the coward was redeemed, and thus it was not a bleak event, wasted and ironic, but an uplifting one, necessary and pointed.

An interesting element of the film is its formal presentation, in which a small group is abandoned and left behind in order to "fool" the enemy and "fake" the sense of a larger combat force. The genre is taking on a falsified presentation of itself, and the combat action is a "staged"event. The look of the film—dictated, of course, by budget considerations—carries out this idea. The film is set for the most part on what is obviously an artificial set, and there is no way a viewer can coherently construct a sense of the geography for the situation vis à vis the men hiding in the cave and the larger world outside which contains the enemy.

The heroes of the film lose their own map of the minefields they have laid, and thus are lost in their own territory. Furthermore, the basic issue of the combat becomes one of staging a show—our side tries to pretend it's a big army, in control of the space, with plenty of ammo. The other side tries to penetrate the disguise, expose the sham and find the reality. The presentation of the film for the viewer alternates from that of being an objective camera, recording information in what might be called the traditional "third-person" in the literary sense, to a subjective presentation in which we are "inside" the mind of the leading character, sharing his thoughts and worries and assuming what we see is his private view of things. In and of itself, this does not change what viewers have seen in other films of the genre, but Fuller's variation of it allows viewers to discover that what they thought was objective may have been subjective and linked to the perception of a single character after all. This nontraditional presentation, which appears in other works of Fuller, gives an audience a sense of strangeness of events. For instance, we are placed in the position of "looking" through a pair of binoculars wielded by a confident commander on our side. Having seen what he sees, we believe, as he does, that the battle can be won. However, we then see the enemy leader in close-up, followed by a shot of our side being wiped out by enemy bombs, an event now seen through the enemy's eyes. This representation of an event, which has to be immediately reevaluated from a different viewpoint, illustrates a modern attitude toward the combat genre. *Fixed Bayonets* seems to say that what we were looking at during the 1940s must be seen again, from a different perspective, to be really understood.

There is a kind of magic and eloquence at work in *Fixed Bayonets*. Any time a film cuts itself off from realism in its visual presentation, particularly when the film is about a real event such as the Korean war, a kind of mystical presence is generated. The characters of *Fixed Bayonets* are intuitive. Rock can "smell the enemy" and he is able to say clearly, "I'm dead," announcing his death before the fact but as if it were a *fait accompli*. The ghostly departure of their comrades, as well as their own final return to their waiting group, take on a magical quality. As they approach their comrades, who had gone ahead to blow up a key bridge while they held the line so the action could occur, those at the bridge (now blown) call out, "Who's there?" and from afar the solemn cry returns, "Rear Guard!" From out of the mist they emerge, looking exhausted and beaten, wearing the ravages of combat, with the dirgelike "On the Banks of the Wabash, Far Away" on the sound track. They are the Ghost Patrol of the Korean War, who have been on duty in an artificial arena, acting out an attitude toward genre, contributing toward its development into myth. "Ain't nobody goes out lookin' for responsibility," says Rock's voice on the soundtrack. "Sometimes you get it whether you're lookin' for it or not."

The Symbiosis of Korea and World War II

The Korean War was largely a war of men on foot or men in airplanes flying overhead. The sea variation was almost totally neglected, except for an occasional sub film and the sea/air variation, in which carriers stood by off the coast of Korea and launched jets and helicopters from their decks (See Filmography). What did happen during this time period was an increase in the number of World War II sea and air stories to compensate, films such as *Flying Leathernecks* (September 20, 1951) and *The Frogmen* (June 30, 1951).

The Frogmen is unique in that it concerns an unusual warfare group, the underwater demolition teams of World War II. Because it is about a service seldom covered in the combat film, it is worthy of observation. Can the typical combat film be made in unusual physical circumstances? Will the basic definition hold up?

First of all, the nature of the work done by the underwater demolition teams is usual, but not totally removed from that done by certain submarine commando groups, such as the underwater teams seen in *Up Periscope* (1959) and *Crash Dive* (1943). Staying underwater is also a condition of the submarine film, even though the men may be sipping coffee in the kitchen instead of fending off jellyfish.

At once, a viewer can see that *The Frogmen* will match its events to the traditional combat film. It opens with a printed dedication and a thank you to the official group being depicted—a dedication *Before* the credits. The basic conflict concerns a new skipper coming in to take over a group who loved the leader they have lost. Thus the death of the original leader is established, a man who died on Iwo Jima saving the life of one of his men. They consider themselves an elitist team—there are only 1000 frogmen out of 3,000,000 Navy men. The new commander, played by Richard Widmark (who would become an icon of combat films) does not subscribe to the elitist concept, and this separates him from his men, who want their original dead father figure back.

Everything generic is in place, even the usual man from Brooklyn. This one explains to us how important Brooklyn really is, by listing the famous people who came from there: Mae West, Danny Kaye, Barbara Stanwyck, Susan Hayward, Houdini. (By not including William Bendix, he blows his credibility.)

The group is one we can recognize: Flanagan, Kinsella, Creighton, Kinskowski, and others, plus two sets of twins. The combat is intense, frightening, and there is plenty of it, played out for its underwater drama. There is a mission to be completed, and there is an enemy, who, up to a point, are never seen. They just don't exist, until their Frogmen come into combat against our team.

The Frogmen are like the old professionals of the 1930s Warner Brothers movies—men who do dangerous work, whether driving trucks, climbing electricity poles, or handling explosives. This film (made by 20th Century-Fox) pays tribute to that kind of story by stressing visually the danger of the job. There is no real ideology presented here. It is a human story of individual bravery, and of personal growth for an unfeeling leader and for childish men who want their daddy back. If accepting new relationships can be seen as a metaphor for our nation's accepting new friendly relations with the Germans and Japanese, then a great article can be written about this film on that basis. Otherwise, it's the war combat film, told in its traditional format, but wedding it to stories about men who do dangerous work with the necessary courage and endurance.

What is interesting here is that, since the combat genre is now firmly in place, it finds fresh variations for its familar story. Using the frogmen makes it unique. Yet it does not break with what an audience will expect. It borrows a bit from an earlier tradition (the working man films), but it definitely puts what it borrows into the acceptable context of the new genre. *The Frogmen* is typical of the World War II films that came out during the outbreak of the Korean conflict. It can be called typical, because even its unique setting doesn't make it different. It is locked into a format, and that format is its genre.

To show how World War II and Korea parallel each other during this wave, there is the curious case of *Cease Fire!* (November 25, 1953). It is difficult to know how to describe this unusual film, except to suggest it follows the Audie Murphy example. Based on a screenplay by Walter Doniger, which was from a story by Owen Crump, *Cease Fire!* is a docudrama, a strange mixture of fact and fiction. With the cooperation of the Department of Defense, Crump and his film crew went to Korea to assemble a cast of non-actors from Army combat personnel. Their plan was to make a film about the everyday dangers of an infantry platoon on reconnaissance patrol behind enemy lines. Thus we have a shot-on-the-spot drama, reenacted by the men who lived it for real, some of whom were later wounded or killed in battle. The men play themselves, taking a hill they once took, all presented to viewers in 3-D! And what are the names of these men, so carefully assembled to be "real"—Thompson, Goszkowski, Elliott, Hofelich, English, Carrasco, Mayes, Kim, Pruchneiwski, Wright—the usual ethnic mix. And who comments on their achievements? A scrappy group of newspaper correspondents at Panmunjom. Thus the Korean War not only had its own documentaries (see Filmography), but also its own semidocumentaries which mixed real heroes and reel heroes in a mindboggling confusion of history and reality.

This typifies the complex third wave, a full decade of films, complicated by the interference of the Korean conflict. It set out intially to celebrate and reconcile, or to put together the two halves of the viewing audience. To do this, it had to touch closely on reality in some way—through using actual combat footage, referring to day-to-day life of the foot soldier, and relating the film closely to actual historical battles. However, it also had to reflect new meanings or to contain postwar messages for viewers. As this happened, the Korean War broke out, and added to the basic definition its own subtle variations, while still keeping the original definition intact. Korea was sucked up into the evolutionary process.

Significantly, the split that occurs between World War I films and World War II films does not take place between World War II and Korea. They are constituted in the same basic terms. What does happen, however, is that Korea seems to inspire certain films to reflect a harsh new cynicism toward war and those who plan it and lead it.[15] This strain, which will be fully developed later in the Inversion wave, begins to appear during the third wave. It can be seen in such films as *Attack!*.

Attack! (September 20, 1956) pulls no punches about combat. Based on a stage play, it is nevertheless one of the great films about World War II combat. Mean and tough, cynical and despairing, it clearly shows how genre works. Keeping strictly to the basic ideas of hero, group, and objective, it begins the demolition of the wholesomeness of the tradition. When a tank slowly runs over the hero, literally leaving tire treads, it can be seen in retrospect as a perfect metaphor for what will happen to the genre in the future. *Attack!* is a signpost to the films of the future, but for a time its type seems to disappear or at least lie low and emerge only in aberrant movies. It finally did emerge in a wave of its own, but not before an entirely different wave—the epic reenactment.

Fourth Wave. January 1, 1960–December 31, 1970
Epic Re-creation of Historical Events

As if to put an official seal on the idea that, unless it has been thoroughly and completely depicted on film it hasn't happened, a period of large-scale epic combat films emerged. These films depicted in detail the battles of World War II. Many were made on actual locales, with international casts, and some contained veterans of the events. Real generals and veterans were replaced with film heroes such as Henry Fonda, John Wayne, and Robert Mitchum. This period of epic recreation, with its attention to minute detail as to timing and place, may be seen as the final evolutionary stage: the true war has been removed, and in its place is its filmed replica. This finally makes the war a legendary story—fully distanced and mythic—suitable to be one of our national stories for all time. Technically, this took place throughout the 1960s, with key films appearing in the first half. However, such films continued to be made even in the 1970s (*Midway*, 1976).

Three films of this era show the various ways in which this happened: *The Longest Day, Battle of the Bulge,* and *Tora! Tora! Tora!* Each is a story about a real historical event. However, the degree to which each film mixes the real events of history and filmed story about those events varies. Taken together, they illustrate the parameters of the era's treatment of history.

1. *The Longest Day* (October 5, 1962) An equal mix of history and narrative, based on D-Day, presented as part narrative, part docudrama.

2. *Battle of the Bulge* (Dec. 18, 1965). Largely a narrative, which mixes all the old movie stories about this battle together into one big movie, but which has true historical reference.

3. *Tora! Tora! Tora!* (1970). A docudrama re-enactment of the Japanese attack on Pearl Harbor, before, during, and after.

The Longest Day

This film, a kind of storytelling newsreel, clearly sets out to present its story as a document. Each character is introduced with the image of the actor playing the part. Underneath is printed information that explains who and what the person is. All foreign language is accurate, with subtitled translations where needed. (This leads to one of my favorite dialogue exchanges of any movie. When dolls dressed as paratroopers are dropped over France to confuse and mislead the Germans, the discovery is announced by incredulous soldiers: "Gummy Puppen!" This is followed by a Mel Brooks round of events in which "Gummy Puppen" is solemnly repeated over and over as the information is sent forward through the lines to Headquarters.) In this film, the official replacement of true heroes with their screen counterparts takes place: John Wayne as Col. Ben Vandervoort, Henry Fonda as Teddy Roosevelt Jr., Robert Mitchum as Brigadier General Norman Cota effectively bawling out, on a Normandy beach, "There are only two kinds of people on this beach—those that are dead and those that are gonna die."

It is curious how this replacement process works. Although moviegoers would have seen photos in magazines and newspapers of war personnel, few would know what men like Teddy Roosevelt Jr. or Norman Cota looked like. Thus it was easy to replace these faceless heroes with faces of heroes the audience *did* know and recognize—

John Wayne in The Longest Day

Fonda, Wayne, Mitchum. If, on the other hand, the image of the hero was fixed in the minds of audiences, the actor must be made to look that way (or he must look that way by nature). In the same vein, if you cast FDR, you must get an actor who looks like him or at least one who can drive a wheelchair and wield a cigarette holder. Who would believe a short, fat-faced Lincoln? A curly-headed Hitler with no mustache? A tall, elegant Napoleon with a wig? To be Jesus, an actor must have long hair, blue eyes, and a white robe with a homespun look. Mickey Rooney cannot play Jesus.

Nowadays, with TV making so many instant biographical films, everyone from Grace Kelly and Rita Hayworth to John F. Kennedy and Jimmy Hoffa is depicted on film, and always by lookalike actors. Statistics indicate the ten characters most frequently depicted on the

Robert Mitchum in The Longest Day

screen include four real people: Hitler, Lincoln, Napoleon, and Jesus. (For the record, the others are Hopalong Cassidy, Tarzan, Sherlock Holmes, Zorro, Dracula, and Frankenstein's monster.)

Why do we know what Lincoln, Napoleon and Jesus look like? We all saw Hitler in newsreels and photos, but what about the others? These three men are images ahead of the era of image. However, Lincoln was on the verge of it; we know him from photographs. And Napoleon and Jesus we know from paintings. Therefore, we know all four from fixed images. Perhaps filmmakers chose to depict only historical figures they assumed the audience could identify by look. This accounts for the media popularity of Lincoln as much as his humble background, his association with the Civil War, and his populist appeal.

Or is it the other way around? Was it the appeal, association, and background that caused him to have his image re-created, and thus known and used by filmmakers? Who becomes a movie historical favorite and who doesn't is mysterious. Teddy Roosevelt should have been a natural for films. He was a glamorous, colorful, feisty figure, but he is not one of our great movie heroes. Whenever he appears, he is usually a comic figure, as in the caricature of him in *Arsenic and Old Lace* (the crazy uncle who pretends to be him and runs around yelling *Charge!* and burying the men his aunts poison as if they were yellow fever victims). He frequently appears in musical films, as a kind of historic touchstone. Conscious of image and perhaps the first great manipulator of media, Roosevelt was *too* exaggerated—a do-it-yourself media hero before media manipulation's time and when heroes seemed to be plentiful. Presidents such as Kennedy and Reagan knew our films have lost their heroes, and they rose by using the media to fill that national void.

At any rate, casting must match the look of known media figures, but is free to re-create unknown faces in the images of known ones. (Later, we come to an era when the face creates the role, as when a man "looks like" a president and actually gets voted into the job.)

As is frequently the case, the real story of the war is somehow more powerful and dramatic than all the made up ones, yet the made up ones are incorporated into the *Longest Day* narrative. Some of those "made up" stories from earlier films had, of course, been suggested by real events in the first place. The film works back and forth from a macrovision of war to the microvision—from the true life leaders, as played by Wayne and Mitchum and Fonda, to the inner stories (presumably true) of the men who fought the war up close. A character on board ship, played by Jeffrey Hunter, tells his personal story of a wartime marriage. This is juxtaposed with the horrible truth of a unit of paratroopers landing in a village where a church is on fire, and falling helplessly into the flames—illuminated by the conflagration for all the Germans to see.

As a semidocumentary re-creation of events, *The Longest Day* has the same problem it would have if it actually were a documentary— no continuous involvement for the audience with a single character. The personal involvement that does come for viewers is that of their involvement with actors, with the big stars and their personae. When John Wayne breaks his leg and continues to walk on it, we remember how he went on when he was shot in the leg in *The Horse Soldiers*. Good old John Wayne! We can count on him. We saw him hang in there before. Being pushed along by his men in an ammo cart, he tells them, "You've got a long walk."

"It's a privilege to serve with you, sir," one replies.

"Well, God willing, we'll do what we came here to do," he says.

His strength and presence, the accumulation of *Flying Tigers, Fighting Seabees, They Were Expendable, Back to Bataan, Sands of Iwo Jima, Flying Leathernecks,* and all the rest of them, is put into those words. Here is the truth of his career—we believe he *is* Col. Vandervoort. More importantly, we believe Col. Vandervoort was him. It could not be so without the genre films behind him. When there is no real viewer involvement with characters, only with star personae, viewers are forced to become involved with and respond to *event.* This means re-living D-Day as a filmed reality.

The film's end title says simply, THE END OF THE LONGEST DAY.

Tora! Tora! Tora!

Tora! Tora! Tora! and *Battle of the Bulge* illustrate additional approaches to the filmed re-creation of historical events. *Tora! Tora! Tora!* is a "who would believe it?" postwar phenomenon—a Japanese–American co-production, with a Japanese crew filming their part of the story, and an American crew filming ours. It is a curious film, deadly dull until the Japanese actually take off to bomb us, and watching it you can only wonder how to react (assuming you're awake to do so at all). The Japanese clearly have the better half, as theirs is the more active story, the more dramatic event. Their characters have dignity and pride, and telling the story of the bombing of Pearl Harbor from their point of view helps, finally, if not to compensate for, at least to offset the indignity of their presentation in so many American films of World War II. Watching *Tora! Tora! Tora!*, one can suddenly see the event of Pearl Harbor from another viewpont—how daring a raid it was, what a military coup, and how bold the men who planned it and how brave the men who flew its mission. Our side appears remarkably inefficient, complacent, and disorganized by comparison, a fact which is doubtless historically correct. *(Tora! Tora! Tora!* thus illustrates the power of film. By filming Pearl Harbor from inside the Japanese bombers, it can inspire the victims to cheer the attackers!) This is not the point of the film,

Combat: The Longest Day

which only sets out to present factually both side of the story, but it is an end result, particularly for an American who has never thought of Pearl Harbor as anything but "a dastardly deed."

Tora! Tora! Tora! treats its material as historical event. Each major character, based on a real person, is introduced by a title underneath his face: "Cordell Hull, Secretary of State," or "Vice-Admiral Yamamoto, Incoming Commander in Chief." Although historical events are dramatized, and conversations are written as dialogue, an attempt is made to "create reality," with a meticulous attention to detail, to timings and characterizations that are not controversial. Watching it, it is as if one has picked up a history book and the words one reads become images. It is a docudrama of the sort that is now done regularly on PBS—a "reenactment" of historical event in a sober manner, as factual

December 7th, from Tora! Tora! Tora!

as possible, following actual newsreels and photographs. Presumably this phenomenon, a twentieth-century curiosity, is a product of making films (images) about real historical events people have already seen in films (newsreels and earlier movies). Previously, people might create tableaux of "Napoleon at Waterloo," based on paintings or drawings, in a similar manner. But when the entire audience *knows*, one has to re-create more accurately. Yet when what the audience knows is perhaps a filmed, or narrative depiction, what, then, is being recreated? When *Tora! Tora! Tora!* presents the actual bombing of Pearl Harbor, it is then that our remembered images are re-created for us. From newsreels, *Life* magazine photos, but also from *December 7th*, which was mostly not real to begin with. In addition, movies we have known and loved come in to play. Into the mess fly the B-17s, en route from San Francisco, from *Air Force*. (This was true to history, but made memorable by the film.) Out of the harbor speed the ships that get away, and

Tora! Tora! Tora!

on a desk appears the infamous date. A viewer thinks, "This is true, I am seeing truth," but the source of visual belief comes from the non-truth of movies.

Battle of the Bulge

Battle of the Bulge presents its credits against abstracted images of combat, which appear to be negatives from actual photographs. This opening presentation speaks of the use of photographed images by calling attention to the photographic process. A narration tells us, "December, 1944. British and American armies were near victory" and we enter a story that is a less factual depiction of events than it is a dramatic retelling of the story for greater accuracy. This is a narrative film, not a docudrama like *Tora! Tora! Tora!* or a mix of the two, like *Longest Day.*

However, in *Battle of the Bulge*, we see clearly that the story being told is a collection of former American combat films. Once again, it's as if the approach to history is to draw together all the movies into one long story from December 1944 to the end of the war. However, these are all separate episodes, unlike A *Walk in the Sun*, which made one long event coherently representational. Psychotic Telly Savalas, a tank corps man, appears to be playing William Bendix, and a group of German soldiers role-play as perfect Americans who can answer the question "Who's your favorite baseball player?" with "Lou Gehrig" in perfect English, just like in *Battleground*. There are many kinds of combat: a big tank battle (without Patton), fighting in the streets, the blowing up of a bridge, a commando raid, bombs, running attacks, seen during both night and day. *Battle of the Bulge* translates the fighting of the Bulge into a traditional American story of how elite Europeans seek to bring underdogs to heel. When the Germans capture territory and find a fresh chocolate cake flown across the ocean from Boston, the German officer comments, "This means the Americans have no conception of defeat. They have the fuel to fly cakes across the ocean. I must break their morale—teach them about defeat." The film also has a sense of America as a vigilante force, hellbent on revenge.

At the end, we read on the screen "This picture is dedicated to the one million men who fought in this great battle of World War II. To encompass the whole of the heroic contributions of all the participants, names, places, and characters have been generalized and action has been synthesized in order to convey the spirit and essence of the battles." Is there any way to say it more directly?

The New Image

There is one other aspect to the fourth wave of epics to consider— the aesthetics of color and CinemaScope. Both technological factors change the look of the combat film, and the look is as important as any other aspect.

Color adds distance. Although events in real life have color, an average person's perception of the war was a black and white perception, based on newsreels, photos in papers and magazines, and the majority of combat films seen.[16] (Yet the first real viewing experience the American public might have had was made by a man undergoing intense

bombing and combat: John Ford's *Battle of Midway*—shot in color.)
Adding color seemed to add unreality, making a subconscious link to
the entertainment films of the same period. It brightened the images,
made them prettier, and seemed to remove the gritty reality they represented. Later, as attitudes toward violence changed, it brought more
blood, but again, with a distanced aesthetic appreciation of its look,
not its reality.

Color, which should add naturalism to films, tends to do the opposite.
Even today, when a filmmaker wants to be gritty and real, as in *Raging
Bull* or *Elephant Man* or *Last Picture Show*, he boldly chooses the
black and white format. For most people, World War II was a black and
white experience, and it remains so. (The 1985 release of George
Stevens, Jr.'s excellent documentary on his father's career, *George Stevens: A Filmmaker's Journey*, may change this. In that film, American
audiences can see World War II combat, including the landings of D-
Day and the liberation of concentration camps, in color. Stevens, Sr.,
a cameraman before he became a director, shot the footage on color
stock with his own cameras.) The newsreels, the photographs in magazines and newspapers, and the films of 1943 and 1944 which defined
the genre, were almost all black and white. As a John Ford film would
later tell us, "When the legend becomes fact, print the legend."
The printed legend of World War II is that it took place in black and
white.

CinemaScope provided filmmakers with a greater space in which to
show events, a larger canvas. Thus, it was perfect for the late war films,
which chose to depict the war as epic event. Widescreen was a technological experiment that took place long before the 1950s, of course,
but the 1950s brought CinemaScope into economic feasability and thus
prominence. (Space does not allow a complete historical analysis of
the changes brought by color and 'Scope to the combat film, but such
technological developments, which change the look and meaning of
film, should not be overlooked—as they usually are—in discussions
of genre.)

One film from the epic fourth wave illustrates the use that can be
made of black-and-white and CinemaScope in relation to the generic
development—*In Harm's Way* (April 7, 1965). It also illustrates an
example of the epic form that is truly a great film—personal and intense
despite the larger canvas. *Longest Day, Tora! Tora! Tora!*, and *Battle
of the Bulge* are so bent on truth and reality that they lose something

In Harm's Way

that great films always have. That is the dramatic sense of a great story
in which the audience becomes involved in the characters and breath-
lessly awaits the outcome of events. As they carefully re-create events,
they create one kind of drama—history brought to life—but they lose
another—life brought to history. Each of the films is successful in its
own way, and all of them have the power of real events working for
them. The story of World War II is a dramatic one, so in a way,
filmmakers can't lose on action and event. But *In Harm's Way* shows
action, event, and character in the epic form—and still maintains the
"objectivity of history" of the epic film.

The director of *In Harm's Way*, Otto Preminger, in collaboration
with his filmmaking team, made films which can be defined as "objective" because they tended to present characters and narratives so that
audiences had to decide for themselves who was good or bad, and what
events meant morally. Obviously, the problem of achieving true objec-

tivity on film is complex. In that he selects, guides, casts, and shapes, Preminger is not really presenting films that are "objective." However, his films provide audiences with multiple points of view, which in turn distance a viewer from the material and prevent an alliance with a single character. Since each character is presented in the narrative line with good and bad action, in the moral sense, audiences tend to make decisions about the characters for themselves. This is a more objective presentation than one in which an audience is allied with a single character and experiences all events through that character. The use of color (with which emotion can be heightened and demonstrated visually), and the use of the small screen, (with which more control on the frame can be exerted, since there is less space for the eye to scan), are good for subjective presentations. By going to black and white (a seemingly neutral look, although obviously it, too, can be used for emotion and subjectivity) and the wide screen, Preminger increased his chances for objectivity in his epic World War II combat film.

In Harm's Way tells multiple stories of individuals in World War II. Its size and scope make it an epic, as it stretches from the night before December 7 through the early years of the war, culminating in a battle based on the Battle of Leyte Gulf. It incorporates a wide range of the war's battle iconography: a land, sea, and air conglomeration that, like several other films of the type, gives a viewer a complete miniature war in one movie. It adds in characters that represent all the various human stories one might connect to war films: father–son conflict, romantic liaisons, interference from bunglers on high, political chicanery, spies and newspapermen, and a long list of others including nurses and rape. A lengthy combat sequence involving airplanes, submarines, PT boats, destroyers, and carriers takes place, magnificent in its presentation and massive in its visual look. This is another type of epic: the epic of style, in which a great filmmaker and his team fuse all the elements into one film. By presenting it in black and white, they ensure neutrality and a strong identification for viewers with the films of the past—their assumed reality. By shooting it in CinemaScope, and increasing the space on which we contemplate the event, the film causes us to contemplate film itself, and thus the concept of filming war over and over again to create genre. An aspect of genre evolution is this technological evolution in which we see the classical becoming the modern within the image.

Fifth Wave January 1, 1965–December 31, 1975
The Testing of the Genre
(Presenting an inverted, parodied, satirical,
and opposite reality)

During this period of time, various World War II combat films were released in which the characteristics of the genre were inverted and/or destroyed. This attempt to destroy the genre acts as a kind of testing of it. It includes *Inversion* (turning the former beliefs and truths inside out, such as equating our side with the Nazis, making us their counterparts in evil), *Destruction* (mocking the beliefs on which the genre is based), *Parody, Satire,* and other types of comedy.[17] Also during this period, the genre was frequently used as the background for another type of story.

The epic fourth wave (1960–1970) had carried on a kind of proud presentation of combat films, not only for those ten years, but also—as in *Midway* (1976)—beyond into the 1970s. At the same time, television shows about World War II became popular, among them *Rat Patrol* and *Combat!,* both of which followed the traditional format of the genre, thus solidifying its existence and further continuation. *Rat Patrol* was a half-hour weekly show on ABC from September 12, 1966 through September 16, 1968, and *Combat!* also on ABC, aired from October 2, 1962 through August 29, 1967. *Rat Patrol* had four commandos (three Americans and one British) fighting the Germans in North Africa during the early days of the war. *Combat!* was the story of a U.S. Army Division engaged in battle across Europe after D-Day. The former show, which contained humor, used footage from *The Battle of the Bulge* and *The Great Escape. Combat!* used some actual battle footage and emphasized realism.

Around the middle of the sixties, subversive films began to appear, so that the fifth wave may be seen to overlap with the fourth. In a sense, the testing of the genre runs as a counterforce to the epic re-creation. This is a parallel to the counterculture at work against the mainstream during the same time period. This may be attributed to American feelings about Vietnam. The testing of the genre, like its birth, was inspired by historical events.

During this period, the war in Vietnam was present as a kind of insane combat film, running continuously night after night, on the evening news. The cast was always the same, and the events were endlessly repeated. There were heroes and villains, but they all seemed to be on the same side. As Pogo might have put it: "I have seen the enemy and they is us." Vietnam was a bad TV show, and there is the sense that Americans caught on to it because they had to watch it every day. When they perceived it as a longrunning cliché, badly directed and planned, they wanted rid of it—off the screen, and out of their lives. This rejection of the military and other authorities was reflected not only in combat films but also in Westerns, gangster films, and other genres. The Vietnam combat film, unlike the Korean, barely existed during these years. It wasn't just a question of who wanted it? Who needed it? It was there on the tube for all to see.

The "Dirty Group" Movies
(subverting conventions, Vietnam's influence)

During World War II itself, combat films tended to be about men making last stands, or men on patrol. Those on patrol had a mission, even if it were nothing more than staying alive. In many cases, the mission was a specific objective so that the action might be thought of as a commando raid. As the genre emerged, the commando variation became increasingly popular. The commando raid is particularly suitable for the testing of the genre, because it implies a maverick unit, highly trained for specialized combat, possibly outside the mainstream of military authority. Two such examples are *The Dirty Dozen* (June 16, 1967) and *Play Dirty* (1969).

These two films ably illustrate the inversion process. Both are directed by men who demonstrate in other works a penchant for anti-generic attitudes, and both present worlds of treachery and questionable values. The films are similar in that both are about tainted groups on questionable missions under the leadership of unwilling realists, but *The Dirty Dozen*, made and released first, was a huge hit and enjoys a solid critical reputation. *Play Dirty* is a nearly forgotten film which was written off as a poor imitation of *Dirty Dozen*, the sort of critical fate that many genre films receive. Both are clearly genre films, however, and *The Dirty Dozen* is as imitative in that sense as is *Play Dirty*.

In both movies, one can observe that the knowledge and experience of other such films enriches the viewing experience and deepens the point of view the films are expressing. Both deliberately subvert the conventions of the genre, so knowledge of the genre is both assumed and used. At the same time, however, both films still function as mass audience, commercial entertainment. These are not films which set out to destroy the genre by being think pieces, self-consciously calling attention to the evils of the medium's presentation of violent combat. On the contrary, both films are jump-from-the-seat entertainments that become think pieces only if they are examined in terms of what generic changes and attitudes they represent. Otherwise, they are war-is-hell-but-damned-exciting films.

The success of *Dirty Dozen* spawned not only *Play Dirty* but many "dirty group" movies that mark the Wave of Inversion: *Kelly's Heroes* (1970) and *Devil's Brigade* (1968), for example. *Kelly's Heroes* is actually the popular caper movie of the 1960s adapted to the combat format. Its group of diverse types includes an Italian, a Jew, Kelly himself, "Cowboy," the Southern drawler, a cranky sergeant, and a bearded, long-haired AWOL soldier dressed in hippie clothing, wearing both an Iron Cross and his dogtags, who refers to a group of drunken bums (a pseudo Hells Angels collection) by saying "These are my boys." They find out a captured German has 14,000 bars of gold camouflaged with lead in a military convoy, and instead of fighting the war, they are busy stealing the gold for personal gain. *Kelly's Heroes* uses World War II to develop the antiwar sentiment of the 1960s, and to celebrate corruption. In order to get this gold, their involved heist plan includes capturing a bank behind enemy lines ("the perfect crime" one of them explains). The film is both a celebration of action and violence and a distinct comment on the foolishness of war.

Devil's Brigade is the story of a company of chronic misfits who hate each other more than they do the enemy and who are trained for a commando raid in Norway. Their leader (William Holden) is presented as noble because he has dared to break the rules (a direct inversion of having to learn to go by the rules to survive in the original films). This is a continuation of the tradition of American films in which the hero is an outlaw, something which may have grown out of our original immigrant defection from friends and families.

The beginning of the "dirty group" movie is found in *Gung Ho!* (January 26, 1944). *Gung Ho!* has a "dirty group" that is presented as just fine, because of the propaganda needs of the time. *Gung Ho!* is the story of Carlson's Makin Island Raiders. It is a factual record of the Second Marine Raider Battalion, following it through its inception three weeks after Pearl Harbor through their first brilliant victory. These words are off the film's opening title card. "Only those men who are prepared to kill and be killed" are selected for the mission. In a series of shocking interviews conducted by Randolph Scott, who plays Carlson, we see the formation of a wartime "dirty group" presented as a collection of realistic, noble heroes:

- Rod Cameron plays a mountain man who says "Down home in Kentucky a feller ain't much of a shot unless he can hit a squirrel in the head." He admits he has already killed ("I've done it"). He has knifed his victim in the dark. Since his chief rival from back home is already in the service (reference to a Hatfield–McCoy type feud), he has to get in, too, or "my daddy'll wallop me if he kills more Japs than I do." In answer to the question, "Why do you want to kill Japs?", he replies calmly, "Isn't that what we're here for?"
- Alan Curtis plays an ordained minister of the gospel with a good background and education. Scott tells him, "We've got our chaplain—what we want now is killers." "I'll do my duty," Curtis replies.
- A kind of John Garfield character, seemingly left over from a 1930s Warner Brothers movie. "Nobody gives me a break . . . Montana's my name, and I'm from Brooklyn . . . They say I'm a no good kid."
- Two brothers who fight all the time because they had the same mother but different fathers and also because they keep wanting the same girl. These are, of course, the vestigial Quirt/Flagg characters.
- A character played by Robert Mitchum who is a former boxing champion called "Pig Iron," a fighter both in and out of the ring who has been in the brig four times.
- The rest of the group who volunteer give as their reasons such comments as "I fought in Spain. I fought in Greece. This fight is all the same." "I haven't been in a fight yet. This is my chance." "I just don't like Japs."

This shocking collection of weirdos, prejudiced and pugilistic, is presented as an appropriate group of men to get a tough job done. They are our heroes, but they are also, seen today, a "dirty group," who will kill or be killed. "Now, Raiders, Let's Go" is the narrator's cry as they hit the beach and dig in. The film presents a blast of combat that is intense, hand-to-hand, fast, furious, ugly, dirty, and, I regret to add, very entertaining if one can detach one's moral and political conscience from it. It is a fast and fierce little movie, with incredible bombing sequences. Perhaps its strength is that it hasn't prettied itself up: it shows its group to be what it is, even in the early years of the war.

In *The Dirty Dozen*, a popular and critically successful film, can be seen the evolutionary process at work. There is still a group of mixed types, but now it's a corrupt and criminal group. The objective is no longer a useful military target, but is, in fact, a whorehouse, a fancy "Rest and Recreation" for German officers. The leader is more of a bully than a noble father figure, more misfit than hero. He is an outsider who has put his own criminal tendencies to work *inside* the system, which is the place he feels that criminality can best be fit. *The Dirty Dozen* suggests that war needs evil and antiauthoritarian attitudes to succeed. The boy next door is going to be a bungling fool. Get a criminal. An orderly leader with a sense of military discipline is not going to be able to solve the problem, because the problem may require a little cheating, a little fudging of the rules.

Without paying tribute to a noble military force, *The Dirty Dozen* begins about as grimly as any war film—or for that matter any film—has ever begun: in a military prison, with a graphic hanging. A scared and whimpering young man ("I didn't mean it. . . I'm sorry") is hanged for a murder. Lee Marvin,[18] the film's "hero" watches, cool and impatient. (He finally walks out, not waiting for the Bible reading to be completed.) At the theater where I first saw the film, the packed audience actually gasped in disbelief as the body dropped with a hideous thunk through the trap.

Marvin plays the antihero of the 1960s. "I'm not interested in embroidery, only results," he says, and given his assignment of shaping a group of condemned criminals into a fighting commando unit, he adds, "Somebody up there must be a raving lunatic." At first, the plan is to offer this group only an alternative to the hideous hanging we have just witnessed. But Marvin says, no, they must have a better goal—if they distinguish themselves, their sentences can be lifted. There is a subversive hint to this, of how war can return criminals and killers to civilian life as heroes.

The group is introduced, face by face, crime by crime, sentence by sentence. ("Death by hanging . . . 30 years of hard labor . . . etc.") They are a Hispanic, a Black, a Mexican, a Pole, a New Yorker—the classic group configuration. One, a big man with the syndicate back in Chicago, shot an old man while doing a stickup in London (John Cassavetes); one (Charles Bronson) is a Silesian coal miner's son who speaks German, hates officers, and who shot the commanding officer who ran off and left his men, taking their medical supplies with him.

Lee Marvin in **The Dirty Dozen**

"You made only one mistake," Marvin advises him, "you let somebody see you do it." There is a pious Bible-quoter (Telly Savalas), a Southerner who sees himself as the Lord's tool, who hates blacks, and who raped and beat a woman to death. " I was in a state of grace." Another (Clint Walker) is a quiet mountain man who killed someone because of his incredible strength, by accident. He has uncontrollable rages. The minority figures include a black man who killed "two Cracker bastards" who tried to castrate him, (Jim Brown), and a guitar-playing Mexican (Trini Lopez).

Marvin has his own way of dealing with their insubordination. Not himself one to be concerned with rules or proper behavior, he takes a troublemaker aside and says, "Look, you little bastard, either you march or I'll beat your brains out."

The Dirty Dozen maintains the sense that teamwork is essential to survival, but it's a kind of unholy teamwork—if any one of them tries to escape, they will all have to go back to prison. The film progresses, showing their commando training with a great deal of violence as well as comedy. Since comedy itself is a stage of genre development, it is appropriate that this violent and inverted film make use of it. It is, in fact, a sort of horrific comedy. As the troops are trained, they get their nickname, "the dirty dozen," by refusing to shave because they have only cold water to use. Marvin manipulates this deprivation to cohere them into a group.

As their training progresses, they have an opportunity to act out a mock inspection, with one pretending to be an officer. This both uses the old "noble officer speaks to men" ploy from genre history and sends it up effectively. Donald Sutherland, posing as a pompous officer, unctuously asks one of the men under inspection, "Where are you from, son?"

"Madison City, Missouri," is the eager reply.

"Never heard of it," says Sutherland.

The sense that the real enemy is us is depicted via another officer (Robert Ryan) who disapproves of Marvin and is suspicious about the group. What they are working against is not so much the Germans as the forces inside our own military who have incarcerated them and whose foolish adherence to military tradition threatens them. Ryan challenges them to a war game, and this game illustrates the new "play dirty" tradition of the combat film. There is no way these guys can lose! They cheat. This illustrates that they understand all too well what war is, and what it takes to win and survive in it. It proves the basic inversion policy of the movie. "We're going to steal everything," says Cassavetes, "We're playing war games, right?" They confidently and cheerfully set out to play, singing and laughing as they move toward what they know will be their win. For once, the joke will not be on them, because the establishment has stupidly agreed to play *their* game. The war game is a brilliant comedy sequence, superbly directed and presented.

The new dirty group: The Dirty Dozen

The war game becomes a convention of latter day combat movies. This device, a play-within-a-play format, illustrates what has happened for movie audiences. The war is over, long since won, and thus a war game is as an effective device with which to present a combat story as an actual depiction of war itself. The growing self-consciousness of the genre is ably illustrated by this convention. When it's time for the actual commando raid, however, Lee Marvin cautions them, "Up until now it's all been a game. Now it gets real." Nevertheless, the game was as real to them as the raid itself, and the raid will be just another game. They learn their procedures by studying a model of the chateau they will storm, and by memorizing the roles they will play. They are to dress in costumes, pretending to be specific characters, and they recite a rhyme to remind themselves of the order the action will take. And the mission itself is a great piece of filmmaking, a sustained effort of tension that ranks among the best of the genre.

There are two heroes in *Play Dirty*,[19] played by Michael Caine and Nigel Davenport, representing the traditional, "two men in conflict" plot device. In earlier waves, one man would have decent values and believe in the conflict, and would shape up the other one or make him understand the worth and necessity of the war. At the very least, one man would be tough (like John Wayne in *Sands of Iwo Jima*) and the other would, through the rigors of combat, learn the practical necessity for that harshness. In *Men in War*, a mature Korean combat film, the two men were seen to be two sides of the same man, or of an attitude to war, and they ultimately unite in understanding, serving one another's primal needs. In *Play Dirty*, however, these expectations of the genre are not met. The potential good guy with decent values would be the Michael Caine character, the only noncriminal in the group. At the beginning of the film, Michael Caine appears to be a romantic hero a la Errol Flynn in *Objective Burma*. The progress of the film's story shows him abandoning that role and embracing the evil of the film in order to survive. Instead of attempting to teach and reform the others, he deliberately sets out to learn the bad guys' ways. "I'll watch," he says, "and I'll learn." Later in the film, he is complimented for having learned to "play dirty" after he calmly mows down Red Cross representatives with his machine gun.

Like *The Dirty Dozen*, *Play Dirty* does not open with the traditional noble words written on the screen. Instead, an excellent pre-credit opening sequence ably establishes the meaning of the film to come, and the new sense of the hero in the genre. Across the desert an army jeep flies at high speed, its radio blaring "Lili Marlene" in German. In it sits a German officer, a dead body slung across the seat next to him. He speeds through the desert as the credits roll and, after reaching what is obviously an established point on his mental map, he calmly changes his hat to that of a British officer[20] and changes the radio to an English-language station playing "You Are My Sunshine." The dead body remains.

While watching this sequence, we make a series of decisions which are used in the inversion of the genre. We first see the man at a distance, and assume he may be the hero. He is not. Then he appears to be a German, our enemy. He is not. Then he appears to be one of our British allies, and thus presumably again the hero. He is not any of those things either. What is he, then? What he has accumulatively appeared to be—a villainous fake hero who owes allegiance to nothing but his own survival and who plays dirty, very dirty, and finally is seen to be the dirty hero who dies for nothing. (In *Film Comment*, which runs a continuing series in which celebrities are asked to list films that were their "guilty pleasures," director Martin Scorsese cited *Play Dirty*, referring to the powerful effect it had on him as a viewer. He then went on to say that it was Michael Caine driving the jeep in the opening sequence. In fact, it is Nigel Davenport, and the error illustrates one of the points of the film—good and bad are interchangeable and Caine has to become like Davenport to survive.)

The basic unit of the war film—the group—is inverted by using a group of outsiders as in *Dirty Dozen*. However, *Play Dirty* takes things a step farther with a group that is truly a foul bunch.[21] Even in *Dirty Dozen*, at least some of the criminals had noble reasons for their imprisonment, an indication of potential for heroism. The black man in that group, for instance, had killed in self defense. Charles Bronson's character had shot an officer who was deserting his men, and big, slow Clint Walker had killed after being goaded into it. No one in the *Play Dirty* group, however, has the slightest shred of decency. Foulest of all, Leach, their leader, had deliberately scuttled his ship full of men to collect the insurance money, leaving his comrades to drown.

Furthermore, for the first time we do not see this motley crew shape up and reform. We do not see them suddenly turn into a fighting force that rides to the rescue of a beleaguered group somewhere, or who suddenly respect Michael Caine. On the contrary, they remain sullen, remote, psychopathic. They do not change, and, in fact, they never really become a unified group, but remain isolated from one another not only in combat, but also in death. (The exception to this would be the two Arab lovers, but in a sense they are a one-character unit.) These men do not discuss things with one another for the common good, but only to preserve their own skins.

The use of the objective further illustrates the evolutionary development. It's a fake. It's just a joke, a Hollywood set, a trick not only on the group trying to capture it but also on us. Although we have clearly followed a map to reach our destination, the objective does not really exist. From the beginning of the film, our knowledge of the traditional combat genre has been used to place us in familiar territory. We think we are in a movie like *Objective Burma*, if not in the geographical and political sense, at least in the cinematic. We know where we are, we know where we are going, and we know to what and for why. Only, it ain't so!

By setting up typical audience expectations and undermining them so directly, André De Toth, the film's director, in addition to making an entertaining movie, makes a comment on genre films. You thought this was an objective like the ones you were familiar with, but it isn't. You thought your heroes would be good guys, but they aren't. You thought war was noble, but it isn't. You thought you understood yourselves, but you don't. The use of a fake objective illustrates physically the inversion present in his film.

Just as the genre is being redefined by *Play Dirty* in newer, less heroic terms, Michael Caine in the plot line redefines their objective. When the group members have expended energy sneaking up in pure commando form on what they have been told are oil storage units but which in fact turn out to be mockups made of chicken wire, papier maché and canvas cloth, Caine in a fury, decides they will not give up, but will press on to find the true oil storage units they were sent to blow up.

However, those in power, the evil and/or incompetent leaders, have themselves redefined the real objective (the true storage units) as a nonobjective, unbeknownst to the commando group. This twist presents the true depth of the cynicism of the film. The objective isn't real, but the real one isn't real either, because an objective is an objective only when that label is placed on it by those in power. It can be changed, just as the rules of the genre can be changed. The objective in *Play Dirty* is the perfect objective correlative for what is going on in the genre, and, incidentally, illustrates the difference between the film that can reach us with visual power as opposed to one that must verbalize this concept. ("Oh, God, Maud, it's all so meaningless.") By taking us through a familiar genre story, *Play Dirty* sets us up for a familiar experience. We go in with the characters, tense and excited, and replay the guts and the glory and the fire and the bang-bang, only there's nothing really there. The revelation of the fake buildings is a deep shock for the viewer. Viewers have to live out the redefinition of the genre at the level at which they first experienced its definition—through excitement and violence. *Play Dirty*, a virtually forgotten film, is actually a masterful filmmaking achievement. In it one sees that the evolutionary process is not just a "we've got to keep the masses entertained with something new" but a serious commentary on the changing society viewing the films.

Vietnam and the Genre

While these "dirty group" films were being released, the war in Vietnam was continuing. It becomes important to ask the same question that was relevant to Korea: would this genre have continued to be as popular if the new war had not come along? Probably not. Since we kept on having wars, we kept on having war movies. Although the wars were not the same, the war movies tended to be the same in certain basic ways. Thus it is possible that the genre would not have gone into this inverted, or destructive phase without the influence of the Vietnam war.

The Vietnam war played as it happened on home screens. Anyone who wanted combat had only to turn on the television set. Thus, no one needed story films about Vietnam itself. What was needed was an adjustment of the old, familiar, more acceptable story forms to incorporate new attitudes generated by Vietnam. This is borne out by the fact that there are very few Vietnam films, although this seems to be changing. In 1984 and 1985, such films as *Uncommon Valor*, *Rambo: First Blood—Part II*, and *Missing in Action* have been released. In these films, combat veterans return to Vietnam to liberate American prisoners of war. As of 1985, Vietnam seems on the brink of cinematic respectability for combat/action films. So far, our approach has been to go back in and rescue ourselves—a convenient way to make a *new* Vietnam war—one in which *we* are victorious. Vietnam thus becomes our fight to free its victims instead of our losing debacle.

Up to now, what we can call the "Vietnam film" takes place at home, which is where the war took place for the viewing public. It tends not to be about combat at all, but about the destructive effect it had on American society. Veterans come home and become crazy killers, or have difficulty readjusting because they are hurt and crippled, and also because people imagine them to have become crazy killers. Young people drop out, go to Canada, and incite political riots.

These films, of course, are the overt manifestation of the pressures of Vietnam. The covert presentation takes place inside the old familiar container, the Western movie. Such films as *The Wild Bunch* (1969), a dirty group movie, *Little Big Man* (1970), in which Cavalry men massacre a Sioux Indian village of people who are remarkably Oriental looking ,and *Soldier Blue* (1970), which questions our mistreatment of the Indians, really are films about our activities in Vietnam to a large degree. The evolution of the Western film, if studied closely, would inevitably reveal the march of American history, as that genre is sensitive to historical pressures as much as, if not more than, any other. (This may be why Westerns are temporarily dead. Vietnam killed them.) Basically, the home front movies and these Westerns with new political attitudes are the Vietnam films of this era.

However, there are some Vietnam combat films. The first important one was inevitably written, produced, and directed by Samuel Fuller, the Grand Old Man of War. It was called *China Gate* (1957). There were also a few films set in Vietnam, such as *Saigon* (1948) and *Rouge's Regiment* (1948), *A Yank in Indochina* (1952), and *The Quiet American* (1958). But mostly, it was not a popular subject. There were ripoff cheapies, such as *A Yank in Vietnam* (1962), *Commandos in Vietnam* (1965), and *The Losers* (1970) in which an incredible plot had the Hell's Angels going over to Vietnam to carry out a suicide mission. The first big movie of Vietnam combat was *The Green Berets* (1968). Couched almost totally in terms of the World War II combat film, and incorporating devices from the Korean War (Hero John Wayne befriends a small Vietnamese boy at the end), it was a film that had no imitators and was denounced by critics. Audiences seemed to like it fine, of course, and other films about Korea and World War II continued to be made that were similar.

From *Green Berets* until 1982, only four significant films were made about Vietnam combat: *Boys in Company C* (1978), *Go Tell The Spartans* (1978), *The Deer Hunter* (1978), *and Apocalypse Now* (1979). *Deer Hunter* is a story about the home front, as well as about combat, and its combat is cut short by the imprisonment of the heroes. *Go Tell The Spartans* contains a character called "Old WWII," played by Burt Lancaster, so we can be sure to get the point that his military style and values belong to a different war, a different era. The film of this group that is most like the established combat genre is *Boys in Company C*, a combat patrol film with a mixed group of types, followed from their leaving home, through basic training, over to Vietnam and into combat. Their chance to liberate themselves from the horrors of war comes through a soccer game.

Similarly, *M.A.S.H.* (1970), the Korean war film about a mobile army surgical hospital that inspired the longrunning hit TV series, contains a football game. The emergence of the game as a unit of the combat genre reflects modern times. These games take the place of the war game units that were seen in films like *Dirty Dozen*, and are linked to the presentation of commando raids. A progression of abstraction takes place here—from straightforward, serious combat to commando raids to war games to noncombat but combative games like soccer and football. Not only does this show genre development, but also changing times in terms of the audience's increasingly non-real, referential understanding gleaned from constant watching of television. The audience that watches football on television can have its physical war combat replaced by a football game, an appropriate metaphor. The ultimate of this games progression is represented by *War Games* (1983) where all activity is brought onto the computer screen, represented by no human activity at all except at the computer board.

Genres must keep step. In the late 1970s and 1980s, movies about professional football (and other games) not only become a mini-genre themselves, but their conventions can stand in for meanings in established genres. This does not represent the replacement of a basic generic convention with another. Rather it represents the abstraction of an old one, or its reduction into primary visual terms. War is a game to be won with rules and opposing teams and uniforms and a final score.

Looking Backward, Looking Forward

The total evolution of the World War II combat genre may be summarized as films which:

Create reality
Self-consciously use the original creation
(Respite)
Relate filmed reality to historical reality

Replace reality officially with filmed version
Invert and thus test the filmed reality

After all this, one is tempted to quit. But the question arises—what will happen next? One can presumably look back in order to see ahead. What has been happening in the last few years shows us that the military comedy still exists *(Stripes, Private Benjamin)*, that the war games variation still exists *(Southern Comfort, with a National Guard unit on maneuvers in a Louisiana swamp)*, that commando raids for various purposes are moving toward a Vietnam milieu *(Uncommon Valor and Rambo)*, that combat arises in some form in new locations *(Under Fire, in Nicaragua)*, that cross-pollinizing continues *(Red Dawn, the teenage movie goes into combat)*, and the old traditional combat film rolls on *(Attack Force Z)*.

At the very beginning of the 1980s, at a time when one might assume the World War II combat film was dead, Samuel Fuller brought out his magnum opus, *The Big Red One*. In terms of genre development, it is an interesting phenomenon. We already have seen how Fuller is unique. His films have honesty in their presentation, but they are distinguished mostly by their amazing energy and dumbfounding abstraction. He's a special case, because of his own World War II combat experience, his tendency to write, produce, and direct his own films, and his having made films about both Korea and Vietnam. *The Big Red One* is the story of his own combat experience, and its resulting blend of reality and unreality make it a fitting finale to the decades of combat films that have been screened and discussed here.

Fuller had previously made one other World War II combat film, *Merrill's Marauders* (1962). It is a variation of the *Objective Burma* story, that of Brigadier General Frank D. Merrill, who commanded the first American infantrymen to fight in Asia, the 5307th Composite Group, who came to be called Merrill's Marauders. They were trained as guerrillas and sent deep behind Japanese lines in Burma.

Merrill's Marauders is a kind of "for real" *Objective Burma*. Looking at it illustrates what happens to genre as it evolves. It plunges a viewer rapidly into war, with an abstracted narrative that offers no explanation or justification for why anyone is fighting. It clearly assumes that an audience has knowledge of, awareness of, and a full understanding of, the combat situation: hero, group, objective, iconography, and even historical fact.

Thus it is solidly based on genre, even though it treats the basic definition in a highly abstracted manner. Part of the epic fourth wave, *Merrill's Marauders* is indeed an epic creation, which replaces a real-life set of heroes with their filmed counterparts. It also has the visual power of the Second Wave, some of the questioning attitudes from the Korean Interruption, and the anticipation of inversion that will follow later. The work of Sam Fuller, as always, defies all rules.

But *The Big Red One* (1980) is the more interesting film because it illustrates the problem of analyzing genre. In Fuller's case, which came first—the chicken or the egg? Since Fuller wrote, directed, and produced his own combat films, it seems safe to conclude he was in charge of the collaborative process, which does not mean that he might not have used ideas from others. Since he also fought in the war, it seems safe to conclude he was creating experience based on reality as much as, if not more than, movies. Significantly, his war films do present the basic pattern of the World War II combat film in terms of group, hero, and objective, but these elements are tempered by real-life experience, by Fuller's personal attitude toward film, and by the demands of his low-budget presentation.

Fuller's "group" is Lee Marvin, the old warhorse who has survived World War I only to have to fight World War II, and four young men for whom he plays both mother and father. Fuller's war, the real one he fought, would have been such a war—his leader and the three closest to him. A foot soldier in combat does not have the big picture, or a very large group, as he engages in fighting. As he fought, Fuller lived while others died. And that's the story of *The Big Red One*. All around the little group of five, men constantly die and disappear and are replaced. This is the truth of the war for Samuel Fuller, from North Africa through Sicily and D-Day and Czechoslovakia. He was a survivor.

The Big Red One is Fuller's abstracted re-creation of the memory of his experience as a young combat soldier. We know that genre re-creates a familiar story, because an audience has the need to know and feel and hear and see war so that they can learn what it is. Since Fuller knew and heard and saw the real thing, he re-creates *experience*, a dramatized version of a personal combat experience. Yet because he is seeking to connect to an audience whose expectations are generic, he has to reconcile experience and genre on a much larger scale than that done by the Third Wave.

Nevertheless, *The Big Red One* can be classified as a genre film. Since a World War II genre exists, *The Big Red One*, by virtue of being a World War II combat film, is a part of it. It contains the iconography of the World War II genre: guns, helmets, tanks, mortars, grenades, ships, landing craft, German soldiers, landscape of war, civilians overrun by war, children of war, hospitals, wounded soldiers, explosions, etc. It has the required list of generic recurring themes and forms: combat/rest, night/day, safety/danger, father figure leaders, ethnic types, discussions of home, mail call, Christmas in combat, new recruits coming up, death, loss, sacrifice, blood, the family unit of combat (mom, pop, etc.), the cook, the taking of an objective, the purposeful journey, maps, directions, walkie-talkies, the newspaper man. However, it also contains nongeneric elements: A scene in an insane asylum and the liberation of a death camp. (The latter did appear in such films as *The Young Lions* (1958) but it is not, oddly enough, indigenous to the war genre film). Rarely does the combat genre story begin as *The Big Red One* does in World War I and come forward to the "present time" (which is ironically past time) of World War II.

In *The Big Red One*, Fuller is like a man telling a story orally (the narration) and as he tells it, the pictures in his mind—those abstracted, partial pictures that we have as memories when we clearly narrate logical events to other people—flash on the screen. It is as if we are seeing into his mind. Images explode, jump forward. Then they calm and settle and are whole. Then they fragment again. Some of the material is generic, because, after all, the genre itself is based on actual historical experience. Some of the material is not generic, because it is personal to Fuller's real experience, in which war is not as it has been presented on screen. Its purpose was not, as in the generic need, to prepare us for death and for a generation of our society's members who learned to kill. Its purpose was, for those who fought it, to live. "That's the only glory of war." Thus, the artistic purpose of the Fuller film is at odds with the genre. Ironically, he must use the genre to make his point. His purpose, however, is not generic, but personal in the sense that it is his autobiography he gives us—both the truth of people he remembers, and the abstracted essence of that truth. Fuller makes no attempt to delineate characters other than one small unit: Lee Marvin and his little band of survivors. They are symbolic—the ones who live through combat. The war genre does the opposite. It seeks to make a larger group of individuals (representative though they are) real, so a

Lee Marvin and the group of survivors in The Big Red One

viewer will feel their loss and death. Fuller lets anyone and everyone die, except for the magic glorious survivors. His whole purpose differs.

Fuller's film demonstrates a primary need—the need for a man to share his story. Where some veterans give us an oral history, Fuller was in the unique position of being able to give us a visual one. We bring our experience of the genre. He brings the experience of the war. We know a little bit about the experience. He knows a lot about the genre. Genre and experience combine.

The importance of understanding genre—in *all* its manifestations (historical, political, and cinematic)—is underlined by *The Big Red One*. The power of genre for the mass audience is so extreme that even Samuel Fuller, a veteran of World War II, cannot film the true story of his experience without coming to terms with genre. Genre's blend of truth and history, and its falsification of both as well as its reality of both, are so strong for viewers that they can no longer understand the story or look of World War II without reference to it. Genre forces reality to its mold. Truth cannot exist without genre. Can genre exist without truth? Since the combat genre is historically determined, its study cannot fully answer this question, which requires a deeper look into a less historical genre example.

A comparison of Fuller's presentation of the landing at D-Day on Omaha Beach with that of *The Longest Day* reveals the difference between the personal and the epic. A viewer is plunged into the D-Day combat of Fuller's film very suddenly, without historical explanation and preparation, much as the individual soldier would have been plunged into it to fight there. The combat sequence breaks down a viewer's perception of coherent events, and also our genre expectation. It presents incoherence, with no overall vision of what the total situation looked like or meant. The water runs with blood as each man's number is called to go forward. "Survivin' is the glory of war," the narrator/hero says, and with those words, the final comment on both World Wars could be made. *The Big Red One* could easily stand as the very last combat film ever made about World War II. Will it? Its final scene is a World War II repeat of its first scene, which was about the end of World War I. "There is no end to this story"—words not spoken on screen here—seem to echo from the ending of *Steel Helmet*.

What we see from the evolutionary process is that a useful container has been built—a set of characters and situations that are familiar and that can be used to teach us new things we need to know. If the new ideologies, problems, and pressures can fit into the old genre, it will remain alive. If not, the concerns will shift to new places, such as the science fiction film, or they will go back to the old ones, such as gangster films and Westerns. When we need the combat film, it is there. If we don't need it, or we want to see its basic configuration in another setting, that will happen.

FOUR

Variations of Genre

Hollywood films are never what they are thought to be, as everyone who studies them learns. It is only the uninitiated who repeat the old assumptions—there's always a happy ending, always a scene where the lover keeps one foot on the floor in bed, never an experimental attitude toward the medium, and never an antiestablishment political statement. None of this is true in reality. For example, *I Am a Fugitive from a Chain Gang* (1932) does not have a happy ending. *The Big Combo* (1955) shows a man's head disappearing out of frame as he kisses his way down a woman's body. *Citizen Kane* (1941) and *Rope* (1948) are truly experimental, one with narrative structure and one with long takes. *They Won't Forget* (1937) is a story of a miscarriage of justice in which an innocent man is wrongfully hanged, and the prosecutor doesn't care because it furthers his own career. These are just a few examples to prove the point. Many mainstream films operate against themselves, containing subversive messages that are the opposite of the surface stories. Part of this comes from the meanings derived from the visual components of film, which act as commentary, intentional or unintentional, on the more literary portions.

It's the same with genre. It's easy to make genre easy, but if one wishes to be complete about it, there are things to be considered which might be eliminated as irrelevant, but which, in fact, turn out to be very relevant indeed. The historical tracing of a genre isolates films which point up genre's complexity as well as its vitality and flexibility. Once established, genre keeps alive. It's hard to kill. A complete historical survey of any one genre indicates how many times what is established as the genre will turn up where it is not expected—in other compatible genres, for instance, or in seemingly incompatible ones.

Let's assume that we are going to be as complete as possible. We won't eliminate anything that is directly related. We have seen what has happened so far: the combat genre was born out of history and defined, and it evolved into a familiar, recurring format long after the historical event that inspired it was resolved. As it did that, its basic definition remained intact, but was used for alternative but related meanings. The concerns of the basic combat film—the list of questions it asked the American public—were more or less built into the evolutionary process. The questions were always there. The answers have changed.

What if the combat genre were varied for a set of questions that were seemingly unrelated? Or what if it were varied by tone or mood? What if it were united with another genre, one that was seemingly incompatible? If so, what would happen?

This is an additional aspect of genre evolution that can't be ignored. As the evolution takes place, it can be undergoing another variation, wave by wave. Another genre, such as the woman's film, might merge with it. A seemingly incompatable attitude, such as a musical variation or a comedy presentation, might be taken toward it.

These variations are too incomplete and too inconsistent to negate the evolutionary process. Yet they are another important proof of genre, because they are based on the assumption that the audience understands the thing to be varied. They are part of the process that fixes the genre in an audience's mind, and they further demonstrate that the basic generic conventions can be flexible in meaning while remaining rigid in form.

Three variations of the combat genre demonstrate how this works: the woman's film, the musical, and the comedy. None of these variations of combat has its own coherent historical evolution. For instance, the woman's combat film appears briefly during 1943, and again in the Korean War. The musical version never really appears, but hides itself in places from time to time. Comedy appears hardly at all during the early stages (at least as a pure form), but grows increasingly important until it plays a key role in the inversion wave.

How is what we now know to be the combat genre altered for these variations? Events, such as mail call and a ritual celebration of a holiday, can remain. The iconography (the guns, equipment, uniforms) may remain, although uniforms (clothing) take on an expanded role in the woman's film. The geography does not need to be altered. The presentations of night and day, safety and danger, action and repose, may still be used in organizing the narrative. The tools of the cinema may be employed in the same manner. The basic definition can remain intact *except* in the units of *hero, group,* and *objective.* Here is where the variance is seen. The average audience thinks of a film as a kind of surface literary experience—who is it about, what happened to him, who were his friends, what did they have to do? These are the primary identification points that determine what is now called "accessibility." The subliminal messages that an audience codes out of the visual presentation are just as important—perhaps more important—but they are not what most people leave the theater talking about. Thus, altering the basic units of hero, group, and objective alters the meaning of the conventions in ways the audience can immediately determine. This works only if what we recognize as genre is present.

This variation pattern is a part of the growth and survival of the genre. It is further proof of the process, built into the evolution as it takes place, stage by stage. To test it, one must ask—can the audience recognize the genre in its varied, or altered, form? If not, there is no genre. The film is not a combat movie.

The Woman's Film Variation

Very few women-in-combat films exist, but in the first wave of war films two important ones emerged: *So Proudly We Hail* (September 10, 1943) and *Cry Havoc* (November 24, 1943). There are also training camp films for the women in military, such as *Keep Your Powder Dry* (1945) and *Ladies Courageous* (1944), and women up front taking charge of combat action (Irene Dunne flying a plane out to bomb the enemy in *A Guy Named Joe,* 1943). Later, there is even a service training musical to match the old Dick Powell films—Esther Williams in *Skirts Ahoy!* (1952), surely one of cinema's noblest titles.

It is not uncommon for the woman's film to use other genres as a background, and many of these other genres are male-oriented: Westerns in *Westward the Women* (1951), biography in *Madame Curie* (1943), prison movies in *Caged* (1950). But the use of the war film presents a set of comparisons and contrasts that help to further define the combat film, as well as the woman's film. In genre terms, the woman's film and the WWII combat film are seemingly diametrically opposed to one another. Consider these comparisons:

Woman's Film	Combat Film
1. About women.	1. About men
2. Story about an individual.	2. Story about a group.
3. Passive.	3. Active.
4. Can be set in any time, any place.	4. Is fixed in wartime, primarily WWII.
5. Love and romance central.	5. Love and romance either not present, or relegated to subplot or flashback.
6. Flexible. Uses other genres as setting to be invaded and reconstituted in female terms.	6. Inflexible because of linkage to real historical event.

The first point is obvious. However, whereas men in combat may or may not think about women or talk about women, and women may or may not appear, men always appear in the woman's film. In fact, frequently the woman's film is about what a woman has to do in order to figure it all out about men. The one film about women that contains no men, *The Women* (1939), is a dog-barks-the-Star-Spangled-Banner joke. See—it can be done! *The Women* is all about men, even if they don't appear physically on the screen. Significantly, when the film was remade as a musical, *The Opposite Sex* (1956), the men do appear.

To reflect its individualistic presentation, the woman's film frequently is titled only with the woman's name: *Mildred Pierce, Lucy Gallant, Nora Prentiss*, and countless others. The notion of a group of women working together is a film rarity. To work as a group, women must set aside petty rivalries, and unfortunately many films present women as petty rivals. Sisterhood is not common. When a woman's film presents a group of women together, it is usually a film linked directly to a profession (a male concept), as in *Dramatic School* (1938) or *Stage Door* (1937). It may also show a group of women banding together to protect themselves from men, as when the women of *Secret of Convict Lake* (1951) pitchfork a rapist to death. It may present a unit of women to make a specific point about how destructive and ridiculous women are in a group, as in *The Women*, a comedy, but also in the later film, *The Group* (1966), a tragedy in intent, a comedy by accident. An exception to this is William Wellman's excellent film, *Westward the Women*, based on a story by Frank Capra. In this film, women work together beautifully, forming a group of sisters who can prove their worth in a difficult situation. This film is an unusual one, however, and it is also an example of placing women in a man's genre, because the film is a traditional Western in every other way. The women can become sisters because they have taken men's roles upon themselves. They have become brothers.

Traditionally, the female film is passive, and the male active. No matter where a woman goes, she takes her restrictive condition of femininity with her. She is trapped in a situation which has been forced on her by a restrictive society and a series of limited choices/bad decisions. She undergoes events of a psychological, emotional, or social nature. She is acted upon, and even if she becomes a murderer, or takes some kind of action, she has generally been forced into it. (The innately evil woman is an inverted aspect of this phenomenon.) The action available to a woman is that of traveling up and down the socio-economic ladder (or possibly that of usurping the male role). From genre to genre, from Brooklyn to Bombay, from cave days to now, she is trapped in the sense that her social limitations restrict her life. Her problem is external (society presses down on her and limits her), and internal (she must figure out what she can do about it).

In the combat film, there is the opposite situation. Even though they are in a war environment, the men in war are free to move about or, if trapped, to make plans of active resistance. The war itself is open-ended, with the possibility of victory and thus, control. These films are filled with action, and in some cases, are almost totally action. The men move horizontally through a geography as they take charge of events across a temporal and spatial framework.

Instead of always being set in one specific time period, such as a time of war as is necessary for the combat film, the woman's film can take place in any time period. It is frequently in a modern setting, but it also fits well into a period with a specific social attitude toward women, such as suffragette days. But love and romance, which are the central concerns, can happen anywhere, and this allows for the essentially passive woman's film to be flexible and invade other genres.

Consequently, the woman's film, unlike the combat film, cannot be as easily identified by one set of generic expectations. After it is identified as being about a woman, it can go in many directions. It tends to be a metaphoric representation of human problems of all sorts, to which audiences, including women *and* men, can bring an individualistic set of attitudes. In a combat film, men go out and do battle with other men. In a woman's film, a woman has an emotional response to whatever varied circumstances are a part of her own life, and her world may consist of only some vague plan for the future, some hopes and dreams. Whatever the emotional issues of the leading woman character's life are, these are the conventions of the film. (Career? Family? Love? Sacrifice? Politics? Science? War? Murder? Evil children? History?) Since the combat film takes place in a world of action, and action brings resolution, a list of conventions can be seen and identified. Since the woman's film is a more internalized situation, in which no action is possible or in which action brings destruction, it is more difficult to identify a set of recurring events. Women tend to be depicted as imprisoned by their emotions, rather than liberated by their actions.

Thus, the woman's universe is a state of mind, rather than a common set of exterior generic conventions. In that these films' preoccupation with the woman's dilemma overrides the specifics of historical time, locale, and visual style, which define most other film genres, the woman's film can be regarded as a super-genre which can encompass others within it.

The woman's film seeks to achieve something on film for women that women presumably cannot achieve in real life: nobility, release, sisterhood, sex, economic power, political power, physical dominance, in short, liberation in all its forms. The woman's film variation, in which women successfully and happily achieve these goals, frequently takes place outside of society's restrictions—in wars, on wagons west, and in whorehouses. The implication is that society, polite society, is the force which holds women down. When women choose to give up these freedoms and accept society's more restrictive role (the alleged "happy ending"—where the woman gets married, returns to her husband, or whatever—or where she is punished for these achievements by death or rejection) the film takes place in a more conventional social arena.

Women in Combat—World War II

What happens when women go into combat? Two films from the year of initial definition, 1943, So Proudly We Hail and Cry Havoc, illustrate the generic merger. Since both were released as the genre was forming, they obviously cannot be thought of as re-creating it. And since we are looking at two films from the 1940s, before the women's liberation movement of the late sixties, we are looking into films which reveal women in contrast with traditional models. Besides these two films, home front movies such as *Tender Comrade* (1943) and *Since You Went Away* (1945) show women in new roles, taking men's places in defense work.

Both *So Proudly We Hail* and *Cry Havoc* maintain the conventions of the combat genre. Thus, the iconography of war is present in the traditional way. Guns, helmets, uniforms, ambulances, ships, soldiers. The enemy is in place, and he is smart, mobile, and attacks aggressively. The historical setting is accurate—on Bataan, as it is about to fall, and events which are recognizable occur: mail call, a Christmas party, rivalries, complaints. However, both films alter the pattern of hero, group, objective. This alteration shows us what the woman's combat film is about. It shifts the meaning of the war onto the primary issues of the woman's film. When women are in the war, the issues of the war are love, motherhood, sex, and choice—four things the woman's film is always about, whether it is set in the West, in the home, in a prison, or in combat.[1]

A woman's film can have a woman play a hero instead of a heroine. This does not mean merely that she plays a man's role, or does a man's job in the film. She is the central figure of the film either way. She takes the role of the hero only when certain attitudes and deeds can be ascribed to her. A woman is hero, as opposed to heroine, if she fits one of the following portraits.[2]

1. A woman who defies conventional roles and redefines her life on her own terms, even if she ultimately chooses to be a wife and mother. She undergoes a process of questioning, as a hero would.
2. A woman who defies society itself, not just the conventions of society. She settles for nothing less than possession of her own life, even if she is destroyed in the fight. A man who fights this way is a hero.
3. A woman who by choice or accident finds herself in a situation or a profession that commonly would be restricted to male participation, and she functions ably in it.
4. A woman who forms and maintains a positive sisterly relationship, a healthy mother/daughter relationship, or who joins a group of women in an important professional endeavor.

The women who go into combat are heroes because they comply with one or more of the ground rules above.

In the woman's film, or in any American film, you frequently have
a woman character who does a man's job, and it's a big surprise, or a
plot point. For instance, K.C. of *Take Me Out to the Ball Game*, the
"man" who is the new owner of the ball team, is Esther Williams, and
"I.V. Hotchkiss" of *You Came Along* is really *Ivy*, the publicity agent
who will tour the United States with three flyers. This calls attention
to the fact that women do not usually hold such jobs, and when they
do no one expects it. The film uses this first by making it dramatic,
unexpected, and exciting for an audience. Except that, after a while,
audiences get wise. A woman! It's going to be a woman, we all begin
to think, and by thinking it, make it acceptable, possible, believable.

Film works in these mysterious and dangerous ways. It takes something that is not true, and makes it dramatic by using it as if it were
true. By doing this, it makes a point about the thing not being true. By
making the point, it also makes it true. It makes the untrue thing
possible, just not very probable. But by making it possible, and putting
it on the screen as if it were a reality, it begins to make it probable. The
impossible then becomes possible and finally inevitable.

Perhaps more than any other variation of the woman's film, *So
Proudly We Hail* demonstrates how two genres can merge. The setting
is purely military, and definitely in the combat tradition: the island of
Bataan during the last days before it fell to the Japanese. (Never mind
that, as the ship carries the nurses toward the place, one says, "I hope
there's a good beauty parlor on Bataan. My hair is a mess.") The
iconography of war is present. The enemy is in place.

The hero of *So Proudly We Hail*, Claudette Colbert, is a tough-
minded professional. She is presented as a career military "man" whose
entire family has been in the service. She is a variation of the Errol
Flynn character of *Objective Burma*. But where Flynn had no conflict
between his duty and anything else to do in life (in the best "a man's
gotta do what he's gotta do" tradition, he was in Burma because that
was where a man must be), Colbert finds conflict between love and
duty. She has to make a choice. Whether it's a melodrama or a light
comedy, a woman's film always forces a woman to make a choice. If
she makes the wrong one, she is punished for it. Thus the woman's
film demonstrates society's way of repressing women. Force the choice
of tradition on her, and punish her if she chooses anything else. (The

Claudette Colbert in So Proudly We Hail

trouble with this method was that films showed women too much of the other choice, and whetted their appetites.)

Colbert's choice involves a man, as these choices almost always do. The film begins on board a troop ship returning the nurses to the United States. Colbert is sitting in a deck chair and staring blankly into space. She is in the catatonic state of the movie-story woman who tried to be a man, but found she was a woman after all. As she sits and stares, her story is told in flashback—a device of the woman's film of the 1940s. (The format is present in *Possessed* (1947), *The Hard Way* (1942), *Mildred Pierce* (1945), and many others.) The flashback places the active part of the woman's story in an appropriately passive presentation. What has happened cannot be changed.

Colbert behaves heroically in combat, and is a reliable soldier. However, she falls in love and decides to marry—a fatal error. Her commanding officer, also a woman, warns Colbert that she should not

Claudette Colbert and George Reeves in So Proudly We Hail

forget her military duty. When she does, she brings down the inevitable punishment of death for her husband and catatonia for herself. She makes a wrong choice. She can be a soldier or a lover, but she can't be both. (Only men get to be both.) Like the men who climb trees and pick flowers, forgetting for a moment that they are in a state of combat, she has momentarily forgotten and responded to nature. She dies—her catatonia being a form of death. Unlike the poor men who are killed, however, Colbert can be resurrected because, since she is a woman, she was only being true to her femininity by falling in love. Her behavior does not have to be punished by true death, only the temporary death of insanity. If she leaves the combat zone (the man's world), she can live again in her rightful place, the woman's world. Thus the film offers liberation and says be true to it, and simultaneously punishes it and says it will kill you.

For women, the war combat film messages were decidedly confused and contradictory. This contradiction, common to the woman's film, is demonstrated through the device of "the happy interlude," in which a woman can have both freedom and love. She can temporarily exist as the creature she wants to be. This interlude is an ironic contrast to what will follow, but it represents the ideal state. In *So Proudly We Hail*, Colbert has her happy interlude when she has a honeymoon in a foxhole. She gets to be a soldier *and* a lover.

This type of contradiction is an important function of the woman's film. Its purpose—show women freedom and take it away from them—is well reflected in the combat film. On the one hand, the women of *So Proudly We Hail* reflect the changing times in which women are going out of the home both to war and to work. They are undergoing an enforced liberation, which will ultimately lay a foundation for a changing social structure. "Time is short," says Colbert. "There's no time to waste it on personal things. We've got a job and a responsibility." This is reflected in the film not only in the heroic actions of the women, but also in their aggressive sexual behavior.

On the other hand, their situation in combat is the kind of subliminal transfer of home life to the battlefield. The men go out to fight (earn a living) and the women stay home and keep house (tend the wounded). Among the messages of freedom, and the sense that sisterhood, like male camaraderie, is a function of sharing meaningful work, are other messages. "Why can't we be pals?" Paulette Goddard asks her lover, Sonny Tufts. "Because only men and men can be pals." he replies. Furthermore, the sense that a loss of love destroys one's life is carried out both in Colbert's character and in one played by Veronica Lake. The death of Lake's loved one has made her hard, and inspires her to suicide.

So Proudly We Hail represents a traditional group of mixed types. Besides the noble "hero," there is a cynical outsider who must be integrated into the group (Veronica Lake). There is the wiseguy G.I., a wolf character who chases men aggressively (Paulette Goddard). There is the female equivalent of the beardless youth, a naive young virgin, Rosemary Larson (Barbara Britton) and the usual parental figure (Mary Servoss) about whose role there can be no confusion: she is called "Ma" MacGregor. The only difference between this group and the ones we've met before is—they are women.

The use of the group is constant in both male and female combat films. The group incorporates conflict, teaches responsibility, initiates and educates its members. However, its organization in *So Proudly We Hail* is altered for the presentation of key issues more indigenous to the woman's film than the combat film. What the group represents—the concerns they have—are changed.

Although these women are in the midst of the war, the primary issues the film brings into focus are those connected with the world of women: love vs. duty and motherhood, for example. Instead of the issues of the war itself, or why we fight, we have romantic entanglement, fear of rape, and issues that might be said to be from the woman's frame of reference. When the question of why we fight does appear, it also emerges from the woman's point of view. We fight because we are mothers, to keep our sons safe.

Motherhood as a concept is reinforced in the plot of *So Proudly We Hail* in two episodes. In one, a baby is born. In another, the group's highest ranking officer, "Ma" MacGregor receives a message that her son has been killed. She has already lost her husband to the war, but, she says, she has a grandson and she'll save him from having to fight. (History has proved her efforts futile).

In these two episodes the war film and the woman's film make a direct connection to one another. They comfortably intermingle, reinforcing one another. Death of a son, loss of a husband, birth of a child—these are events one associates with pictures about a woman's life. The visual presentation of them on screen in the midst of combat seems to provide a point of fusion or unity for the two genres. This is in direct contrast to the male-oriented combat film.

For instance, when babies are born in *Stand by for Action* the event acts as a denial of the male combat situation. It brings the home front into the war, and undercuts the genre. In a sense, this difference proves the point of the genre variance—if birth and motherhood are to be important issues of the plot, then the combat film needs to be about women-in-war to maintain its combat integrity. In fact, when the very male-oriented combat film, *The Big Red One*, presents a birthing scene, it is used for bizarre contrast and as a comment on how far removed men-in-combat usually are from such events.

Costume is a key element in this film. The war film, in its way , is always a costume film, because soldiers, sailors, and marines must wear the proper uniforms and carry the proper weapons to be identified. We know their war by their uniforms, just as we know their military force, theater of war, and combat specialty. We can decode this information, because it is a part of our culture, our common language. (Children in World War II proudly learned to identify uniforms, branches of the service, kinds of airplanes. The war and its costumes were part of their education.)

However, in the woman's film, costume is not just clothing; it's fashion: What women wear matters. (Fashion shows often turn up in the middle of the woman's film, as in *The Women* (1939) and *Mannequin* (1937).) Using this tendency. *So Proudly We Hail*, which after all is about a bunch of nurses on Bataan, makes fashion important because it's a film about women. The sweet young character receives a hat through the mail—a feminine hat, representing what she has given up to serve her country and, since she will die, what she will never have in life. She is like the Robert Walker character in *Bataan*, whose Walter Mitty like stories are the life he will sacrifice.

One of the biggest plot developments of *So Proudly We Hail* involves a black lace nightgown. When a Christmas dance is held aboard ship, the women scramble to make themselves attractive. They try to look like the girls back home. Most of them have only uniforms to wear, but Paulette Goddard has hoarded a sexy black lace nightgown and some perfume. This nightgown becomes an important symbol to her, a link with her past as a woman, not a soldier, and proof of her sexual power.

The group all demonstrate difficulty with their clothing. One can never manage the zipper on her jump suit, and when Colbert decides to marry, they all decide she needs a skirt. What symbolism! However, this is demonstrated more practically in a more combat related device. On their first night on Bataan, the women find their nursing uniforms, stark white and crisp, show up clearly in the dark jungle night, marking them as easy targets.

Furthermore, within two minutes of work in their jungle hospital, these whites are filthy. Told their costumes aren't appropriate, they agree and start dressing as men. They accept clothing that is right for the genre they have moved into. They ditch fashion.

The group of women in *So Proudly We Hail* are strong and intelligent. They work hard, and are good at what they do. In this sense, the film reflects the changing times in terms of the woman's role. Because of the war, and the absence of men on the home front, women have begun to work outside the home. Some have actually gone off to fight the war themselves. No one in the film says to the women, "Why are you girls out here?" The women are also not presented as sexually naive, or frightened by sex. (After all, they *are* nurses.) On the contrary,

the women are more matter-of-fact than the men. When Claudette
Colbert comes in to bathe George Reeves, he is embarrassed, and she
is amused at his attitude. Paulette Goddard's character completely
dominates the man she falls for, played by Sonny Tufts. She's the male
aggressor, and he's the pursued victim. The women of *So Proudly We
Hail* burst forth into acts of real male heroism, or male behavior, in
three episodes:

1. When Claudette Colbert runs into a burning jungle hospital in an
   attempt to save Barbara Britton.
2. When Paulette Goddard socks Sonny Tufts on the head with a rock,
   so she can take him off Bataan and row him over to Corregidor to
   temporary safety.
3. When Veronica Lake committs suicide to save the group. Her sacrifice,
   although a genre convention, is particularly shocking because she uses
   her femaleness to achieve it. Since rape is a horror of war, and since
   women are vulnerable on the front lines in this regard, this spectre
   hangs over the women. The film makes a shocking covert reversal of
   this vulnerability, by having Lake both exploit it (she lures the Japanese
   toward her for this purpose) and reverse it (as they move forward, she
   kills them, suggesting that ultimate sexual power belongs to women).
   This link between sex and violence is one of the major memories
   people have from World War II combat films. "Remember when
   Veronica Lake put the grenade in her blouse and blew up the Japs?"
       Everyone does. She places a hand grenade inside her blouse (the
   symbolism doesn't have to be dwelled on) and walks slowly toward the
   enemy in her combat fatigues. As she nears them, she takes off her
   helmet, and releases her long, very blonde hair over her shoulders.
   When they come near her, in obvious delight, she pulls the pin on
   her grenade and everybody blows up.

In these three actions, the women take the male prerogative for
themselves. They are behaving like heroes from male combat films.
Presumably, this is necessary to preserve the accepted and known genre.
At the same time, because the film is about women, some conventions
of the woman's film must be present, too. The women who go to
combat have taken their issues into another genre.
    In changing the combat film from a male-oriented story to a female-
oriented one, the removal of a clear objective removes the need for
action. If men must go out to blow up a radar station, or if they must

dig in and hold the fort, they have an objective. Even if it involves staying in one place—the "last stand" motif—action must be taken in order to complete this goal. The women, with no objective, have no action to take. They do not have the option of going out on patrol to resolve the situation they are in by killing the enemy. The women in both *So Proudly We Hail* and *Cry Havoc* have a job to do—they stay behind and nurse the men who have been wounded. To do this they stay in one place. They are not making a "last stand." Because they are on Bataan, they are, of course, contained within a larger last stand situation, but they will survive. They are making a kind of eternal stand, and since they are healing people, they are almost an external unit from the combat, a Red Cross, King's X unit. (For propaganda purposes, this quality is seen as being violated by the enemy, who bomb hospitals.)

There is no real objective or series of objectives in *So Proudly We Hail*. The women are more or less stationary in their combat environment, first on the ship that takes them to Bataan and then in their jungle hospital as the war rages around them (and sometimes upon them, through bombs). Thus, they are dependent on the men who fight the war and plan the war to do a good job.

However, they take woman's action. Veronica Lake makes a last stand, in which she buys time and safety for the women, by luring the enemy through her sex. Goddard rescues her lover, and Colbert marries hers. The story, although set on Bataan, is *actually* the story of Colbert's doomed romance with George Reeves. The ending of the film is positive. A letter her dead husband wrote her is read aloud, and Colbert comes alive again in the "it's all suddenly clear now" tradition of old movies. She says that she understands she must give up the military and return to her husband's farm to "make things grow." This is an obvious feminine ending to a masculine genre film which asks the question (heard in the dialogue): "What is a heroine?" Like a finely balanced scale, the film maintains an objective physical presentation of one genre (combat) while it presents the subjective issues of another (the woman's film).

Cry Havoc is a film based on a successful stage play. It adapts the combat film for the woman's variation by concentrating on the group. It has no real hero, and it has no real objective. Most of it takes place inside the bunker-like living quarters the women inhabit on Bataan.

Like *Bataan*, it presents a character configuration of 13 diverse types who come from many different professions. As the men in *Bataan* were a mix of military units, these women are a mix of what might be seen as typically female forces. They are rounded up in the last days of Bataan as volunteers to help a nursing unit. The opening narration, spoken by a male voice, says: "This is the story of thirteen women. Only two of them, Captain Alice Marsh and Lieutenant Mary Smith, were members of the Armed Forces. The others were American women who, until that fateful day in December, knew no more of war than did you or your nearest neighbor." The nine volunteers are:

- Pat Conlin (Ann Sothern). She describes herself as a "lady in waiting." She was a garment worker in New York, a clerk in a dime store in Detroit, a soda jerk in Los Angeles—a waitress deluxe.
- Constance Booth (Ella Raines). "I wrote fashion articles in the Manila Telegram." (This is a candidate for my all-time favorite movie job.)
- Stephena Polden (Gloria Grafton). Called "Steve," she was a supervisor of machine operators in a Manila cannery. She is the identification point for the female war workers in the audience.
- Nydia Joyce (Diana Lewis). "Back home where I come from, women aren't allowed to do a blessed thing." She is the traditional Southerner, the feminine stereotype this film will unseat.
- Luisita Espiritu (Fely Franquelli). "I live in the village with my mother." This Philippine character has the same last name as an actor who played a male equivalent in *Bataan*.
- Susan and Andra West (Dorothy Morris and Heather Angel). Two sisters, with Susan a student of art and Andra a student of music. They represent the artistic, sensitive pursuits associated with the feminine spirit.
- Helen Domeray (Francis Gifford). A PBX switchboard operator.
- Grace Lambert (Joan Blondell). A burlesque queen. "You know what you do to a banana before you eat it? Well, I do it to music."

The other four women are:

- The tough top commander, Captain Alice Marsh (Fay Bainter).
- The professional nurse, Lieutenant Mary Smith (Margaret Sullavan). If there is a hero in the film, she would probably be the choice, as she goes on no matter what. She is depicted as working herself to death. She is seriously flawed, however, as she refuses to admit she has malaria, and also to admit that she is secretly married, which is against military rules. Her husband is a lieutenant who runs a nearby message center, and who becomes the object of another woman's desire, causing conflict.

- Flo Norris (Marsha Hunt). The original volunteer from civilian life. Although she is not a nurse, she is presented as a top professional, a kind of professional volunteer. To indicate this status, she is dressed in male clothing from the very beginning of the film.
- Sadie the cook (Connie Gilchrist). Sadie was a dietitian before the war. She is also the comedy relief. Since preparing food and eating it is an association with the home front, or safety, it is logical that the one who does it can not only be a comedy figure, but also a mother substitute.

Although two women in this group were military professionals before the war, only four of them had no careers of any sort. The others are all working women. Their group contains no real ethnic or racial stereotypes. Although there is a Filipino woman, and there is an alleged Irish type (Pat Conlin, but she isn't very Irish), this woman's group is more of a class or social mix than an ethnic one. This fits with the woman's film, which is usually a story about class, or a social climb.

Besides being separated into high and low class, or into educated and uneducated, they also might be separated into those who work for a living and those who do not. The richest one of the group is the one who most desperately wants to work, and who has come to Manila to pursue a career as a fashion writer. (Her sense of direction may be poor, but her impulse is sincere.)

The point of this group is to show what ordinary women can do if given a change. They arrive in high heels, fussy dresses, and silly hats. But when they change into fatigues, they also change into competent workers, braver than they thought possible, stronger than they knew. In more traditional times, they accepted lowly roles, either as waitresses or strippers, or no roles at all ("where I come from, women aren't allowed to do a blessed thing"). When extraordinary times give them a chance to do what men do, they do very well indeed.

Men are hardly seen in *Cry Havoc*, except as patients. They have a few lines of dialogue here and there. The story is about women. The film's hero, and oddly enough it does have a male hero, is the officer who runs the communication post in the jungle. The women know he is there, because he is seen in long shot, at a distance, outside his post. He is talked about constantly, but we never see him up close at all, a visual equivalent of the film's meaning. These women, cut off from their traditional world, are accepting new roles for themselves. Thus their traditional role, that of loving and depending on men, is demonstrated through the device of having no man up close in their lives.

The women of Cry Havoc *before combat.*

The two weak members of this group of thirteen are women who are linked to concerns which might be thought of as primarily feminine: Susan, the art student, and Constance, the fashion writer. Susan is buried alive after a bombing, and has to be dug out. She has gone insane as a result of the experience. Constance is a crybaby, who is terribly frightened in the situation. She is also the most useless of the group, the one who knows how to do nothing (except dress well). As the women are initiated into the experience of war, and thus into the male world, they all begin to cope, however. (The music student even shoots a plane down off screen by helping an aerial gunner.) They find reserves of courage and humor. When Blondell wants to help keep their spirits up during bombing, she shows them how she did her strip number. Later, when wounded in the legs, she laments "Why couldn't it have been in my face where no one would have noticed?" When confronted with the news that there is no hope of getting off Bataan—

*Fay Bainter, Diana Lewis, Fely Franquelli, Marsha Hunt, Ann Sothern, Joan
Blondell, Margaret Sullavan, Ella Raines, Francis Gifford, Dorothy Morris,
Heather Angel, Gloria Grafton in* Cry Havoc, *dressed for World War II.*

they are surrounded—they accept the news calmly and dig in further
to the work. Margaret Sullavan says, "They're Americans. They believe
in a happy ending." (Fay Bainter replies, "I'm an American. I don't.")

The happy interlude, by its nature, is doomed in both the woman's
film and the war film. In this case, the women go swimming. They
play, happy and relaxed and clean for the first time in weeks. They get
a chance to be soldiers *and* bathing beauties, but we know that can't
last. Suddenly, they hear planes and Constance (Ella Raines), who has
swum out too far, cannot return to safety in time. She is machine-
gunned, and killed in the water. (Don't relax in the environment in
wartime. Climb a tree, or pick a flower, or swim in the cool water, and
you die.)

When they go through the effects of the dead men ("What did you

do in the great war, daddy?" asks one of them, ironically), they find
the toys of childhood, a marble, a rabbit's foot. The men who are dying
are like children. Thus, the issue of motherhood is indirectly
introduced.

Women in Combat After the War

Perhaps the most significant thing about the women's variation of
the combat film is that, unlike the men's, it did not evolve and reappear
so frequently that it became readily recognizable. On the contrary, it
nearly disappeared after World War II.[3] Not only did the need to see
women in war go away, but apparently the need to teach them to go
back home became important. A particularly large group of films in
which women are punished, victimized, driven crazy, or presented as
evil were made in the immediate postwar period. When combat broke
out again in Korea, the women-in-combat film briefly reappeared,
presenting two more films of the type: *Flight Nurse* (January 30, 1954)
and *Wild Blue Yonder* (January 2, 1952).

In both *Flight Nurse* and *Wild Blue Yonder*, the women in combat
are nurses. (It's important to remember that this is historical truth—
the only women up front in close combat areas *were* nurses.) Both these
films carry out the pattern established by the two earlier women-in-
combat films—a respect for the basic generic conventions, tempering
them for the new concerns of motherhood, love, sex and choice, and
making the primary adjustments in hero, group, and objective. They
both repress the group unit, making it small and unrepresentational,
and remove all sense of a physical objective from the story. Both make
the hero a woman.

The voiceover narration of *Flight Nurse* is that of the title character,
a flight nurse played by Joan Leslie. This narration informs the viewer
that she came out to Korea, not knowing what to expect, because she
wanted to be near her sweetheart, a helicopter pilot she expects to marry
(Arthur Franz). She tells the story of her first flight out, to bring the
wounded back from up front. (These "hospital planes" were a phenomenon of the Korean War.) As she tells the story, she is seen from the
male point-of-view by three different wounded men. (Those interested
in the view of women taken by traditional Hollywood films should
know this movie.) At first, she is seen by a young boy as if she were his

mother. Her face fades, and his mom's superimposed over it. The next man sees her as a madonna. Her face again disappears and a dark lady in white lace shawl takes her place. Finally, the third one imagines that she is the girl he is going to marry. For a third time, her face disappears and she becomes this wholesome, fresh-faced girl from back home. Here we have the three roles available to decent women spelled out for us in overt visual terms: mother, madonna, wife.

The presentation of the detailed group disappears in *Flight Nurse*. There are only five women. One never appears and the two are so minor they *hardly* appear.

- An off-screen presence, the girl back home in Rocking Chair, Texas, who loves Joan Leslie's man. She sends him gingerbread ("nice and gooey" observes Leslie). She never appears in the film, but we do see her photograph. She is an Elizabeth Taylor lookalike, a true beauty.
- The Sisterhood character, the heroine's friend. (Jeff Donnell.) *Flight Nurse* has true sisterhood. This character is also prophetic, because she tells the heroine that she once had a guy back in a small town in Vermont, but when she went to visit him there, it was awful. She found it dull, not for her. She lost him to his old home-town girlfriend. "Flight nurses always lose their men," she says.
- The heroine's superior officer, another sisterhood figure, who lost the man she loved in a bombing raid over Tokyo. She still listens for the engines in the skies.
- A minor character, Kit, a nice young woman.
- The heroine. She is presented as a hero. She is the flight nurse of the title, and the film presents her growth into a dedicated professional. She is not only a great nurse, but also a brave soldier. She never gives up, and never panics in the face of danger. ("I'm a nurse, remember?") When the plane she is on is about to crash, she calmly stands in front of the frightened wounded and slowly applies her lipstick. What a gesture! She uses it to reassure the men, calm them, and prove her bravery. It represents the status quo of women in normal life. One can see the men thinking—if she's putting on her lipstick, she must not be afraid. If she's not afraid, why should we be afraid. We're men. She's not.

A Ph.D. thesis could be written on the use of lipstick as a woman's weapon of war and defiance. When Eleanor Parker, the innocent girl who has been corrupted by prison life, walks out the door of *Caged*, she demonstrates her attitude toward life by applying lipstick—thick, dark, lipstick—with a generous hand on an open, welcoming mouth. This represents her kind of bravery, as she leaves one combat (prison life) for another (presumably the life of a prostitute among criminals). In *Tender Comrade*, one of the women hoards lipstick. Why not sugar? Because lipstick is more important. Priscilla Lane knows that. She writes a message that saves her life with hers (*Saboteur*, 1942). Lana Turner drops her lipstick, and it rolls over to her open-toed white shoes in *The Postman Always Rings Twice* (1946), and it's her gauntlet thrown down. It's how we meet her—follow the lipstick to the foot, and then the legs, and then the body, and then the defiant, sexy face. It's also how we leave her, as her dead hand falls and drops her lipstick, releasing forever her sexual power of which it has been the symbol. The ultimate use of the lipstick motif is when Marlene Dietrich faces the firing squad at the end of *Dishonored* (1931), wearing her customary veils and furs. When they hestitate, not able to bring themselves to shoot the woman who stands before them, hand on hip, high-heeled, and without blindfold, she takes out her lipstick and generously applies a new coating. While they compose themselves, she defies them with her feminine symbol. While they fear to use their weapons on her, she proudly uses hers on them. She also demonstrates her contempt for the male world of politics and war.

The finale of *Flight Nurse* has the nurse, in hospital herself from injuries sustained in the plane crash, reject her lover. "I wouldn't be right for you," she tells him matter-of-factly, indicating he should go back to Rocking Chair and marry the gingerbread lady. He still loves her, however, and for that matter, she still loves him. But what he represents is no longer what she wants or feels she must do in life. She chooses her career, actually a form of duty and sacrifice, over love. Although there is another man in her life, he is the man who flies the plane she works in, and what she is choosing is not the other man, but a way of life. She wants the work and the excitement. She is proud of her profession. "I will set the skies ablaze," she says, which is a part of her credo as a flight nurse. *Flight Nurse* maintains the idea that a woman can't have both love and a career, but it suggests she can survive happily by knowing which she wants. To make such a point, the film presents an effective merger between two genres. The woman's film *needs* the combat film to verify the position.

Wild Blue Yonder is also about nurses, but during World War II, not Korea. It, too, works by removing the group and the objective and concentrating on the "hero" who is a heroine. Vera Ralston, the hero/heroine, talks to Ruth Donnelly, her commanding officer about the job. Donnelly informs her that nurses are important partly because men want their mamas when they are out in the war. "We're out here on the Pacific Ocean substituting for all their moms."

Wild Blue Yonder is a strange film. It may be the only World War II combat film with a Ouija Board. There is a great deal of stock footage in use, and the plot is a kind of rerun of World War II battles in the Pacific. Its presentation of the generic merger of the woman's film and the combat film seems to represent an attempt to re-do the whole Pacific war with a woman in the lead role instead of a man. It replays the war via woman's issues.

Wild Blue Yonder also demonstrates a phenomenon of a later evolutionary stage. Not only does it take on new issues, including a kind of preparatory peptalk for the Korean War, but it also provides us with Phil Harris, playing a character in the film, but stopping the action to sing his then current hit record, "The Thing." This strange occurrence is not a single case. Bob Newhart stops the action in the midst of *Hell Is for Heroes* (1962) and does one of his famous telephone routines. In fact, several later combat films feature popular singers and/or comedians doing their hits or familiar schticks. These hit performances are a way of touching base with the current audience, of integrating them into a genre that originally touched base directly through history and propaganda. "The Thing" thus becomes an event equal to the fall of Bataan in film terms! It also represents another step in a weird progression of presenting minorities as group members. From Mexicans and blacks in World War II, to orientals and Native Americans after the war, and finally to comics and singers. Presenting comics and singers as a new minority is a surprising phenomenon that may reflect two things: an attitude that says such men are not macho enough for real war and they can become our new disposable characters, or the public's new awareness that former attitudes toward minority characters were becoming unsuitable for the times. Whatever the reason, the progression is observable in *Wild Blue Yonder,* and is pertinent because the film itself is about another "minority"—women.

Women in Training Camp Films

There are women's training films, but few of them. Three interesting films of this type are *Ladies Courageous* and *Keep Your Powder Dry* from the war years and *Skirts Ahoy!* from the Korean period. *Ladies Courageous* is "sanctioned by the United States Army Air Force as the official motion picture story of the Women's Auxiliary Ferrying Squadron, now known as the WASPS, Women's Air Force Service Pilots." (WASPS is an unfortunate title choice for more than one reason.) These women ferry bombers, but their story is a bit depressing because, as the *New York Times* succinctly put it, they "are portrayed as a bunch of irresponsible nitwits." They keep deliberately crashing their planes to get publicity, to punish straying husbands, and things like that.

Keep Your Powder Dry and *Skirts Ahoy!* are glamorous entertainment films. The latter is a musical in which Esther Williams swims. Each is about three women who join the armed forces, and what happens to them once they are enlisted. In the earlier film, made during the war itself, the women join the WACs and the Quirt/Flagg conflict is between two women (Lana Turner and Laraine Day). *Skirts Ahoy!* takes place during peacetime, and the women's problems are all with men. The theme song of *Keep Your Powder Dry* says that women can fight and file in the army way, can drive a truck and take their places with the men. A Wac's a soldier, too. This stirring number is bellowed out over the credits, but it gives itself (and the film) away when it then segués into a romantic version of "I'll See You in My Dreams."

In both *Keep Your Powder Dry* and *Skirts Ahoy!*, we see the importance of clothes demonstrated, as long sequences show how the women are measured for uniforms and redressed. Presumably these new fashions will change them from mindless clotheshorses into efficient working people. In all these training films, as in the combat films, the female variations reflect a basic usage of the iconography and plot and character devices of the male versions. However, again they are temporized to fulfill the problems inherent to the woman's film. The combination of these two unlike genres generates its own new information. We learn that when women are allowed to work together like men, they can become sisters.

Using established generic conventions to reflect new issues is a part of the evolutionary process. As the evolution takes place over a period of years, it is to be expected that the issues must shift. However, it is not as expected that within the evolution, an incompatible genre like the woman's film might comfortably bond with it. The fact that it can happen helps explain genre. The women's combat film—the merger of two opposite genres—clarifies the characteristics and concerns of both, and also proves that both genres exist in audience's minds.

The Musical Variation

At first glance, it seems possible to eliminate the category of the musical variation of World War II combat. No images of our troops cha-cha-ing through the jungle leap to mind. Skits and satirical revues, including things like the "Springtime for Hitler" number in *The Producers* don't really apply. The well-known British film *Oh, What a Lovely War!* (1969, Richard Attenborough's directorial debut) is about World War I, and is actually a series of skits, only some of which are musical numbers. As is traditional with World War I, its message is antiwar, as its release date would suggest.

However, a few observations are important here. While it is true that musical combat films are not common, the use of war and combat in musicals, and the use of music in combat films, does happen. Not only is the combat film scored with stirring music, but popular songs, folk songs, and military songs are used within its narrative.

A musical number is a stylization of true behavior. A boy and girl talk and share thoughts in dialogue in a nonmusical film and fall in love as a result. In a musical, they sing and dance together and do the same thing. Thus, a musical film can provide a stylization of combat, complete with hero (lead dancer), group (the chorus), objective (patroling through the music to completion), and all the iconography of war. Musicals alter the basic definition by stylizing everything, making it all representational. By repressing everything, they repress nothing. This could never happen if genre were not fully recognizable.

In uniting the musical film and the combat film, two opposites are combined. The lighthearted format is temporarily sacrificed to a more serious one. It becomes apparent that the abstract presentation of a musical number, with its sensuous use of sound, light, and action (dance) is very much like that of the combat film, with its presentation of sound, light, and action. A battle and the movement forward of a patrol is almost a choreographed event. The sound of music and the sound of bombs—both have rhythms, and both are part of what a viewing audience takes in as part of the meaning and the visual/aural/visceral experience of the combat film. The medium makes its own connections, because of its own properties.

The most interesting aspect to the linkage of war and music is the interaction between musicals and war films in plot terms. When World War I moved out of the combat film and off the screen after its transitional use during the last pre-war days, it didn't go away, it just moved to a new neighborhood. World War I turns up as a musical number.

During World War II, Hollywood created many colorful, tuneful musicals for home audiences to enjoy as escapist entertainment. Many of these musicals bore no relationship to the war. Others contained indirect reference. The leading man might be a sailor on leave (*Anchors Aweigh*) or a man who goes overseas into combat while his girlfriend waits back home (*Gang's All Here*) or a man who joins up late in the conflict to entertain troops (*Cover Girl*). However a curious link is forged between the musical and combat through the use of World War I in many musical stories during this time period. In films like *For Me and My Gal* (1942), *Yankee Doodle Dandy* (1942), *The Dolly Sisters* (1945), *Night and Day* (1946) and others, World War I is seen on the screen either through actual combat or through the device of entertainers going overseas to sing for the troops.

In these musicals with World War I references, there appears more than once a scene in which the soldiers who are going to combat are called directly from the theater (where they may be an audience, or part of the performance) to board their war ships. Such a scene makes a powerful visual metaphor for the leaving behind of a joyous, peaceful life (a "musical" life) to enter the life of war. It also calls to mind the fact that both performing a musical number and carrying out battle orders are actions which must be planned, or "staged" to work properly. They must be directed and controlled to succeed. When we speak of heavy drama as needing comedy relief, we are talking about the need for all forms of story presentation (novels, plays, films, whatever) to contain within themselves an opposite. Thus if we need "comedy relief" in a serious piece, perhaps we need "serious relief" in a musical film— that moment in which reality intrudes itself to connect directly to viewers. Perhaps a bad musical is one with no serious relief. Certainly the best musicals contain a successful presentation of a dark force— one that can even make an audience cry. In *Meet Me in St. Louis*,

Judy Garland sings the melancholy "Have Yourself a Merry Little Christmas," followed by Margaret O'Brien's hysterical breakdown. It is not only an effective musical moment, but an effective dramatic moment, and it is part of what makes the film a great musical.

Meet Me in St. Louis is not an isolated case. Even in minor musicals, such as Show Business, there is tragedy. George Murphy and Constance Moore's baby dies—right between numbers, as it were. There is murder (Down to Earth), gangsterism (Love Me or Leave Me), alcoholism (When My Baby Smiles At Me), and plenty more in mainstream so-called escapist musicals of the 1940s and 1950s. People just don't want to remember it that way. (Another aspect of genre!) Thus it is not unlikely that war, a subject on everyone's mind in the 1940s, would and could be incorporated into musical films, and a linkage made. At no time in film history would we have needed any more "serious relief" in our musicals. People who had the luxury to remain outside combat at home (and go to musicals) could have their guilt assuaged by these reminders.

The presentation of combat inside a musical is not uncommon in World War II, or after. In The Gang's All Here (1943), an escapist musical if there ever was one, Alice Faye's boyfriend is seen briefly slogging through a Technicolor jungle, in intense combat, while a series of newspapers fly out from the screen, screaming headlines about Japanese defeats. This brief, miniature World War II movie verifies the character of the leading man as a soldier, and also touches on relevant issues for the then-current viewing audience. It is presented both in recognizable combat film images and as a kind of musical montage, a number in and of itself. Few may remember that the Andrews Sisters are torpedoed right in the middle of "Shoo Shoo Baby" in Follow the Boys (1944). Nevertheless, they are. What's more, they are not seen again in the film, and their shipboard companion, George Raft, dies in the explosion. And the film is definitely a musical.

In later years, both The Sound of Music (1965) and Darling Lili (1969) illustrate the merger of the musical and the war situation. Darling Lili contains startling sound overlaps in which the World War I flying combat sequences are linked to Julie Andrews' musical numbers. The music from her song is played over the images of a combat sequence.

Another curious phenomenon is the 1944 musical comedy, Up in Arms, starring Danny Kaye and Dinah Shore. If a movie features a scene in which the hero singlehandedly captures a platoon of Japanese soldiers on a Pacific island, is it a combat film? A biography like *Sergeant York* or *To Hell and Back*? In this case, no. It is a musical comedy. *Up in Arms* illustrates that genre really does respond to something that is on people's minds—so much so that it has to become a part of all kinds of films, whatever is around. A musical comedy about a hypochondriac who is drafted, *Up in Arms* illustrates events of the war years, and of the war movies, in musical terms. The leading characters make a phonograph record to take along on combat, and we see the homefront side of cutting the records that are mailed overseas to men in combat, as in *Story of G.I. Joe*. The men depart for combat, marching onto a troop ship, singing their heads off and looking well rehearsed in their choreography, the musical variation of many a serious film departure. On board the troop ship, a big band plays jump tunes up on deck, and the soldiers and nurses jitterbug. Dinah Shore does a number, and everyone has a swell time. How far away from this is the troop ship scene in *Guadalcanal Diary*? They, too, sing and talk and share their memories. The cheerful enjoyment of sailing into Pacific combat in *Up in Arms* may be seen as the musical variation of the more serious presentation of the same event, yet the serious event contains music and laughter, too. Furthermore, the musical version has its totally serious moment: standing on deck at night, looking out at the troop ships and destroyers that make up the convoy, Dana Andrews and Constance Dowling, the second leads, talk:

> ANDREWS: It'll seem funny, forty years from now, after the war, taking these uniforms out, shaking the mothballs out of them, and wearing them to march in a 4th of July parade.
> DOWLING: Joe, do you really think it will be a better world?
> ANDREWS: *(with conviction)* I'm sure of it.

Later, Danny Kaye captures the Japanese army, and gets the girl. Is this really any different from Sergeant York or Audie Murphy capturing hundreds of Germans? Or from Katharine Hepburn poisoning the entire Japanese army in *Dragon Seed*? It represents film fantasy, but more importantly, it represents a ritual act on behalf of the moviegoing public. Thank you, Danny Kaye. Thank you, Gary Cooper. Thank you, Katharine Hepburn. If you can do it, we can do it. Alone, together, with music or without. It is what is on our minds and what we want to see happen. Seeing is believing. Believing is doing. Doing is winning.

Danny Kaye in Up in Arms

The more we see it, the more we know we can do it. It's why we like genre films.

After the combat genre of World War II has been fully established and defined, it can appear as a referential moment in a musical film. This is observed in *I'll Get By* (1950), made during the Korean conflict.[4] Leading lady June Haver is out entertaining the boys in the Pacific. Earlier she has split up from her true love, William Lundigan, and he has gone to war. As she stands on the stage, singing her heart out to an audience of cheerful soldiers, the film shifts to a traditional war film image. It's as if two separate films have been spliced together by mistake. From out of nowhere comes a World War II combat patrol. From over a distant hill they straggle, battle weary and dirty from jungle warfare. They file down the hill slowly, hot and worn, carrying their guns. When Haver sees Lundigan among them, she runs from the stage to his arms. Haver is fresh and crisp. Her hair is perfectly coiffed, and she has fresh violets in it. Her pale yellow dress is spotless, and fully puffed out by starched crinolines. Her high heels fly over the combat turf, and she embraces him.

What is going on here?

Genre is going on here! The Musical meets the War Film. An audience can see the combat patrol and read this image of war for what it represents in terms of hero, group, objective, and everything else. We can assimilate it into the musical story. It's a traditional image that we know and recognize. Furthermore, we accept it as compatible. The image not only speaks to us of *Bataan, Guadalcanal Diary, Sahara,* et al., it also tells us more, something about the leading man's character. It says, having lived through *Bataan, Guadalcanal,* and *Sahara,* he has now grown up. This man who treated June Haver badly will be different because he went on "patrol in combat with a group of mixed types, and his leader died, and he had to take over, and they went for their objective." We know his story. Furthermore, this combat movie is the resolution of the musical story. Without the combat genre, the film cannot complete itself. These films show how genres with seemingly incompatible characteristics can use one another. Again, it could not happen without the genre being clearly established and recognized by the audience.

The Comedy Variation

Comedy in combat is almost always present. We take it along on patrol, because that's the American way. Men joke, tease, and gripe with humor. The man who steals eggs and carries them in his helmet— who has to put that helmet on when the bombers come over—makes a Laurel and Hardy egg-on-face joke. We've always had the film that mocked war, from Charlie Chaplin in *Shoulder Arms* (1918), with Chaplin effectively camouflaged as a vigilant and particularly active tree, to *Dr. Strangelove* (1967), with its powerful comment on the madness of nuclear war. Even as early as 1946, Sid Caesar was doing a standup comedy routine in which he acted out a lampoon of Hollywood combat movies—a little skit in which a fighter pilot captures the entire German air force.[5] But war is not a funny subject, and making pure comedies about it is difficult, especially when the medium is one that can make real such things as bombs and explosions. The comedy variation of combat is a tricky business. By its nature, it fits best in peacetime, with no threat of real war, and most easily is used for an antiwar statement.

First of all, there is the question—is a comedy combat film a comedy, or is it a combat film? Is comedy a genre, or an attitude toward genre? Screwball comedies have their own characters, conventions, and narrative structures, as do groups of comedy films by certain directors (Preston Sturges, Frank Capra) whose work is a genre unto itself. The unique comic worlds of Charlie Chaplin and Buster Keaton are probably genres, as are the Marx Brothers and W. C. Fields. And comedy can invade certain seemingly incompatible genres, much as the musical and combat film can commingle. For instance, consider the comedy horror film, which is sometimes only a spoof of horror films, but which other times is an honestly scary film with laughs (*Ghost Breakers*, 1940).

The comedy variation of combat involves its own tempering of hero, group, and objective. The hero must be flawed, so that comedy can happen to him. He must be unattractive (by sex symbol standards), or cowardly, or sickly, or inept, or uninformed, or shy. Something must be wrong with him. If he is a sex symbol, he must be put upon on some way that limits his heroic capacities. He must be temporarily emasculated. The group configuration either does not exist, so that the hero can be the comedy star, or it exists as an inept extension of him, or as his nemesis. The objective is a search for dignity, just keeping free of or in control of the comedy, and it can take many, many forms.

Obviously, the early days of the war did not encourage a comedy look at combat. Real combat was serious. Comedy relief was to be found in other kinds of films, or in the training film variation of combat, in which the war was not a war, but a war game. (Comedians in uniform also dealt with the saboteur issue.) This tradition existed during World War II, with Abbott and Costello in various service-related comedies, and after World War II with other comedy teams, such as Martin and Lewis. Full-scale comedies involving men on actual patrol in the real war did not appear until *after* World War II. Then they became a jolly way to reminisce about the good old days of the war, not only on film but also on television. (*McHale's Navy* is an example of the combat comedy, and *Hogan's Heroes* is the example of the comedy concentration camp film, a melancholy variation indeed.)

During the war, *See Here, Private Hargrove* (March 22, 1944) was one of the most popular comedies released, but it was a training camp film involving a war game. Its sequel, *What Next, Corporal Hargrove?* contains comedy in actual combat, but it was released after the war (December 26, 1945).

Two films illustrate the true comedy version of combat, *Operation Petticoat* (December 5, 1959) and *What Did You Do in the War, Daddy?* (September 1, 1966). Both were co-written, directed and produced by Blake Edwards, a man whose work frequently concerns comedy variations of established genres, as can be seen in his popular Pink Panther films. When talking about the comedy variations of the combat film, it is important to understand that these films are different from antiwar comedies (even if they indirectly make such a statement) and films which make a soldier's life funny. We are talking about a true combat film, following the conventions of the genre, being treated as a comedy. Comedy combat, not combat comedy. *Operation Petticoat* and *What Did You Do in the War, Daddy?* illustrate two methods of honestly presenting the real genre in comedy terms. *Operation Petticoat* does it by the same method as the woman's film—alter the basic unit of hero, group, and objective—and keep everything else intact. (Interestingly, women play a big part in *Operation Petticoat*, further proof that the methods are similar.) *What Did You Do in the War, Daddy?*, a unique film, does it by keeping all generic conventions intact, but treating them as a distanced event.

Operation Petticoat

Operation Petticoat is *Destination Tokyo* feminized. The hero is a comedy star, with a comic variation of himself at his side. The group is a Keystone Kops unit, and the objective is a series of jokes. This film follows a pattern that is frequently used by the naval film, that of having a man return to his old ship. He remembers his World War II combat story in flashback. This character is played by Cary Grant, who is now boss of submarines in the Pacific and who once was the skipper of the *Sea Tiger*, which is about to be sent down for scrap metal. He has come to his old sub for nostalgic reasons, carrying the former ship's log, because he is himself the man who must give the order to scuttle her for scrap.

Consider the casting of Cary Grant. Here one genre unit intersects another. Grant is himself a genre, master of the Cary Grant film. Over the years since World War II he has become a legendary master of comedy. His presence automatically speaks of elegance, grace, talent, legend, persona . . . and comedy. Yet the film *Destination Tokyo*, which he made during the war, was not a comedy. His comedy persona had to be abandoned for the sober role. His association with that film, and with his role of submarine skipper, is built into his appearance here. He brings meaning with him, some of which is specific to the submarine film.

The second lead of *Operation Petticoat* is played by Tony Curtis, a Cary Grant variation. Not only is Curtis a latter day comedy player with smooth good looks, he is also associated with his ability to do Cary Grant imitations, as in *Some Like It Hot*. His role here is that of an "idea man" who used to design navy posters for Hollywood. He comes on board carrying his golf clubs.

Curtis and Grant confront one another. When Curtis hears the *Sea Tiger* has been trying to get toilet paper since 1941, he says he'll handle the problem. "You'll ruin your manicure," says Grant, skeptically. "Don't let the manicure fool you," replies Curtis. "I was born in a neighborhood called Noah's Ark. If you didn't travel in pairs, you just didn't travel." This establishes Tony Curtis' own persona. Born in a slum as Bernie Schwartz, he developed a career as a teen idol, partly as a comedy player and partly as a misunderstood juvenile delinquent. Grant and Curtis provide a self-conscious comic updating of Quirt and Flagg. Grant's persona is imitated by Curtis, with Curtis' own persona relating back to Grant's personal life, as they both come from humble origins. Together, they make a comedy team for a combat movie which will treat the hero like a concept, rather than a human being.

Not only is there real combat in *Operation Petticoat*, there is even a mock commando raid for the toilet paper. Most interesting of all, there is a situation in which the submarine must take on women and children from an island (and some of the women are pregnant) as well as a group of nurses. This incorporates all the possibilities from old Navy movies—except nuns! When the women come on board the submarine, the formerly masculine spaces (in which men move with confidence and assurance about their jobs), suddenly become problem areas. To walk past a woman on a submarine, a man must rub against her. This puts him in her power, or at her mercy. A woman's bosom

Cary Grant and Joan O'Brien in Operation Petticoat

juts out into the passageway of the submarine and forever transposes it into a danger area. It takes possession of the space. It attacks and intimidates. The enemy is among us!

During the action of *Operation Petticoat*, babies are born, including a set of twins. And, through plot complications too entangled to explain, the submarine is painted pink. Thus we see what happens in the comedy variation of the war film—emasculation. If war is a macho thing, requiring brave men to fight it away from the comforts of home and women, then a way to make it a comedy is to put the women back into it, which is exactly what happens here. Edwards paints the whole genre pink.

To be successful, combat comedy must remove the sting of war. It must take away the serious issues, defuse the masculine intensity and sense of male honor linked to combat, and make the practice of combat into an unreal experience, that is, a game of some sort. This allows us to laugh. We are at the appropriate distance from an event that, seen close and felt as real, would not be funny. (As Mel Brooks says, "Tragedy is when I cut my finger. Comedy is when you fall in a sewer and die.")

What Did You Do in the War, Daddy?

What Did You Do in the War, Daddy? demonstrates effectively how to treat combat as comedy. In doing so, it provides a checklist of devices that all film comedy uses to provide an audience a place to laugh at things it might not laugh at in real life. By manipulating all these devices at top speed and making them ridiculous, it is able to maintain the generic configuration of hero, group, objective.

Can films really make unfunny subjects funny? Can we see death, murder, and suicide, and laugh at them? Let's put it this way—how funny is Hitler? Hitler, an unfunny subject by anyone's terms, is as funny as any filmmaker can make him. Over the years he has been treated as a joke in many films: *The Great Dictator, To Be Or Not To Be, The Producers, The Lambeth Walk,* and cartoons such as *Der Fuhrer's Face.* Of course, these films do not produce the real Hitler, cheerfully bawling out, "What are we baking in the ovens today, Hermann?" and expecting to get a laugh. Instead, Hitler is treated as a cartoon, an exaggerated parody of his physical self, strutting and uniformed to a ridiculous level. This demonstrates one of the ways to make Hitler, or any unfunny subject, funny—cartooning or exaggeration. Some form of distance, to provide for viewers a humorous perspective as well as a margin of safety, must be created. Comedy is commentary, as well as surprise. An audience can unload its anger and aggression at Hitler by laughing at him and, on that basis, he is probably an excellent subject for humor.

Film can provide many different devices to create distance for viewers in comedy: Flashbacks, dream worlds, film-within-film devices, narration, use of color, verbal and visual incongruities and ellipsis, as well as cartooning and exaggeration. There are also traditional methods such as using the theater as a setting, having a play-within-a-play, roleplaying, parody, satire, gameplaying. All the tools of cinema—camera angles, camera movement, lighting, composition, cutting, and the soundtrack—can be used to intrude on a viewer and self-consciously say, "See this? It's only a movie. You're not laughing at a real murder—only a picture of a murder." This gives viewers distance. All these devices involve distancing the audience, and treating the *results* of combat (death) as if they do not matter or do not really exist.

In a cartoon, the hero can get up and walk off after the cannon blows up in front of his face. His head may be charred to a stump, but in the next frame, he is himself again, ready for the fresh disaster. This eternal resurrection is indigenous to cartoons, and perhaps accounts for their popularity with children and adults alike. And, of course, the cinema has readily available another important tool for mass audiences—the familiarity with genre. Using genre as a basis of "reality" and creating distance from it by spoofing it is both a part of the inversion wave of evolution, and a continuing variation within each wave.

What Did You Do in the War, Daddy? is a play on genre and a comment on war. Its particular type of comment could not be made without the knowledge of genre. Thus, it is—unlike other variations we have seen—able to maintain the basic unit of hero, objective, and group. It builds an additional layer between these traditional devices and the viewing audience—the layer of comedy,—or, perhaps of unreality and distance.

The very title, *What Did You Do in the War, Daddy?* is in itself a device which uses a once-respected inquiry line as an ironic question. This announces the film as, if not a comedy, at least ironic in attitude. Significantly, the title of the film is not the first thing an audience sees as the film opens. What one sees is a massive explosion—followed by the simple printed statement: "Sicily, 1943." A skilled genre viewer might feel uneasy; there is no printed "thank you" for the armed services and their cooperation, no insignia or stirring military music. Just a wild visual explosion and a calm statement of place and time—a nongeneric opening juxtaposition to set the alert viewer on edge. As the film opens, it first presents traditional combat in straightforward terms. Then it moves into a scene inside a tent between Dick Shawn and Carroll O'Connor that does not tip its hand. At first, it could be a typical scene from a combat film that we have seen many, many times before. But as it plays itself out, it slowly begins to come apart at the seams—it descends into comedy. The recognizable and straightforward military conversation about tactics that O'Connor and Shawn are having suddenly takes on a parodistic nature, in which O'Connor seems to mock Shawn and Shawn is revealed to be a silly martinet, acting out his role from having watched old war movies. The scene is a perfect example of what will happen in the film that follows—establish real combat and let it fall into the chaos of comedy.

Dick Shawn leaves the tent and goes up front to confront his new command, a hardbitten patrol unit of tough World War II combat types if we've ever seen them—C Company, who've had more combat experience than God. This is a familiar situation of genre—the schoolbook lieutenant who comes in to take over the old pros. Shawn bawls orders which are received with studied indifference by the patrol, who are busy getting chow. At the end of this sequence, as Shawn's jeep pulls away, the old pros are seen looking at one another with a "what the hell is going on here" attitude. Only then does the film's title appear for a viewer: *What Did You Do in the War, Daddy?* Now we know the film will be a comedy, but until then, no one could really be sure. Thus it builds itself solidly on the truth—not about the war, but about the combat genre.

As it unfolds, *What Did You Do in the War, Daddy?* turns out to be a war combat film, but also a comedy film which suggests that all war should be seen as the farcical situation it really is, essentially meaningless. It is presented as a sort of gameplaying event, with a little-boy mentality that starts it and keeps it going. Unlike the frequently pretentious antiwar films that give an audience a direct unambiguous message, *What Did You Do in the War, Daddy?* gives a viewer a true comedy. It is rowdy, chaotic, and very funny. Whatever message it contains is in the tradition of Hollywood's action films. Its meaning is implied, not told.

As was said earlier, war by its nature is a kind of theatrical event. We even refer to the theater of war. World War II had the ETO and PTO,—European and Pacific Theaters of Operation. People have roles to play with titles and appropriate costumes, insignias, and prescribed behavior. There are "leads" (generals) and "bit players" (privates), and when it is all over, there are the inevitable reviews—by historians. *What Did You Do in the War, Daddy?* uses this idea of theater to the hilt.

After the pre-credit sequence, Edwards takes viewers into a brilliant passage in which the combat unit moves into the city of "Valerno" via traditional combat movement. This passage forms a visual basis for what will be repeated in the film. As the patrol moves forward, ducking, hiding, looking around them and above them, they present a ballet of combat. It's as if an avant-garde Manhattan dance troup has discovered a brilliant idea for a new dance—the dance of the combat movie. It is absolutely true to the form, yet stylized and representational. As the men dance forward on patrol through the empty city, we await the inevitable moment of danger. And it comes—in the form of a soccer ball! Out of nowhere, like a ridiculous missile of some desperate war, a soccer ball flies through the air, impales itself upon a patrolman's bayonet, and slowly deflates cartoon-style. This flying ball acts as a punctuation mark. It marks the end of any assumption the audience might have had about this perhaps turning out to be a traditional genre film after all. It deflates the pomposity of war, and the purpose of combat. It's as if an avant-garde Manhattan dance troupe has discovered another, at the same time establishing the "war is a game" level of meaning in the film. The combat patrol now becomes enmeshed into the village life of Valerno, and the film takes off from there. The pre-credit scene has established the genre, and the opening sequence after the credits establishes the attitude to be taken to the genre.

What Did You Do in the War, Daddy? uses the full genre definition. Its group is presented as a true combat unit, including the device of having Aldo Ray, a star of many serious combat films, as one of its members. Its objective is initially established as serious, and presented as an actual combat patrol entry into a dangerous village. Its hero, as in *Operation Petticoat*, is a dual figure: a serious side played by James Coburn, and a comedy variation, Dick Shawn. The same emasculation process as in the submarine takes place, and the same legitimate presentation of actual visual combat occurs.

The level of sophistication about genre of *What Did You Do in the War, Daddy?* is even higher than in *Operation Petticoat*. Both films work from an assumption of genre, and take an attitude that says "this is a filmed event." *What Did You Do* works at a very high level of assumed audience awareness. The film not only suggests that war is a game, just as soccer is a game, but that filmmaking is a game, too. One must know both sets of rules: the conventions of genre *and* the properties of the medium.

Edwards treats the action as a filmed event. He makes jokes on space, by making a laugh out of the CinemaScope frame. When the Italian beauty makes her first entrance into the film, her bosom enters, not her. It completely takes over and dominates the entire CinemaScope space. Edwards moves a candle across the screen in the same comedy manner, uses joke music on the soundtrack, and refers to films overtly in having an Italian say an American is like "Giovanni Wayne."

All the devices of comedy are brought into use: role-playing (including men dressing as women), chases, dialogue, satire, and slapstick physical comedy. Events include a man going mad in the catacombs, Communists who are trying to poison a German, and two bank robbers tunneling under the town to rob the bank. In the middle of it all, Hitler appears. The maddest figure of them all, the biggest role player, the craziest and most chaotic of human beings, Hitler is played straight. In the world of *What Did You Do in the War, Daddy?* who needs a comedy Hitler? There's enough else.

Structurally, the narrative presents real combat, mock combat, a movie of mock combat that is mistaken for real combat, and, as if that weren't enough, it weaves another combat metaphor (a wild party) into the sequence and presents a party/combat scene with its aftermath of "death"—drunken sleep, and partied-out bodies lying all over the city square. After the first "party" (read "combat") scene, we see the next morning, the wounded lying about the city square as if they were dead. The chaos of party is both the chaos of war and of comedy. The exploding firecrackers and noise of the party parallel those of combat. Added into this madness is the knowledge that the party, besides being a combat metaphor, is also another kind of game. Edwards builds a multi-layer comedy which, against a background of real war, demonstrates the chaos and destruction of comedy itself. The chaos of war equals the chaos of comedy. ("What is war?" says one character. "The survival of the loudest" is the reply. One might substitute "funniest" for "loudest".)

The film pulls off an enormous coup. In the beginning, the audience watches a "real" combat unit move into a "real" village for "real" combat reasons.[6] The soccer ball destroys that reality. Later, we see the same patrol pretend to be in combat, rehearsing for a movie they will make to send back to their commanders as their excuse for remaining in the village. (They'll pretend they're still fighting there.) The original action from the film's opening is thus replayed, once again looking real, but this time the whistle that blows is the director's whistle, not the soccer official's.

As this happens, a German plane flies overhead and photographs the action, and it becomes real again, because when the Nazis see the pictures, they believe it. Here is the evolution of the combat genre in miniature, contained within the plot of a movie. A film event becomes real because someone "saw" it and believed it. By believing it, the Germans make it real, and turn the town into a true combat zone by invading it. This puts the heroes of the patrol in an awkward position. In film language, they have nothing to go on but comedy experience, so they fight the war on that basis. They deal with the Germans, who now control the village, in comedy terms. They dress up either in drag, or in enemy uniforms, and crawl out of the catacombs and bonk the Germans on the head, one by one. "Everybody go out and get one German," is their plan. Ultimately, they succeed. The entire German army is captured, dressed in American uniforms, and put in prison. The Americans, dressed as Germans, are totally in control. The substitution of one army for another—what's the difference?—makes its point. The village explodes in celebration, and a lot of the audience leaves the film with a headache. As the film unfolds, the pace is increasingly speeded up, so that the experience of viewing is the experience of sinking into chaos. But with genre as guide, the viewer can follow the event.

It is fitting and appropriate that the film end with yet another mad party, with noise, music, explosions, and above it all an insane general standing on the church roof crying out "Back to the reservation! You'll get no more rifles from Kincaid!" To him, it all looks reasonable, familiar, logical. He has undergone the process of war, of comedy, and of filmmaking. He is fully integrated into madness. He has been our guide, and he represents us. He can see the genre that holds it all together, even if he is academic in his equating of the combat genre with the western.

Summary

These three types of variation on the combat film are important because they are all based on an assumption of genre. They prove that filmmakers and audiences both understood the same language when the concept of the World War II combat film was introduced into any kind of movie. Genre exists, because it can be used not just to re-create itself, or to teach new ideology, but also because it can be put to work to verify musicals, to mingle with other genres, and to self-destruct in comedy. Finally, it can be made to question itself.

FIVE

Problems of Genre

A war broke out. America entered. The film industry made films about the events of that war. People watched them. A way of telling people about the war emerged, and was defined as the combat genre. After the war, combat films briefly disappeared, and then reappeared—again and again and again.

By tracing the birth and growth of the combat film, we determine a set of observations about genre:

1. It is born, grows, and becomes fixed into a basic definition that is recognizable, even though its characteristics are imaginatively varied by filmmakers.
2. After it is established, it goes through an evolutionary process in which it remains recognizable even though its ideological meanings change, its narrative expands, or its characteristics become abstracted to the point of being referential.
3. During its evolutionary process, it may be varied by seemingly incompatible attitudes or generic mixes.

That's what has happened so far. Any problems? Yes. Consider, for instance, the *Brute Force* phenomenon. That 1947 film contains these characteristics:

- There is a group of representative men from diversified backgrounds and nationalities.
- They are thrust together in difficult circumstances in primitive, close quarters (not unlike a foxhole).
- They wear uniforms.
- They are not "free" but are bound to follow orders or be punished for lack of obedience.
- They are without female companionship.
- They have "jobs" to do that are not "civilian" jobs, and they have a goal or purpose, which is to endure and survive.

- They dream and talk of home, and of their former lives before they were forced into this group and situation.
- One cracks under the strain of the situation.
- They share a common enemy.
- They have a mission or objective which is not only like a military strategy, but is expressed in exactly those terms.
- They tell their stories as the situation unfolds, and these stories are presented as flashbacks.
- They look at a "pinup" and fantasize about women.
- They send mail and receive mail, and the mail is of paramount importance to their sanity and well-being.
- They all die by gunfire, trying to achieve their objective.

Is *Brute Force* (even the title is appropriate to a combat film) a combat film? No. It is a prison movie. The men are closed in cells, not foxholes, and their common enemy is a cruel warden. Their mission is to escape, and one of the planners of this escape inspires them by telling them of "Hill 633" and how his old World War II military unit outwitted the Germans in Italy. When this man (Howard Duff) tells his story, it is an actual World War II story seen in a flashback.

Is it only the setting (prison vs. combat) that separates these films? Even the apparent difference of "free" forward movement across and through space for the combat patrol as opposed to forced physical enclosure for the prisoners is similar. There is, of course, no real freedom in combat, and often enough the military situation is likened to prison. Furthermore, the regimented life convicts live is actually styled along military guidelines.

So, what then is genre? Only a setting?

The *Brute Force* observation leads to the understanding that, in genre, there is an inner story (a group of men undergoing duress in an attempt to remain free) and an outer story (the actual setting which identifies the genre as prison or combat). Genre is the method of telling the story. In the shifting patterns of storytelling, the costumes and setting of a genre film might be called its objective parts, and its morality, its humanistic issues, might be called its subjective part. Each genre film has an objective/subjective makeup. The subjective can change its meanings, be varied, and thus evolve. It responds to interpretation. The objective remains the same and is quickly recognized. In fact, it can be so easily recognized that it can become increasingly referential and abstract. We have already see how this takes place in the evolution of the combat film. Simply, stated, we know ideology shifts over a period of time, but the "genre" remains the same. New ideas are taught through familiar forms. In this way, for example, a science fiction story can be used to tell the same story as a Western. We know this can happen because we've seen *Lost Patrol* become *Bad Lands* and *Bataan*. We've seen *Brute Force*.

It becomes possible to think genre is the way we dress a story that we need to tell about an act we must perform. "The attempt to remain free" then becomes the main idea behind both the combat and prison films. This meaning can be equated with a need to know oneself, to understand the universe, to contemplate God, to figure out life, or ultimately to decipher death.

This is important because *Brute Force* is not an isolated case. The Western *Rocky Mountain* (1950), can further demonstrate the phenomenon. Consider these characteristics:

- A patrol on a combat mission in hostile territory.
- A representative group of soldiers.
- An entrapment on a high place, resulting in a last-stand destruction of the entire group.
- A little dog as a mascot.
- Hostile, savage forces in huge numbers.
- Attempt by one of the group to "go for help," resulting in death.
- A second attempt, resulting in success which comes too late for the victims of the last stand, but not too late for a patriotic point to be made for the audience.

All these characteristics are clearly those of the combat genre. Yet the film defines itself as a Western. The hostile forces are Indians. The terrain is the American West, and the "high place" is Ghost Mountain, in California.

Curiously, although it is classified as a Western, *Rocky Mountain* really is a Civil War combat film. As has been pointed out, few films after the silent era directly depict the combat of the Civil War. Civil War films often contain combat as one event in a larger story, which includes tales of family differences (representing the "brother against brother" aspect of the war), sexual pressures (a staple of the Southern film, play, or novel—but that's a subject for someone else's book), and economic development (rags to riches, or riches to rags).

After World War II, the combat film about the Civil War was frequently removed from the South and real battles and reset in the West as a Western. If we can believe our Hollywood films, the West was a hotbed of Civil War intrigue, with plots to take over California, spies under every cactus, attempts to steal payrolls and seize gold and silver mines. Presumably, the nature of the Civil War—the sense of family conflict, the threat to our very existence as a nation, and the sight of destruction of American property—was abhorrent to us. Shifting it West made it acceptable, and the Indians made an acceptable enemy. Instead of us against us, it was us against them, even if national shame should be connected to the conflict. Also, the West is a traditional setting of fighting, conflict, death, killing, and destruction. It is the place where we accept it as a necessary event. There is a strong link between the Western and the combat film, part of which is natural to their common patrols-in-hostile-territory situation. Both also have actual historical roots, and both undergo the evolutionary process, reflecting changing ideology. (The western evolves from a celebration of American colonialism to a criticism of it.) It is always interesting to compare the two. Westerns are based on myths, even though there was a real West. World War II films are based on reality, even though there is a myth. This has to do with the development of film. We never saw the real West of the 1870s captured on moving film for us, but we did have the real World War II on film. This changes a viewer's relationship to filmed narratives.

Observing *Brute Force* and *Rocky Mountain*, we gain further understanding about genre. The basic combat story can be relocated to another equally well established genre without changing the original generic definition. In other words, what defines one genre can appear in another without damaging either. (This is different from the variations we observed, in which the "other" is subservient to the combat genre.) What becomes apparent is the narrative link among genres. Consider this chain: *Bataan* leads to *Brute Force* which leads to *House of Bamboo* which leads to *Rocky Mountain* which can link back to *Bataan*, or from combat to prison, prison to gangsters, gangsters to Westerns, Westerns back to combat.

All four of these movies are linked by a basic configuration involving a hero, a group, a conflict between the hero and a second lead, a designated enemy for the group, an objective in the form of a last stand or a commando raid, guns, uniforms, military iconography, and ritualistic behavior or set of rules to follow. In each, a group is trying to work together to achieve something: win the war, get out of prison, steal for wealth . . . and keep alive. Each ends with an intense battle with guns, and three are last stands in which all are killed by their "enemies."[1]

Boiled down, their story is the same—a group of men of different types confront an enemy to achieve a goal. This illustrates what is commonly designated "transference"—that a story can move across an objective field, through a series of genre settings (the West, a prison, World War II, and Japan's underworld). As it goes, it changes its generic designation accordingly.

We might also construct another, longer chain: *Lost Patrol* to *Bataan* to *Brute Force* to *House of Bamboo* to *Dirty Dozen* back to *Gung Ho!* and then to *Rocky Mountain*. The World War I prototype of the combat film brings us its nearly identical counterpart in *Bataan*, which is itself repeated in the prison movie. The criminal element introduced in *Brute Force* is carried out through the criminal former war heroes in *House of Bamboo* whose evil is a kind of "dirty group" as in *Dirty Dozen*. The original "dirty group" of World War II was to be found in *Gung Ho!* who are linked to the hard-riding, hard-fighting Southern rebels of *Rocky Mountain*. These games can be played with many film titles—as many as one's historical knowledge can dig up. The chains can be made as long as one wishes, and the links can be forged at differing points. They can be circular or linear. What is proved is that the same story can be told as several different genres.

The complexity of genre may be further illustrated by a 1953 film, *South Sea Woman*, starring Burt Lancaster, Chuck Connors, and Virginia Mayo. Coming at the end of the Korean conflict, it reflects a new interest in the characters and situations of war, for it contains at its base a Quirt/Flagg relationship, that of the competitive camaraderie between Lancaster and Connors. It is set in the context of a military court being held in San Diego in 1942. Burt Lancaster is on trial for desertion, and the story unfolds in "flashback" testimony from a series of characters who witnessed various portions of the total events. The use of the flashback is interesting, because the 1953 audience would already associate World War II with the past.[2] It represents a return to a time of more coherent feelings, a more acceptable and clearcut war than Korea.

The film is a latter-day hybrid of the type described as popular during the historical period in which it is set (1940–42, such films as *Somewhere*

I'll Find You, A Yank in the R.A.F., and *They Met in Bombay*, as described elsewhere.) It takes a fundamental military service comedy plot from the 1930s in which Lancaster and Connors (Quirt and Flagg) are opposing forces. Lancaster is a True Marine, devoted to his duty, and Connors runs away. Lancaster follows him to save him from his folly, and they embark on a series of madcap adventures: they sink a saloon (yes, don't ask), destroy a Chinese junk with firecrackers, and swim to shore on a tropical island. Layered over this 1930 service plot is a World War II initiation-to-duty plot, in which they learn on the island that the Japanese have bombed Pearl Harbor, and the United States is at war with Japan and Germany. Because the island is held by Vichy French, they pretend to be deserters so they can roam free. They spend their time in a hotel run by a French woman (reminiscent of the French canteens of World War I) and end up releasing all the Free French that are being held in dungeons on the island. This portion of the film reflects the typical tongue-in-cheek, dashing adventure story that Lancaster made popular at that time with *Crimson Pirate*, *Flame and the Arrow*, and *Ten Tall Men*. It is pure, fastpaced adventure.

Next, Lancaster—still trying to prevent Mayo from marrying Connors—enlists the aid of a motley group of islanders (a drunk, an embezzler, and a true deserter), in a miniature forerunner of the *Dirty Dozen* unholy group. Lancaster and these cohorts break up the wedding ceremony of Mayo and Connors by dressing up in chicken suits! Now it appears we are in the midst of a typical Bob Hope and Bing Crosby Road picture. Yet just as we have settled in for comedy, they are chased through the deep jungle, pursued by a German Captain and his troops, and shadowy lighting, tension, and real bullets place us in the depth of a typical jungle warfare combat movie. As it turns out, the island is near Guadalcanal!

As if this weren't enough, the heroes steal a yacht which is well stocked with weapons and set out to do battle on the ocean. They bump into a group of Japanese in a landing craft, under protection of a destroyer. While underway there, they have found Virginia Mayo hidden on board and they have also found time to rehabilitate the drunk they took with them. (There is no development of the drunk's rehabilitation. The narration tells us about it.) Our heroes open fire on the destroyer, and what happens? True combat breaks out before the viewer's eyes. The crew is killed. The Japanese are wiped out. The destroyer is sunk. The character played by Chunk Connors—the one who has been antimilitary and who was trying to desert—climbs aboard the Japanese ship and loses his life while dropping grenades down her smokestack into the arsenal. This is serious combat, culminating in death for a hero. All ends well, with Lancaster giving a speech that says marines are crazy but we need that kind of craziness. He sweeps Virginia Mayo into his arms, kisses her, says he'll marry her, and when she faints, remarks, "Now all we need is a preacher. . . and a motel."

Why bother with a film like *South Sea Woman*? Because it seeks to disguise its genre by its title, and it is, in fact, a significant mixture of established genres: adventure, comedy, the service comedy of the 1930s, the south seas film, the star vehicle (Hope/Crosby Road pictures), the pirate movie, the prison escape picture, and the costume drama. It is possible to say that *South Sea Woman* does not count, because it is a mixture of genres. . . or because it is not a recognizable genre. . . or even because it is a mess. However, that's a bit too easy. A film like *South Sea Woman* illustrates the point that the story patterns of genre and/or its central issues can move from setting to setting, and that once the conventions are established, they do not have to be used in a pure form. Films like *South Sea Woman* keep generic traditions alive in times when they are not popular, but they could not do so if the traditions were not established. They act as tenders of the flames in times when certain patterns are not right for what is in the minds of the viewers.[3] They don't complete any one of their genre stories, or fully develop them, but they use them as if they are known.

Battle Circus (1953) is another example of these films in which other genres haunt the situation. It is a war film, a combat film, an airplane movie, a circus movie, a screwball comedy, a romance, and a hospital movie. It contains a sequence in which a pilot is fighting bad weather to return to a M.A.S.H. unit with blood plasma in time to save a life. We've met this pilot before, in other genres, other films, where this desperate flight and race against time would be the high point, the whole story. Here it's just a unit of plot, mixed in with other units to make a film to be released. Having been presented to us earlier, in its pure, strong, generic form, we can accept it here as a little reminder of what those other movies were all about. We *know* how that pilot has to suffer, and we *know* the danger he's in. We also know he'll make it.

Battle Circus also gives us a little screwball comedy, in which Humphrey Bogart accidentally walks in on June Allyson while she is show-

ering. He goes back out in the rain, but she follows, and they fall in
the mud, get soaked to the skin, laugh and kiss. (When it rains on two
people in films, and they fall in the mud, they will also kiss. I first
learned this in *Julia Misbehaves*.) Keenan Wynn plays a former circus
roustabout who is in charge of dismantling and repitching the hospital
tents as the mobile unit moves about in combat. His job was learned
in earlier films, too—the circus movie. And so it goes.

One thing any sensible filmgoer knows is that a film entitled *The
Black Shield of Falworth* will be about medieval knights and ladies, and
it most certainly will not have anything in common with the World
War II combat genre. Well, perhaps a jousting scene, or some scenes
with combat, or even knights "on patrol" might apply. But who could
be prepared for *The Black Shield of Falworth* having a traditional basic
training motif? Tony Curtis, playing the hearty peasant who is really a
nobleman with a ring "placed on him at birth," comes to the "squire
school" at Herbert Marshall's castle. This school, which has a heirarchy
of squires, knights, etc., is set up as a traditional boot camp. Curtis is
issued his regulation gear, and is seen walking with it stacked neatly in
his arms as he enters the "barracks" and begins a dialogue with friends
and enemies among his fellow trainees. There is even a tough sergeant
(Torin Thatcher, in black, with a hood and an eyepatch) along with a
series of training events (hand-to-hand combat, which looks suspi-
cioiusly like the judo training of World War II, and archery, reminiscent
of "Maggie's drawers" rifle training). There is a "bugle" to signal for
"lights out" ("snuff those candles!") and there are uniforms with insignia
that indicate the "rank" and "class" of those in training.

What is one to make of this? Besides demonstrating the limitations
of genre art, *Black Shield* leads to the assumption that, offstage, the
Korean War has reactivated the training genre and reminded the viewing audience, as well as the screenwriters and filmmakers, of certain
filmic events they have come to know and understand. Even without
the Korean War, presumably the audience remembers and accepts
"visual description" as reality. A training camp is a training camp. We
depict it in terms we know and understand and have come to expect.
That is genre.

This reinforces the knowledge that a genre film is not always used
for the same purpose. Genre, once established, can be used in many
ways. Genre is a coin to be spent and, once spent, becomes an invest-
ment that returns dividends. It is a coin with an increasing value, too,

because the more it's spent, the more it's worth. Once an audience recognizes Quirt and Flagg, a little vignette of their quarrelsome selves reminds us of their full story.

Looking at films which are not combat films leads to the observation that genre cannot be understood without taking into consideration its presence in pure, impure, and merged forms. If it had to always be in a pure form, it simply would grow too boring and too obvious for viewers.

There are three uses of genre:

1. The pure form, what we recognize as the genre film.
2. The hidden form, in which what we recognize as one type of genre film appears in disguise, or in another form (*Brute Force*, the prison film that is a combat film).
3. The impure form, in which a miniature genre film appears as part of a larger plot, which may itself be a genre, or may be a mix or collection of familiar genres stuck together.

Each of these uses has its important function, and without considering them all, one cannot really understand the properties of genre. As in chemistry, a genre is an element. It can stand alone, merge equally with another compatible element such as the woman's version of a combat movie, lie dormant inside other elements, or become part of an alloy involving the combination of many elements. And just as would be true in chemistry, its basic properties never change, but are transposed into another thing by reaction with other elements. History and society are the catalysts which trigger these reactions.

Some things about genre which appear to be fixed turn out not to be. For instance, if a song makes a film a musical, what can one do about *Rio Bravo*, a Western in which a group of cowboys sit around the jail and perform an extended song? It is a real musical number, taking its time and demonstrating important things about all the characters who are involved. It is characterization through music, presumably a mark of musical films. This does not make *Rio Bravo* a musical, however. It is still a Western. And three songs don't make *To Have and Have Not* a musical either. Furthermore, a Western setting doesn't make a film a Western exclusively, and Westerns are not always set in the West either. What about the Florida Western, such as *Seminole?*

This brings forward the next observation: genres make multiple usages of the same events and settings. We can define genre by recurring events, or characters, or settings—but these things have no fixed meanings in and of themselves. We know concepts are represented by the things an audience sees on the screen—the coding to be identified by clothing, furniture, architecture, behavior—anything and everything. Is what makes a genre recognizable the meanings of the things presented to a viewer, or is it the things themselves? Is a Western defined by civilization vs. wilderness, or is it defined by hats and horses?

Let's start out with a doctor. He appears in a hospital/medical film, of course. He is allegedly restricted to the requirements of his profession, and to the kinds of stories that involve illness and provide him with a chance to practice his profession. But doctors appear as heroes in Westerns (The Hanging Tree), combat films (The Story of Dr. Wassell, Homecoming, Battle Circus), comedies (M.A.S.H., People Will Talk, The Disorderly Orderly), women's films (And Now Tomorrow), melodramas (Magnificent Obsession) and so many others that it's pointless to go on. There's nothing about being a doctor that keeps a hero from appearing in different genre movies. His is a profession that is needed anywhere, anytime, so, of course, he can turn up, bringing his medical baggage with him, in any kind of film as a hero.

The same thing applies to a setting like a kitchen. A kitchen obviously can appear in any genre, because people have to eat. This does not mean, however, that when a kitchen turns up as a primary setting in a Western, as in The Man Who Shot Liberty Valence (1962), that it is not merely peculiar, but striking. It is the very unusualness of the kitchen in Liberty Valence that contributes to the film's theme of civilization encroaching on the wilderness. Instead of sitting around a campfire to eat, these Western heroes come into a restaurant, which has a kitchen, and in which the hero, James Stewart, works as a waiter. However, from chuckwagons to mess halls to Park Avenue spreads, the kitchen is a place that appears out of necessity. But what about a small shack on top of a high mountain? It can be seen in genres such as gangsters, Westerns, combat, literary adaptations, woman's films, screwball comedies, horror films. It could be used in a musical, a comedy, or a tragedy. It could be in the Northeast, the South, the West, or even the East. The same is true for many such specific settings.

Consider the desert. Many different genres have been set there, from World War I and World War II combat to harem films to fantasy films to Foreign Legion films to melodramas to woman's films to comedy to whatever you want to do with it. A setting is never generically fixed, not even if it is real geography. Units of action can be associated with more than one genre, too. For instance, does a mail call ever appear in a film *not* associated in some way, however distant, with the military? Yes it does, in a girl's sorority movie, with all the girls away at school getting boxes of cookies except one poor scholarship girl from the orphanage. But then, maybe it's there because the girl's sorority movie has a vestigial link to the boy's military school movie, and thus to the same basic military motif. Mail call, another situation linked to the military, is also indigenous to the prison movie and the sorority film, which is also a kind of prison movie.

Consider the use of skiing, which appears in a great many comedy films of the late thirties and early forties. *Two Faced Woman, Tell It to The Judge, I Met Him in Paris* are a few. The ski lodge as a setting is important also, appearing in *Sun Valley Serenade, Mr. and Mrs. Smith,* and more. Does this make skiing exclusively a unit of screwball comedy? No. Why not? Because it also appears in films after screwball comedy died, as in the Esther Williams musical *Duchess of Idaho* (1950). It appears in its dark form in Hitchcock's *Spellbound* and in the Nazi Germany melodrama, *The Mortal Storm.* Today, it is still with us, in James Bond films.

Does the use of skiing in so many different kinds of films at least always reflect the same meaning when it is used? That is the key point. And why did it become popular in the late thirties and early forties? The latter question may have a simple answer. Skiing became a fashionable sport in Hollywood during the late thirties, having been imported from Europe as a leisure pastime for the moneyed set. Ski suits replaced riding habits as the chic thing to have in one's wardrobe.[4] If people in Hollywood liked to ski, and thought it was the chic thing to do, could movies with ski sequences be far away? It gave them an excuse to go to Sun Valley on location, or at least simulate the beauty of Sun Valley in the studio.

Skiing as a unit for a fashionable comedy, then, may be seen as having practical origins. Skiing comes over from Europe. Clothes and outfits are developed for it and sold. People making films perceive it as glamor, so films begin to re-create it that way. It is placed in its appropriate filmic setting—romantic, screwball comedies that feature clothes, laughs, glamor. Putting it all together, we get visual meaning. Skiing = fashion, glamor, money, romance, sex, laughter and escape.

Seeing these films today, we can understand something about the times and what these films meant to audiences. Rich people skied. Poor people—a lot of people who went to the movies—did not. Rich people could ski for real, but poor people could ski at the movies. Skiing came to mean freedom—*any* kind of freedom—economic to the poor, sexual to the repressed, etc.

This means skiing can be used anywhere to mean escape or release of some sort. Perhaps one ought to think of skiing as "the runaway unit." Besides people careering down hills on two sticks of wood, we have runaway horses, cars, carriages, trains, buses, and airplanes. Something in nature or something man-made carries a human being pellmell through space and time. If it's a comedy, he hangs on, flying through bushes, over trees, horror a mask on his face while the audience laughs hysterically. If it's not a comedy, he leans forward grimly, controlling as best he can his destiny, and the audience leans forward tensely involved and frightened. Thus, an extended sequence on skis is available for story use in a Sonja Henie musical, a comedy (screwball or otherwise), a love story, a psychological thriller, a melodrama, a spy movie, a commando raid movie, and a combat movie. Realizing this, we can understand that listing "skiing" as a genre unit only for screwball comedies may be misleading. If one listed all the characteristics of any specific genre, and then eliminated, or marked, all those which appear in another genre one would presumably have almost nothing left. If anything were left, it would be a list of unique properties used only in that genre. This provides us with two observations: (1) Any property appearing *only* in one genre is fundamental to defining that genre, and (2) Many key elements in genre definitions may have key usages in other genres. Either these things have only one true meaning, and all genres are the same, or all meaning is not fixed.

Another observation about genre is an awareness that there are modes (comedy, drama, and their subtle variations—satire, melodrama, etc.) and there are active and passive forms of telling the same kind of story. For instance, if the story is about men having to fight for their freedom, a combat film about men on patrol presents an active variation of the story, while men locked into prison is a passive presentation. A man fighting another man who is trying to kill or destroy him is an active version of a story which might be seen as passive if the man is psychologically destroying himself. There are perhaps also male and female versions of all basic stories.

The issue of tone in genre study is important. Are Western comedies such as *Cat Ballou* or *Support Your Local Sheriff* to be classified as Westerns or comedies? Should all genres simply be divided into two halves, comic or tragic? Or is comedy itself a genre which should contain all the comic variations of other genres? And are musical variations a third tone, or an offshoot of the comedy variation? Take *Love Me or Leave Me*, for example. This tale of the life of the singer Ruth Etting, who was involved with gangsters, has a sad ending. Is it a musical variation of the gangster genre, or are musicals themselves a genre that can have either comic or tragic tones? Or should the film perhaps be classified as a biography?

What, for instance, separates American comedy from the traditional horror film? Consider films such as *Bringing Up Baby* and *Hail the Conquering Hero*, to take two samples from many possibilities. In both films characters emerge from nowhere and take over the life of the hero, dominating him, pulling him forward into a series of events and a lifestyle that he himself does not approve of, does not want to participate in, and cannot control. His life plunges into chaos. He behaves as he does not wish to behave. He is altered. If this is not a horror film, what is?

When the six marines emerge from out of the fog outside a bar in *Hail the Conquering Hero*, enter, and take over the life of Eddie Bracken, it is possible to see a parallel to a horror movie set on the misty moors, with a tiny pub, and an innocent victim inside. Thus it is not character and event alone that determine genre, but also mood and tone, setting and costume. It is the attitude taken toward the event that separates comedy from tragedy, laughter from screams.

When a comedy pokes fun at something too close to the audience's heart, it is described by critics as offensive. Later, it can be called "ahead of its time." "Out" of its time is more appropriate, and this illustrates something about genre. Certain settings and characters work well in certain times for mass audiences. The ideological meanings they contain, or can be made to contain, speak to the current concerns of viewers.

In seeking genre definition, scholars go to the films for an intrinsic generic definition, but are also seeking to capture the extrinsic circumstances for the original audience when the film first appeared, as well as for the audience now. The extrinsic circumstances for the original audience have disappeared, and as we seek to mesh the extrinsic and the intrinsic of today and yesterday (and, for genre, tomorrow), we are always slightly off in our attempts. We are seeking to analyze intrinsically what is an extrinsic situation.

We must think about not only genre, but also about the people who made the film, the film itself, and the people who watched the film then and who watch it now. In genre, we all share a common denominator. But what is it?

Genre is a recipe. At any given historical time filmmakers have a list of ingredients. All the things that could possibly go into the recipe are present in history and available to the storyteller—event, tone, attitude, plot, character, mood, form, language of the medium, etc. The recipe (the genre) is prepared to the vision of the cooks (the filmmakers) and/or the desires and needs of those to be fed (the audience). It may be a mix of ingredients or a pure dish. An egg (a concept) may be present as a poached egg, part of a cake, or the binder in a meat loaf. Need—that is to say, historical or cultural event—dictates desires for dishes. We feed ourselves. (This neat analogy also allows for the "different drummer" school of cuisine—the artists who are "ahead of their time" or "out of step with the times" or "behind the times" and who cook up diet dishes when audiences want kugel!). In the study of genre we have to deal not only with what is butter and what are eggs but also with what do people feel like eating and why?

A final observation in looking at groups of genres is that many can be set anytime and anyplace (horror films, musicals and comedies— and women's films, if one wishes to call those genres). Some which appear to have specific settings, such as Westerns, may in fact appear in places like Florida, Canada, Eastcoast America, or Australia. Furthermore, a Western is not locked into as narrow a time period as one might think. Westerns can appear in Revolutionary War times, as well as in modern times. In *Massacre*, Richard Barthelmess lassoes the villain from his speeding convertible, and Gene Autry films were mostly set in the time of their release. The most common time setting for Westerns is around 1870, but as the genre lost popularity in the late 1960s, we observe the time period most commonly used became closer to 1910. And why not call a Western a costume picture, which, after all, is what it is? Although war films need to be in a time of war, the war can be an imaginary one, as in *Star Wars*. Some people say *Star Wars* is a Western, but what they really mean is that it is the *Brute Force* case— a story from one genre moved to another. It *is* a science fiction fantasy, because people don't want to see it as a Western. If ideology can be made to shift as we saw in the evolutionary process of the combat film, and if conventions of the genre can be moved intact to another setting, as we see in *Brute Force*, what is genre, really? A fad? A business accident? People say it is a story that "needs to be told." Actually, it is a story that needs to be told in a specific way. Don't tell it to us as a Western when we want it told as science fiction. This point reaffirms the importance of the objective "things" which form the basic definition of any genre.

How does one define genre in film as a working concept? Perhaps it is "something recognized and understood from prior experience," real or unreal. It is a thing unfixed, in a state of flux or change. It is a story that needs to be told or heard, but it must be told in a certain way and that way is genre. Genre is the clothes the story wears, and fashion, of course, changes. In any given period of time, there is taste, so several different attitudes toward fashion (the clothes the story wears) coexist. Fashion appears, disappears, reappears. It adapts itself as it goes. Always within the current scene are the seeds of the future fashions.

Part of the purpose of genre has to be to provide us a familiar story with which to teach us new ideological messages. Its comfortable characteristics soften the blow of change for us, and they help us to learn the new lesson. This would not, could not, be possible without an important and frequently overlooked aspect of genre—its visual component. A great deal has been written about certain aspects of this—churches in the West represent civilization, and men who wear hats are cowboys (unless, of course, they are wearing fedoras, in which case they are gangsters). A group of men who ride into town and tie up their horses at a saloon are immediately understood by an audience for what they are—good or bad cowboys—by the way they ride, dress, and just plain *look*. However, even this important coding of information and meaning is only part of the whole visual package. The narrative structure of events, the camera movement, the cutting, the camera angles—all these things have specific meanings themselves which can be interpreted and varied by filmmakers. Much of what we understand to be genre lies in this area, and individual artists of film who wield these tools with skill make generic awareness, too. Because film is a visual medium, genre is not only seeing familiar things. It is also seeing things in a familar way. When a combat unit takes a church in a small village, we learn how it's done, and recognize it without explanation and words when we see it again—even if it takes place on another planet or in a Western town or becomes, in an urban environment, a besieged bank. In fact, it is our ability to recognize such events, and know their referential origins, that helps to prove a genre.

Why does the sun look largest when it is about to set? Why does the moon hang in the sky, centered, as Li Po said, "like a single pale flower" at certain times of the month? Both the sun and the moon appear larger to our eyes when they are rising or setting. Although there is no significant variation in the distance they are from the earth, and certainly no variation in their apparent size, we believe them to be larger when we see them on the horizon rather than overhead. Scientists call this perceptual phenomenon "the moon illusion" and have, over the years, put forth various theories in explanation. Some say that when the moon gets low in the sky, it comes into closer juxtaposition with known objects, and, by inviting comparison, seems larger. Some say that the act of looking upward strains our muscles, and thus presumably renders judgment inaccurate. (What an explanation for most of film study, as we all stare dumbly up at the screen!) Perhaps some blame lycanthrophy—that most cinematic of scientific causes. However many theories exist, scientists do agree on this: there is no real answer to the question of the moon illusion.

Why does a seemingly meandering river, operating by the process of chance, form a strikingly geometric pattern of regularity? In other words, why do regular forms emerge from random processes? There exist things that are called "river meanders"—patterns of striking geometric regularity that have been formed by the path of a winding river. "Meanders," say scientists, are the form that the river takes to do the least work in turning, and that makes them the most probable form the river can take. A predictable form. In reading about river meanders, I found these words: "The fact that logical irregularities cannot account for the existence of river meanders does not rule out other random processes as a possible explanation, because chance may be involved in other subtler, more continuous ways. As it turns out, chance operations can explain the formation of regular meanders. It is a paradox of nature that such random processes can produce regular forms. The striking geometric regularity of a winding river is no accident."

Genre in film is a moon illusion and a river meander. Like the moon illusion, it comes and goes according to our perception. Like the river meander, it is a regular form of storytelling that was produced by a random form, a series of business deals.

I have heard of an Indian tribe that has one gigantic story they tell and different people know different parts of it. No one person knows the total story. Certain parts of it are told more often than others, and periods of stress require that certain parts be recounted. In fact, some parts are told only at times of stress. Thus, the story can be told as a series of parts, but each part can be told separately, as a thing unto itself. Maybe all tribes do this, and our film genres are the separate parts of our story.

Can a basic story be flexible enough to become many genres? Suppose it were the story of a journey, and of the need to make a journey— a long, arduous, hazardous journey. In order to make this journey, you need courage, daring, foresight, and a touch of ruthlessness, even selfishness, and certainly an ability to see things as they are. You must want the frontier, as it were. You leave behind safety, loved ones, status quo, and/or misery. Thus when you arrive at the end of the journey (or achieve the new status), you must pay or be punished, because you broke with the past, with tradition, with family members, with safety, with society's rules. As a result, you got lucky, found love, enjoyed a better life, got rich, whatever. This story can exist doubled. It can be happy or sad. It can be tragic or comic. It can be male-oriented, or it can be female oriented, active or passive. It can end in triumph, or in death and ruin.

The journey can pass through space and time (the horizontal mode) or up and down the social ladder of success (the vertical mode). It can also be in and out of sanity, or sanity's counterpart, love (the internal variation). In the space and time mode, the characters move and actually act out the journey (the wagon trains West). In the passive mode, the characters are acted upon.

Besides the male and female, there is the light (comedy) and dark (tragedy). The creation of a thing (inventing it, putting on a show) counts as a journey, because in all forms of creating one goes from not having a thing to having it. That's the journey of creation. The journey can also be historical, a man's biography, his life. The main types would probably be (1) an actual journey; (2) historical; (3) creative; and (4) psychological.

All of these many kinds of journeys are not rigid forms, but can each be found in their purest stages. Thus, there would also be the pure and impure versions. Naturally, as the stories based on this form become familiar, impurity would begin to dominate, in order to provide variation and orginality. (Perhaps genres die when they become too impure to live.) It would never matter if the story were a simple tune or a symphonic opus. The ideologies of these stories can change, and the evolutions can be rapid, as they are in the horror genre, or slow, as they are in the Western. Genre is the method or form in which this all-purpose story is presented. It varies according to historical pressures.

Genre can be observed as it grows, waxes, and wanes, even buries itself in other forms. It has a diabolical ability to disappear and reappear. It can dilate itself inside a larger film, break off, and become the total film. After this dilation, it can further expand itself and allow back into its story the portions it shucked off in the first place. It evolves. Its conventions can shift their ideology, and they can appear in other genres, used for the same or different meanings, and they can be varied in many ways. Ultimately, a genre can take in conventions from other genres. It can become a *container* for other stories.

Nongenre films, particularly those which abound with the formulae of genres, exist in abundance throughout film history. These films keep alive and hold in themselves several generic story patterns and referential forms of iconography. As the story pattern undergoes the generic evolutionary process, it is like a pawn that has been made into a queen. It has undergone a journey and ennobled itself.

The ordinary definition of a specific genre that has been prevalent in our culture (or in certain areas of film study) appears not to be incorrect, but to be incomplete. Each blind man defining the portion of the elephant he has in hand is not wrong about what he perceives. He just doesn't have the larger picture. A thorough description of the tunnel into King Tut's tomb, without the additional information of the treasures it leads to, may seem like a major archaeological study if the door to the tomb is never unsealed.

Genre is alive. It is fickle and inconstant, and must be constantly watched. Will there be more World War II combat films? As Samuel Fuller says at the conclusion of *The Steel Helmet*: "There is no end to this story."

Annotated Chronological Filmography
of World War II and Korean Combat Films

The combat films of World War II and Korea are listed here in chrono-logical order by dates from The New York Times. *Films described in the text are designated by an asterisk* before the title.*

December 7, 1941–December 31, 1942.

A Yank on the Burma Road (Jan. 29)

Director (hereafter Dir): George B. Seitz. Screenplay (hereafter Sp): Gordon Kahn, Hugo Butler and David Lang. With Laraine Day, Barry Nelson, Keye Luke, Philip Ahn.

This film was in the theaters in New York City a scant seven weeks after Pearl Harbor. Its subject was timely enough—a former New York cabbie leads a group of Chinese guerrillas in an attack on the Japanese after he learns about December 7. (Although this is not a frivolous subject, the idea of sending a fleet of New York cab drivers to run over the Japanese has always seemed to me a practical suggestion greatly overlooked by the War Department.)

This is the first film about fighting the Japanese after Pearl Harbor, but it is not a combat film in the tradition we know. It is a film to cash in on the news about the war. What is suggested is that we civilians, like the hard driving hero, will have to get involved, sacrifice our selfish needs, and fight a tough war. It teaches us and initiates us. It is a beginning, but it begins in terms of other kinds of films, other kinds of fights. The hero is not allied with any military force, and there is no group mixture of hearty Americans fighting alongside him. There is a hero, however, and there is a group . . . and there is a big fight. The main plot line is a story about how the cabbie leads a convoy of trucks carrying medical supplies through landslides and bombed bridges to its destination. Its concerns are those of the truckdriving film, and it is an initiation story in which the hero starts out driving just for money, falls in love, and ends up doing it for patriotism.

Our Russian Front (Feb. 12)

Documentary. A compilation of Soviet newsreels and fact-films, edited by Lewis Milestone and Joris Ivens. Photographed at the Russian front. Commentary written by Elliot Paul and delivered by Walter Huston. Produced under the auspices of Russian War Relief, Inc.

Submarine Raider (June 22)

Dir: Lew Landers. Sp: Aubrey Wisberg. With John Howard, Philip Ahn.

This film is really insignificant, and only compulsive accuracy forces its inclusion here. However, it initiates a ritual event, re-enacting Pearl Harbor in narrative form, a phenomenon that would continue to occur long after the war was over. It unites narrative with reality by using newsreel footage, but this accident of poverty cannot claim too much significance without cheating the truth. It shows "the enemy" planning and perpetrating the Pearl Harbor attack, presenting a narrative that covers the 24 hours preceding the assault. The central event has a hide-and-seek chase between an American submarine and a Japanese aircraft carrier. Done cheaply by Columbia Pictures, *Submarine Raider* is designed to exploit current events. There is always historical relationship in film between "first" and "quick and cheap," or money and current events. Genre study should not overlook this.

Eagle Squadron (July 3)

Dir: Arthur Lubin. Sp: Norman Reilly Raine, from a story by C. S. Forester. With Robert Stack, Diana Barrymore, Jon Hall, Eddie Albert, Nigel Bruce, Leif Erikson, Evelyn Ankers, John Loder, Gladys Cooper.

A truly transitional film. Although it lacks the passionate intensity and commitment of the films that would define the new genre, it nevertheless prepares us to understand the war we are embarked on. In this initiation film, the heroes, like the audience, must learn to be professionals and to accept the new responsibilities and sacrifices. These elements would be a part of the new genre, but at the same time, the film's derring-do, its sense of "men are eagles," make it seem to be looking backward toward WWI (*Wings, Hells Angels*, and the two *Dawn Patrols*) for its inspiration. It is a story in which American fliers join the R.A.F. and must be initiated into the typical "stiff upper lip" tradition of the British aces. However, it is a difficult case to evaluate. It contains a great deal of action—enough to qualify as a combat film despite its basically ground-ridden plot line—including a dogfight between British and Nazi planes over the Channel, and evacuation of a bombed hospital, and a Commando raid on the French coast. This is WWII combat! With *Eagle Squadron*, we see the new genre beginning to emerge, but as is true to a lesser degree in *Wake Island*, it is a language not yet spoken by either the audience or the filmmakers.

United We Stand (July 3)

Documentary. Feature-length compilation of newsreels produced by Fox Movietone News for 20th Century-Fox. Narrated by Lowell Thomas. Explains reasons for WWII, including some scenes of war.

*Wake Island (Sept. 2)

Dir: John Farrow. Sp: W. R. Burnett and Frank Butler, "From the records of the United States Marine Corps." With Brian Donlevy, Robert Preston, Macdonald Carey, William Bendix, Albert Dekker, Walter Abel.

The World at War (Sept. 4)

Documentary. Compilation written and produced by Samuel Spewack for the Bureau of Motion Pictures of the Office of War Information. Narration spoken by Paul Stewart. Released through the Motion Picture Industry's War Activities Committee and distributed by M-G-M, 20th Century-Fox, Paramount, Warners, and RKO.

The Battle of Midway (Sept. 15)

Documentary. Photographed in color by a crew of Navy camera men under the supervision of Commander John Ford, USNR. Produced by the War Activities Committee, which designated 20th Century-Fox as the distributing agent.

*Desperate Journey (Sept. 26)

Dir: Raoul Walsh. Sp: Arthur T. Horman. With Errol Flynn, Ronald Reagan, Nancy Coleman, Raymond Massey, Alan Hale, Arthur Kennedy.

Manila Calling (Sept. 28)

Dir: Herbert I. Leeds. Sp: John Larkin. With Lloyd Nolan, Carole Landis, Cornel Wilde.

In this *Manila Calling* variation of the *Lost Patrol* format, a small group of fighting men take a high-ground military position, and, after being joined by a group of various civilians, hold the ground until they are all blasted off their rock by bombers. The last two survivors are a man and woman played by Lloyd Nolan and Carole Landis. Nolan is seen in his traditional role of cynic and Landis in her traditional role as Landis. At the film's end, before their deaths, they attempt to send a message out to the free world about what is happening, a device used in other early World War II films, such as *Foreign Correspondent* and *Somewhere I'll Find You.*

The *Times* review criticizes *Manila Calling* heavily, and refers to how the authors and the director "simply made use of clichés"—the old critical bugaboo of genre. The "clichés" referred to most likely include the familiar presentation of how the individuals respond to their entrapment: one goes mad from the strain, one tries to escape at the expense of the others and one is forced to reveal the previously concealed tragic story of his life. Because the plot devices and characterization of *Manila Calling* later become staples of the combat genre, it might be said that it is a combat film of sorts. However, the combat is guerrilla effort, and the presence of civilians removes it from the mainstream of the genre.

*Flying Tigers (Oct. 23)
Dir: David Miller. Sp: Kenneth Gamet and Barry Trivers, from story by Mr. Gamet. With John Wayne, John Carroll, Anna Lee, Paul Kelly.

The Navy Comes Through (Nov. 12)
Dir: A. Edward Sutherland. Sp: Roy Chanslor, Aeneas MacKenzie, adapted by Earl Baldwin and John Twist from magazine story by Borden Chase. With Pat O'Brien, George Murphy, Jane Wyatt, Jackie Cooper.

Although there are effective scenes of battle excitement (a merchant marine ship, with practically no armaments, runs the gauntlet of battle through Nazi subs and bombers) most of this film is a battle between a chief petty officer and his former lieutenant, a pre-war plot. Furthermore, as the *New York Times* put it, "a picture dealing with such a hazardous occupation as getting munitions through the submarine zone of the Atlantic calls for something more inspiring than the comic-strip daring that the script writers unblushingly thought up in this case."

We Are Marines (Dec. 14)
Documentary. Directed and produced by Louis de Rochemont for March of Time. Script by James L. Shute, J. T. Everitt, J. S. Martin and Lt. John Monks, Jr. Narrated by Westbrook Van Voorhis and the marines themselves. Distributed by 20th Century-Fox. (Shows how marines get to be marines.)

Notes for December 7, 1941–December 31, 1942:
A glance at release titles might suggest that a great many more combat films were released than are indicated. However, a check reveals that they are not combat films, but training comedies, musicals, rowdy Quirt/Flagg adventures, or war background films with romance. Some of these titles which were eliminated for very specific reasons after research include: *You're in the Army Now, Pacific Blackout, Call Out the Marines, To the Shores of Tripoli, Canal Zone, The Bugle Sounds, Two Yanks in Trinidad, This Above All, Suicide Squadron, Remember Pearl Harbor, Ten Gentlemen from West Point, Ship Ahoy, True to the Army, Atlantic Convoy, Pacific Rendezvous, Spy Ship, Parachute Nurse, Flight Lieutenant, Wings for the Eagle, Sabotage Squad, Invisible Agent, Bombs Over Burma, Thunder Birds,* and *Army Surgeon.* Many of these concern spies and saboteurs. An important British film, *In Which We Serve,* was released on December 24, 1942. *Flying Fortress* (December 19, 1942) was made at Warner Brothers' Teddington Studios in England, and is only partly a combat film (bombing raid sequence).

1943

*Air Force (Feb. 4)
Dir: Howard Hawks. Sp: Dudley Nichols (uncredited: William Faulkner). With John Ridgely, Gig Young, Arthur Kennedy, John Garfield, Harry Carey, George Tobias, Faye Emerson

*Immortal Sergeant (Feb. 4)

Dir: John Stahl. Sp: Lamar Trotti from the novel by John Brophy. With Henry Fonda, Thomas Mitchell, Maureen O'Hara, Reginald Gardiner.

*Stand By for Action (March 12)

Dir: Robert Z. Leonard. Sp: George Bruce, John L. Balderston, Herman J. Mankiewicz, from story by Capt. Harvey Haislip, USN and R. C. Sherriff, suggested by the story "A Cargo of Innocence" by Laurence Kirk. With Robert Taylor, Charles Laughton, Brian Donlevy, Walter Brennan, Marilyn Maxwell.

At the Front (March 20)

Documentary. Army Signal Corps film on November and December 1942 action in Algeria and Tunisia. War Activities Committee of the Motion Picture Industry release. Col. Darryl F. Zanuck in charge of unit that photographed and edited film. (Note for trivia buffs: Col. Zanuck is seen in film several times, once brandishing a Tommy gun. Also seen is John Ford, riding a donkey.)

Desert Victory (April 14)

Documentary. British Ministry of Information. British 8th Army in the field. El Alamein assault. Included even though it's British, because it won Oscar for Best Documentary, 1942.

*Crash Dive (April 29)

Dir: Archie Mayo. Sp: Jo Swerling, from story by W. R. Burnett. With Tyrone Power, Anne Baxter, Dana Andrews, James Gleason.

Action in the North Atlantic (May 22)

Dir: Lloyd Bacon. Sp: John Howard Lawson, with additional dialogue by A. I. Bezzerides, W. R. Burnett, from story by Guy Gilpatric. With Humphrey Bogart, Raymond Massey, Alan Hale, Julie Bishop, Ruth Gordon.

One of the most interesting things about this film, in retrospect, is its presentation of a scene in which a torpedoed American ship goes down. The German sub who sunk it comes in, taking a film of them, and tries to run them down, showing no mercy to those in the icy water. The dramatic scenes of the flaming ship and the desperate escape of the crew are one of the high points of the movie. Almost forty years later, the excellent German film *Das Boot* (1981) shows a similar episode from the point of view of the German sub. In *Action*, the Germans are heartless and cold, ruthlessly filming their movie, and moving off, laughing at the hapless men in the water. "We'll pay ya back," shouts Massey defiantly. In *Das Boot*, the horror of the situation is subtly presented, as the German sub's crew, carrying on necessary combat, soberly sees their U.S. counterparts hit the water. They know they are to take no prisoners and, in fact, that space and rations, as well as their orders for a long patrol, prevent it. Silently, grimly, they pull back out of frame in a visual presentation almost directly linked to the earlier movie. Given the nature of genre, one imagines the German film crew and creators to have seen *Action* sometime in the postwar period, and to have answered it directly with *Das Boot*, without propaganda, without apology, in a tragic explanation of the horror of war.

*Bataan (June 4)
Dir: Tay Garnett. Sp: Robert D. Andrews (called "original screenplay") With Robert Taylor, George Murphy, Thomas Mitchell, Lloyd Nolan, Robert Walker

Victory Through Air Power (July 19)
Documentary. An animated film from the Disney Studio, a thesis on the use of airplanes in modern warfare. Based on the book by Major Alexander P. deSeversky.

*Report from the Aleutians (July 31)
Documentary. U.S. Army Signal Corps film, photographed by a unit commanded by Capt. John Huston. Produced for the War Department, released through the Office of War Information and distributed and exhibited through the auspices of the War Activities Committee of the Motion Picture Industry.

Destroyer (Sept. 2)
Dir: William A. Seiter. Sp: Frank Wead, Lewis Meltzer, Borden Chase, based on Wead's story. With Edward G. Robinson, Glenn Ford, Marguerite Chapman.

Destroyer makes its hero an old man, Edward G. Robinson, who served on the *John Paul Jones* in World War I, and who desperately wishes to serve on her again in active combat in the new war. This same device is used for the Walter Brennan character in *Stand by for Action*. The ship contains a group who represent the usual mix: Boleslavsky, Donahue, Yasha, Kansas Jackson, Clark, Morgan, Sarecky. The basic plot conflict concerns youth versus age, as Robinson fights with a shipmate, Glenn Ford, who also falls in love with Robinson's daughter, Marguerite Chapman. Dynamic combat scenes are well represented, especially a climactic sequence against the enemy in the North Sea. Edward G. Robinson, like Humphrey Bogart, represents the "tough guys are needed in times like these" tradition. These stars, closely associated with gangster roles, make perfect heroes for war movies. The Gangster Goes to War tradition includes this film, *Fighting 69th* (Cagney), *Sahara* (Bogart), and such films as *All Through the Night*, not a combat film, but one in which gangsters literally gang up on the Nazis.

*So Proudly We Hail (Sept. 10)
Dir: Mark Sandrich. Sp: Allan Scott. With: Claudette Colbert, Paulette Goddard, Veronica Lake, George Reeves, Sonny Tufts.

Corvette K-225 (Oct. 21)
Dir: Richard Rosson (Howard Hawks, producer). Sp: Lt. John Rhodes Sturdy. With Randolph Scott, James Brown, Ella Raines, Barry Fitzgerald.

A semi-documentary presentation which was produced by Howard Hawks (and rumored to be partially directed by him). It starts out as a training film, with a romantic subplot, but goes into combat. It is about the small escort ships (the Corvettes) that accompanied the big, slow transports that took supplies over from Canada to England in wartime. This example of those ships, the Corvette K-225, is a Canadian ship manned by a Canadian crew, and it crosses the Atlantic from Halifax to England under maximum attack. The *Times* referred to the film as "a virtually documentary treatment of the experience." The details of the plunging sea, the cramped quarters, the tension and danger are excitingly presented. A good many of the backgrounds were actually photographed aboard Corvettes at sea, and that adds to the realistic feeling. The heroes of the Corvette face danger from both the enemy and the ocean.

*Sahara (Nov. 12)
Dir: Zoltan Korda. Sp: John Howard Lawson and Korda, adaptation by James O'Hanlon from story by Philip Macdonald, based on an incident "in the Soviet photoplay, *The Thirteen*." With Humphrey Bogart, Bruce Bennett, Lloyd Bridges, Dan Duryea, Rex Ingram.

*Guadalcanal Diary (Nov. 18)
Dir: Lewis Seiler. Sp: Lamar Trotti, adaptation by Jerry Cady from book by Richard Tregaskis. With Preston Foster, Lloyd Nolan, William Bendix, Richard Conte, Anthony Quinn, Richard Jaeckel.

*Cry Havoc (Nov. 24)
Dir: Richard Thorpe. Sp: Paul Osborn, based on the play by Allan R. Kenward. With Margaret Sullavan, Ann Sothern, Joan Blondell, Fay Bainter, Marsha Hunt, Ella Raines.

1943 notes
Newsreels of Tarawa were in theaters on Dec. 7, 1943. The War Department also previewed a film made to be shown to war workers, called "War Department Report: about the enemy's strength and our need to build supplies. . ." on this anniversary date.

Misleading titles: *Corregidor, Mission to Moscow, Commandos Strike at Dawn* (Norwegian guerrillas), *Pilot No. 5* (flashback to civilian life is bulk of story, with resolution provided by Franchot Tone, who plunges his plane into an enemy aircraft carrier); *Aerial Gunner, This Is the Army, Minesweeper, Bomber's Moon, Tonight We Raid Calais*, and *Salute to the Marines*, which ends in combat.

Problem films: *Bombardier* (July 2) in which the climax is the bombing raid over Japan, with the torture and execution of one captured member of the Flying Fortress's crew. The majority of the film takes place in a U.S. training camp for high-level bombing techniques; *We've Never Been Licked*—an odd-ball movie in which half the action is on a college campus, and half in Japan, with the hero acting as a spy to guide his former buddies to bombing a Japanese carrier; *A Guy Named Joe*, which mixes romance, fantasy, combat, and the woman's film in equal portions.

The *Why We Fight* series released two of its films to civilian audiences during this period: *Prelude to War* and *The Battle of Russia*.

1944

*Destination Tokyo (Jan.1)
Dir: Delmar Daves. Sp: Daves and Albert Maltz, from story by Steve Fisher. With Cary Grant, John Garfield, Alan Hale, John Ridgely, Dane Clark.

*Gung Ho! (Jan. 26)
Dir: Ray Enright. Sp: Lucien Hubbard, based on the factual story "Gung Ho!" by Capt. W. S. LeFrancois, USMC. Additional dialogue by Joseph Hoffman. With Randolph Scott, Grace McDonald, Alan Curtis, J. Carrol Naish.

With the Marines at Tarawa (March 3)
Documentary. Photographed by the Second Marine Division. Shot by 15 marine photographers (two of whom were killed) under the command of Capt. Louis Hayward. Edited at Warner Brothers. Released by Universal under the auspices of the War Activities Committee of the Motion Picture Industry.

The Fighting Seabees (March 20)
Dir: Edward Ludwig. Sp: Borden Chase, Aeneas MacKenzie, from story by Chase. With John Wayne, Susan Hayward, Dennis O'Keefe.

The labeling of films as truly "combat" is particulary difficult in the early days of the war, before the genre clearly emerged and defined itself. Nowhere is this better illustrated than in *Fighting Seabees* and in *Marine Raiders* (see below), two difficult cases. I am well aware that these two films often appear on lists of World War II combat films. This is especially true of *Fighting Seabees*, a well-known film starring John Wayne and Susan Hayward. *Fighting Seabees* is not really a combat film, and neither, to a lesser degree, is *Marine Raiders*. Neither reflect the hero, group, objective triumvirate necessary to the definition, and there is an absence of actual combat for the majority of running time in both. I am placing them in my filmography in detail to illustrate the problem, and also to offset the sense that I had arbitrarily eliminated films closely associated with the genre. No one who has seen it recently would actually place *Fighting Seabees* in the same cateagory as *Bataan*. It belongs in a larger context—war background, military service, or Films of World War II. *Fighting Seabees* is the story of a group of civilian construction workers, whose boss is John Wayne, and of their attempts to build airstrips in the Pacific islands. It is actually the story of how the Construction Battalion (the "Seabees") came about, as it was illegal to arm civilians, and many such workers lost their lives when the islands came under attack. When the workers were enlisted as military personnel, they were able to bear arms to protect themselves as they built airstrips, bridges, etc. under difficult—and sometimes combat—situations. *Fighting Seabees* is the story of a colorful gang of tough workers, their dynamic boss, and his romance with a beautiful newspaper correspondent (Hayward, who at first is on an island with them—an indicator of the level of seriousness of the plot line). There is an early "combat" sequence—a kind of skirmish with the Japanese. As the enemy lands on the island, supported by offshore firepower, the naval forces on the island to supervise the construction workers prepare to engage them in battle by drawing them into an ambush. Before this can happen, the workers themselves attack the Japanese, roaring forward on tractors, trucks, road graders, and various oddball vehicles. The ensuing battle is a disaster, and many Americans are killed. After the Seabees are firmly established as a military force, they go back to the islands for combat conditions, wearing traditional military gear. The final portion of the film is a combat movie, with snipers, patrols, and full-out battle.

Tunisian Victory (March 24)
Documentary. M-G-M release, made by Great Britain and the United States jointly. U.S. Army Signal Corp. and British Army Film Unit.

*The Memphis Belle (April 14)
Documentary. Dir: Lt. Col. William Wyler. Distributed by Paramount for the War Department and the Office of War Information.

Eve of St. Mark (May 31)
Dir: John M. Stahl. Sp: George Seaton, from play by Maxwell Anderson. With Anne Baxter, William Eythe, Michael O'Shea, Vincent Price.

Tells stories of a group of Americans from their pre-Pearl Harbor training days to their final elimination in a last stand by the Japanese (and malaria) in the Philippines. Combines the training camp film with the last stand.

Attack! The Battle of New Britain (June 21)
Documentary. Signal Corps and Air Force film under Lt. Col. Robert Presnell. Commentary written by L. Jesse Lasky, Jr. Released through War Activities Commission of Motion Picture industry.

Marine Raiders. (July 1)
Dir: Harold Schuster. Sp: Warren Duff, from original story by Duff and Martin Rackin. With Pat O'Brien, Robert Ryan, Ruth Hussey.

(See *Fighting Seabees*) This film comes in three parts: an opening section set on Guadalcanal, which runs about twenty minutes; the heart of the film, which moves from Australia to San Diego back to Australia, and in which there is no combat (but there are training camp battle maneuvers), and it becomes a story of love, romance, duty, training-of-men, and more; and a final sequence "on a Japanese-held island" in which the men return to combat for the final approximately 20 minutes. Thus, it can be seen that the combat film is used as a kind of parentheses around a traditional and detailed romantic love story. The majority of the movie does not take place in combat, but because it begins and ends there, because it does actually present full-out blasting combat, and because the discussion of war and combat is ever-present, it cannot be overlooked. It is truly a problematic case, as it barely reflects the basic genre characteristics in other ways. It has a hero-friend configuration (Ryan and O'Brien) and a comedy cook, but not the detailed mixed group. It is clearly the old service movie, with its central problem of "dedication to the corps" as a motif, updated with true World War II combat.

Wing and a Prayer (Aug. 31)
Dir: Henry Hathaway. Sp: Jerome Cady. With Don Ameche, Dana Andrews, William Eythe, Richard Jaeckel.

Salute to the Navy airmen who helped cripple the Japanese fleet in the Battle of Midway. Life aboard a floating airfield—a composite of adventures from such ships as the *Enterprise, Lexington, Hornet, Torpedo*. The iconographic Betty Grable surfaces again here, as the men watch her and Alice Faye on "Tin Pan Alley" while at sea. One of the characters is a former movie star (William Eythe) who tells the men about working with such glamor girls. Movies-within-movies!

The Battle for the Marianas (Sept. 20)
Documentary. Marine Corps film regarding fighting in Saipan, Tinian, Guam.

Thirty Seconds Over Tokyo (Nov. 16)
Dir: Mervyn LeRoy. Sp: Dalton Trumbo, based on the book by Capt. Ted Lawson and Robert Considine. With Van Johnson, Spencer Tracy (as Doolittle), Robert Walker, Phyllis Thaxter.

Biography. "131 days after December 7, 1941," the Doolittle Raid over Tokyo took place, and this film tells the story of one man who flew on that raid. It is based on a real event, and on a real character, but it is a war effort movie which stresses the team as a group, well-trained by their noble leader.

It is a curious thing that a film like *Thirty Seconds*, obviously a war film, if not as obviously a combat film, can be officially designated as "combat" whereas no one would think of including a George Raft–Carole Lombard semimusical film, *Bolero*, as a war/combat film. And yet, *Bolero* contains more actual running time of combat than *Thirty Seconds*! Based on a true story, *Thirty Seconds* is the story of Captain Ted Lawson's marriage, his training to be part of the Doolittle raid, his arrival on ship board to hear of his mission over Tokyo, the raid itself, his crashing in China, the amputation of his leg, ultimate rescue, and return home. The actual combat sequence takes just about thirty seconds indeed! First they fly over the coast of Japan and are not spotted. Then, in the air over Tokyo, bombing their targets, they are shot at for less than one minute. There is no other combat in the film. The rest is a domestic drama, a training film, and a personal-battle-with-a-handicap story.

Bolero, on the other hand, is a musical about a coal miner who becomes a dancer, goes to Paris, uses women to climb to the top, and forms a dancing partnership ("strictly business") with a beautiful blonde (Lombard). When World War I breaks out, he goes into combat. He is seen in the trenches, and a bombing, exploding, shooting, running combat sequence of a few minutes screen time is unleashed, culminating in a wound which puts him in a hospital, with a doctor warning him he will never dance again. "You're all torn up inside." Raft does dance, and he dies from it, presumably because of his combat experience. Van Johnson, the hero of *Thirty Seconds Over Tokyo,* does not die; in fact, he lives on happily with his wife, taking up a normal life, and writing a book about his experiences.

Beachhead to Berlin (Dec. 16)
Documentary. Film shows the various responsibilities of the Coast Guard during the Normandy invasion.

1944 notes
Winged Victory (Dec. 21), based on a famous Broadway hit, is not a combat film. It tells the story of a group of young men who go into training as pilots, but only one survives the various pressures and dangers to be seen leaving for Japanese combat at film's end. Excellent scenes, detailed and involving, of the men's training as pilots. Human story of their former lives, romances, families included.

Abroad with Two Yanks (October 26), referred to in Dorothy Jones' list as a combat film, has no combat. It is a comedy, including a musical revue called the "Marine Follies" in which our two heroes go in drag. The *New York Times* review commented: "They're a sort of Quirt and Flagg team" about these two men.

The Story of Dr. Wassell (June 7)—An epic biography of a real-life doctor, including, among many incidents, his experiences in Java under combat conditions.

Purple Heart (March 9) contains no real combat. It is the fictionalized story of eight flyers shot down in the Doolittle raid over Japan, and of their torture, trial, and execution by the Japanese Black Dragon Society. This is probably the world's only combat movie in which the Japanese agents arrive in a station wagon.

Home Front: *Mr. Winkle Goes to War, The Fighting Sullivans* (brief combat sequence).

Comedy: *See Here, Private Hargrove* (training only).

Women Ferrying Bombers: *Ladies Courageous.*

1945

Brought to Action (Jan. 13)
Documentary. Footage shot by Navy cameramen of the second Battle of the Philippines (October 1944). Released by the War Activities committee of the motion picture industry, in conjunction with the Office of War Information. Footage prepared by the O.S.S.

*The Fighting Lady (July 16)
Documentary. Narrated by Lt. Robert Taylor. Supervised by Rear Admiral Arthur W. Radford and Capt. Edward J. Steichen. 20th Century-Fox distributor.

Story of an *Essex*-class carrier (27,000 tons), a floating city of 3000 men, chosen to represent all the aircraft carriers in the Pacific fleet. Film shows carrier repelling a torpedo-bomber attack, a crash landing on the deck, and the carrier's role in attacks on Marcus Island, Kwajelein, Truk, and the Marianas. Prod. by Louis de Rochemont.

*Objective Burma (Jan. 27)
Dir: Raoul Walsh. Sp: Alvah Bessie (orig. story), Ranald MacDougall, Lester Cole. With Errol Flynn, William Prince, James Brown, George Tobias, Henry Hull.

Fury in the Pacific (March 23)
Documentary. Shot in combat by 39 cameramen under the direction of Comdr. Bonny M. Powell, USNR, at the invasion of Pelliu and Angaur Islands. Distributed for the OWI by Warner Brothers, by arrangement with the War Activities Committee.

God Is My Co-Pilot (March 24)
Dir: Robert Florey. Sp: Peter Mine, based on the book by Col. Robert L. Scott. With Dennis Morgan, Dane Clark, Raymond Massey, Alan Hale.

Set in Kunming, China, in 1942, this film is based on a book by the army colonel who is its central character, yet it is treated somewhat more as fiction than biography. A story told in flashback, it presents the entire life of the hero from childhood through West Point, his love and romance, and over into war in China. In war combat (and there are air combat sequences), the young man finds religion. This motif is the main thrust of the film. Traditional use of group, et. al., to achieve story of faith, love, and politics intertwined with combat.

To the Shores of Iwo Jima (June 7)

Documentary. Shows preliminary bombardment of Iwo by sea and air, and then the action from Mount Suribachi to the northern tip of the island. Called "the toughest 26 days in Marine Corps history." Office of War Information releases. A 20-minute film.

*The Battle for San Pietro (July 12)

Documentary. Signal Corps film. Depicts 5th Army attack on the town of San Pietro of December 1943. Shot by Signal Corps front-line photographers under the command of Major John Huston.

The Fleet That Came To Stay (July 27)

Documentary. Visual story of Japan's Kamikaze pilots, made during the three-month campaign of the Battle of Okinawa, from Easter Sunday morning, April 1, 1944, through the end of the action. Released throught War activities committee at the request of the Office of War Information. Navy, Marine and Coast Guard photographers.

Pride of the Marines (August 25)

Dir: Delmer Daves. Sp: Albert Maltz, based on the book by Roger Butterfield, adapted by Marvin Borowsky. With John Garfield, Eleanor Parker, Dane Clark.

    Biography. Based on the story of Marine Sergeant Al Schmid, who won Navy Cross for defending a machinegun post throughout the night on Guadalcanal. He was blinded by a grenade burst, after he had killed 200 of the enemy. His combat experience, taking place historically at the Tenaru River, is carefully and superbly depicted in the film. However, the combat unit is a single-story experience, surrounded by the prior civilian life of Schmid and his girl, and by his post-combat adjustment to blindness.

The True Glory (Sept. 7)

Documentary. Full film record of the European War, produced by a joint committee of British and American filmmakers. Anglo-American planning committee, headed by Capt. Garson Kanin and Carol Reed. Columbia Pictures release, on behalf of the Office of War Information and the film industry's War Activities Commission.

Back to Bataan (Sept. 13)

Dir: Edward Dmytryk. Sp: Ben Barzman and Richard Landau, original story by Aeneas MacKenzie and William Gordon. With John Wayne, Anthony Quinn, Beulah Bondi.

Not a traditional combat film, because it depicts guerrilla fighters in the Philippines. Shows liaison between civilian Philippine patriots and the American fighting men left behind. Opens with an enactment of the freeing of the American prisoners from Cabanatuan, and goes into flashback story.

*The Story of G.I. Joe (Oct. 7)

Dir: William Wellman. Sp: Leopold Atlas, Guy Endore and Philip Stevenson, patterned on the newspaper columns of Ernie Pyle. With Burgess Meredith, Robert Mitchum, and "combat veterans of the campaigns in Africa, Sicily, and Italy."

Thunderbolt (Oct. 27)

Army Air Force film about the 57th Fighter Group, based on Corsica, and how the employment of tactical air power in support of ground troops was used for five months at the Gustav Line in Italy. Dir. and edited by Lt. Col. William Wyler and Capt. John Sturges.

Appointment in Tokyo (Dec. 8)

Documentary. The Recapture of the Philippines, including landing on Leyte and the fighting east of Lingayen Gulf plus the battle in Manila's streets. Written by Capt. Jack Handley and Capt. Jesse Lasky, Jr. Dir: Major Jack Hively.

*They Were Expendable (Dec. 21)

Dir: John Ford. Sp: Frank Wead, based on the book by William L. White. With Robert Montgomery, John Wayne, Donna Reed, Jack Holt, Ward Bond.

What Next, Corporal Hargrove? (Dec. 26)

Dir: Richard Thorpe. Sp: Harry Kurnitz. With Robert Walker, Keenan Wynn.

Here is the first of the WWII combat comedies, in that its comedy is actually set in real combat: the capture of a French village. However, most of the comedy takes place during an A.W.O.L. trip to Paris.

1945 notes

Keep Your Powder Dry is a training camp film for women who join the WACS. *This Man's Navy* puts Wallace Beery, who must have made a film about every possible military service, in the blimps at Lakehurst. There is no real combat, except a short sequence when Beery's blimp goes against a submarine off the coast. *Counterattack* is a misleading title, because it takes place in one room, a basement, in which Paul Muni as a Russian dominates a group of German prisoners. *Note for trivia buffs: First Yank Into Tokyo* is probably the first movie to exploit the news about the atomic bomb. A cheap quickie, it tells a story of a young man who, believing his girl died on Bataan, allows his face to be altered so that he looks Japanese. He goes to Tokyo to save a scientist who has the secret of the atomic bomb.

1946

*A Walk in the Sun (Jan. 12)
Dir: Lewis Milestone. Sp: Robert Rossen, from the novel by Harry Brown. With Dana Andrews, Richard Conte, John Ireland, Norman Lloyd

1946 notes
Two films about the activities of the O.S.S. were released during this year: O.S.S. (May 27) and *Cloak and Dagger* (October 5). Perhaps officially marking the end of the war, the hugely successful and critically acclaimed film, *The Best Years of Our Lives* (Nov. 22) depicted the difficulties of the returning veterans and their adjustment to civilian life. *Courage of Lassie* has a war background, in which the famous collie is trained for combat and rescues a soldier before being returned to the care of Elizabeth Taylor and his peaceful life as a sheep dog.

1947

No combat films were released.

1947 notes
A third film about the O.S.S. activities, 13 *Rue Madeleine* (Jan. 16) came out, and so did the story of the making of the atomic bomb (*The Beginning or the End*, Feb. 21). One movie, *High Barbaree* (June 6), tells an involved flashback while two flyers drift at sea after their plane has crashed. It is not a true combat film, however.

1948

Homecoming (April 30)
Dir: Mervyn LeRoy. Sp: Paul Osborn. With Clark Gable, Lana Turner, Anne Baxter, John Hodiak.

Told in flashback, the story of a smug doctor who learns about reality during World War II, mainly from falling in love with a down-to-earth nurse, even though he's a married man. Uses war and combat as a background, as they tend wounded men.

*Fighter Squadron (Nov. 20)
Dir: Raoul Walsh. Sp: Seton I. Miller. With Edmund O'Brien, Robert Stack, Henry Hull.

1949

Command Decision (Jan. 20)

Dir: Sam Wood. William R. Laidlaw, George Froeschel, based on the play by William Wister Haines. With Clark Gable, Walter Pidgeon. Van Johnson, Brian Donlevy.

The film concerns itself with the traditional air force film problem: the pressures of command. It is a story of one general's fight with politics. The film has added dramatic encounters obviously not in the original play: grim takeoffs of heavy bombers off on dangerous missions; a dramatic "talk down"of a plane in trouble, which crashes on the field; and the intense "memory" of combat sound and death on the part of the general as he thinks of the men in combat. Basically, this is not a combat film, however.

Home of the Brave (May 13)

Dir: Mark Robson. Sp: Carl Foreman, based on play by Arthur Laurents. With James Edwards, Douglas Dick, Lloyd Bridges.

This film illustrates how the combat situation will be used to tell a story about a current sociological problem. Foreman altered the orginal play, which was a story about a Jewish soldier, to be about a black man. Because of racial prejudice, this character goes to pieces during combat on a South Pacific island. The story is told in flashback after the black man comes in from the mission in a state of shock and paralysis. Through talk and narcosynthesis, the story is brought out. The *New York Times* called this "the first in the cycle of Negro-prejudice pictures which Hollywood now has in the works."

*Task Force (Oct. 1)

Dir: Delmer Daves. Sp: Daves. With Gary Cooper, Jane Wyatt, Wayne Morris.

"Now that sufficient interval has passed since the end of World War II for the public to look back on its torments with reflection and sentiment." Film springs to life when it depicts actual combat involving carriers and planes, done with great documentary detail.

*Battleground (Nov. 12)

Dir: William Wellman. Sp: Robert Pirosh. With Van Johnson, Ricardo Montalban, John Hodiak, George Murphy.

*Sands of Iwo Jima (Dec. 31)

Dir: Allan Dwan. Sp: Harry Brown, James Edward Grant, based on story by Brown. With John Wayne, John Agar, Adele Mara, Forrest Tucker.

1950

Twelve O'Clock High (Jan. 28)

Dir: Henry King. Sp: Sy Bartlett, Beirne Lay, Jr., based on the novel of the same name. With Gregory Peck, Hugh Marlowe, Gary Merrill, Millard Mitchell, Dean Jagger.

"Dedicated" to the daylight precision bombing teams of American pilots who were in Europe in 1942, this famous film won an Academy Award for best supporting actor (Dean Jagger). It begins in London in 1949 and, as is typical of many war films, is a story told in flashback—Jagger's wartime experience, introduced with a famous poetic passage, evocative of war and memory, when he stands alone on the deserted airfield from which bombers once were launched. It is a traditional story of the air corps—concerning the problems of leadership, of sending men to death, the pressures of command, etc. It presents detailed, honest, and seemingly accurate scenes of combat planning and bombing, no doubt influenced heavily by *Memphis Belle*. Actual combat footage is used.

Cassino to Korea (Oct. 4)
Documentary. By the Signal Corp. on the Italian Campaign, based on the experiences of two men. Sgt. James M. Logan of the 36th Infantry Division (Medal of Honor winner) and Capt. David Ludlum, an Army Air Force meterologist who forecast the important weather break during the Cassino seige. Because battle footage from Korea was not yet available, the editors used a commentator, Quentin Reynolds, to draw parallels between the Italian campaign and the Korean.

American Guerrilla in the Philippines (Nov. 8)
Dir: Fritz Lang. Sp: Lamar Trotti, based on the novel by Ira Wolfert. With Tyrone Power, Micheline Prelle, Tom Ewell.

This film takes up the story of the Motor Torpedo Squadron No. 3 and their guerrilla activities when left behind in the Philippines. It's as if the cast of *They Were Expendable* were picked up where they left off at film's end, and put into *Back to Bataan*. The story is narrated by its hero, Tyrone Power, which provides distance and a sense of history to the events.

Breakthrough (Nov. 18)
Dir: Lewis Seiler. Sp: Bernard Girard, Ted Sherdeman, from a story by Joseph Bren Jr. With David Brian, John Agar, Frank Lovejoy.

The story of an infantry platoon during the Normandy campaign. Very definitely couched in the tradition of what has come to be the WWII combat film, with a representative group "cut from long familiar stencils."

1950 notes
Flying Missile (Dec. 25) returns to the format of the inventor movie, in which a submarine commander attempts to install V–2 rockets on subs. War game format for the most part. War combat as background: *Chain Lightning* (first section only), *Malaya*, *When Willie Comes Marching Home*, *Francis* (comedies)

1951

The Halls of Montezuma (Jan. 6)
Dir: Lewis Milestone. Sp: Michael Blankfort. With Richard Widmark, Jack Palance, Reginald Gardiner, Robert Wagner, Karl Malden.

Stresses psychoses and hatred among men as they undergo an intense assault on a Pacific Island, which might be Okinawa. Traditional combat format, with detailed battle enactment. Filmed with the assistance of the U.S. Marine Corps. A true combat film.

*The Steel Helmet (Jan. 25)
Dir: Samuel Fuller. Sp: Fuller. With Gene Evans, James Edwards, Robert Hutton, Steve Brodie, Richard Loo. A review calls it "the first fiction film in circulation on the subject of the Korean War."

*Operation Pacific (Feb. 3)
Dir: George Waggner. Sp: Waggner. With John Wayne, Patricia Neal, Ward Bond.

A Yank in Korea (April 2)
Dir: Lew Landers. Sp: William Sackheim, from a story by Leo Lieberman. With Lon McCallister, William ("Bill") Phillips, Brett King, Tommy Farrell.

Film is dedicated to Pfc. John J. McCormick, whose letter to his children, written before he died in Korea, is supposed to have inspired the film. After an opening in which a young man is inducted into service on his wedding day, film is set in combat.

Fighting Coast Guard (May 12)
Dir: Joseph Kane. Sp: Kenneth Gamet, from story by Charles Marquis Warren. With Brian Donlevy, Forrest Tucker, Richard Jaeckel, Ella Raines.

Military service film, but contains actual footage of Pacific fighting.

Go for Broke (May 25)
Dir: Robert Pirosh. Sp: Pirosh. With Van Johnson, Lan Nakano, Henry Nakamura.

A tribute to the men of the 442d Regimental Combat team, composed largely of Japanese-Americans. Shows the regiment's story from training into World War II combat.

*The Frogmen (June 30)
Dir: Lloyd Bacon. Sp: John Tucker Battle, based on a story by Oscar Millard. With Richard Widmark, Dana Andrews, Gary Merrill, Jeffrey Hunter, Robert Wagner.

Suicide Attack (July 14)
Documentary. Dir: Irving Lerner. Narrator: Louis Pollock. Footage captured from Japanese newsreels compiled into film showing their propaganda machine at work. Review says "the events depicted, unless you were a part of them, will have only a passing historical interest. . . . one wonders if it was worth the effort."

Force of Arms (Aug. 14)

Dir: Michael Curtiz. Sp: Orin Jannings, from a story by Richard Tregaskis. With William Holden, Nancy Olson, Frank Lovejoy, Gene Evans.

Combat is presented throughout this film, which is a love story set in "a lull in the Battle of San Pietro." Primary focus is on romance, not combat, however.

Flying Leathernecks (Sept. 20)

Dir: Nicholas Ray. Sp: James Edward Grant. With John Wayne, Robert Ryan, Don Taylor.

Wayne fights for air coverage of Guadalcanal ground forces, at expense of his own flying squadron.

The Desert Fox (Oct. 18)

Dir: Henry Hathway. Sp: Nunnally Johnson, from the biography of Brig. Desmond Young. With James Mason, Cedric Hardwicke, Luther Adler.

Story of German General Irwin Rommel. *Biography*. An intelligent and sympathetic story of the German General's African campaign and his ultimate return to disillusionment and death in Hitler's Germany.

*Fixed Bayonets (Nov. 21)

Dir. Samuel Fuller. Sp: Fuller, suggested by the novel by John Brophy. With Richard Basehart, Gene Evans, Michael O'Shea. Korea.

The Tanks Are Coming (Dec. 6)

Dir: Lewis Seiler. Sp: Robert Hardy Andrews, from a story by Samuel Fuller. With Steve Cochran, Philip Carey.

A minor film that demonstrates generic proof, with a sergeant who wears cowboy boots and sixshooters, and the traditional group of melting-pot names. It's about WWII in Europe, the activities of the 3d Armored Division, "America's Iron Fist," from St. Lo to the German border in the summer of 1944.

1951 notes

Comedies: *U.S.S. Teakettle* (latter retilted *You're In The Navy Now*) and *Up Front*, based on Bill Mauldin's cartoon characters.

Training Film for Jet Pilots: *Air Cadet*.

German Soldier Helping U.S. Against War Background: *Decision Before Dawn*.

Key Literary Influence Filmed: *Red Badge of Courage*, the Civil War novel brought to life and revealing an early example of the concept of a group of mixed American fighting types.

1952

*The Wild Blue Yonder (Jan. 2)

Dir: Allan Dwan. Sp: Richard Tregaskis, from a story by Andrew Geer and Charles Grayson. With Wendell Corey, Vera Ralston, Forrest Tucker, Phil Harris. (Title in England: *Thunder Across the Pacific*)

Submarine Command (Jan. 19)

Dir: John Farrow. Sp: Jonathan Latimer. With William Holden, Nancy Olson, William Bendix.

Although it contains a great deal of footage not involved in combat, it is a significant film because its story covers both World War II and Korea. Its hero suffers guilt from having dived his sub during WWII and left his commander wounded on the bridge. Thus the plot makes an entire film out of the psychological ramifications of a fictionalized Howard Gilmore incident. This hero redeems himself through Korean combat.

Retreat, Hell! (Feb. 20)

Dir: Joseph H. Lewis. Sp: Milton Sperling, Ted Sherdeman. With Frank Lovejoy, Richard Carlson, Anita Louise.

United States Marines First Battalion exploits in Korea. Depicts the Inchon beachhead, the drive inland to Seoul and North Korea, and their ultimate retreat. ("Retreat, hell!" said the colonel. "We're just attacking in another direction.") Traditional format established in World War II repeated here in group of characters. Film begins on the home front, goes to Korean combat.

Okinawa (April 24)

Dir: Leigh Jason. Sp: Jameson Brewer, Arthur Ross. With Pat O'Brien, Cameron Mitchell, Richard Denning.

Navy destroyer standing offshore in Okinawa, resisting kamikaze attacks. Newsreel footage. Traditional.

Red Ball Express (May 30)

Dir: Budd Boetticher. Sp: John Michael Hayes, based on story by Marcel Klauber, Bill Grady, Jr. With Jeff Chandler, Alex Nicol, Charles Drake, Hugh O'Brien, Sidney Poitier.

Story of the nonstop trucking of supplies during the final assault on Europe that came to be known as the "red ball express." Most members of this group in the real war were from the black Quartermaster units, so Poitier's presence is key.

One Minute to Zero (Sept. 20)

Dir: Tay Garnett. Sp: Milton Krims, William Wister Haines. With Robert Mitchum, Ann Blyth, Charles McGraw. Korea.

Demonstrates the difference between Korea and WWII films by stressing family, wives, romance, Korean refugees and guerrillas.

Battle Zone (Nov. 1)

Dir: Lesley Selander. Sp: Steve Fisher. With John Hodiak, Stephen McNally, Linda Christian.

The updating of Quirt and Flagg into the Korean War. They are now two marine photographers shooting combat action in the Yalu Zone and fighting over a Red Cross Girl.

Flat Top (Dec. 6)

Dir: Lesley Selander. Sp: Steve Fisher. With Sterling Hayden, Richard Carlson, John Bromfield.

Life aboard a carrier in the Philippines. Uses very good authentic combat footage.

Torpedo Alley (Dec. 20)

Dir: Lew Lander. Sp: Sam Roeca, Warren Douglas. With Mark Stevens, Dorothy Malone, Douglas Kennedy.

Stevens plays a carrier pilot from WWII who accidentally killed two crewmen. In the subs during Korea, he redeems himself with great valor. Good scenes of conditioning submarines made on location at New London sub base.

1952 notes

Musicals: *About Face* (a remake of the non-musical military school film, *Brother Rat*) and *Skirts, Ahoy!* (training film about women).

Service comedies: *Jumping Jacks* and *At War With the Army* (both with Martin and Lewis).

Remake of World War I film: *What Price Glory?* (this time directed by John Ford).

Misleading Titles: *Glory Alley* (about a Congressional Medal of Honor winner from the Korean War who has trouble adjusting to his return to civilian life in New Orleans), *Operation Secret* (a cloak-and-dagger movie about the French underground, set in postwar times and told in flashbacks. The hero is accused of a murder committed in the last days of the war, and he is on trial among his Maqui comrades, one of whom turns out to be a Communist villain. Thus the old war is updated for new cold war purposes).

1953

Eight Iron Men (Jan. 2)

Dir: Edward Dmytryk. Sp: Harry Brown, based on his play. With Bonar Colleano, Arthur Franz, Lee Marvin.

The original play, called *A Sound of Hunting*, was done in 1945 on Broadway and concerned a platoon of weary soldiers of representative types and names. They were stuck in an Italian town trying to rescue a comrade who had been pinned down by an enemy machine gun, alone out in the streets. In the film version, when he is finally rescued, he is found comfortably asleep. He has missed all the turmoil. This climax was not in the original play. Contains dream sequences with women. Mostly talk.

Above and Beyond (Jan. 31)
Dir: Melvin Frank, Norman Panama. Sp. Frank, Panama, and Beirne Lay, Jr.
With Robert Taylor, Eleanor Parker, James Whitmore.

Biography. Story of Col. Paul Tibbets Jr., who organized the bomb crew
for the atom bomb and the first strike on Hiroshima. The training of the crew,
etc, and his personal story as well.

Thunderbirds (March 12)
Dir: John H. Auer. Sp: Mary C. McCall Jr. from a story by Kennedy Gamet.
With John Derek, John Barrymore, Jr., Gene Evans.

A tribute to a distinguished National Guard unit called the Thunderbirds.
Follows their exploits from just before Pearl Harbor through various WWII
campaigns. Actual combat footage.

Fear and Desire (April 1)
Dir: Stanley Kubrick. Sp: Howard O. Sackler. With Frank Silvers, Kenneth
Harp, Paul Mazursky.

Interesting because done by a young group of independent filmmakers.
Story of four soldiers stranded behind enemy lines after their plane is shot
down. We see what they do, and hear what they are thinking as they undergo
stress of war. One is gentle, one introspective, one is tough, and one is callow
and crazy from fear.

The Desert Rats (May 9)
Dir: Robert Wise. Sp: Richard Murphy. With Richard Burton, Robert New-
ton, James Mason.

Tribute to the Australian and British stand at Tobruk with Mason once again
playing Rommel.

*Battle Circus (May 28)
Dir: Richard Brooks. Sp: Brooks, based on story by Allen Rivkin, Laura Kerr.
With June Allyson, Humphrey Bogart, Keenan Wynn.

Destination Gobi (May 30)
Dir: Robert Wise. Sp: Everett Freeman, based on story by Edmond G. Love.
With Richard Widmark, Don Taylor, Casey Adams.

An unusual WWII story, based on the meterological teams that went into
the Gobi desert wastes to send weather reports to the Allied forces. Widmark
is detached from carrier *Enterprise* to head the team, and we end up seeing
sailors out in the parched desert wastes. The review says, "Ever hear of the
First Mongolian Cavalry, United States Navy; or the Sino-American Coop-
erative Organization, or Argos VI in Inner Monglia?" Despite unusual setting,
traditional presentation of patrol. Since they come under attack by Japanese,
this is a combat film, mixing traditional characteristics with unusual variations.

The Glory Brigade (Aug. 15)

Dir: Robert D. Webb. Sp: Franklin Coen. With Victor Mature, Alexander Scourby, Lee Marvin.

United Nations motif, in which a reconnaissance patrol of U.S. Army engineers and Greek infantrymen meet in Korea and burrow deep into enemy territory. There's a great deal of heavy combat. Mature plays a Greek-American who clashes with Scourby, the Greek leader, but the two ultimately learn respect. A rescue from a hilltop siege by helicopter is the film's climax.

Mission Over Korea (Sept. 19)

Dir: Fred F. Sears. Sp: Jesse L. Lasky, Jr., Eugene Ling, Martin M. Goldsmith, from a story by Richard Tregaskis. With John Hodiak, John Derek.

American Air Force valor during early stages of Korea. A low-budget film full of war film references.

Sabre Jet (Nov. 3)

Dir: Louis King. Sp: Dale Eunson, Katherine Albert, based on a story by Carl Krueger. With Robert Stack, Coleen Grey, Richard Arlen, Julie Bishop, Leon Ames.

Story of the bravery of fighter jet pilots who fly missions over Korea from air bases in Japan. True to Korean variation of combat, the film is as much about the bravery of the wives who wait for them in Japan as it is about the men.

*Cease Fire! (Nov. 25)

Dir: Owen Crump. Sp: Walter Doniger, based on story by Crump.

Filmed in 3-D with men who were footsoldiers in the hills of Korea.

Paratrooper (Dec. 31)

Dir: Terence Young. Sp: Richard Maibaum, Frank Nugent, adapted by Sy Bartlett from book, The Red Beret by Hilary St. George Saunders. With Alan Ladd, Leo Genn,

Originally titled The Red Beret, and officially a British film despite Ladd's presence as a troubled man forced to assume command during a raid to recapture an air field in North Africa during WWII.

1953 notes

Military comedies: Off Limits, Never Wave at a Wac.

Atomic war movie: Invasion, U.S.A. (showing U.S. invaded by an unnamed, but obviously Soviet army, done in stock WWII format).

WWII prison Drama: Stalag 17

Epic novel, about peacetime up through December 7th, with military setting: From Here to Eternity.

Training camp film, in traditional format: Take the High Ground.

Service background musical: *Three Sailors and a Girl*.
Misleading Title: *Sea Devils*. (smugglers).

1954

*Flight Nurse (Jan. 30)
Dir: Allan Dwan. Sp: Alan LeMay. With Joan Leslie, Forrest Tucker, Arthur Franz.

Beachhead (April 17)
Dir: Stuart Heisler. Sp: Richard Alan Simmons. With Tony Curtis, Frank Lovejoy, Mary Murphy.

Marine reconnaissance on a primitive Pacific Island in WWII. Basic plot concerns conflict between two leaders for control of authority.

Men of the Fighting Lady (May 8)
Dir: Andrew Marton. Sp: Art Cohn, based on stories by James Michener and Commander Harry A. Burns, USN. With Van Johnson, Louis Calhern, Walter Pidgeon, Dewey Martin, Keenan Wynn.

Story of a jet fighter squadron aboard an American carrier operating off Korea in the sea of Japan. Documentary in style, but with traditional storylines: representative group; hardboiled squadron leader who pushes men past their limits; a brave pilot leading a blinded comrade in another plane back to the ship, with the resulting "talk down," etc. New iconography: the helicopters rescuing pilots downed in the sea and on the land.

1954 notes
Misleading titles: *This Is Your Army*, (a documentary about army life, not combat); *Hell Raiders of the Deep*, (an Italian film); and *Hell and High Water*, (a submarine film, but not combat, in which a sub goes to investigate word that an atomic bomb has been exploded by a "foreign power.")

War Prison Camp: *Prisoner of War*, (Ronald Reagan volunteers to be captured to check out stories about what is happening to Americans in Korean prisoner of war camps).

War Background: *The Caine Mutiny*, (based on the famous novel which depicts the tensions among the crew and officers of a Navy destroyer-mine-sweeper during World War II).

1955

Bridges at Toko Ri (Jan. 21)
Dir: Mark Robson. Sp: Valentine Davies, based on the novel by James Michener. With William Holden, Grace Kelly, Fredric March, Mickey Rooney.

Navy fliers in Korea, with Holden tragically killed at end. Story of combat and family life entwined.

Battle Cry (Feb. 3)

Dir: Raoul Walsh. Sp: Leon M. Uris, based on his novel. With Aldo Ray, Van Heflin, James Whitmore, Raymond Massey, Mona Freeman, Nancy Olson.

U.S. marines in the Pacific. Long, episodic film that takes individuals from boot camp into combat, with personal stories as well as combat stories being told. Traditional.

The Purple Plain (April 11)

Dir: Robert Parrish. Sp: Eric Ambler. With Gregory Peck. Bernard Lee.

RAF wartime bomber crashes in Burma jungle, and survivors must get to safety. Combat related.

*To Hell and Back (Sept. 23)

Dir: Jesse Hibbs. Sp: Gil Doud, from autobiography by Audie Murphy. With Audie Murphy, Marshall Thompson, Charles Drake, Jack Kelly.

Target Zero (Nov. 16)

Dir: Harmon Jones. Sp: Sam Rolfe, from a story by James Warner Bellah. With Richard Conte, Charles Bronson, L. Q. Jones, Chuck Connors, Peggie Castle.

A squad of American soldiers on a dangerous Korean war patrol.

Battle Taxi (no review date)

Dir: Herbert L. Strock. Sp: Malvin Wald. With Sterling Hayden, Arthur Franz, Marshall Thompson.

Korean War. Hayden is the head of a helicopter rescue squadron who has to convince his feisty group that they are on missions of mercy, not combat patrols. Stock combat footage is used.

1955 Notes

Combat related: *Court Martial of Billy Mitchell*, (the trial of the famous flyer who advocated air power) and *Mr. Roberts*, (the celebrated comedy about life on the *Reluctant* during World War II).

Misleading titles: *Hill 24 Does Not Answer*, (about Jerusalem and the Holy Land, not World War II); *Three Stripes in the Sun*. (life in post-war Japan, not combat).

World War II Background: *The Sea Chase*, (with John Wayne as a German freighter captain who does not agree with the Nazis, but who tries to bring his crew home from Sydney, pursued by the British—action and tension, but not those of traditional military battle maneuvers).

1956

The Bold and the Brave (May 26)
Dir: Lewis R. Foster. Sp: Robert Lewin. With Wendell Corey, Mickey Rooney, Don Taylor.

Italy in WWII. Combat setting in traditional format, but with emphasis on internal struggles and character developments of three very different men.

D-Day, The Sixth of June (May 30)
Dir: Henry Koster. Sp: Ivan Moffat, Harry Brown, based on the novel *The Sixth of June* by Lionel Shapiro. With Robert Taylor, Dana Wynter, Richard Todd, Edmond O'Brien.

Film illustrates how basic combat situation and familiarity with historical fact can provide setting for a romantic story. As men move toward landing of D-Day in Normandy, Taylor and Todd on shipboard remember the story of how they have both loved Dana Wynter. Taylor is married, but falls for her, even though she is engaged to Todd. This takes up most of the story, which climaxes in combat on D-Day, with Todd stepping on a land mine.

The Proud and the Profane (June 14)
Dir: George Seaton. Sp: Seaton, based on the novel *The Magnificent Bastards* by Lucy Herndon Crockett. With William Holden, Deborah Kerr, Thelma Ritter, Dewey Martin.

Another story about a love affair, and about war's effect on women. Kerr is Red Cross worker at Noumea in South Pacific during WWII. Her husband was killed on Guadalcanal, and she falls in love with married Holden. Combat referential.

Away All Boats (Aug 17)
Dir: Joseph Pevney. Sp: Ted Sherdeman, based on the novel by Kenneth Dodson. With Jeff Chandler, George Nader, Lex Barker, Julie Adams, Richard Boone.

About naval ships that transported assault troops to the beaches in the Pacific Islands during WWII. Combat presented, as ship goes through minefield, survives kamikaze pilots, fire, etc. Traditional presentation of tough-minded captain who appears at first to be ruthless, but who turns out to be efficient and aware that such toughness is necessary for survival in combat. Long interlude seen in flashback involves George Nader remembering how he met, courted, and wed his wife. This type of story expansion through flashback is common at this period of time.

Attack! (Sept. 20)
Dir: Robert Aldrich. Sp: James Poe, from the play *Fragile Fox* by Norman Brooks. With Jack Palance, Eddie Albert, Lee Marvin, Richard Jaeckel.

Set in Europe in 1944, the film plunges viewers directly into combat, with the credits superimposed over the image of an empty helmet rolling down a hill. It is an Inversion film of the fourth wave type, but one that appears during the third wave as an example of the undercurrent working against the mainstream. It is a tale of cowardice, not bravery, and worthy of a book of its own. It works against estabished genre traditions, consciously undermining them by telling of corruption, desire for political power, incompetence, and, above all, cowardice during the war. Beautifully shot and cut, it presents war as a mad, almost surreal experience. The plot concerns a psychological story about a father-son relationship, demonstrating how aspects of the basic definition are used for another purpose in late stages of evolution.

Between Heaven and Hell (Oct. 12)
Dir: Richard Fleischer. Sp: Harry Brown, based on the novel by Francis Gwaltney. With Robert Wagner, Terry Moore, Broderick Crawford, Buddy Ebsen, Brad Dexter.

Set in combat situation on an island in the Japanese-occupied Pacific. Story concerns the regeneration of a hardheaded G.I.

Battle Stations (no review date)
Dir: Lewis Seiler. With John Lund, William Bendix, Keefe Brasselle, Richard Boone.

War with Japan in the Pacific.

1956 notes
Training camp: *The Girl He Left Behind*
Test pilots: *Toward the Unknown*
Comedy: *The Lieutenant Wore Skirts, Teahouse of the August Moon*
British-made: *Cockleshell Heroes*—a traditional combat format
Military trial concerning collaboration: *The Rack:* Korea.

1957

Battle Hymn (Feb. 16)
Dir: Douglas Sirk. Sp: Charles Grayson, Vincent B. Evans. With Rock Hudson, Anna Kashfi, Dan Duryea, Martha Hyer, Don Defore, Alan Hale.

Biography. Story of Air Force Colonel Dean Hess, the "flying parson" who cared for orphans during Korean War, as an atonement for having accidentally bombed a school yard during WWII. Shows the staples of the WWII combat film linked to those specific to the Korean: children, refugees, marital conflict. Central generic event: Hudson steers his WWII buddy home after he has been hit, their planes flying in close formation, Hudson "talking home" the friend.

Heaven Knows, Mr. Allison (March 15)
Dir: John Huston. Sp: John Lee Mahin and Huston, based on the novel by Charles Shaw.

Combat setting of a Pacific Island during WWII, with a nun and a marine corporal isolated amidst the enemy. Action qualifies it as combat, despite the unusual "group" configuration.

Men in War (March 20)
Dir: Anthony Mann. Sp: Philip Yordan, based on the novel, *Combat!* by Van Van Praag. With Robert Ryan, Aldo Ray, Robert Keith.

An outstanding combat film set on patrol with the infantry in Korea. Maintains traditional units of the combat film, varied for Korea, and still remains a fresh work of artistic merit. My book on Anthony Mann contains an extensive analysis of this film.

China Gate (May 23)
Dir: Samuel Fuller. Sp: Fuller. With Gene Barry, Angie Dickinson, Nat King Cole, Lee Van Cleef.

Set in Vietnam, with story concerning combat patrol which included an American veteran of Korea going to destroy a Communist ammunition dump. They are a French Legionnaires group, aided and guided by Dickinson. The group includes a veteran of both WWII and Korea (Cole), an ex-cop from Paris, a Greek expatriate, and ex-German and ex-Czech soldiers.

The Enemy Below (Dec. 26)
Dir: Dick Powell. Sp: Wendell Mayes, based on the novel by Commander D. A. Rayner. With Robert Mitchum, Curt Jurgens, Al Hedison, Theodore Bikel, Kurt Kreuger.

A detailed physical chase and fight between an American destroyer-escort (in the book it was British) and a German submarine has a psychological parallel between the two captains. Classic naval battle.

Hellcats of the Navy (no review date)
Dir: Nathan Juran. With Ronald Reagan, Nancy Davis, Arthur Franz.

The WWII action of a submarine and its crew, with Davis as a nurse. The President of the United States and First Lady appear in their only film together.

Bitter Victory (no review date)
Dir: Nicholas Ray. Sp: Rene Hardy, Nicholas Ray, Gavin Lambert based on Hardy's novel. With Curt Jurgens, Richard Burton, Ruth Roman.

Beautifully shot in CinemaScope and Sepiatone, the very first image of this film announces it will break the tradition of the combat film and be a personal, individualistic one. Its music is modern, discordant, not military, and its cinematic presentation is in every way unusual. Shots are held for a seemingly endless time and then suddenly quick, hard cuts follow. Narrative development in the traditional sense is eliminated, contributing to a strange, delirious quality to the story. Like *Attack!* and *Hell Is for Heroes*, *Bitter Victory* demonstrates the inversion process beginning its work in earlier waves. Restrained and formal on the surface, and concerned with the rules of war and military behavior, as with stories reminiscent of *Gilda* and *Casablanca*, *Bitter Victory* has a madness underneath. Thus it is like war itself—all planning and tactics, but basically an insane endeavor. The story is about a commando operation behind the German lines at Bengazi in North Africa during the early days of World War II.

1957 notes
British: *Above Us the Waves, Reach for the Sky, Baby and the Battleship* (comedy), *Pursuit of the Graf Spee* (set in 1939, based on fact)

Training camp: *The D.I., Bailout at 43,000, Bombers B-52* (actually set at a base, not a training camp)

World War I: *Paths of Glory*, a pacifist film

Comedy: *Operation Mad Ball, Sad Sack*

Military Personnel: *Sayonara*

Misleading titles: *Battle Hell* (British on Yangstze in 1949), *Jet Pilot, Until They Sail, Time Limit, Kiss Them for Me* (three men on leave in WWII) *Bridge On the River Kwai* (prison during WWII, with some combat)

1958

*The Deep Six (Jan. 16)
Dir: Rudolph Mate. Sp: John Twist, Martin Rackin, Harry Brown, as adapted from novel by Martin Dibner. With Alan Ladd, Dianne Foster, William Bendix, Keenan Wynn, James Whitmore, Joey Bishop.

WWII Navy drama, with Alan Ladd as naval gunnery officer, simultaneously in conflict with the Japanese and his own Quaker upbringing. Begins in advertising world of Madison Avenue (his civilian life) and travels out into the Aleutians, where he serves on a combat destroyer.

Darby's Rangers (Feb. 13)
Dir: William Wellman. Sp: Guy Trosper, suggested by the book by Maj. James Altieri. With James Garner, Jack Warden, Edd Byrnes, Venetia Stevenson, Etchika Choureau.

Special combat forces in WWII. Goes from Scottish training camp into combat in the Italian campaign. Uses traditional group and story conflicts. However, training and combat are given second status, and romance—a love story for each major character—is equally as important to storyline.

Run Silent, Run Deep (March 28)
Dir: Robert Wise. Sp: John Gay, based on the novel by Cmdr. Edward L. Beach. With Clark Gable, Burt Lancaster, Jack Warden, Brad Dexter, Don Rickles, Nick Cravet.

WWII submarine combat. Excellent film, with tense combat in the tradition of the type, taking sub out of Pearl Harbor into the Bungo Straits near the Japanese islands. A shoreline story is sketched in, to help delineate the characters of the two leads, but the majority of the film is traditional sub combat. Dives and drills, torpedoes and depth charges, conflicts on board—it's all here, but done with great skill and pace.

The Young Lions (April 3)
Dir: Edward Dmytryk. Sp: Edward Anhalt, based on the novel by Irwin Shaw. With Marlon Brando, Montgomery Clift, Dean Martin, Maximillian Schell, Lee Van Cleef.

This film may mark the emergence of the truly epic form that would be seen during the 1960s. Based on a successful novel, it tells the story of three different men (two Americans, one German) and their pre-war, combat, and furlough lives during World War II. It actually contains a minimum of combat, the best of which is in the African desert campaigns. The stories of the three men are interwoven, and they cover the traditions of training camp and combat films.

Kings Go Forth (July 4)
Dir: Delmar Daves. Sp: Merle Miller, based on the novel by Joe David Brown. With Frank Sinatra, Tony Curtis, Natalie Wood.

WWII, set in the area of the Maritime Alps, where Americans are trying to dislodge the Nazis. This concerns combat, but the majority of the film takes place when the men go on furlough to rest in hotels, villas and bars on the French Riviera. Major plot concern is racial—Sinatra and Curtis both fall in love with a girl whose father was black. Film illustrates how traditional combat setting and characters are used for another concern or social issue.

A Time To Love and a Time To Die (July 10)
Dir: Douglas Sirk. Sp: Orin Jannings, based on the novel by Erich Maria Remarque. With John Gavin, Jock Mahoney, Don Defore, Keenan Wynn, Lilo Pulver, Erich Maria Remarque.

Begins and ends in WWII combat in Europe. Young Nazi soldier goes on leave in the middle, meets and falls in love and marries a young girl in the ruins of a 1944 German city. He is killed at Russian front at finale.

The Naked and the Dead (Aug. 7)
Dir: Raoul Walsh. Sp: Denis and Terry Sanders, based on the novel by Norman Mailer. With Aldo Ray, Cliff Robertson, Raymond Massey, Richard Jaeckel, James Best, Joey Bishop, L. Q. Jones.

One of the very biggest and most successful novels of WWII brought to life, as an indication of the new epic form. Despite the literary success behind the film, it was apparently inspired by old WWII movies. Characters include a comic Jew, a hillbilly, an Indian scout, a cynical loner, a Southern religious boy, a beardless youth, a former playboy who grows up in combat, a general who is convinced he has to make the men hate him to gain their respect (he has learned that from watching *Sands of Iwo Jima!*). The personal stories of each key character are told to the audience via the flashback device.

Torpedo Run (Oct. 25)

Dir: Joseph Pevney. Sp: Richard Sale, William Wister Haines, based on stories by Sale. With Glenn Ford, Ernest Borgnine, Dean Jones, L. Q. Jones, Diane Brewster.

WWII submarine warfare in the Pacific. Traditional, with the guilt theme often connected to subs. Ford has had to sink an enemy transport he knew was carrying his wife and child. A climactic scene has the crew of this sub having to get out of it from the bottom, through the device of Momsen-lungs, even though they are in Arctic waters. The use of the Momsen lung is rare in sub movies, oddly enough. It was the device we saw tested in the prewar "inventor" style film, *Submarine D-1*.

In Love and War (Nov. 1)

Dir: Philip Dunne. Sp: Edward Anhalt, based on novel by Anton Myer. With Robert Wagner, Jeffrey Hunter, Bradford Dillman, Dana Wynter, Hope Lange, Sheree North.

Story of three representative marines during WWII. Emphasis is more on love than war, as the stories of what happens to them before they ship out constitute the majority of the film.

China Doll (Dec. 4)

Dir: Frank Borzage. Sp: Kitty Buhler, based on a story by James Benson Nable, Thomas F. Kelly. With Victor Mature, Ward Bond, Bob Mathias, Stu Whitman, Li Li Hua.

Army Air Force in China during 1943. Most of the film takes place on the ground until the finale, which is a well executed air-combat sequence. War is always present, however, with bombings, missions, etc. Story once again, however, is linked to prejudice theme—Mature's romance and marriage to Chinese woman.

Tarawa Beachhead (no review date)

Dir: Paul Wendkos. With Kerwin Mathews, Ray Danton, Julie Adams.

Traditional WWII action, involving military assault plus romance and problems of individuals in troop.

1958 notes

World War I: *Lafayette Escadrille*

British: *Night Ambush*, *Count Five and Die* (espionage), *Dunkirk*, *A Town Like Alice*, *Orders To Kill*

Comedy: *No Time for Sergeants, Imitation General, Onionhead*
Postwar Germany: *Fraulein*

1959

The Last Blitzkreig (July 31)
Dir: Arthur Dreifuss. Sp: Lou Morheim. With Van Johnson, Kerwin Mathews, Dick York, Larry Storch.

Battle of the Bulge, World War II in final days. Here is a genre inversion indeed—Van Johnson, hero of *Thirty Seconds Over Tokyo, Battleground, Go for Broke,* and *Men of the Fighting Lady,* this time plays a German commando! Because he speaks such perfect English and looks so American (amen to that), he has been sent to infiltrate American lines as a saboteur and spy. Combat.

Up Periscope (March 5)
Dir: Gordon Douglas. Sp: Richard Landau, based on the novel by Robb White. With James Garner, Edmond O'Brien, Alan Hale, Carleton Carpenter, Andra Martin.

WWII submarine film, set in the Pacific. Traditional sub episodes and conflicts. Sub undertakes a combat mission, with Garner going into enemy-held island, somewhat reminiscent of the similar mission in *Crash Dive.*

Pork Chop Hill (May 30)
Dir: Lewis Milestone. Sp: James R. Webb, based on factual material by S. L. A. Marshall, USAR. With Gregory Peck, Harry Guardino, Rip Torn, George Peppard, James Edwards, Bob Steele, Woody Strode.

American infantry assault upon a position in Korea. The enemy is presented physically, but also psychologically through the device of a battlefield loudspeaker that broadcasts discouraging information to the attacking infantrymen. Here is Tokyo Rose updated! It also demonstrates the "brainwashing" element of the Korean conflict. The group of men are traditional, and also include another touchstone of the Korean war, a group member who is a Nisei.

*Operation Petticoat (Dec. 6)
Dir: Blake Edwards. Sp: Stanley Shapiro, Maurice Richlin, based on story by Paul King, Joseph Stone. With Cary Grant, Tony Curtis, Gene Evans, Arthur O'Connell, Dina Merrill.

Battle Flame (no review date)
Dir: R. G. Springsteen. With Scott Brady, Robert Blake, Elaine Edwards.

Misleading title has Korean War setting, with some combat situations, but mostly romance between Brady and Edwards.

Battle of the Coral Sea (no review date)
Dir: Paul Wendkos. With Cliff Robertson, Gia Scala, Gordon Jones.

Robertson plays a sub captain on a Japanese-held island during WWII, who seeks to signal key information to U.S. fleet.

1959 notes
Comedy: *Perfect Furlough, Don't Give Up the Ship, Private's Affair.*
Atomic war with sub: *On the Beach*
WWII Setting, with guerrillas or some variation: *Angry Hills, Ten Seconds to Hell, Five Gates to Hell* (first two are WWII, later is Vietnam)

1960

Never So Few (Jan. 22)
Dir: John Sturges. Sp: Millard Kaufman, from novel by Tom T. Chamales. With Frank Sinatra, Peter Lawford, Steve McQueen, Richard Johnson, Brian Donlevy, Charles Bronson, Paul Henreid, Gina Lollobrigida.

Burma jungle fighting during WWII, including an extended raid on a Japanese air strip. Wild and lurid combat scenes, plus romance in wealthy Oriental homes and fun in Calcutta bars.

The Gallant Hours (June 23)
Dir: Robert Montgomery. Sp: Beirne Lay, Jr., Frank D. Gilroy. With James Cagney, Dennis Weaver, Ward Costello, Richard Jaeckel.

Biography. Story of Admiral of the Fleet William F. Halsey Jr. A behind-the-scenes look at the pressures and courage of a military commander in time of war. No actual naval battle is depicted. In this reverent story, told in flashback, can be observed a very conscious creation of the myth of World War II. It presents reality in image and story, comments on reality by including a narration that constantly explains and tells the fates of characters being seen, and adds mythic distance by music that can only be described as holy. Halsey says, "there aren't any great men, just great challenges that ordinary men like you and me are forced by circumstances to meet." The portrait, however, definitely presents him as a great military leader. It is a loving and affectionate film.

All the Young Men. (Aug. 27)
Dir: Hall Bartlett. Sp: Bartlett. With Alan Ladd, Sidney Poitier, Ingemar Johansson, James Darren, Mort Sahl.

Marines in Korea, set in 1951. Key problem is racial integration.

Hell to Eternity (Oct. 13)
Dir: Phil Karlson. Sp: Ted Sherdeman, Walter Robert Schmidt, based on a story by Gil Doud. With Jeffrey Hunter, David Janssen, Vic Damone, Sessue Hayakawa.

Biography in the tradition of Sergeant York and Audie Murphy. A Japanese-speaking young American, Guy Gabaldon (played by Jeffrey Hunter) single-handedly caused the surrender of 1000 Japanese on Saipan. His story of combat is dramatized, but so is his personal story, that of a boyhood in California in which he was the ward of Japanese-Americans. An antiwar film, actually, and an interesting story. The middle section of the film is very savage and well-directed combat, thrilling and intense, despite the antiwar message.

1960 notes
British: *Sink the Bismarck, Yesterday's Enemy*
Musical/Comedy: *Wake Me When It's Over, G.I. Blues*
  Spies in WWII setting: *The Enemy General*
  Sci-Fi: *Atomic Submarine*
  Italy-America co-production: *Under Ten Flags,* Ends in WWII combat
  Postwar Germany: *Verboten*
  Interesting cross-genre: *Ocean's Eleven,* a gang of wartime buddies and heroes get together to mount a military-style operation in which they will use their wartime skills to rob five major Las Vegas gambling casinos on New Year's Eve.

1961

The Guns of Navarone (June 23)
Dir: J. Lee Thompson. Sp: Carl Foreman, from the novel by Alistair MacLean. With Gregory Peck, David Niven, Anthony Quinn, Stanley Baker, Anthony Quayle, James Darren.

A tough team of allied saboteurs secretly land on a Nazi-held Greek island during WWII in order to blow up two big guns which control a vital sea lane. Here we see the phenomenon of the 1960s—the international cast in an international production. The war is as much internal among the group as external with the Nazis, and the format is that of the commando raid variation. Still, its attitudes are traditional, and this is a combat film.

Marines, Let's Go. (Aug. 16)
Dir: Raoul Walsh. Sp: John Twist. With Tom Tryon, Tom Reese, David Hedison, William Tyler. Korea.

Begins and ends in combat, with long, tedious R & R section in between. This portion of the film is largely comedy in the *What Price Glory?* tradition.

The Battle at Bloody Beach (Aug. 17)

Dir: Herbert Coleman. Sp: Richard Maibaum, Willard Willingham. With Audie Murphy, Gary Crosby, Alejandro Rey.

Set in Philippines during WWII. Murphy is American scout, bringing help to guerrillas, and also searching for his bride left behind when war broke out.

Sniper's Ridge (Aug. 24)

Dir: John Bushelman. Sp: Tom Maruzzi. With Jack Ging, Stanley Clements, John Goddard.

Korea. Low budget story of G.I.s who are battle-fatigued, and just want to go home. They are more concerned with that than the enemy, although the leader steps on a mine and can't take his foot off it or it will explode. This happens frequently in Korea films, and is the central event of this 61-minute movie. The *Times* review refers to this film's negative attitude about war, compared to "the patriotic propaganda efforts of World War II currently invading television's late shows."

Operation Bottleneck (Sept. 7)

Dir: Edward L. Cahn. Sp: Orville H. Hampton. With Ron Foster, Norman Alden, John Clarke.

WWII in Burma, with small group of American paratroopers dropping on a Japanese held area. Among other things, they rescue the women of a tea house, but also manage to blow up some strategic supply lines.

Armored Command (Oct. 7)

Dir: Byron Haskin. Sp: Ron Alcorn. With Howard Keel, Earl Holliman, Burt Reynolds, Warner Anderson, Tina Louise.

Vosges mountains during WWII, with Louise shot by Nazis and left as appealing victim to be found by American troops. Actually she is there to demoralize them and spy.

1961 notes

International films: *The Bridge, The Great War* (WWI) *Two Women, Fate of a Man* (horrors of war in Russia), *Invasion Quartet* (British mockery, a lampoon, but done straight-faced, of films like *Guns of Navarone*)

1962

*Merrill's Marauders (June 14)

Dir: Samuel Fuller. Sp: Fuller and Milton Sperling. With Jeff Chandler, Ty Hardin, Peter Brown, Claude Akins, Will Hutchins.

Hell Is for Heroes (July 12)
Dir: Don Siegel. Sp: Richard Carr, from a story by Robert Pirosh. With Steve McQueen, Bobby Darin, Fess Parker, Harry Guardino, Bob Newhart, Nick Adams, James Coburn.

Set in Montigney, France, a rest area near the Siegfried Line in 1944, this film tells the story of a war hero who is never a part of a group, and who, in fact, is totally unable to relate to the group. This character is well played by Steve McQueen, an actor whose persona is that of a loner. A visually powerful film, presenting an empty, surreal landscape of war, its combat is among the most intense and graphic in all the war films. Its plot and characterizations refer directly to other genre films, most notably *Sahara*, despite differences in geographical settings.

In its searing finale, Steve McQueen functions as a kind of human war machine, running forward, shooting, throwing packages of explosives into the pillbox under attack. He is shot, falls onto his back into a hole, arms outspread like a Christ figure. But he staggers to his feet, and arises out of the hole like a Frankenstein monster. He falls to his knees again, but repeats his actions, finally throwing himself and the explosives into the pillbox.

His suicide/sacrifice demonstrates with dynamic image that only the McQueen character, the "war hero," understands what is wanted from men who fight our wars. They are to die, because that's what war asks of young men. His repeated action of falling down, getting up, falling down, getting up, and pressing onward causes a viewer to feel that he is watching endless reruns of war movies. We've seen this action repeated before, and we keep repeating it in history, too.

At the end, the camera moves in on the pillbox, and the image is grained out, frozen, and changed to a newspaper image. Image becomes history, and seems to ask the question—can we finally put such things in the past, where they belong? One of the great war films. Inversion type, working against fourth wave when released.

War Hunt (Aug. 8)
Dir: Denis Sanders. Sp: Stanford Whitmore. With John Saxon, Robert Redford, Sydney Pollack, Gavin McLeod.

Korea. Uses traditional group format, to question mentality of someone able to kill in war. Takes place near Panmunjom just before ceasefire, and "the hero" (Saxon) is actually a psychotic killer.

*The Longest Day (Oct. 5)
Dir: Ken Annakin, Andrew Marton, and Bernhard Wicki. Sp: Cornelius Ryan, adapted from his book, with additional episodes by Romain Gary, James Jones, David Pursall, Jack Seddon. With a huge cast, including John Wayne, Robert Mitchum, Henry Fonda, Sean Connery, Richard Todd, Red Buttons, Eddie

Albert, Paul Anka, Fabian, Jeffrey Hunter, Edmond O'Brien, Richard Burton, and more.

No Man Is an Island (Oct. 11)
Dir: John Monks Jr. and Richard Goldstone. Sp: Monks and Goldstone. With Jeffrey Hunter, Marshall Thompson.

Based on the experiences of George R. Tweed, an American sailor who became the only serviceman on Guam to avoid capture by the Japanese during the early years of WWII.

Smashing of the Reich and Kamikaze (Oct. 3)
Documentaries: Two compilation films using battle footage of World War II. Two films produced by Perry Wolff.

1962 notes
British: *Desert Patrol* (WWII campaign in Libya), *Junglefighters* (Burma) *The Valiant*

Comedies: *The Horizontal Lieutenant* (hero must capture a Japanese thief stealing gefulte fish on a Pacific Island during WWII—that's the truth); *The Best of Enemies* (British capture tired Italians in desert, 1941)

Related films: *The Outsider, biography* of Ira Hayes, flagraiser at Iwo Jima, his sordid postwar story; *Four Horsemen of the Apocalypse* (famous novel reset in WWII, with combat finale);

Spies: *Counterfeit Traitor, Five Finger Exercise.*

Prisoner-of-War: *Password is Courage.*

World War I: *Lawrence of Arabia.*

Korea-related drama: *Manchurian Candidate.*

1963

The War Lover (March 7)
Dir: Philip Leacock. Sp: Howard Koch, based on the novel by John Hersey.
With Steve McQueen, Robert Wagner, Shirley Ann Field.

Air Force B–17s, flying out from England on bombing runs, combined with story of mixed-up pilot who tries to steal friend's girl.

PT-109 (June 27)
Dir: Leslie H. Martinson. Sp: Richard L. Breen, from an adaptation by Howard and Vincent X. Flaherty of the book by Robert J. Donovan. With Cliff Robertson, Ty Hardin, James Gregory, Robert Culp, Grant Williams.

Biography. The story of President John F. Kennedy's heroic combat experience in the Pacific on a PT boat.

Cry of Battle (Oct. 12)
Dir: Irving Lerner. Sp. Bernard Gordon based on the novel, *Fortress in the Rice* by Benjamin Appel. With Van Heflin, James MacArthur, Sidney Clute, Rita Moreno.

Americans of different backgrounds are caught in the Philippines at the start of WWII. They join a guerrilla band.

The Victors (Dec. 20)
Dir: Carl Foreman. Sp: Foreman. With George Hamilton, George Peppard, Eli Wallach, Vincent Edwards, James Mitchum.

American riflemen fighting WWII in Europe. An epic antiwar statement, showing traditional combat characters and situations, plus "human" stories in bars and bedrooms. Former characteristics are deliberately undercut, such as when one G.I. adopts a little dog, the other Americans use it for target practice, finally killing it. Film also presents the execution of an American soldier by a firing squad on Christmas Eve, a close parallel to the execution of Private Eddie Slovik in France on January 31, 1945. To make comments, film does such things as cut back and forth between scenes of horror in combat and newsreels depicting the cheerful home front.

1963 notes
Prison drama, based on true incident: *The Great Escape*.
Training camp: *Soldier in the Rain*.
Saving of the Lippizan stallions: *Miracle of the White Stallions*.
Korean Prisoners: *The Hook*.

1964

War Is Hell (Jan. 23)
Dir: Burt Topper. Sp: Topper. With Tony Russell, Baynes Barron, Burt Topper.

Low-budget. Set in Korea. There is nothing new here, but it is notable that the action is introduced by Audie Murphy.

A Yank in Vietnam (Feb. 6)
Dir: Marshall Thompson, Sp: Jane Wardell, Jack Lewis. With Marshall Thompson.

A small Hollywood company put together a crew of Vietnamese technicians, recruited a native cast (except for director Thompson), and went into the "danger zone" to film this English-language production. "First came the Japanese," says the film, "then came the French, and now the Communists. We've been fighting all our lives." Frequently cited as the first Vietnam movie.

Flight from Ashiya (April 23)
Dir: Michael Anderson. Sp: Elliott Arnold, Waldo Salt, from novel by Mr. Arnold. With Yul Brynner, Richard Widmark, George Chakiris, Shirley Knight.

United States Army Rescue corps., picking up survivors in North China sea. Each of three men has a flashback which explains their current character, and Richard Widmark's story explains why he hates the Japanese. It is because of the death of his war correspondent sweetheart during WWII. Film is not a WWII combat film per se.

633 Squadron (June 25)

Dir: Walter E. Grauman. Sp: James Clavell, Howard Koch, from a novel by Frederick E. Smith. With Cliff Robertson, George Chakiris, Harry Andrews.

WWII aviation movie, about British squadron's mission to bomb a Norwegian rocket factory.

The Secret Invasion (Sept. 17)

Dir: Roger Corman. Sp: R. Wright Campbell. With Stewart Granger, Raf Vallone, Mickey Rooney, Edd Byrnes.

Five convicts sent on dangerous mission into Nazi-held Yugoslavia. They are promised their freedom if they succeed. Here is the "dirty group" variation.

The Thin Red Line (Oct. 29)

Dir: Andrew Marton. Sp: Bernard Gordon, from the novel by James Jones. With Keir Dullea, Jack Warden, Ray Daley.

Set on Guadalcanal during WWII, story of internal conflicts and problems of command, etc.

The Finest Hours (no review date)

Documentary. Based on Sir Winston Churchill's memoirs. Sp: Victor Wolfson. Dir: Peter Baylis. Newsreel footage.

1964 notes

World War I documentary: Guns of August
Heroism of WWII debunked: The Americanization of Emily
Army hospital in last years of WWII: Captain Newman, M.D.
WWII trials: Man in the Middle
Comedy: McHale's Navy, Ensign Pulver, Father Goose, (New Guinea island during WWII)
Atomic Nightmares: Dr. Strangelove, Seven Days in May, Fail Safe

1965

None but the Brave (Feb. 25)

Dir: Frank Sinatra. Sp: John Twist, Katsuya Susaki, from a story by Kikumru Okuda. With Frank Sinatra, Clint Walker, Tommy Sands, Brad Dexter, Tony Bill.

Japanese vs. marines on a small island. Since island is cut off from all communications, they have to exchange assets—the Japanese trade water for the skills of an American medical corpsman. They make a technical truce until war intrudes, and they fight again. Combat.

*In Harm's Way (April 7)
Dir: Otto Preminger. Sp: Wendell Mayes, based on novel by James Bassett. With John Wayne, Patricia Neal, Kirk Douglas, Henry Fonda, Dana Andrews, Tom Tryon, Burgess Meredith, and all-star cast.

Up from the Beach (June 10)
Dir: Robert Parris. Sp: Stanley Mann, Claude Brule, based on *Epitaph for an Enemy*, novel by George Barr, adapted by Howard Clewes. With Cliff Robertson, Red Buttons, Marius Goring, Slim Pickens.

American invaders on D-Day plus one, confused and lost, involved with Normandy villagers.

Ambush Bay (August 31)
Dir: Ron Winston. Sp: Marve Feinberg, Ib Melchoir. With Hugh O'Brian, Mickey Rooney, James Mitchum, Harry Lauter.

A typical World War II combat film—nine men on a dangerous patrol in the Philippine. The story concerns these marines who land secretly at night with only 96 hours in which to get through Japanese held territory to contact an informant who has information concerning the planned invasion. (As it turns out, the informant is a Japanese girl originally from Long Beach!) Traditional problems arise—death of the leader, a botched mission that enforces new action, the blowing up of mines underneath the ocean, etc. The group is the usual mix, and the excitement is quite good, with plenty of action. Trivia buffs may appreciate that this film, shot on location in Luzon, may be the only movie in history whose cinematographer was actually a Manila University chemistry professor.

The Walls of Hell (Nov. 18)
Dirs: Gerardo DeLeon, Eddie Romero. Sp: Ferde Grofe Jr., Cesar Amigo, and Romero. With Jock Mahoney, Fernando Poe, Jr., Mike Parsons.

A Filipino-made, English-language film, with some American actors and financed with American money. Shot on site, tells story of an assault by American and Filipino guerrillas on the 10,000 Japanese marines who held 20,000 Filipinos captive behind the 20-foot-thick walls of Intramuros.

*Battle of the Bulge (Dec. 18)
Dir: Ken Annakin. Sp: Philip Yordan, Milton Sperling, John Nelson. With Henry Fonda, Robert Shaw, Robert Ryan, Dana Andrews, George Montgomery, Ty Hardin, James MacArthur, Telly Savalas.

The Cavern (Dec. 26)
Dir: Edgar Ulmer Sp: Michael Pertwee, Jack Davies. With John Saxon, Larry Hagman, Peter Marshall, Brian Aherne.

Seven people trapped underground for five months during the end of WWII. Six soldiers, one female civilian, of an international mix: American, British,

German, Canadian. No flashbacks tell their story, and no philosophizing explains about war and life. Just urgent tension, in a combat situation.

1965 notes

International: *Taxi for Tobruk, The Naked Brigade, Italiano Brava Gente* (seen on U.S. TV as *Attack and Retreat*)

Saboteurs and Tricksters: *36 Hours, The Train, Operation Crossbow, The Saboteur (Code Name: Morituri)*

Prisons and Escapes: *King Rat, Von Ryan's Express, The Hill*

WWI Documentary: *Over There, 1914–1918*

Comedy: *Operation Snafu*

Note: Because of a newspaper strike in 1965, some titles may have been omitted. For instance, television guides frequently refer to a 1965 movie, *Once Before I Die*, directed by John Derek, starring Derek, Ursula Andress, Richard Jaeckel, and Ron Ely, which is an offbeat story of a band of American soldiers in the Philippines during World War II trying to survive the Japanese attack.

1966

The Heroes of Telemark (March 10)

Dir: Anthony Mann. Sp: Ivan Moffat, Ben Barzman. With Kirk Douglas, Richard Harris, Michael Redgrave, David Weston.

WWII in Norway, with resistance fighters and saboteurs, but also with a combat section.

*What Did You Do in the War, Daddy? (Sept. 1)

Dir: Blake Edwards. Sp: William Blatty, from a story by Edwards. With James Coburn, Dick Shawn, Aldo Ray, Harry Morgan, Carroll O'Connor.

Is Paris Burning? (Nov. 11)

Dir: René Clément. Sp: Gore Vidal, Francis Ford Coppola, from the book by Larry Collins and Dominique Lapierre. With Jean-Paul Belmondo, Charles Boyer, Leslie Caron, George Chakiris, Alain Delon, Kirk Douglas, Glenn Ford, and an all-star cast.

The liberation of Paris in 1944, reenacted with epic detail, including combat.

1966 notes

International: *Weekends at Dunkirk*

World War I: *King and Country, The Blue Max*

Fiction—if Nazis had invaded England: *It Happened Here*

Dienbienphu: *Lost Command*

1967

Tobruk (Feb. 9)

Dir: Arthur Hiller. Sp: Leo V. Gordon. With Rock Hudson, George Peppard, Nigel Green, Guy Stockwell, Jack Watson.

A group of 90 men are sent on a secret mission to blast the fuel bunkers that supply Rommel and his tank battalions. Set against the African battle of Tobruk, and reported to be true. Film updates old combat format by having German-Jewish commandos go with the British, with the two groups disguised as Nazi captors and British prisoners of war. Peppard is a young Jewish leader. Hudson is a "Canadian" major.

First To Fight (March 30)

Dir: Christian Nyby. Sp: Gene L. Coon. With Chad Everett, Dean Jagger, Gene Hackman, Claude Akins.

About the marines. *Times* review says, "old style, flag waving tribute" and refers to the film's having "every war cliché except the soldier from Brooklyn." Here is a film that indicates how important old films are in our lives, as when the hero freezes in battle and hears the strains of "As Time Goes By." He and his wife watched *Casablanca* together. Two big combat scenes.

*The Dirty Dozen (June 16)

Dir: Robert Aldrich. Sp: Nunnally Johnson, Lukas Heller, from the novel by E. M. Nathanson. With Lee Marvin, Ernest Borgnine, Charles Bronson, Jim Brown, John Cassavetes, Richard Jaeckel, George Kennedy, Robert Ryan, Telly Savalas, Donald Sutherland, Clint Walker.

Beach Red (Aug. 4)

Dir: Cornel Wilde. Sp: Clint Johnson, Donald A. Peters, Jefferson Pascal, from the novel by Peter Bowman. With Wilde, Rip Torn, Patrick Wolfe, Burr DeBenning.

Filmed on location on former Japanese battle site in the Philippines. Story of Marine infiltration of an enemy-infested island. A semi-documentary, using the flashback technique and following traditional combat group format, etc. An honest and tough movie, with first half hour full-out combat with marines from LST into landing on beach. *Beach Red* is an interesting film. It is as if Americans had a morbid desire to return to the combat conditions of the World War II movie, and see them done real, in living color, with all the blood and horror now possible in the moviemaking of the 1960s. Except for brief flashbacks, when characters remember the loves in their civilian lives, the film is nothing but intense combat. There is practically no dialogue, and except for a few screamed-out words, brief exchanges, and the sound of thoughts in each soldier's head, nothing at all is said. Men just fight and move forward across the Pacific island, inch by inch. The bloody business is seen for what it is—lost limbs, a severed foot or arm, floating in the water or abandoned on the beach, flamethrowers and grenades reducing the enemy to ashes, dead bodies used as shields when advancing, vomit, the whole ugly thing. And throughout it all, a man with the movie camera, who landed with them, taking picture after picture. His response to a wounded man—"get out of my way, you're ruining the shot." His attitude toward the look of combat— "I'll try another lens." His retort to someone who begs him to stop taking his picture just after he's killed a man—"You do your job, Sir Galahad, and I'll do mine."

Beach Red is nothing but combat. There is no story at all except the story of taking a Pacific island under terrible conditions. This would not be possible if the genre were not solidly established. Instead of a story, with character, intercut by intense fighting, this film presents combat, with referential character touches, intercut by intense story. It can reverse the normal narrative pattern, because genre exists.

Far from Vietnam (Oct. 2)
Documentary. Compilation of film material, newsreels, interviews, etc. with a strongly anti-Vietnam message. By Alain Resnais, William Klein, Joris Ivens, Agnès Varda, Claude Lelouch, and Jean-Luc Godard.

North Vietnam (Dec. 11)
Documentary. By Felix Green. Anti-American involvement.

The Anderson Platoon (Dec. 18)
Dir: Pierre Schoendorfer.

Originally shown on CBS television, this hour-long movie was released this date in American theatres. Follows the activities of an American platoon under the command of Lt. Joseph Anderson, through the central highlands of Vietnam—in combat—in 1966.

1967 notes
WWII German setting: The Night of the Generals
Rumanian peasants during WWII: The 25th Hour
Spoof of WWII spy movies: Triple Cross
World War I: King of Hearts
Misleading Western film title: War Wagon
Comedy/Farce variation (British) : How I Won the War

1968

The Young Warriors (Feb. 8)
Dir: John Peyser. Sp: Richard Matheson, based on his own story. With James Drury, Steve Carlson, Jonathan Daly.

WWII drama with traditional combat for men on patrol against Nazis. Director Peyser also directed television's hit show, "Combat!"

The Face of War (May 11)
Documentary. Dir. Eugene S. Jones. Combat troops in Vietnam.

The Devil's Brigade (May 23)
Dir: Andrew V. McLaglen. Sp: William Roberts, based on a book by Robert H. Adleman and Col George Walton, USAR. With Cliff Robertson, Vince Edwards, William Holden, Michael Rennie, Dana Andrews, Claude Akins, Carroll O' Connor, Richard Jaeckel.

WWII setting. Story of a mixture of Canadian and American troops who are brought together for commando raid in Norway. Two groups fight among themselves during training, indulging in a huge barroom brawl at completion. Norway is cancelled, but they go through major commando operations in Italy. *Times* review "There's hardly a character, a situation, or a line of dialogue . . . that has not served a useful purpose in some earlier movie or television show."

The Long Day's Dying (May 29)
Dir: Peter Collinson. Sp: Charles Wood, based on the novel by Alan White. With David Hemmings, Tom Bell, Tony Beckley.

WWII. The story is about three English parachutists who get cut off from their unit. Their survival through violence makes an effective antiwar film, although as the review in the *Times* pointed out: "One of those pictures that go on the assumption that if you avow your sensibility early enough as tough antiwar, and if you dismember your characters incessantly, an eye at a time, with mud, and gore and blood vomiting, you can make the same picture the prowar people have been making all along and find an audience warmed by its humanism."

Attack on the Iron Coast (June 6)
Dir: Paul Wendkos. Sp: Herman Hoffman, based on a story by John C. Champion. With Lloyd Bridges, Andrew Keir, Mark Eden.

Commando raid on Nazi-held coast town in France. Low-budget British film released by United Artists.

The Green Berets (June 20)
Dirs: John Wayne, Ray Kellogg. Sp: James Lee Barrett, based on the novel by Robin Moore. With Wayne, David Janssen, Jim Hutton, Aldo Ray, Raymond St. Jacques, Bruce Cabot.

Big-scale combat in Vietnam, from training camp into combat and commando raid. Conscious re-creation of the war in Vietnam in the terms of the WWII movie and the Western film.

Anzio (July 25)
Dir: Edward Dmytryk. Sp: Harry A. L. Craig, based on the novel by Wynford Vaughan-Thomas. With Robert Mitchum, Peter Falk, Arthur Kennedy, Robert Ryan, Earl Holliman.

The January 1944, Allied landings at Anzio 20 miles south of Rome and 55 miles behind the German lines. Robert Mitchum plays a tough newspaperman who has covered the war "for seven years, from China to Italy" in this inversion plot about World War II Rangers in Italy and about the incompetent leadership that cost so many of their lives. Since it is a part of the inversion wave, it begins at a point other combat movies might (or might not, depending on the wave) reach later in the narrative—with soldiers carousing and swinging on the chandeliers (literally) with Italian prostitutes. Arthur Kennedy, playing a general, passes among his troops in the *Red Badge of Courage* variation, "You fellas get enough to eat tonight?" he asks, in a mocking version of the noble general's visit to settle down his green troops from the Stephen Crane story. A reenactment of the landing at Anzio is presented, with the action of this film placed in the hands of an objective observer—a newspaper man, who is questioning the war. It is a "why do we do it?" movie, and the question is asked out loud. Finally, Arthur Kennedy says to Robert Mitchum: "You think this is a game," and Mitchum replies, "Isn't it the ultimate game? Men kill each other because they like to." "You found the answer then," says Kennedy, but adds, "it's a hell of a condemnation of mankind."

"Maybe if we admit it, recognize it, we might be able to live with each other," replies Mitchum.

"We hope," says Kennedy. At the triumphant entry into Rome of the American troops that finishes this film, Mitchum comments. "Nothing changes except the uniforms and the transportation . . . well, we've seen the conquering heroes, let's go home." Despite the cynical speeches, the film follows the tradititional combat mold.

The Hell with Heroes (Sept. 5)
Dir: Joseph Sargent. Sp: Halsted Welles, Harold Livingston, based on a story by Livingston. With Rod Taylor, Harry Guardino, Kevin McCarthy, Peter Deuel, Claudia Cardinale.

Two WWII flyers run an air cargo smuggling ring, and this film is interesting because, as the *Times* review said, it was "a throwback to the movies that Hollywood ground out in the panic of 1946 . . . even has the physical texture of a 1946 film . . . Universal Pictures is developing something entirely new—

the imitation 1946 movie. Because all movies are necessarily imitations (if only of life), the imitation movie (really, an imitation mutation) tends to come out looking like a last carbon copy whose form is familiar, but whose content is extremely fuzzy." (Vincent Canby).

Hell in the Pacific. (no review date)
Dir: John Boorman. With Lee Marvin, Toshiro Mifune.

An American and a Japanese, alone on a deserted island, enact a miniature and personal war.

17th Parallel: Vietnam in War.
Documentary. Dir: Joris Ivens. A convincing and disturbing case against American involvement in Vietnam. Focuses on peasants and their families, showing their banding with guerrillas under North Vietnamese Army leadership.

1968 notes
Comedy: *Secret War of Harry Frigg, The Private Navy of Sergeant O' Farrell*
WWII Prison: *Counterpoint*
Korean war and prison trial: *Sergeant Ryker*
Submarine tradition, but not in combat: *Ice Station Zebra*
Misleading title: *The Bofors Gun, The Glory Stompers* (juvenile delinquents, not war)
Heist involving army personnel: *Dayton's Devil.*

1969†

The Bridge at Remagen (June 25)
Dir: John Guillermin. Sp: Theodore Straus, William Roberts, Ray Rigby. With George Segal, Robert Vaughn, Ben Gazzara, Bradford Dillman.

Story of Allies in combat at key bridge. Based on real event. Intense combat.

Castle Keep (July 23)
Dir: Sydney Pollack. Sp: Daniel Taradash, David Rayfield, from the novel by William Eastlake. With Burt Lancaster, Peter Falk, Patrick O'Neal, Jean-Pierre Aumont, Tony Bill, Bruce Dern.

Focuses on eight soldiers on the French border, and is a kind of allegory on war. Uses traditional combat format to make its antiwar, and somewhat pretentious point.

---

†From here on, dates from *Variety*, not *The New York Times.*

Extraordinary Seaman (Jan. 22)

Dir: John Frankenheimer. Sp: Philip Rock, Hal Dresner, based on the story by Philip Rock. With David Niven, Faye Dunaway, Alan Alda, Mickey Rooney, Jack Carter, Juano Hernandez.

Niven captains lost ship during WWII. A comedy. Despite the use of real newsreels from the 1940s, it is essentially a comedy.

*Play Dirty (Jan. 15)

Dir: Andre De Toth. Sp: Lotte Colin, Melvyn Bragg, story by George Marto. With Michael Caine, Nigel Davenport, Nigel Green, Harry Andrews, Aly Ben Ayed. (A United Artists release, technically listed as British film.)

Where Eagles Dare (Dec. 11, 1968)

Dir: Brian G. Hutton. Sp: Alistair MacLean. With Richard Burton, Clint Eastwood, Michael Hordern, Mary Ure.

Commando unit goes in to free an American held captive in a mountain castle during WWII. International film released by M-G-M, and in the tradition of group objective, but done in the new "commando group on glamorous assignment" tradition.

Submarine X–1 (Aug. 27)

Dir: William Graham. Sp: Donald S. Sanford, Guy Elmes. With James Caan, Rupert Davies, David Sumner, William Dysart.

Submarines. Follows pattern in which captain loses his sub but gets a second chance against the Germans in combat involving midget subs. Traditional.

The Battle of Britain (Sept. 17)

Dir: Guy Hamilton. Sp: James Kennaway, Wilfred Greatorex. With Harry Andrews, Michael Caine, Trevor Howard, Curt Jurgens, Ian McShane, Laurence Olivier.

Based on the brave deeds of British airmen who prevented the German invasion of England. Called a "spot the star" epic re-creation of events. Excellent aerial sequences.

1969 notes

Italian peasants and Germans in WWII: Secret of the Santa Vittoria
Italian International Productions: Battle of El Alamein; Battle of the Commandos.
World War I musical revue: Oh What a Lovely War

1970

M.A.S.H. (Jan. 21)

Dir: Robert Altman. Sp: Ring Lardner Jr., from novel by Richard Hooker. With Donald Sutherland, Elliott Gould, Tom Skerritt, Robert Duvall, Gary Burghoff, René Auberjonois, Sally Kellerman.

Korean comedy about mobile army surgical hospitals, with references to movies being shown each night that are traditional WWII and Korean combat films, and with serious implications. Was turned into one of the most successful television shows in the history of that medium.

Patton (Jan. 21)
Dir: Franklin J. Schaffner. Sp: Francis Ford Coppola, Edmund H. North, based on factual material by Ladislas Farago and Omar N. Bradley. With George C. Scott, Karl Malden, Stephen Young, Michael Strong.

Biography of General G. S. Patton Jr., involving the sweep of the events and battles in which he participated in WWII. Winner of eight Oscars, this film is one of the most successful and influential of all the military biographies.

Catch-22 (June 10)
Dir: Mike Nichols. Sp: Buck Henry, based on the novel by Joseph Heller. With Alan Arkin, Martin Balsam, Richard Benjamin, Art Garfunkel, Jack Gifford, Bob Newhart, Orson Welles, Anthony Perkins, Paula Prentiss.

Army life during World War II, used to reflect the novel's depiction of the insanity of army life during combat.

Kelly's Heroes (June 17)
Dir: Brian G. Hutton. Sp: Troy Kennedy Martin. With Clint Eastwood, Telly Savalas, Don Rickles, Donald Sutherland, Carroll O'Connor, Gavin MacLeod.

The heist movie meets the combat movie in this story of a group of misfits who band together to go behind the lines to steal confiscated German gold. A "dirty group" movie, with comedy and action, including combat.

*Tora! Tora! Tora! (Sept. 23)
Dir: Toshio Masuda, Kinji Fukasaku for Japan, Richard Fleisher for United States: Sp: Larry Forrester, Hideo Oguni, Ryuzo Kikushima, based on books by Gordon W. Prange and Ladislas Farago. With Martin Balsam, Jason Robards, Joseph Cotten, E. G. Marshall, Soh Yamamura, Tatsuya Mihashi.

The Virgin Soldiers (Oct. 29, 1969)
Dir: John Dexter. Sp: John Hopkins. With Lynn Redgrave, Nigel Davenport, Nigel Patrick, Jack Shepherd.

British soldiers learning about sex and combat in Malaysia.

Too Late the Hero (May 6)
Dir: Robert Aldrich. Sp: Robert Aldrich, Lukas Heller, from a story by Aldrich and Robert Sherman. With Michael Caine, Cliff Robertson, Henry Fonda, Ian Bannen, Harry Andrews.

A suicide mission on a Japanese-held island. Excellent film illustrates how a traditional combat genre definition and characterization can be varied to contain new ideology and excitement. Film was retitled *Suicide Run*. Much action and excitement.

Hornet's Nest (Sept. 2)

Dir: Phil Karlson. Sp: S. S. Schwetzer, from his story. With Rock Hudson, Sylva Koscina, Sergio Fantoni, Jacques Sernas.

WWII, in which Hudson, with a group of Italian children, blows up a German-held dam.

Mosquito Squadron (July 8)

Dir: Boris Sagal. Sp: Donald S. Sanford, Joyce Perry. With David McCallum, Suzanne Neve, David Buck.

A Canadian born RAF pilot and his cohorts go on mission behind German lines to destroy secret weapon during WWII.

The Last Escape (July 1)

Dir: Walter Grauman. Sp: Herman Hoffman, based on story by John C. Champion, Berry Trivers. With Stuart Whitman, John Collins, Matin Jarvis.

Set near end of WWII, with an O.S.S. captain given the assignment to sneak a rocket expert out of Germany (this plot of the German scientist who must be rescued was used many times).

1970 notes

Prison escape of Germans from Scottish prison: *McKenzie Break*

WWII combat comedy: *Which Way to the Front?*

Misleading titles: *Suppose They Gave a War and Nobody Came?*; *Five Man Army*; *The Last Grenade*

1971

Raid on Rommel (Feb. 24)

Dir: Henry Hathaway. Sp: Richard Buel. With Richard Burton, John Colicos, Clinton Greyn, Wolfgang Preiss.

Uses old combat footage, some of which is from *Tobruk*. Standard combat film.

Murphy's War (Jan. 27)

Dir: Peter Yates. Sp: Stirling Silliphant, based on the novel by Max Catto. With Peter O'Toole, Sian Phillips, Philippe Noiret, Horst Janson.

Set near the end of WWII, this film is a kind of combat anecdote in which a fighting Irishman (O'Toole), whose merchant ship has been torpedoed by a scouting German U-Boat, never gives up until he blows the sub to smithereens. Story involves rescue, a Quaker mission, a refurbished airplane, and great adventure. World War II becomes a personal vendetta for Murphy.

1971 notes
World War I: *Von Richthofen and Brown; Johnny Got His Gun.*

1972

No significant examples of the combat genre were released.

1973

Eagles Over London (Jan.)
Dir: Enzo G. Castellari. Sp: Alejandro Ulloa. With Van Johnson, Francisco
Rabal.
   Example of the International low-budget film that uses a WWII military,
combat setting—tells story of Germans infiltrating British high command on
eve of Battle of Britain.

Hitler: The Last Ten Days (May 9)
Dir: Enni de Concini. Sp: de Concini, Marie Pia Fusco, Wolfgang Reinhardt.,
English sp. adaptation by Ivan Moffat. Based on Gerhard Boldt's *Last Days
of the Chancellery*. With Alec Guinness (Hitler), Simon Ward, Adolfo Celi,
Eric Porter. (World War II related)

Battle of Okinawa (Sept.)
Dir: Kihachi Okamoto. Sp: Kaneto Shindo. With Kejiju Kobayashi, Yuzo
Kayama.
   Japanese version of events much used in American combat films.

Triple Echo (May 23)
Dir: Michael Apted. Sp: Robin Chapman. With Brian Deacon, Oliver Reed,
Anthony May, Glenda Jackson.
   Here is an example of how the WWII film was updated to accommodate
modern attitudes. A sensitive young deserter, who does not wish to fight, is
helped by a woman who persuades him to pose as her sister. (He is a trans-
vestite.) Retitled *Soldier in Skirts*, this is a British film.

1974

   Despite titles such as *Heroes* (a documentary on home movies!) and *The
Great Battle* (a five-hour Russian release), there were no significant war films
of any sort in 1974.

1975

Undercovers Hero (Aug. 20)
Dir: Roy Boulting. Sp: Leo Marks and Boulting. With Peter Sellers, Lila Kedrova, Curt Jurgens.

A British comedy about WWII, with Sellers playing a series of roles, one of which is Hitler. Released in the United States, but not to television, film was retitled *Soft Beds and Hard Battles*. No wide release.

1976

All This and World War II (Nov. 17)
Dir: Susan Winslow. Unusual *documentary* covers WWII through newsreels and 20th Century-Fox film footage. Called a documentary on "the last of the world's great conflagrations," it has all been set to the music of the Beatles.

Midway (June 16)
Dir: Jack Smight. Sp: Donald S. Sanford. With Charlton Heston, Henry Fonda, James Coburn, Glenn Ford, Hal Holbrook, Toshiro Mifune, Robert Mitchum, Cliff Robertson, Robert Wagner, James Shigeta.

An epic film of the fourth wave type, *Midway* re-creates the June 1942 battle in detail. The real battle of Midway is depicted in loving detail, with Henry Fonda cast as Fleet Admiral Chester W. Nimitz and Toshiro Mifune as Admiral Yamamoto. Running alongside actual historical storytelling is a soap opera narrrative involving Charlton Heston as a Captain whose son (Edward Albert Jr.) has fallen in love with a Nisei girl whose parents get sent to an internment camp. Thus, the epic form is constructed to both give a detailed inspirational reenactment of a great naval battle and to provide a story which is critical of America's government policies. Something for both the young (who identified with its Vietnam-type theme) and old (who remembered World War II and its films more fondly). Actual 16mm combat footage is used for this 70mm Sensurround production.

1977

A Bridge Too Far (June 8)
Dir: Richard Attenborough. Sp: William Goldman, based on book by Cornelius Ryan. With Dirk Bogarde, James Caan, Michael Caine, Sean Connery, Edward Fox, Elliott Gould, Gene Hackman, Laurence Olivier, Robert Redford, Ryan O'Neal.

Technically a British production, this all-star international film details the action surrounding a true-life 1944 military operation botched by both the

Allied and German troops. It is typical of the 1970s in that, instead of cele-brating the nobility of American World War II victories, it depicts the futility of war and the wretchedness of a specific military debacle. An example of how images of World War II are used for new generic purposes is demonstrated by the film's opening, in which black-and-white newsreel footage in the original aspect ratio is put on screen.

MacArthur (June 29)

Dir: Joseph Sargent. Sp: Hal Barwood, Matthew Robbins. With Gregory Peck, Ed Flanders, Dan O'Herlihy, Dick O'Neill.

Biography. This film tells the story of MacArthur's highly publicized life from the fall of Corregidor in 1942 to his dismissal from his command in the middle of the Korean conflict. The story is told in flashback, as MacArthur delivers his famous "old soldiers never die" address at West Point. Although there are action sequences involving combat, the focus of the film is not on action or war itself. Rather, it is a more personal or introverted story. It is significant, however, that a biographical film about MacArthur would be undertaken in 1977.

1977 notes

Documentary on World War I: *Men of Bronze* (true story of black regiment).

Tortured Prisoner of War Returns Home: *Rolling Thunder.*

Vietnam Veterans: *Heroes.* (Not to be confused with 1974 documentary of same title or with *The Heroes,* 1972 heist-of-lost-military money film)

1978

Force Ten from Navarone (November 29)

Dir: Guy Hamilton. Sp: Robin Chapman, based on screen story by Carl Foreman and novel by Alistair MacLean. With Robert Shaw, Harrison Ford, Edward Fox, Franco Nero, Barbara Bach.

Although this is not a sequel to the 1961 World War II commando raid movie, *The Guns of Navarone,* it begins with the end of the earlier film, to link the alleged survivors of that caper (now played by Robert Shaw and Edward Fox) to this one. The two films are very similar. This one concerns a commando raid to destroy a bridge between partisan troops in Yugoslavia and the advancing Nazis. The seemingly indestructible target is finally done in by nature—when a huge dam is exploded, and its surging waters bring down the bridge. (This effectively combines the World War II combat film with the popular "force of nature destruction" films of the early 1970s.) A film in the tradition of the WWII commando film—with a representative international group involved in traditional action.

Brass Target (December 13)
Dir: John Hough. Sp: Alvin Boretz, based on the novel *The Algonquin Project*, by Frederick Nolan. With Sophia Loren, John Cassavetes, George Kennedy, Robert Vaughn, Patrick McGoohan, Bruce Davison, Edward Herrman, Max Von Sydow.

Like *The Eagle Has Landed* before it, this film speculates on a "what would have happened if. . ." motif from World War II—in this case, "what would have happened if" Patton had been assassinated. Although not a combat film per se, this is definitely a World War II movie in terms of background and attitude.

1978 notes
Mercenaries in Africa, structured like old films: *Wild Geese*.

Vietnam veteran's adjustment to home life: *Coming Home*.

World War I background: *The March on Paree 1914*.

Vietnam Combat Films: *Go Tell the Spartans*, *The Boys in Company C*, *The Deer Hunter*, *Good Guys Wear Black*. These four films illustrate four approaching attitudes toward Vietnam combat. *Go Tell the Spartans*, set in 1964, uses the WWII format in presenting a cross-section group, this time commanded by Burt Lancaster who is nicknamed "Old WWII," in case the audience doesn't catch on to the film's contrast of attitudes, morals, and purposes between that war and this one. The film uses certain traditions of the earlier combat movie to point up the mistakes made in Vietnam. *The Boys in Company C* follows the tradtitional format closely, in its story of a mixed group of representative types who go through training and into Vietnam combat. It is a *direct* updating of the old genre format, as the group faces not only death and combat, but also danger from drugs, incompetent leaders, and government cynicism. The finale finds the group getting a chance to get out of Vietnam forever through the device of playing a soccer game. Thus, as pointed out elsewhere, the device of a game is brought into the combat film. Space does not permit a detailed writeup of this significant example of the old group updated, but *Boys in Company C* is perhaps the most interesting of the Vietnam films to date. The most critically celebrated of these four films was undoubtedly *The Deer Hunter*, but it is a film which takes place only partially in Vietnam. Although it does present intense combat, it distinctly tries to break with the past and the combat presentation is cut short by the imprisonment of its characters. In retrospect, it can be said that the most generically significant of these 1978 films might have been *Good Guys Wear Black*, a film that was totally ignored at the time because it starred Chuck Norris, the kung fu star who is only now creeping toward the edge of respectability. Loaded with action, the movie is the story of a former top Vietnam Army commando unit that used to rescue American POWs behind enemy lines. As of today, it appears that this concept will be the most popular generic one for the Vietnam combat film—the rescue mission. However, *Good Guys Wear Black* is set years later in America. It tells of government corruption as the mystery of how Norris' group got left stranded in the jungle on a mission is unraveled and avenged by Norris and his buddies.

1979

Sam Fuller and *The Big Red One* (May 23)

Dir: Thijs Ockersen. Dutch documentary on the filming of *The Big Red One* and on Samuel Fuller's entire career.

1979 notes

Vietnam: *Apocalypse Now*; *More American Graffiti* (has Vietnam combat sequences as part of overall tracing of character's stories into the 1960s—excellent combat)

World War II Background: *Yanks* and *Hanover Street* (in Britain) and *1941* (in USA). *Hanover Street* is one-half woman's film and one-half combat, including both aerial bombing raids and a commando special mission.

1980

*The Big Red One (May 14)

Dir: Samuel Fuller. Sp: Samuel Fuller. With Lee Marvin, Mark Hamill, Robert Carradine, Bobby DiCicco, Stephane Audran.

The Sea Wolves (July 9)

Dir: Andrew V. McLaglen. Sp: Reginald Rose, based on the novel *The Boarding Party* by James Leasor. With Gregory Peck, Roger Moore, David Niven, Trevor Howard.

Advertised as "the last great untold action story of the war," this international movie (technically, a British production) tells of a volunteer mission by a part-time regiment of settled older business men (what a comment on the former glory of the genre!). They undertake to destroy three German freighters off the coast of Portugese Goa. The *Variety* review said, "For those who complain they don't make them like that no more, this one's a reasonably entertaining answer."

The Final Countdown (July 16)

Dir: Don Taylor. Sp: David Ambrose and Gerry Davis, Thomas Hunter and Peter Powell, from a story by Hunter, Powell, and Ambrose. With Kirk Douglas, Martin Sheen, Charles Durning, James Farentino, Katharine Ross.

Not technically a WWII combat film, this film nevertheless warrants inclusion because of its bizarre combination of wartime combat plot with the science fiction film. Its story is that of the USS *Nimitz*—and it's shot on the gigantic carrier itself—and of how a mysterious storm transports it back in time to December 6, 1941, in the waters between Pearl Harbor and the Japanese fleet. There is stock footage of the ultimate attack, briefly presented. However, the documentary-like presentation of the huge carrier itself is beautifully done, and the story can't help but fascinate a World War II film buff.

Note

The Filmography ends in 1980, which omits the excellent 1981 German submarine film, *Das Boot*. Although I referred to the emergence of the Vietnam combat film, I did not pursue this. An excellent Vietnam Filmography, including films not set directly in combat, has been published in *Journal of Popular Film and Television* (Spring 1981), volume 9, number 1. Prepared by Lawrence Thompson, Richard Welch, and Philip Stephens, it is introduced by these words: "Since 1948, fewer than 60 American-made films have dealt with Vietnam." A comprehensive listing follows.

John Ford's *officially* credited war documentaries include *Sex Hygiene* (1941), *The Battle of Midway* and *Torpedo Squadron* (1942), *December 7th* (1943), *This is Korea!* (1951), *Korea* (1959), and *The Growler Story*, made for the Navy in 1957 to teach Navy cameramen, using the story of Howard Gilmore. Ford was also the executive producer on *Vietnam, Vietnam*, directed by Sherman Beck for the United States Information Agency.

The Filmography does not include made-for-television movies, such as *Carter's Army* (1970).

World War II continues to be a setting for films and TV: *Swing Shift* (home front) and *Winds of War* (depicting December 7 again).

Author's Note

Since the original publication of this book in 1986, the VietNam movie has come into its own, most notably with the critical and commercial success of PLATOON, directed by Oliver Stone, a 1987 release. Other later releases include FULL METAL JACKET, HAMBURGER HILL, and GOOD MORNING, VIETNAM, with more to come.

Selected Titles Relevant to Prior History of World War II Combat Films

World War I

The Battle Cry for Peace (1915)
A Submarine Pirate (1915)
Civilization (1916)
Hearts of the World (1918)
The Kaiser—Beast of Berlin (1918)
My Four Years in Germany (1918)
Shoulder Arms (1918)
The Big Parade (1925)
The Road to Glory (1926)
What Price Glory? (1926)
Barbed Wire (1927)
Wings (1927)
Four Sons (1928)
Lilac Time (1928)
The Cockeyed World (1929)
She Goes to War (1929)
All Quiet on the Western Front (1930)
Dawn Patrol (1930)
Hell's Angels (1930)
The Man from Wyoming (1930)
Seas Beneath (1931)
Sky Devils (1932)
Hell Below (1933)
The Eagle and the Hawk (1933)
Today We Live (1933)
Crimson Romance (1934)
Lost Patrol (1934)

The Dark Angel (1935)
The Road to Glory (1936)
Suzy (1936)
Dawn Patrol (1938)
Submarine Patrol (1938)
The Fighting 69th (1940)
Sergeant York (1941)

Post World War II Films About World War I:

Lafayette Escadrille (1958)
Paths of Glory (1958)
Lawrence of Arabia (1962)
The Blue Max (1966)
Darling Lili (1969)
Oh, What a Lovely War (1969)

Training Camp/Military Service Films:

Tell It to the Marines (1926)
Hell Divers (1931)
Here Comes the Navy (1934)
Shipmates Forever (1935)
Sea Devils (1937)
Wings of the Navy (1939)
I Wanted Wings (1941)
The Bugle Sounds (1942)

Hybrid Films, Military and Non-Military

International Squadron (1941)
They Met in Bombay (1941)
A Yank in the RAF (1941)
Captains of the Clouds (1942)
The Lady Has Plans (1942)
Once Upon a Honeymoon (1942)
Somewhere I'll Find You (1942)

Notes

Introduction

1. Not official remakes.
2. There is almost too much in even one film for any scholar to master. Besides what we learn about our culture, about the medium itself, and about the mystery of communication, we also learn how we are to behave outside the classroom. A famous newsreel of World War II shows General Eisenhower going among his troops on the eve of D-Day, talking to them, laughing with them, just being one of them. Did he learn to do that at West Point? From reading *The Red Badge of Courage?* From his natural instincts as a born leader of men? Or did he learn it from going to the movies? More importantly, once his newsreel was made and shown and reshown, would the generals who come after him learn to go among their own men from seeing Ike? Or would behavior, since taught from movies, now be altered by them, as the new generals *refuse* to go among their men, considering it obsolete behavior, an empty ritual remembered from old movies and newsreels. Maybe it will then become an old-fashioned concept, with no significance at all except in the art or religions of war, useless in the nuclear age, unless you want to make a movie about World War II. What was taught as the thing to do can become the thing *not* to do—all learned and unlearned from staring at the screen.

1. Definition

1. Dorothy B. Jones, "War Films Made in Hollywood, 1942-44," Hollywood Quarterly (October 1945), 1(1):18, 19.
2. One of these, *In the Rear of the Enemy*, has my all-time favorite combat film title.
3. *Call Out the Marines* (January 26, 1942) is about blondes and secret agents, not combat, but its review in the *New York Times* does carry an interesting reference: "Now that World War I has made way for World War II, Victor McLaglen and Edmund Lowe, the rowdy Quirt and Flagg of the earlier fracas, have dropped their old aliases and bobbed up as McGinnis and Curtis."
4. To standardize release, all dates reflect date of film review in the *New York Times*. Review dates were favored over release or production dates, because they indicate mass-audience viewings.
5. This out-of-step-with-the-times element of comedy probably hit its apotheosis with a curiosity called *The Devil with Hitler* (October 19, 1942). Not a combat film, it tells the story of how the devil tries to save his personal prestige by having Hitler do one decent thing on earth. Hitler looks like an ape, and in this hideously unfunny comedy, he and Mussolini and a Japanese ambassador cross and doublecross one another in a series of depressing events. *The Devil with Hitler* was a Hal Roach film, released through United Artists, written by Al Martin, and directed by Gordon Douglas. To add to the insult, this film was shown in theatres on a double bill with *Mask of Nippon*,

about Japanese atrocities in China (a propaganda film) and a short called *Salvage*, an appeal for scrap metal with which to help the war effort, one of the World in Action series. What a night at the movies!

6. Richard Slotkin, author of *Regeneration Through Violence*, has discussed this phenomenon in lectures and writings in eloquent terms, in which he identifies familiar patterns of loss and defeat by a group as a typically American film story.

7. Such films as *Commandos Strike at Dawn* (a Norwegian guerrilla action) and *Corregidor* (which uses the tragedy at the island fortress as a background for some awful love stories, with a few battle scenes thrown in, along with plenty of rhetoric about why we are fighting) do not apply. As usual, films with misleading titles were examined, but eliminated.

8. It is interesting to speculate why sound films have not mythologized The Revolutionary War (too sacred?), or why they have not filmed the great battles of the Civil War very often. Both these wars share a common characteristic: an us-against-us aspect that, brought to life and demonstrated, may be unsettling for viewers. They also share a costume problem—expensive to produce—and the revolutionary war uniform is beautiful, but perhaps unmasculine to the eye of the average movie goer.

9. It is possible that this film, and others like it, were inspired by the glamorous story of the famous Lost Battalion of World War I, which was cut off by German forces after the launching of an American attack in the Argonne Forest in early October of 1918. The 600 men put up a heroic defense for five days without food, water, or reserve ammunition. They refused all offers to surrender, and were ultimately rescued, but not before two-thirds of them had died. In 1919, a film called *Lost Battalion* was released—a careful reenactment of the event, starring some of the men who were real members of the group.

10. A figure my students have dubbed "mom."

11. See Filmography for the films which follow, from *Gung Ho!* onward, all of which fit the basic pattern whether written up in detail here or not.

2. Prior History

1. *Formula* (a story pattern that has not become a genre, has not been ennobled). *Genre* (a story pattern or formula that has undergone an evolutionary process).

2. There is an additional category, which includes all the Nonmilitary Preparation for War films of the 1930's such as espionage films, set both in Europe and America, and various films which educated the public to Fascism both at home and abroad. However, since these are not connected to the military, they are not referred to here.

3. A detailed book on the subject of World War I on film, both narrative and documentary, is Michael T. Isenberg's *War on Film: The American Cinema and World War I, 1914–1941*. I highly recommend it for a fuller explanation of the World War I film, and for a sense of how real combat footage was obtained in the field. Isenberg points out that early newsreels often were staged events passed off as the real thing, and that many presented shots of "Great Men Doing Great Things" (Wilson signing the Declaration of War, for instance). Actual Signal Corps combat footage, he says, was relatively rare due to the cumbersome photographic equipment and the nature of trench warfare. The book is an exemplary historical study.

4. What is the "first" war film? The word "first" is one all film historians avoid if at all possible, since so much has been lost forever. However, just for the record, specu-

lation on the first fight on film suggests Thomas Edison's "Barroom Scene" from 1894, and first sights of war on film suggest the 1900 British movie of the Boxer Rebellion, *Attack on a China Mission*. In 1906, the British also showed viewers the Zulu wars in *How a British Bulldog Saved the Union Jack*. By 1910, movies in the Vitagraph presented "Scenes From True Life" by J. Stuart Blackton, about the war of independence. In 1911, D.W. Griffith warmed up for *Birth of a Nation* with "The Battle," also about the Civil War. By 1912, Hollywood was already making 500 movies a year, including one of the first to be based on the Charge of the Light Brigade. In 1914, newsreel film with trench warfare was available, killing the romantic vision of war forever by beginning to show people what war really looked like.

5. Two later films, *The Eagle and the Hawk* (1933) and *The Road to Glory* (1936) are also of this "glory" type. The former is an air film, too, but the latter concerns trench warfare. It is about Frenchmen in the war, and some film historians believe it contains actual World War I battle footage from French Archives. Others disagree.

6. The second *Dawn Patrol* (reviewed December 24, 1938) starred Errol Flynn and David Niven in the roles created by Richard Barthelmess and Douglas Fairbanks Jr. Technically this remake falls at a time when the transition-to-war films were beginning to appear. This places it in direct conflict with its own subject matter. If the World War I film is about the tragedy of war, in a no-win situation, with even the most glorious having an undercurrent of defeat, how can this same film be used to excite people into an enthusiasm for the necessity of a new war? The remake of *Dawn Patrol* is an odd film. It's like the old situation—"is this glass of water half empty or half full?" It depends on your attitude. Some find the second *Dawn Patrol*—practically a direct remake with even the same aerial footage—a serious film about the horrors of war. Others find it quite a peppy adventure, which makes war look like a heck of a lot of fun!

7. David D. Lee, "Appalachia on Film." In Warren French, ed., *The South and Film* (Columbia: University of Mississippi Press, 1981, pp. 207–21. Quote is on pg. 211.

8. This real life priest wrote his autobiography, *Father Duffy's Story*, in 1919. According to the Wisconsin Research Center, his book formed the basis for the movie. A priest/chaplain, who is a former football hero, would turn up as a character type in other combat films.

9. Inventiveness in this case means the development of new weapons or safety devices. In such films as *Submarine D-1* (1937), *Dive Bomber* (1941), and *Flight Command* (1941), military personnel invent and test, respectively, the diving bell, the high altitude pressure suit, and an instrument for flying in the fog. These films teach us about military life and equipment, and prepare us for the dangers associated with that world. Inventiveness, or inventing things, may thus be seen as an appropriate substitute for the dangers of war. All three are actually a form of the popular movies about inventors that appeared in the same period. If *Young Tom Edison* (1940), *Edison The Man* (1940), *The Story of Louis Pasteur* (1936), and *Dr. Ehrlich's Magic Bullet* (1940) can be box office and critical successes, you can be sure that inventing things will turn up somewhere in another genre of the time. In the military movies, one sees the ingenuity of inventiveness moved into a situation that directly demonstrates the dangers involved in it. Ingenuity is thus equated with bravery, and originality with courage. The testing of military equipment becomes the equivalent of the doctor's taking his own serum himself, to test it. Joseph Reed has equated these inventor movies with movies about composers and further linked both types to the horror film. This illustrates an important property about genre, which will be discussed in the final chapter.

3. Evolution

1. E. L. Doctorow, *New York Times, Book Review*, September 22, 1980.

2. This footage was used in newsreels and "Combat Bulletins" as well as in documentaries.

3. "World War II on Film, " National Audio Visual Center Distribution Catalogue.

4. The excellent *Why We Fight* series was made not for the home audience, but to give the American G.I. a sense of his American heritage, his reasons for fighting the war, knowledge of his new enemies, and the responsibilities of his mission. However, some of the titles in the series *were* shown in movie theaters.

5. "World War II on Film," National Audio Visual Center Distribution Catalogue. Ford made other World War II documentaries—*Sex Hygiene* (1941), about an entirely different sort of combat; *Torpedo Squadron* (1942); and *We Sail at Midnight* (1943). (A list of his other documentaries is included at the end of the Filmography.)

6. Hollywood was booming during the Depression, and falling on bad days during the prosperity of the 1950s. Its economic history does not always match that of the rest of the country.

7. My experience in interviewing people who worked on old films on this subject is that if you say you think it's good, the person says he did it. If you say you think it failed, he says someone else did it.

8. This excellent book, *Hollywood Genres*, one of the best ever written on the subject, clearly defines many elements important to an understanding of Hollywood films. It covers the studio system, the question of authorship, specific genres (although not the combat film), explanations of the mythmaking process, and theoretical aspects of genre study for which there is no room in this book. I highly recommend it.

9. In August of 1943, Wanger gave a speech in New York City to newspapermen, in which he made the observation that war films so far were mostly "westerns and gangster plots, dressed up in Army uniforms." Genre was no secret in those days.

10. See *Merrill's Marauders*.

11. The first films of each wave tend to be films about the Air Force. There are obvious reasons for this: the inherent glamor of the airplane, the ease with which characters can be removed from combat, and the resulting plot flexibility which can provide an appeal to a wide audience.

12. The film ends with O'Brien established as a legendary figure who is maybe "not really dead but on his way to see a girl in Paris." Legendary heroes on film sometimes are represented after death as "living on" in the form of an animal, such as Marlon Brando as a white horse in *Viva Zapata!* There's even a female variation—Gene Tierney as a red fox in *Belle Starr!*

13. Both *Battleground* and *Sands of Iwo Jima* also contain actual combat footage.

14. The concept of a real-life hero playing himself on film is not unique with Audie Murphy. Pancho Villa and Buffalo Bill both appeared as themselves, and one has only to think of Sophia Loren's magnificent hubris in playing herself *and* her mother in her own life story for television to take the measure of this type of event. Other war heroes besides Murphy had their stories told, with an appropriate actor (Gary Cooper as Sergeant York and Dr. Wassell, Jeff Chandler as Merrill, etc.). Sports figures, religious leaders, and presidents all undergo the same phenomenon in their own lifetimes.

15. Partly, this new cynicism and breakdown of faith—which obviously reflects historical attitudes—can count as one of the many plot expansions that take place, to allow the films to incorporate new storylines to keep them relevant. (The father–son conflict is one of these. It is seen elsewhere in the films of the decade in juvenile

delinquent films, Westerns, and family comedies.) It is important to point to the cynicism as a factor, however, particularly since so many people erroneously remember the films of the fifties as bland, status-quo films. This is historically inaccurate, as the fifties movies definitely reflect the audience's breakdown of faith.

16. During the 1950s and the 1960s, combat films would be increasingly made in color and the new CinemaScope format. Although at the beginning of World War II, films such as *Crash Dive* and *Dive Bomber* were made in Technicolor, mostly it was used for the gorgeous escapist musicals of the era. The combat films of the key definition year, 1943, are all in black and white.

17. Comedy about combat exists in all stages, but obviously exists less at the beginning of the genre than in the later stages. However, such films as *What's Next, Corporal Hargrove?* (somewhat less than 50 percent combat) in the first wave and *When Willie Comes Marching Home* (also less than 50 percent) from the third wave are there (see chapter 4).

18. Lee Marvin is a World War II veteran. He enlisted in the Marine Corps when he was barely seventeen years old, and saw action in the Pacific. As a member of I Company, 24th Marine regiment, 4th Division, he assaulted 21 beaches from Kwajelein to Saipan. At Saipan, he was one of six survivors out of 247 men in his company. Wounded in action, he still receives his disability pension from the government. An interesting sidelight to his colorful story is that while he was doing all this in the Pacific, his own father was an Army sergeant fighting in active combat in Europe. Marvin brings a note of realism into his role as the ruthless major that, in fact, comes from hard experience.

19. It is possible that *Play Dirty* was inspired by the true-life story of Popski's Private Army, a British reconnaissance unit that used armored jeeps for rapid mobility and who patrolled North Africa to gather information and destroy enemy supplies. Commanded by Vladimir Peniakoff, they were an ad hoc group of about 200 men who allegedly operated somewhat outside the usual military controls.

20. The wearing of an enemy uniform by the heroic group is something that either appears very early, as in *Desperate Journey*, which is almost a comedy, or very late in the more downbeat war films. It is considered a despicable thing to do. It is established in *Battleground* that the nasty Nazis do it, and, of course, it was against the rules of the Geneva convention.

21. There are only two women in this film. One appears briefly, and is the indirect cause of Caine's being assigned to the group mission. He is dating her, and a rival who outranks him has Caine conveniently reassigned to combat and thus removed from their competition. The other is a German nurse, but there is no love story associated with her. A rape is attempted on her, but she is much too tough to be taken. She fights—another convention upset.

4. Variations of Genre

1. Without straying too far from the subject of combat films, it is important to point out that the woman's film was undergoing its own evolution during this time period. As women's roles changed to meet the needs of the war, the woman's film changed, too.

2. See my article, "Ten That Got Away" in Karyn Kay and Gerald Peary, eds., *Women and the Cinema*.

3. Later, *M.A.S.H.* would be released (1970), set in Korea, but reflecting attitudes inspired by Vietnam. *M.A.S.H.* involves men and women not in active combat, but

once again behind the lines as nurses and doctors. These women are clearly under the domination of the doctors, who are the key figures in the mobile hospital. This is not the case in either *So Proudly We Hail* or *Cry Havoc*, where the women are really the important personnel. There are no doctors seen in *Cry Havoc*, and the ones in *So Proudly We Hail* are operating around the clock, assisted by the women, and allowing the women to run things otherwise. There has been a subtle shift in attitudes toward women. *M.A.S.H.* is an interesting variation on a film which appeared during the Korean war, *Battle Circus*, starring an unlikely romantic combination, Humphrey Bogart and June Allyson. *Battle Circus* is practically a forgotten Bogart film today. A characteristic of persona is that if actors play roles that don't fit the popular concept, the audience discards them. Thus, people don't remember John Wayne *did* die on film and that Bogart was not always a tough guy. Here he romances June Allyson, and once he played a mad doctor with a skunk stripe in his hair (*Return of Dr. X*, 1939). This type of throwing away of what doesn't fit is a trait of genre, also. What audiences do for genre films, they also do for stars, which is a kind of proof that a star is his own genre.

Watching *Battle Circus* today, it's not hard to imagine the people who wrote *M.A.S.H.* seeing it and saying, "ye gods, this is accidentally hilarious. It should be done as a comedy."

4. *I'll Get By* is a semi-remake of *Tin Pin Alley* (1940), which used World War I as a reference point.

5. This proof of genre appeared in *Tars and Spars*. (February 15, 1946).

6. It is an interesting parallel to *Play Dirty*, a serious film, in which viewers saw a commando unit go in for real on a fake objective, and then repeat the action on a real one.

5. Problems of Genre

1. *House of Bamboo*, a major gangster film directed by Samuel Fuller, is the exception in that its hero lives. It is very much a combat film, however, because its group of gangsters were all war buddies, skilled in commando tactics which they use for robberies. It, too, ends in a major shootout. Although the hero, a government agent, lives, the "combat group" of gangsters all die.

2. It also reflects a dominant tradition of the postwar period, the fatalistic flashback so popular in films of the *film noir* tradition. Flashbacks, of course, were also frequently used in musicals and comedies, such as *Yankee Doodle Dandy* and *My Favorite Brunette*.

3. This occurs both before *and* after a story pattern is fully established as a genre.

4. This phenomenon can be verified by looking at the movie star paper dolls of the era. At first, they all have riding habits, and within a year or two, they all have ski suits.

Bibliography

Andrew, Dudley. *Concepts in Film Theory*. New York: Oxford University Press, 1984

"The Bataan Scripts." The American Film Institute Script Collection, Louis B. Mayer Library, American Film Institute, Los Angeles, California

Braudy, Leo. "Film Genre: A Dialogue. The Thirties, The Forties." Post Script (Spring/Summer 1982), vol. 1, no. 3.

Bureau of Motion Pictures; Domestic Radio Bureau (Office of War Information). National Archives, Washington D.C. (General file on all aspects of film during World War II)

French, Warren, ed. *The South and Film*. University Press of Mississippi, 1981. (Esp. "Appalachia on Film: The Making of Sergeant York, by David D. Lee)

Grant, Barry K., ed. *Film Genre: Theory and Criticism*. Metuchen New Jersey: Scarecrow Press, 1977

"Hollywood and the War." *Newsweek*, September 18, 1939, pp. 38–39

Hughes, Robert, ed. *Film: Films of Peace and War*. New York: Grove Press, 1962

Isenberg, Michael T. *War on Film, The American Cinema and World War I, 1914–41*. Rutherford, N.J.: Associated University Presses, Fairleigh Dickinson University Press, 1981

Jacobs, Lewis. "World War II and the American Film," *Cinema Journal*, Winter 1967–68, pp. 1–21

Jones, Dorothy B. "War Films Made in Hollywood, 1942–44." *Hollywood Quarterly* (October, 1945) 1(1): 1–19

Kaminsky, Stuart M. *American Film Genres: Approaches to a Critical Theory of Popular Film*. New York: Dell, 1974

Kay, Karyn and Gerry Peary. *Women and the Cinema, A Critical Anthology*. New York: E. P. Dutton, 1977

Lingemann, Richard R. "Will This Picture Help Win the War?" In *Don't You Know There's A War On? The American Home Front, 1941–45*, pp. 168–233. New York: Putnam.

Look, Editors of. *Movie Lot to Beachhead: The Motion Picture Goes To War and Prepares For the Future*, New York: Doubleday, 1945.

Manvell, Roger. *Films and the Second World War*, South Brunswick, N.J.: A.S. Barnes, 1974

McCombs, Don, and Fred L. Worth. *World War I Super Facts*. New York: Warner Books, 1983

Roscoe, Theodore. *United States Submarine Operations During World War II*. Anapolis: Naval Institute Press, 1949

Salmaggi, Cesare, and Alfredo Pallavisini, compil. *2194 Days of War. An Illustrated Chronology of the Second World War*. Italy: Gallery Verona, 1977

Schatz, Thomas. *Hollywood Genres: Formulas, Filmmaking, and the Studio System*. Philadelphia: Temple University Press, 1981

Smith, Julian. *Looking Away: Hollywood and Vietnam*. New York: Scribner's, 1975

Suid, Lawrence Howard. Introduction to "Air Force" Script from the Wisconsin/Warner Bros. Screenplay Series, Published for the Wisconsin Center for Film and Theater Research. Madison: University of Wisconsin Press, 1983

Thompson, Lawrence D., Richard Welch, and Phillip Stephens. "A Vietnam Filmography." *Journal of Popular Film and Television*. (Spring, 1981), vol 9. no. 1.

——*World War II on Film*. Distributed by the National Audio Visual Center (which lists holdings of the National Archives, the U.S. Army, the U.S. Navy, and the U.S. Air Force).

Index of Films

Subject Index

Abbott, Bud, 251

Abstraction, 1, 17, 46, 214, 264–65; in Fuller's films, 215, 216, 217; *They Were Expendable*, 152

Action (generic), 4, 18, 74, 225, 226; multiple uses of, 273–74; *Objective Burma*, 139; in woman's films, 225, 234–35; *see also* Combat (action)

Actors, 132

Adventure films, 27, 36, 107, 118, 269; military service, 13, 108, 110–12

Agar, John, 164–66, 167, 169

Air combat, 18, 21, 34

Air Corps, 96

Air films, 34, 90, 96–97, 126, 153, 185, 269, 341n5

Air force films, 21, 22, 342n11

Air hero movies, 96–97, 114

Air Service, 42, 95, 97

Alamo, 30, 34, 45

Alcoholism, 247

Alienation, 75

Allan, Moses Anderson, 129

Allegory, 151

All Quiet on the Western Front (Remarque), 98

Allyson, June, 269–70, 344n3

America, American: meaning of, In combat film, 144; national persona of, 35, 71

American Film Institute, Louis B. Mayer Library, 6, 45

Americanism, 34, 79, 80

Andrew, Dudley, 7

Andrews, Dana, 42, 146, 150, 248

Andrews, Julie, 247

Andrews Sisters, 247

Angel, Heather, 236

Antiestablishment political statements, 221

Antihero(es), 205

Antiwar films, 88, 91, 95, 97, 98–100, 252, 257; comedy combat films, 251

Antiwar sentiment, 203; *see also* Pacifist films

Archetypal story; war as, 181

Arizona (battleship), 108, 109

Armed forces: cooperation with studios, 112, 115

Arnaz, Desi, 51, 56, 57

Art directors, 24, 132

Attenborough, Richard, 245

Attitude(s), 41, 151–53, 184, 185, 263, 275, 276, 277; of audience, 62; distanced, 134, 142, 145, 151; experimental, 221; incompatible, 222; toward violence, 198; in war, 205

Attitude toward war, 209; Korean combat films, 178–79, 188; legendary, 145, 146, 151; mocking, 250; new, 169; Vietnam war, 179; *see also* Pacifist films

Audience(s), 7, 33, 54, 56, 78, 84, 138, 170, 276, 344n3; breakdown of faith, 343n15; concerns of, 275; cynical role and, 54; emotional release for, 38, 40, 75; ennobled, 75; expectation in genre, 41, 63; film as surface literary experience to, 223; ideological meanings of setting, characters to, 275; involvement with actors, 192–93, 199; knowledge of genre, 4; non-real, referential understanding of, 214; and nontraditional presentation, 184; participatory relationship, 44 (*see also* Viewer participation); power of genre for, 218–19; in postwar era, 78; prior life of, 84; recognition of conventions, types, 1–2, 124, 131, 139–40, 151, 155, 215,

Training Camp Films (continued)
338; comedies as, 251, 252, 284; women in
military, 223; World War I, 90
Training-camp-into-combat films, 91, 164
Transference, 267
Transition-to-sound films, 90, 95, 98, 112
Transition-to-war films, 105–07, 108, 341n6;
see also Preparation-for-war films
Tregaskis, Richard: Guadalcanal Diary, 71, 152
Truth: in comedy combat film, 257; in/and
film, 228; in genre, 218–19; in World War
II combat film, 152, 158–59; see also
Reality
Tucker, Forrest, 164
Tufts, Sonny, 231, 234
Turner, Lana, 2, 3, 113–114, 242, 244
20th-Century-Fox, 186
Tyne, George, 146
Tyrone Power role, 106

Understanding chaplain (type), 102
Underwater demolition team, 185–87
Uniforms, 16, 23, 73, 232–33, 266–67, 270;
new, 115; World War I, 87
Union strikes, 86
United Artists, 339n5
United Nations (classification), 22, 178
U.S. Army, 115
U.S. Department of Defense, 187
U.S. Navy, 109, 110, 112, 130, 171
U.S.S. Copperfin, 106
U.S.S. Saratoga, 171
Unit of fighting men divided (theme), 134,
135, 136, 183–84

Valley Forge, 34
Vandervoort, Ben, 189, 193
Variety, 3
Veterans, 50, 218; in audience, 156, 158–59,
162, 163, 187; in casts, 163, 170, 175, 188;
Vietnam war, 212–13
Victory, 44, 75, 80, 81; possibility of, 21, 69;
World War I films, 94
Vietnam, 14
Vietnam combat films, 202, 212–14, 215
Vietnam War, 122, 123, 143, 153, 201–02;
attitude toward, 179; and genre, 212–14;
television coverage, 25, 176
Viewers: relationship to film, 266; role of,
126; see also Audience
Viewer participation, 125, 126, 148, 149;
through visualization of concepts, 130–31;
understanding through, 140–41

Villa, Pancho, 342n14
Violence, 80; celebration of, 203; linked with
sex, 234
Visual (the): belief, 195–196; business, 139;
components of film, 221; components
of genre, 277; language, 78; links between
genres, 175–176; meaning in multiple
use of action units, 273–74; power of, 44,
124
Visual presentation, 33–34, 142, 143, 144,
155, 218, 277–78; subliminal messages in,
221, 223; viewer participation through, 141,
149, 151, 184; in woman's films, 232
Visual shorthand, 122, 139–40, 142, 155, 176;
for narrative concepts, 124, 130–31, 134,
149, 151–52
Vitagraph, 341n4
Voiceover narration, 29; Flight Nurse, 240;
Walk in the Sun, 146 (see also Narration)

Wake Island, 33–34
Walker, Clint, 206, 210
Walker, Robert, 511, 55, 59–61, 233
Walsh, Raoul, 92, 132, 135, 153, 154
Wanger, Walter, 132
War(s), 10; ancient, 86; imaginary, 86, 276; as
issue, 178; meaning of, 227; as no-win
situation, 134, 152; prior history of, 83; as
surreal event, 148–49; as theater, 257–
58; unpredictability of, 137–38
War background films, 284
War correspondent (type), 102
Ware, Darrell, 105
War effort, 80, 84
War film(s), 1, 14, 33, 34, 98, 269; conven-
tions of, 86; disappearance of, 89; first,
340–41n4; as genre, 9; influence of combat
film on, 9–10. non-genre, 86; pre-Pearl
Harbor, 85; prior history of, 83; settings, 276
War games, 207; as comedy, 251, 252; as
stand-in for war, 109, 208, 214, 215
Warner Brothers, 101, 103, 104, 105, 109, 110,
114, 115, 116, 186; aided by armed forces,
112
Warner, Jack, 102, 132
War On Film (Isenberg), 340n3
War orphans, 179
War photos, 21
War preparedness (theme), 107
Wartime Films, 12–13; see also War films
Wassell, Dr., 342n14
Waste of youth (theme), 55, 58, 89, 90, 91,
94, 95, 97, 98, 101